FUNDAMENTAL RIGHTS VIOLATIONS BY PRIVATE ACTORS AND THE PROCEDURE BEFORE THE EUROPEAN COURT OF HUMAN RIGHTS

Human Rights Research Series, Volume 98.

The titles published in this series are listed at the end of this volume.

Fundamental Rights Violations by Private Actors and the Procedure before the European Court of Human Rights

A Study of Verticalised Cases

Claire Loven

INTERSENTIA
Antwerpen – Gent – Cambridge

Intersentia Ltd
8 Wellington Mews | Wellington Street
Cambridge | CB1 1HW | United Kingdom
Tel.: +44 1223 736 170
Email: mail@intersentia.co.uk
www.intersentia.com | www.intersentia.co.uk

Distribution for the UK and the rest of the world (incl. Eastern Europe):
NBN International
1 Deltic Avenue, Rooksley
Milton Keynes MK13 8LD
United Kingdom
Tel.: +44 1752 202 301 | Fax: +44 1752 202 331
Email: orders@nbninternational.com

Distribution for Europe:
Lefebvre Sarrut Belgium NV
Hoogstraat 139/6
1000 Brussels
Belgium
Tel.: +32 3 680 15 50 | Fax: +32 3 658 71 21
Email: mail@intersentia.be

Distribution for the USA and Canada:
Independent Publishers Group
Order Department
814 North Franklin Street
Chicago, IL60610
USA
Tel.: +1 800 888 4741 (toll free) | Fax: +1312 337 5985
Email: orders@ipgbook.com

Fundamental Rights Violations by Private Actors and the Procedure before the European Court of Human Rights. Fundamental Rights Violations by Private Actors and the Procedure before the European Court of Human Rights

Cover design by Danny Juchtmans / www.dsigngraphics.be
Cover illustration by Maaike Canne / www.maaikecanne.com

ISBN 978-1-83970-283-9 (paperback)
ISBN 978-1-83970-284-6 (PDF)
D/2022/7849/96

British Library Cataloguing in Publication Data. A catalogue record for this book is available from the British Library.

ACKNOWLEDGMENTS

I really enjoyed the last four years, the whole process that led to this book. This is for a large part owed to my supervisors, colleagues, friends and family. I like to compare this with music, which can also inspire you, help you to see things more clearly, put things into perspective, or just make things even more enjoyable than they already are.

First of all, I would like to thank my wonderful supervisors, Janneke Gerards and Cedric Ryngaert, who have been incredibly supportive over the last years. Janneke, I can hardly describe how your kindness, enthusiasm and unparalleled knowledge have helped and motivated me. I have still not figured out how you do it, but despite your busy schedule, you always made time to patiently discuss my research and thoughts and to give the most valuable feedback and advice. Cedric, I am thankful for your always instant willingness to read my work and your supportive comments, which helped me to not forget the broader picture. I would also like to thank the members of the assessment committee for their willingness and time to read and assess my dissertation.

Thanks to my colleagues and former colleagues at Utrecht University, I could write my PhD among and supported by a group of wonderful people. In particular, I would like to mention Leonie, Manon, Melanie, Sim, Tim and, of course, Elif, one of my paranymphs. Although we did not know each when we started our PhD at the very same day under the supervision of Janneke, we have been partners in crime ever since. I will never forget our first international conference together as well as many other PhD and non-PhD related activities including case law lunches, blog posts, concerts, dinners, baby visits and weddings.

Over the last four years, my beloved friends and family have offered welcome distraction and support. Nils and Cindy, my dear geographers, you are both very good in always being there, making me laugh and reminding me to not take life too seriously. I have lost count of all the (Christmas) dinners, board games, holidays, concerts, festivals and baking sessions, but each and every one of them was memorable and I hope that many more will follow. Jonas, due to some considerable distance, we do not see each other that often, but when we see (or call) each other it always feels like yesterday and we can keep talking for hours. You are also one of the persons that has always been truly interested in my research and expressed sincere belief in me making it to the finish line, for which I am grateful.

I am also grateful to my parents who have, both in their very own and unique way, supported and encouraged me to follow my own path. The same goes for my brother, Ta.

Together with Tania, you also bring some lovely Spanishness into my life. Finally, my sister, Cha. Asking you to be one of my paranymphs was one of the easiest decisions I had to make. You are a big sister in the best possible way, always helping and encouraging me while I stumble through life. Even more importantly, you are one of my dearest friends, and love (trail)running adventures as much as I do.

3.7. Protection of Convention rights in employer-employee relations....... 90
4. Conclusion 91

Chapter 6. Detailed Analysis of Verticalised Cases before the ECtHR 93

1. Introduction 93
2. Origins of verticalised cases: underlying conflicts and involved parties 94
2.1. Cases related to one's surroundings 95
2.2. Right to reputation and private life versus freedom of expression cases 96
2.3. Family life cases 98
2.4. Employer-employee cases.. 99
2.5. Conclusion 100
3. The Court's examination of verticalised cases 100
3.1. Cases related to one's surroundings 101
3.2. Right to reputation and private life versus freedom of expression cases ... 104
3.3. Family life cases 110
3.4. Employer-employee cases.. 116
3.5. Conclusion 120

Conclusion 123

PART III.
PROBLEMS IN VERTICALISED CASES 125

Introduction... 127

Chapter 7. Problems that may arise during the Court's Proceedings............ 129

1. Introduction 129
2. Private actors 129
2.1. Defending acts, interests and rights: an analysis of the four case studies... 130
2.1.1. Cases related to one's surroundings 130
2.1.2. Right to reputation and private life versus freedom of expression cases 130
2.1.3. Family life cases 131
2.1.4. Employer-employee cases.................................. 132
2.1.5. Concluding observations: consequences for procedural rights.... 133
2.2. Possible problems further explored 134
3. Convention States and the ECtHR 137
3.1. Convention States 137
3.2. The ECtHR... 139
4. Conclusion 142

Chapter 8. Problems that may arise after the Court's Proceedings 143

1. Introduction 143
2. Effects of a judgment for the disappeared party 143
   2.1. Article 46 ECHR and the nature of the Court's judgments 145
      2.1.1. The indication of general or individual measures by the Court ... 145
      2.1.2. Impact of the indication of specific measures on the disappeared party 150
   2.2. Execution process: practice at the domestic level 151
      2.2.1. Cases related to one's surroundings 153
      2.2.2. Right to reputation and private life versus freedom of expression cases 153
      2.2.3. Family life cases 154
      2.2.4. Employer-employee cases 156
   2.3. Conclusion 157
3. Implications of a judgment for Convention States and the Court itself 158
4. Conclusion 161

Conclusion 163

PART IV.
TOWARDS A NEW APPROACH TO VERTICALISED CASES 165

Introduction 167

Chapter 9. Current Third-party Intervention Procedure 169

1. Introduction 169
2. Procedural requirements 169
3. Different types of third-party intervention 173
   3.1. Amicus curiae interventions 174
   3.2. Actual third-party interventions 177
   3.3. Conclusion 180
4. Influence of third-party interventions on the Court's judgments 181
5. Conclusion 184

Chapter 10.
Proposal to Redesign the Third-party Intervention Procedure 187

1. Introduction 187
2. Scope of a right to third-party intervention for actual third parties 188
   2.1. Personal scope 189
   2.2. Procedural scope 192

3. Additional Procedural Issues in Relation to a Right to Third-party Intervention ... 194
3.1. Becoming aware of the Court's proceedings and the possibility of intervening ... 195
3.2. Third-party submissions and the Court's reasoning ... 197
4. Redesigned third-party intervention procedure in practice ... 199
4.1. Right to reputation and private life versus freedom of expression cases .. 200
4.2. Family life cases ... 201
4.3. Employer-employee cases ... 202

Conclusion ... 205

CONCLUSION ... 207

Chapter 11. Conclusion ... 209

1. Introduction ... 209
2. Characteristics of verticalised cases and the Court's approach to them ... 211
3. Problems in verticalised cases ... 216
4. Towards a new approach to verticalised cases ... 220
5. Final remarks ... 223

Summary in Dutch ... 225

1. Inleiding ... 225
2. De aard van geverticaliseerde zaken en de aanpak van het EHRM ... 227
3. Problemen in geverticaliseerde zaken ... 233
4. Naar een nieuwe aanpak van geverticaliseerde zaken ... 236
5. Afsluiting ... 239

Bibliography ... 241
Appendix I: Overview case law sample ... 253
Curriculum Vitae ... 257

INTRODUCTION

CHAPTER 1
INTRODUCTION

1. SETTING THE STAGE

The well-known case of *Von Hannover (No. 2)*[1] ranks highly on the list of seminal judgments of the European Court of Human Rights (ECtHR or the Court). The applicant in this case, Princess Caroline von Hannover, had previously brought domestic proceedings against several publishing companies, seeking to prevent German magazines from publishing, or further publishing, photos of her and her husband's private life. These legal actions were only partly successful as the domestic courts did not grant an injunction against the further publication of all photos. This prompted the princess and her husband to lodge a complaint at the Court, where they complained about the lack of adequate State protection of their right to respect for private life (Article 8 European Convention on Human Rights (ECHR or the Convention)). The Court found that the domestic courts had not failed to comply with their positive obligations under Article 8 as they had carefully balanced the applicants' right to respect for private life against the publishing companies' right to freedom of expression.[2] In reaching this decision, the Court formulated a set of criteria that domestic courts have to take into account when balancing the right to reputation and private life of one individual against the right to freedom of expression of another individual.[3]

Although this is what the case is still famous for, it has yet another important feature. What happened in the case of *Von Hannover (No. 2)* is that a private actor who had first brought a procedure against another private actor before the domestic courts then brought a complaint about State action (on inaction) in relation to the same case before the ECtHR, thereby transforming it from a 'horizontal' case (i.e. between private actors) into a 'vertical' one (i.e. between a private actor and the State). This 'verticalisation' is a logical consequence of the design of the Convention's monitoring system, given that Article 34 of the Convention allows any person, non-governmental organisation

---

1 *Von Hannover v. Germany (No. 2)* App No 40660/08 (ECtHR (GC) 7 February 2012).

2 *Von Hannover v. Germany (No. 2)* App No 40660/08 (ECtHR (GC) 7 February 2012), paras 124–126.

3 *Von Hannover v. Germany (No. 2)* App No 40660/08 (ECtHR (GC) 7 February 2012), paras 108–113. This case, including the criteria formulated by the Court, is discussed in detail in Chapters 5 (Section 3.3) and 6 (Sections 2.2. and 3.2).

or group of individuals to bring an application before the Court regarding an alleged violation of a Convention right by one of the Convention States. Complaints directed against private actors (e.g. individuals or companies) are thus incompatible *ratione personae* with the provisions of the Convention and will be declared inadmissible.[4]

The obligation for individual complaints to be directed against States has to be seen in the light of the drafting history of the Convention. This dates back to the years directly following the Second World War, which had provided horrific examples of how States can misuse their sovereign powers to deeply violate individuals' autonomy, dignity and freedom. In those early drafting years, there was also a growing fear of a communist threat coming from Eastern Europe and a third global conflict between East and West.[5] This drafting history was also recalled by the President of the Court during a conference marking the 70th anniversary of the Convention in autumn 2020. In his speech, President Spano reminded the audience that the Convention is a 'constellation of rights and values with the primordial aim of averting conflict, strife and, ... human tragedy and suffering'.[6] In other words, the Convention was conceived as an early warning system against totalitarianism and aimed at protecting the fundamental rights of individuals against violations by States.[7]

The system's background and function notwithstanding, the case of *Von Hannover (No. 2)* illustrates that the Convention system does not entirely ignore private actors' infringements of the values, rights and liberties enshrined in the Convention. On the contrary, over the years, the Court has increasingly offered substantive protection of Convention rights in relations between private actors. It has done so by imposing horizontal positive obligations on Convention States, with the result that the latter are required to take action to secure the rights and liberties guaranteed in the Convention in relations between private actors. States may do so by, for example, enacting criminal law or other types of legislation, guaranteeing effective law enforcement, taking operational measures, or having effective legal remedies in place.[8] These horizontal positive obligations are based on the Convention States' responsibility for their own

---

4 See, for example, *Bogomolova v. Russia* App No 13812/09 (ECtHR 20 June 2017), para. 40. On incompatibility *ratione personae* see also the 'Practical Guide on Admissibility Criteria' (updated on 1 August 2021) prepared by the Registry of the Court. A more detailed discussion of the admissibility criteria is provided in Chapter 4 (Section 2.1).

5 For a detailed overview of the history of the Convention system see, for example, J.G. Merrills and A.H. Robertson, *Human rights in Europe: a study of the ECHR,* Manchester University Press 2001 (4th edition); A.W. Brian Simpson, *Human rights and the end of empire,* Oxford University Press 2001; D. Nicol, 'Original intent and the European Convention on Human Rights' (2005) *Public Law* 152; E. Bates, *The evolution of the European Convention on Human Rights: from its inception to the creation of a permanent Court of Human Rights,* Oxford University Press 2010. The history of the Convention system is also discussed in Chapter 2.

6 Opening remarks by President Robert Spano during the conference 'The European Convention on Human Rights at 70: milestones and major achievements' (Strasbourg 18 September 2020).

7 See also Bates 2010 (n 5), pp. 44–45ff and pp. 104–107.

8 These different means by which the Court has required Convention States to protect Convention rights in relations between individuals were distinguished by Gerards (J.H. Gerards, *General principles of the European Convention on Human Rights,* Oxford University Press 2019, pp. 147ff). Horizontal positive obligations are discussed in detail in Chapter 5 of this study.

acts and omissions in relation to the acts of private actors and their obligation to make sure that Convention rights are effectively protected, also in relations between private actors.[9]

Horizontal positive obligations are often imposed in what this study terms 'verticalised' cases; in other words, cases arising from a conflict between private actors at the domestic level.[10] The case of *Von Hannover (No. 2)*, which involved a conflict between the right to reputation and private life of one individual and the right to freedom of expression of a private publishing company, is just one example of such a case. Examples could also include applications pertaining to relations between family members, such as cases concerning custody and access rights arising from a conflict between separated or divorced parents[11], or cases in which a child starts proceedings to establish whether a man who denies paternity is her biological father.[12] Other examples could include employment-related cases, such as when an employee is dismissed for wearing religious symbols at work[13], or cases concerning the right to respect for one's private life and home and involving noise disturbance caused by privately owned bars or discotheques.[14] All these cases can be referred to as verticalised cases as they all originate from a conflict between two private actors at the domestic level (i.e. a horizontal conflict) and, therefore, have to be transformed into a case between an individual and the State (i.e. a vertical case) to be admissible at the Court.

It has long been recognised that such verticalised cases exist[15] and even make up a large portion of the Court's case law. Nevertheless, the particular characteristics of verticalised cases and the Court's approach to them have remained underexplored, with little being known about the exact nature of the underlying conflicts and the parties involved. The same holds true for the Court's examination of verticalised cases. Does the Court, for example, take a particular approach in assessing verticalised cases? And to what extent does the Court consider the rights and interests of the private actor involved in the conflict at the domestic level, not being the applicant? These

---

9 See, for example, the Court's reasoning in *X and Y v. the Netherlands* App No 8978/80 (ECtHR 26 March 1985), para. 23 and in *O'Keeffe v. Ireland* App No 35810/09 (ECtHR 28 January 2014), para. 168.

10 On the term 'verticalised' cases as used in this study, see further Section 3.

11 See, for example, *A.M. and Others v. Russia* App No 47220/19 (ECtHR 6 July 2021).

12 See, for example, *Mifsud v. Malta* App No 62257/15 (ECtHR 29 January 2019).

13 See, for example, *Eweida and Others v. the United Kingdom* App No 48420/10 (ECtHR 15 January 2013).

14 See, for example, *Moreno Gómez v. Spain* App No 4143/02 (ECtHR 16 November 2004).

15 See, for example, P. Ducoulombier, 'Conflicts between fundamental rights and the ECHR: an overview' in E. Brems (ed.) *Conflicts between fundamental rights*, Intersentia 2008, pp. 217–247; S. Smet, *Resolving conflicts between human rights: a legal theoretical analysis in the context of the ECHR*, Ghent University (diss.) 2014; S. Smet, *Resolving conflicts between human rights: the judge's dilemma*, Routledge 2017. In the 2000s, 'verticalisation' was also criticised because of its contributing to an increasing influence of fundamental rights on private law ('constitutionalisation' of private law). On this, see, for example, R. Kay, 'The European Convention on Human Rights and the control of private law' (2005) 5 *European Human Rights Law Review* 466; O. Cherednychenko, 'Towards the Control of Private Acts by the European Court of Human Rights?' (2006) 13 *Maastricht Journal of European and Comparative Law* 195.

unanswered questions have become even more relevant since several scholars and ECtHR judges pointed to procedural issues that may arise in verticalised cases.[16] They have, for example, criticised the fact that, in verticalised cases, one of the private actors involved in the original conflict is unable to defend his acts, interests and rights in the Court's proceedings, while these aspects may be part of the Court's examination and the relevant private actor may eventually be affected by a judgment of the Court.[17] Furthermore, it has been claimed that this may cause difficulties for the Court by confronting it with a situation in which it has to examine a case without having a full and balanced account of the facts of the case and all the rights and interests at stake.[18] This, in turn, raises the question as to whether there may also be consequences for Convention States, for example if domestic courts have to apply and enforce a judgment of the Court in a case in which the original parties to the domestic proceedings are a party.[19]

Just like the characteristics of verticalised cases and the Court's approach to them, these issues require further examination to define the exact extent and implications of the procedural consequences of verticalisation. Exploring these issues will not only provide necessary insight into verticalised cases and how the Court deals with them, but also shed light on how to address the issues arising from the current approach to verticalised cases. Indeed, the Convention system has not been designed to deal with

---

16 See, for example, A. Nussberger, 'Subsidiarity in the Control of Decisions Based on Proportionality: An Analysis of the Basis of the Implementation of ECtHR judgments into German Law' in A. Seibert-Fohr and M. Villiger, *Judgments of the European Court of Human Rights: Effects and Implementation*, Nomos Verlagsgesellschaft 2014, pp. 165–185; N. Bürli, *Third-party interventions before the European Court of Human Rights: Amicus Curiae, Member-State and Third-Party interventions*, Intersentia 2017; C.M.S. Loven, 'A and B v. Croatia and the concurring opinion of Judge Wojtyczek: the procedural status of the "disappearing party"', *Strasbourg Observers* 16 July 2019 <www.strasbourgobservers.com/2019/07/16/a-and-b-v-croatia-and-the-concurring-opinion-of-judge-wojtyczek-the-procedural-status-of-the-disappearing-party/> accessed 31 January 2022; P. Pastor Vilanova, 'Third parties involved in international litigation proceedings. What are the challenges for the ECHR?' in P. Pinto de Albuquerque and K. Wojtyczek (eds.), *Judical power in a globalized world (Liber amicorum Vincent de Gaetano)*, Springer 2019, pp. 377–393; A. Nussberger, '"Second-hand justice" and the rule of law. Dilemmas in implementing the judgments of the European Court of Human Rights' in R. Spano et al (eds.) *Fair trial: regional and international perspectives (Liber amicorum Linos-Alexandre Sicilianos)* Anthemis 2020, pp. 349–363; K. Wojtyczek, 'Procedural Justice and the Proceedings Before the European Court of Human Rights: Who Should Have the Right to be Heard?' in R. Spano et al (eds.), *Fair trial: regional and international perspectives (Liber amicorum Linos-Alexandre Sicilianos)*, Anthemis 2020, pp. 741–755; Concurring Opinion of Judge Wojtyczek in *Bochan v. Ukraine (No. 2)* App No 22251/08 (ECtHR (GC) 5 February 2015) (Judge Wojtyczek expressed similar criticism in his concurring opinion in *A and B v. Croatia* App No 7144/15 (ECtHR 20 June 2019), which originated from a criminal vertical case on (alleged) sexual abuse); Dissenting Opinion of Judge Koskelo in *Kosmas and Others v. Greece* App No 20086/13 (ECtHR 29 June 2017); Partly Dissenting Opinion of Judge Kjølbro in *Orlović and Others v. Bosnia and Herzegovina* App No 16332/18 (ECtHR 1 October 2019); Joint Concurring Opinion of Judges Ravarani and Elósegui in *A.M. and Others v. Russia* App No 47720/19 (ECtHR 6 July 2021).

17 See, for example, Bürli 2017 (n 16), pp. 157ff. This is discussed in detail in Chapter 7 (Section 2).

18 See, for example, Joint Concurring Opinion of Judges Ravarani and Elósegui in *A.M. and Others v. Russia* App No 47720/19 (ECtHR 6 July 2021), para. 1. This is discussed in detail in Chapter 7 (Section 3).

19 This is discussed in more detail in Chapter 8 (Section 3).

such verticalised cases, and they create particular challenges for all actors involved: private actors, Convention States, as well as the Court itself. The Court's legitimacy, for example, may be affected if parties involved in the conflict at the domestic level do not feel that they are being heard by the Court, even though a judgment of the Court may affect their rights and interests.[20] To give another example, the relationship between domestic courts and the Court may be upset if domestic courts face difficulties in applying and enforcing a judgment of the Court in a horizontal case owing to the Court having had to decide on it in a verticalised form.[21] Such challenges to the Convention system give cause to rethink the Court's approach to verticalised cases. Doing so is all the more important because the Court is increasingly being confronted with cases originating in disputes between private actors.[22] An important explanation for this rise in the number of verticalised cases can be found in the Court's own willingness, over time, to increasingly offer substantive protection of Convention rights in relations between private actors by way of imposing horizontal positive obligations.[23] This development also cannot be separated from the fact that the issue of violations of fundamental rights by private actors, particularly companies, has increasingly attracted attention.[24] Indeed, more and more private actors seem to be bringing cases to court in which they hold other private actors accountable for alleged violations of fundamental rights. These include cases involving a private individual's responsibility to delete certain information from his webpage on the basis of another individual's right to be

---

20 More generally, Brems and Lavrysen held that '[t]he crucial lessons from procedural justice research is that if sufficient attention is paid to the requirements of procedural justice, then … individuals will … accept the outcome of the case and the legitimacy of the Court and its case law will not be diminished' (E. Brems and L. Lavrysen, 'Procedural justice in human rights adjudication: the European Court of Human Rights' (2013) 35 *Human Rights Quarterly* 176, 183–184). See Chapter 4 for more details.

21 This is illustrated by, for example, the reasoning of the German Federal Constitutional Court in the case of *Görgülü* concerning the enforcement and application of a judgment of the Court in a verticalised case (BVerfGE, Order of the Second Senate of 14 October 2004, 2 BvR 1481/04 (*Görgülü*) (official English translation). For a detailed discussion of this judgment, see Chapter 8 (Section 3).

22 See also Joint Concurring Opinion of Judges Ravarani and Elósegui in *A.M. and Others v. Russia* App No 47720/19 (ECtHR 6 July 2021), para. 6.

23 See also Concurring Opinion of Judge Wojtyczek in *Bochan v. Ukraine (No. 2)* App No 22251/08 (ECtHR (GC) 5 February 2015), para. 6.

24 The UN Guiding Principles on Business and Human Rights (also known as the 'Ruggie Principles') are a good illustration in this regard. These principles were adopted by the UN Human Rights Council in 2011. A lot have been written on these principles, see, for example, N. Jägers, 'UN Guiding Principles on Business and Human Rights: making headway towards real corporate accountability' (2011) 29 *Netherlands Quarterly of Human Rights* 159; M. Addo, 'The reality of the United Nations Guiding Principles on Business and Human Rights' (2014) 14 *Human Rights Law Review* 133; R. Mares (ed.), *The UN Guiding Principles on Business and Human Rights – foundations and implementation*, Martinus Nijhoff Publishers 2012. In 2014, the UN Human Rights Council established a working-group to develop an international and legally binding treaty on business and human rights. On this development see, for example, O. de Schutter, 'Towards a new treaty on business and human rights' (2016) 1 *Business and human rights journal* 41; S. Deva and D. Bilchitz (eds.), *Building a treaty on business and human rights*, Cambridge University Press 2017; J.L. Černič and N.C. Santarelli (eds.), *The future of business and human rights: theoretical and practical considerations for a UN treaty*, Intersentia 2018.

forgotten[25], or the responsibility of large oil companies to protect the environment.[26] Although such complaints directed against private actors clearly cannot be lodged at the Court directly, this development is ultimately likely to be reflected in the applications brought before the Court, as facilitated by the possibility of verticalisation.

2. RESEARCH AIM AND QUESTIONS

This study aims to provide an in-depth analysis of verticalised cases, given that such cases remain an underexplored aspect of the Convention system while nevertheless accounting for a large share of the Court's case law, and the risk that they may give rise to procedural issues. This general aim of providing an in-depth analysis can be broken down into two sub-aims, which means the research has a dual purpose. First, it seeks to offer insight into the characteristics of verticalised cases and the Court's approach to them; in other words, it aims to conceptualise verticalised cases. Second, it seeks to evaluate the exact extent of the problems in the Court's current approach to verticalised cases – for private actors, Convention States and the Court itself – and to offer an answer to these problems by designing an alternative approach to verticalised cases. The latter means that part of this research is a search for practical solutions that fit the Convention system.[27]

Against this background, the main research question underlying this study is as follows:

> *What are the characteristics of ECtHR cases originating from a conflict between two private actors and how can the Court deal with such verticalised cases while taking due care of the procedural rights of private actors, as well as the position of Convention States and the Court itself?*

---

25 See, for example, the case of *Hurbain v. Belgium* App No 57292/16 (ECtHR 22 June 2021) in which, at the domestic level, an individual had requested a newspaper's publisher to remove a certain article from its electronic archives, or at least to anonymise the article. This case was referred to the Grand Chamber on 11 October 2021.

26 See, for example, the Dutch case of *Milieudefensie [Friends of the Earth Netherlands] v. Shell* (First Instance Court The Hague 26 May 2021, ECLI:NL:RBDHA:2021:5339 (official English translation)). In this case, the NGO Milieudefensie argued that Shell was guilty of hazardous negligence and of violating human rights because of its climate policy (or lack of it). In its argument, Milieudefensie relied, inter alia, on Articles 2 and 8 ECHR. For a more detailed discussion of Milieudefensie's claim, see, for example, C.M.S. Loven, 'Milieudefensie summons Shell: similar obligations for States and companies when it comes to CO2 reduction?', *Blog of the Montaigne Centre for Rule of Law and Administration of Justice* 26 June 2019 <www.blog.montaignecentre.com/en/milieudefensie-summons-shell-similar-obligations-for-states-and-companies-when-it-comes-to-co2-reduction-2/> accessed 31 January 2022.

27 In other words, the research can also be said to have a 'prescriptive voice' (J.M. Smits, 'What is legal doctrine? On the aims and methods of legal-dogmatic research' in R. van Gestel, H.W. Micklitz and E.L. Rubin (eds.), *Rethinking legal scholarship. A transatlantic dialogue*, Cambridge University Press 2017, pp. 207–228, pp. 213ff) or also to be 'reform oriented' since it recommends change (T. Hutchinson, 'The doctrinal method: incorporating interdisciplinary methods in reforming the law' (2015) 3 *Erasmus Law Review* 130, 132).

To answer this question, four sub-questions are addressed:

1. What are the main features of the Convention system and the proceedings before the Court in particular, and what procedural rights do parties have in these proceedings?
2. What are the characteristics of verticalised cases and how are they approached by the Court?
3. What problems does the Court's current approach to verticalised cases give rise to for private actors, Convention States and the Court itself?
4. What possible ways are there, within the Convention system, for addressing the problems identified in question three?

In line with the dual purpose of the research, the four sub-questions concern different types of questions. The first two sub-questions are primarily descriptive and analytical, while the third and fourth are more evaluative and designing in nature. This is further illustrated in Section 4 of this chapter, which elaborates on the research methods employed in this study. First, however, it is useful to further delineate the notion of verticalised cases, as used in this research.

3. DELINEATION OF THE SCOPE OF THE RESEARCH

As explained earlier, this study defines verticalised cases as cases before the Court that originate from a horizontal conflict; that is, a conflict between private actors at the domestic level. To delineate the scope of this research, the present section further elaborates on the notion of verticalised cases and the terminology used. In this regard, it should be noted, first, that a deliberate choice has been made to refer to 'conflicts between private actors' instead of, for example, to 'civil law cases'. In other words, the notion of verticalised cases is not defined on the basis of the type of procedure governing a conflict at the domestic level. This is because the States comprising the Council of Europe all have different legal systems in place. Accordingly, the same situations may be governed by different kinds of procedures. A conflict between the right to reputation and private life and the right to freedom of expression, for example, may be determined under civil law, criminal law, or even both, depending on the applicable domestic legal system.[28] To allow for these differences, it has been chosen to refer, more neutrally, to conflicts between private actors.

---

28 To illustrate, the French Law of 29 July 1881 on the Freedom of the Press establishes that defamation is a criminal offence (Art. 29). Public prosecution, however, is normally undertaken only upon the request of the offended party. In the Dutch system, defamation is criminally sanctioned on the basis of Articles 261–262 of the Criminal Code, but private individuals can also initiate tort proceedings (Article 6:162 Civil Code). The situation in Germany is fairly similar: the German Criminal Code contains provisions on defamation (Section 185 and further), but proceedings can also be of a civil nature and based, for example, on the Copyright Act [Gesetz betreffend das Urheberrecht an Werken der bildenden Künste und der Photographie] or Article 823 of the Civil Code (unlawful act).

Yet this does not mean that all criminal law cases involving a conflict between private actors fall within the scope of this research. Indeed, criminal law cases in the more classical sense (that is, cases relating mainly to the use of violence by individuals that affects other individuals' fundamental rights, such as the right to life, or the prohibition of inhuman or degrading treatment)[29] are outside the scope. Even allowing for differences between the legal systems in Europe, and regardless of the fact that the victim is always an individual, such criminal cases at the domestic level always oppose an individual (the accused) and the State. Put differently, it is the State, in most legal systems, that can act against the accused through prosecution and by bringing court proceedings, and, in many legal systems, the victim is not a party to these proceedings.[30] Therefore, although similar issues may arise in such cases in the sense that one of the individuals involved in the conflict at the domestic level may not be involved in the Court's proceedings[31], such cases generally have a distinct (procedural) nature and give rise to a different set of procedural questions, for example regarding the presumption of innocence and *res judicata*. Furthermore, in criminal law cases concerning violence by individuals against other persons, the underlying conflict and interests at stake are of a specific nature. Admittedly, and just like in many horizontal conflicts, the Convention rights of two individuals – for example, the prohibition of inhuman or degrading treatment (Article 3 ECHR) or the right to liberty (Article 5 ECHR) – may be at stake. Unlike, however, cases involving a conflict between, for example, the right to reputation and private life and the right to freedom of expression, such cases do not centre around the relationship between these rights; that is, the possibility of reconciliation or striking a fair balance between the opposing rights. This was aptly described by the former Judge and Vice-President of the Court, Nussberger, who has argued that 'in these conflicts one right is not the flipside of the other right; the protection of these Convention rights is not mutually exclusive, a balancing exercise is not necessary'.[32] To illustrate this

---

29 Examples of such cases include *E. and Others v. the United Kingdom* App No 33218/96 (ECtHR 26 November 2002); *Opuz v. Turkey* App No 33401/02 (ECtHR 9 June 2009); *Karaahmed v. Bulgaria* App No 30587/13 (ECtHR 24 February 2015).

30 See also Concurring opinion of Judge Elósegui in *A.M. and Others v. Russia* App No 47220/19 (ECtHR 6 July 2021), para. 3. In some legal systems, however, victims can join the criminal proceedings as, for example, *partie civile* (France, Article 2 Code of Criminal Procedure) or as *Nebenkläger* (Germany, Article 395 Code of Criminal Procedure).

31 On this, see also the Concurring Opinion of Judge Wojtyczek in *A and B v. Croatia* App No 7144/15 (ECtHR 20 June 2019) and the Partly concurring opinion of Judge Wojtyczek in *Sabalić v. Croatia* App No 50231/13 (ECtHR 14 January 2021). See also Pastor Vilanova 2019 (n 16).

32 Nussberger 2014 (n 16), p. 173. Cf. Lazarus, who argues that the Court should pay more attention to the fact that 'coercive duties' (protective or preventive positive obligations to protect individuals from harm by other individuals) have to be balanced against the rights of the potential accuser or the accused (L. Lazarus, 'Positive Obligations and Criminal Justice: Duties to Protect or Coerce' in J. Roberts and L. Zedner (eds.), *Principled and values in Criminal Law and Criminal Justice: Essays in Honour of Professor Andrew Ashworth,* Oxford University Press 2012, pp. 135–155; L. Lazarus, 'Preventive obligations, risk and coercive overreach' in L. Lavrysen and N. Mavronicola (eds.), *Coercive Human Rights: Positive Duties to Mobilise the Criminal Law under the ECHR,* Hart Publishing 2020, pp. 249–266).

Nussberger referred to the Court's reasoning in preventive detention cases in which it considered positive obligations to be limited:

> [i]n other words, the Convention obliges State authorities to take reasonable steps within the scope of their powers to prevent ill-treatment of which they had or ought to have had knowledge, but it does not permit a State to protect individuals from criminal acts of a person by measures which are in breach of that person's Convention rights, in particular the right to liberty as guaranteed by Article 5 §1.[33]

For those reasons, and to keep a clear focus, criminal law cases involving violence by private individuals fall outside the scope of this research.

4. RESEARCH METHODS

To achieve the various research aims and answer the central research question, different, but primarily legal doctrinal[34], research methods were employed. This is explained in more detail below, with the research methods being described in relation to each of the four sub-questions.

First, the large body of academic literature on topics such as the drafting history, the guiding Convention principles and the features of the Court's proceedings has allowed for a literature review that provides a description of the main features of the Convention system (the first sub-question). This body of literature includes leading handbooks on the Convention system in general, as well as detailed studies on, for example, the history of the Convention system, and journal articles on particular aspects of the Court's proceedings or guiding Convention principles. In addition to the academic literature, the Rules of Court and the Court's own Admissibility Guide[35] have been explored for the description of the Court's proceedings and characteristics.

To describe and analyse the characteristics of verticalised cases and the Court's approach to them (the second sub-question), a selection of the Court's case law on verticalised cases was qualitatively analysed. To do so, the case law on horizontal

33 *Jendrowiak v. Germany* App No 30060/04 (ECtHR 14 April 2011), para. 37.

34 This means that the Court's case law, as well as legal documents and academic literature, have been rigorously studied to provide an in-depth analysis of verticalised cases before the Court. Dobinson and Francis, for example, defined legal doctrinal research as research in which the researcher 'seeks to collect and then analyse a body of case law, together with any relevant legislation. This … may also include secondary sources as journal articles or other written commentaries on the case law and legislation' (I. Dobinson and J. Francis, 'Legal research as qualitative research' in M. McConville and W. Hong Chui (eds.), *Research methods for law,* Edinburgh University Press 2017 (2nd edition), pp. 18–47, p. 21). See also J. Vranken, 'Exciting times for legal scholarship' (2012) 2 *Law and Method* 2012 42, 43; M. McConville and W. Hong Chui, 'Introduction and overview' in M. McConville and W. Hong Chui (eds.), *Research methods for law,* Edinburgh: Edinburgh University Press 2017 (2nd edition), pp. 1–17, p. 4; Smits 2017 (n 27), pp. 210ff.

35 'Practical Guide on Admissibility Criteria' (updated on 1 August 2021) as prepared by the Registry of the Court.

positive obligations was first generally explored so as to gain insight into different types of verticalised cases coming before the Court. To enable a detailed description of verticalised cases and the Court's approach to them, four types of verticalised cases were subsequently selected for this study: (1) cases related to one's surroundings, (2) cases involving a conflict between the right to reputation and private life and the right to freedom of expression, (3) family life cases, and (4) employer-employee cases. These four sets of verticalised cases were selected because they highlight different types of relations between private actors for which the Court has offered substantive protection of Convention rights through the concept of horizontal positive obligations. These cases also form relatively homogenous groups that represent a good variety of the types of horizontal conflicts from which verticalised cases can originate in four areas forming a significant part of the Court's standard case law. Accordingly, they can be considered illustrative case studies for helping to unravel the notion of verticalised cases and the Court's approach to them.

A case law sample allowing for an in-depth analysis was then put together. For each type of verticalised case, between 15 and 25 judgments were analysed, amounting to an overall sample of nearly 80 judgments.[36] These judgments were selected by making use of references in literature (in standard reference works, peer-reviewed articles and case comments), the Court's factsheets on topics relevant for this study[37], and reports on key cases issued by the Court.[38] In addition, a 'snowball' method was used[39], meaning that some cases were identified as being relevant because of often being cited by the Court in the judgments found in first instance. As this might not yet include the most recent case law, newly published judgments were also followed closely so as to detect new cases relevant for this study.[40] These different selection methods have allowed for primarily analysing judgments that are considered to be part of the Court's standard and most important case law. Accordingly, the sample consists primarily of 'key cases' and 'level 1' and 'level 2' cases.[41]

---

36 A complete overview of the sample can be found in Appendix I.

37 Specifically, the factsheets on 'children's rights', 'parental rights', 'protection of reputation', 'right to protection of one's image', 'surveillance at the workplace', 'work-related rights', and 'environment'. These factsheets are compiled by the Court's Press Service and can be found on the Court's website (<www.echr.coe.int/Pages/home.aspx?p=press/factsheets&c>).

38 Every quarter, upon recommendation of the Jurisconsult, the Bureau, comprising the President, the Vice-Presidents and the Section Presidents of the Court, selects the most important cases dealt with by the Court. These selections can be found on the Court's website (<www.echr.coe.int/Pages/home.aspx?p=caselaw/reports&c=>).

39 This term is often used to describe a sampling technique in which the network of research participants is used to find additional research participants ('snowball sampling'). See A. Bryman, *Social Research Methods*, Oxford University Press 2008 (3rd edition), pp. 184–185.

40 This was done until 1 September 2021. The case law sample consequently does not include judgments issued after this date.

41 These importance levels are assigned by the Court. Key cases are cases with the highest level of importance (see also n 38). Level 1 cases are 'all judgments, decisions and advisory opinions not included in the Case Reports which make a significant contribution to the development clarification or modification of it's [the Court's] case law, either generally or in relation to a particular State'. Level 2 cases are 'other judgments, decisions and advisory opinions which, while not making a significant

Subsequently, the selection of verticalised cases has been qualitatively analysed. To answer the second sub-question, this analysis focused on two aspects: the characteristics of the underlying conflict and the Court's approach to the case. The characteristics of the underlying conflict could be construed on the basis of the description of the facts of the case included in the Court's judgments, which contain a description of the proceedings at the domestic level. To understand and describe the Court's approach to verticalised cases, the judgments were studied by looking at the nature of the Court's review (i.e. substantive, procedural or a mix of both) and the rights and interests that were visibly taken into account by the Court, according to its own reasoning. In addition, it was identified for each case whether the private party involved in the conflict at the domestic level, not being the applicant, was involved in the Court's proceedings by way of third-party intervention and, if so, how the Court dealt with these third-party submissions in its judgment.

Regarding the third sub-question in this study, the findings on the characteristics of verticalised cases and the Court's approach to them were evaluated to examine the problems to which the Court's current approach to verticalised cases gives rise for private actors, Convention States and the Court itself. The research conducted for the first and second sub-question formed an important basis for doing so. The evaluation was conducted in the light of, for example, the procedural rights of parties in the Court's proceedings and the guiding Convention principles as explored in answering the first sub-question. In addition to the findings for the first and second sub-questions, relevant academic literature and separate opinions were analysed to obtain insight into problems identified by scholars and ECtHR judges.[42] In relation to the third sub-question, it should lastly be mentioned that a distinction was made between problems arising *during* the Court's proceedings and problems arising *after* the Court's proceedings. To explore the latter, an analysis was made of the execution process in the verticalised cases examined for this study. For these cases, documents of the Committee of Ministers of the Council of Europe on the execution of judgments[43] – more specifically, resolutions, action plans and action reports – were studied to obtain insight into the specific measures taken by Convention States to execute judgments of the Court in verticalised cases. This analysis focused on whether proceedings were reopened or new proceedings were initiated after the Court's judgment.

The above provided the basis for answering the fourth sub-question on possible ways to address the problems arising in verticalised cases as identified in relation to the third sub-question. It is explained in Part IV that the insights obtained from the first three sub-questions lead to the conclusion that, within the Convention system, a redesigned third-party intervention can be a useful way to address the problems arising in verticalised cases identified in the light of sub-question three. In order to draft a proposal for redesigning the third-party intervention of Article 36 ECHR, the form and features of the

contribution to the case law, nevertheless go beyond merely applying existing case law' (see 'HUDOC FAQ' accessible on <www.echr.coe.int/Documents/HUDOC_FAQ_ENG.pdf>).

42 These separate opinions were issued in cases included in the research's case law sample, as well as in some cases not included in the sample.

43 These documents can be accessed at: <www.hudoc.exec.coe.int>.

current third-party intervention procedure were explored, based on a study of the Rules of Court in combination with a literature review. The final proposal was drafted in the light of these findings. Inspiration was also drawn from several non-judicial and judicial writings by scholars and judges at the Court on a right to third-party intervention for private actors involved in the conflict at the domestic level, not being the applicant.

Finally, in relation to how the research was conducted, it should be mentioned that the author was a visiting researcher at the Court for three months in autumn 2019, when she was part of the Court's research division and contributed to several research projects. Since the Court's proceedings form an important aspect of the research, it was considered important to have an understanding of the workings of the Court based not only on books, but also on experience and conversations with judges and lawyers working at the Court. The research stay allowed for this. In particular, being part of the research division and having several conversations with both lawyers and judges at the Court helped to get a better understanding of how the Court's judgments come about, the challenges the Court faces in general, and in dealing with verticalised cases in particular, and the need for and feasibility of alternative approaches to verticalised cases. In autumn 2021, the author returned to Strasbourg to discuss the provisional findings of this study with several judges. As, however, these discussions were used merely as background information, and do not provide a separate basis for this study or its findings, they have not been recorded or coded, and the interlocutors can remain anonymous.[44]

5. OUTLINE

This book consists of four parts, each focusing on one of the sub-questions central to this study. The Convention system is introduced in Part I, starting with the history of the Convention system (Chapter 2). The aim of this is to provide insight into why the Convention system requires complaints about interferences with Convention rights to be directed against one of the Convention States. The chapter also aims to provide a basis for understanding the nature and characteristics of the Convention system, as described in the subsequent chapters. These characteristics include the effectiveness and subsidiarity principles, two guiding Convention principles that play an important role in interpreting and applying the Convention, and in the functioning of the Convention system as a whole, and that are therefore discussed separately in Chapter 3. As a final step in introducing the Convention system, the main characteristics of proceedings before the ECtHR are explored (Chapter 4). This is done by discussing procedural rules and standards that apply to proceedings before the ECtHR, including the procedural rights of parties in these proceedings, with particular attention being paid to procedural standards following from Article 6 (the right to a fair trial) and Article 13 (the right to an effective remedy) of the Convention. Although these standards are directed to domestic authorities, this study

44 The author is very grateful to the Court lawyers and judges for finding time to discuss the issues with her.

takes the view, in line with commonly accepted principles, that they must also apply to proceedings before the ECtHR. As such, this discussion serves as a basis for analysing the Court's current approach to verticalised cases from private actors' perspective.

Following the introduction to the Convention system in Part I, Part II provides a detailed analysis of verticalised cases before the Court. To this end, the concept of horizontal positive obligations is discussed in Chapter 5. These obligations are discussed first and separately because they are often imposed in cases originating from a conflict between two private actors at the domestic level. Accordingly, their discussion allowed a selection to be made of different types of verticalised cases coming before the Court. The notion of verticalised cases is further unravelled in Chapter 6, in which – focusing on the four types of verticalised cases mentioned in Section 4 (cases related to one's surroundings, cases involving a conflict between the right to reputation and private life and the right to freedom of expression, family life cases, and employer-employee cases) – the characteristics of and the Court's approach to verticalised cases are set out. The characteristics of verticalised cases are explained by discussing differences in the nature of, and the parties involved in, the conflict at the domestic level. When exploring the Court's approach to verticalised cases, specific attention is paid to the Court's type of review (i.e. procedural, substantive, or a combination of the two), the rights and interests that are taken into account by the Court when examining a verticalised case, and the question of whether the private party in the conflict at the domestic level, not being the applicant, is involved in the Court's proceedings by way of a third-party intervention.

The analysis of verticalised cases presented in Part II demonstrates that an important aspect in verticalised cases is that one of the private actors involved in the conflict at the domestic level is not formally part of the proceedings before the ECtHR. Part III examines which specific challenges this creates for the Convention system. More specifically, a more evaluative approach is taken by highlighting problems that may arise *during* the Court's proceedings (Chapter 7) and problems that may arise *after* the Court has handed down its judgment in a verticalised case (Chapter 8). It follows from the findings presented in these chapters that the problems concern private actors, Convention States and the Court itself.

To address these problems, the final part of this book (Part IV) presents a proposal for a new approach to verticalised cases. More specifically, it explains how the problems arising in verticalised cases could potentially be addressed by redesigning the third-party intervention procedure of Article 36 ECHR to grant third parties with a legal interest in the case ('actual third parties') a right to intervene in the Court's proceedings. To this effect, the form and features of the current third-party intervention procedure are first described (Chapter 9), followed by the proposal for redesigning the third-party intervention procedure (Chapter 10).

Chapter 11 concludes this study by providing a synthesis of the most important findings and by discussing verticalised cases – and particularly the proposal for a new approach to verticalised cases – in the light of the main characteristics of the Convention system.

PART I

INTRODUCTION TO THE CONVENTION SYSTEM

CHAPTER 2
SHORT HISTORY OF THE CONVENTION SYSTEM

1. INTRODUCTION

This chapter introduces the Convention system by first providing a short analysis of its history.[45] The aim of this analysis is to give further insight as to why the Convention requires complaints about interferences with Convention rights to be directed against one of the Convention States. This chapter also serves as a basis for understanding the nature and characteristics of the Convention system as described in more detail in the subsequent chapters. To this end, the intentions behind the Convention system (Section 2) are discussed first, followed by the legal obligations imposed by the Convention (Section 3), and the creation and evolution of the Convention's enforcement mechanisms (Section 4). This discussion shows how the Convention system evolved from primarily offering an inter-State safeguard of democracy to protecting individuals against a wide range of interferences with Convention rights by the State.

2. INTENTIONS BEHIND THE CONVENTION SYSTEM

The Convention was drafted in the years after the Second World War, which had provided horrific examples of how States can misuse their sovereign power and deeply violate individuals' dignity, autonomy and freedom. Or, as Tomuschat put it, '[i]t had been learned during the horrendous years from 1933 to 1945 that a state apparatus can turn into a killing machine, disregarding its basic function to uphold and defend the human dignity of every member of the community under its power'.[46] As the Second World War had exposed the consequences of allowing States to hide behind the shield of

---

[45] This chapter relies heavily on the work of Bates (E. Bates, *The evolution of the European Convention on Human Rights: from its inception to the creation of a permanent Court of Human Rights*, Oxford University Press 2010) which provides an extensive, detailed and excellent overview of the history of the Convention system. For a detailed discussion of this history, see also J.G. Merrills and A.H. Robertson, *Human rights in Europe: a study of the ECHR*, Manchester University Press 2001 (4th edition); A.W. Brian Simpson, *Human rights and the end of empire*, Oxford University Press 2001; D. Nicol, 'Original intent and the European Convention on Human Rights' (2005) *Public Law* 152.

[46] C. Tomuschat, *Human rights: between idealism and realism*, Oxford University Press 2014 (3rd edition), pp. 27–28.

national sovereignty[47], it became accepted that the protection of human rights could not be left to the domain of the States. In other words, international and regional systems were needed to protect citizens from State interference with their fundamental rights.[48] This was contrary to the general stance, which had been dominant for centuries, that international law governed only relations between States and did not deal with matters within States' domestic jurisdiction.[49] This idea of State sovereignty relied on the notion that States were fully at liberty to make their own decisions and set their own rules, and thus potentially free to commit 'wicked barbarism'[50] against their own people.[51]

The first achievements of the internationalisation of human rights were the Charter of the United Nations (UN) in 1945 and the Universal Declaration of Human Rights (UDHR) in 1948.[52] The UN Charter names '... promoting and encouraging respect for human rights and fundamental freedom for all without distinction as to race, sex, language or religion'[53] as one of the objectives of the UN. The preamble to the UDHR states, moreover, that 'human rights should be protected by the rule of law'.[54] Although the UDHR has no legally binding force (being only a recommendation of the UN General Assembly) it has gained moral, political, and legal force through customary law.[55] Consequently, the UDHR has been called a 'momentous achievement for the international law of human rights'[56] and '[the] accelerat[or] [in] the evolution of international human rights'.[57] This is illustrated by its being used as an important source of inspiration for codifying human rights in national constitutions, as well as in human rights treaties.[58] These treaties include the European Convention on Human Rights, which explicitly states in the preamble that '[c]onsidering the Universal Declaration of Human Rights...', 'the Governments of European countries ... take the

47 P. Lauren, *The evolution of international human rights: visions seen*, University of Pennsylvania Press 2011 (3rd edition), p. 138.

48 Lauren 2011 (n 47), p. 138; N. Rodley, 'International human rights law' in M. Evans (ed.) *International law*, Oxford University Press 2014 (4th edition), pp. 783–820, p. 816.

49 See, for example, J. Wouters et al. (eds.), *International law: A European perspective*, Hart Publishing 2019, pp. 676–677.

50 Bates 2010 (n 45), p. 34.

51 Brian Simpson 2001 (n 45), pp. 12 and 92.

52 Lauren 2011 (n 47), p. 225. See also D. Shelton (ed.), *The Oxford Handbook of International Human Rights*, Oxford University Press 2013, p, 195; B. Rainey (ed.), *Jacobs, White and Ovey: the European Convention on Human Rights*, Oxford University Press 2017 (7th edition), p. 3. For an extensive discussion of the origins of the UDHR see, for example, J. Morsink, *The Universal Declaration of Human Rights: origins, drafting and intent*, University of Pennsylvania Press 1999.

53 Article 1, para. 3 UN Charter. See also Article 55(c) UN Charter.

54 Preamble to the UDHR.

55 Lauren 2011 (n 47), p. 225; Wouters et al. (eds.) 2019 (n 49), p. 678. Eleanor Roosevelt, the US representative at the UN General Assembly when the UDHR was drafted, stressed, for example, that the UDHR did not 'purport to be a statement of law or of legal obligations' (E. Roosevelt cited in E. Bates, 'History' in D. Moeckli, S. Shah, S. Sivakumaran (eds.), *International human rights law*, Oxford University Press 2014 (2nd edition), pp. 3–21, p. 19). The fact that the UDHR had no legal force is considered to be an important reason for its acceptance by the 48 States (Bates 2014, p. 19).

56 Bates 2010 (n 45), p. 38.

57 Lauren 2011 (n 47), p. 225.

58 Wouters et al. (eds.) 2019 (n 49), p. 165.

first steps for the collective enforcement of certain of the Rights stated in the Universal Declaration'.

The Convention was the first legislative achievement of the Council of Europe, which came into being on 3 August 1949.[59] Human rights, democracy and the rule of law have been the three pillars of the Council of Europe from the outset.[60] Article 3 of the Statute of the Council of Europe, for example, provides that '[e]very member of the Council of Europe must accept the principles of the rule of law and of the enjoyment by all persons within its jurisdiction of human rights and fundamental freedoms'. The maintenance of human rights and fundamental freedoms are not only objectives of the Council of Europe, but also a condition for membership.[61] This follows from Article 4 of the Statute, which provides that only European States that are 'able and willing to fulfil the provisions of Article 3 may be invited to become a member of the Council of Europe'.[62]

Like the UN Charter, the Statute of the Council of Europe paved the way for the creation of a human rights document. On 4 November 1950, only a year after the Council of Europe came into being, the Member States signed the final version of the text of the European Convention on Human Rights, the first binding regional treaty on human rights. According to Tomuschat it was 'only natural' that the Council of Europe immediately started working on a treaty instrument designed to provide effective protection of human rights by means of mechanisms of collective enforcement, given that the Council of Europe was regarded as an institution that could help prevent the recurrence of tragedies similar to those of the Second World War.[63]

It readily follows from the above that the Second World War was one of the immediate causes for drafting the Convention. However, the years in which the Convention was drafted were also characterised by fears of a communist threat coming from Eastern Europe and the risks of a third global conflict breaking out between the East and the West. These circumstances, taken together with the aftermath of the Second World War, are widely viewed as the immediate reason for drafting the Convention.[64] The Convention was thus intended to provide a means for avoiding

59 Bates 2010 (n 45), p. 49.

60 J. Sweeney, *The European Court of Human Rights in the post-Cold War era: universality in transition*, Taylor and Francis 2013, p. 10; N. Weiss, 'Origin and further development' in S. Schmahl and M. Breuer (eds.), *The Council of Europe: its law and policies*, Oxford University Press 2017, pp. 3–22, p. 16; M. Breuer, 'Establishing common standards and securing the rule of law' in S. Schmahl and M. Breuer (eds.), *The Council of Europe: its law and policies* Oxford University Press 2017, pp. 639–670, p. 639.

61 See also Merrills and Robertson 2001 (n 45), p. 3; O. Dörr, 'The European Convention on Human Rights' in S. Schmahl and M. Breuer (eds.), *The Council of Europe: its law and policies*, Oxford University Press 2017, pp. 465–506, p. 466.

62 It even follows from Article 8 of the Statute that violation of this condition can lead to the suspension or expulsion from the Council of Europe.

63 Tomuschat 2014 (n 46), p. 34.

64 See, for example, Merrills and Robertson 2001 (n 45), p. 4; Nicol 2005 (n 45), p. 155; M.R. Madsen, 'From cold war instrument to Supreme European Court: the European Court of Human Rights at the crossroads of international and national law and politics' (2007) 32 *Law & Social Inquiry* 137, 140; Bates 2010 (n 45), p. 44; Sweeney 2013 (n 60), p. 11; Rainey 2017 (n 52), pp. 3–4; A. Drzemczewski,

repeating the most serious human rights violations seen during the Second World War and protecting States against communist threats and potential new tyrants.[65] In other words, it was intended to function as a 'rampart against tyranny and oppression'[66] and to 'facilitate democratic stability across the union by preventing the emergence or re-emergence of totalitarian regimes'[67] by acting as an 'alarm bell'[68] for democratic Europe. In a similar vein, former President of the Court, Wildhaber, spoke of 'an international law insurance policy or early warning system to prevent democracies from relapsing into dictatorship'.[69]

The idea of the alarm bell was widely supported as the primary objective of the Convention at the time it was drafted, although some held that the system also could serve more far-reaching objectives and regarded the Convention as a European Bill of Rights.[70] Proponents of these more far-reaching objectives sought to lay down an extensive list of all the rights that a human being should enjoy, including social and economic rights, instead of a list including merely political and civil rights.[71] This discloses a lack of consensus regarding the Convention's ultimate goals[72] or, as Bates put it, that 'the Convention meant different things to different people'.[73] This is further illustrated by the debate about the enforcement mechanisms to accompany the Convention, which will be highlighted in Section 4.

Despite a lack of consensus regarding the Convention's ultimate goals, the foregoing shows that the Convention's aim was to protect individuals against violations of fundamental rights by States or, in other words, to 'restrain States' exercise of power'.[74] According to some legal scholars, this is also reflected in the absence of references in the Convention to private law-related interests such as freedom of contract and testamentary freedom.[75] The rights closely related to relations between individuals

'The role and authority of the European Court of Human rights', *2018 International Conference: Constitutional Courts and Human Rights Protection*, 1–2 October 2018, organised by Judicial Yuan (Constitutional Court, Taipei, Taiwan), p. 118; S. Greer, J.H. Gerards, R. Slowe, *Human rights in the Council of Europe and the European Union*, Cambridge University Press 2018, p. 3.

65 Rainey 2017 (n 52), pp. 3–4.

66 Bates 2010 (n 45), p. 45.

67 Bates 2010 (n 45), p. 53.

68 Bates 2010 (n 45), p. 54.

69 L. Wildhaber, *The European Court of Human Rights 1998–2006: history, achievements, reform*, N.P. Engel Publisher 2006, p. 137.

70 This idea was in particular supported by Teitgen, who had a prominent role in the drafting of the Convention (Bates 2010 (n 45), pp. 63ff). See also Nicol 2005 (n 45), pp. 155ff.

71 Nicol 2005 (n 45), p. 157.

72 Nicol 2005 (n 45), p. 155.

73 E. Bates, 'The birth of the European Convention on Human Rights' in J. Christoffersen and M.R. Madsen (eds.), *The European Court of Human Rights: between law and politics*, Oxford University Press 2011, pp. 17–42, p. 25.

74 J.H. Gerards, *General principles of the European Convention on Human Rights*, Oxford University Press 2019, p. 136.

75 I. Leigh, 'Horizontal rights, the Human Rights Act and Privacy: lessons from the Commonwealth' (1999) 48 *International and Comparative Law Quarterly* 57, p. 73; O. Cherednychenko, *Fundamental rights, contract law and the protection of the weaker party: a comparative analysis of the*

can also be regarded as reflecting the idea that the Convention was first and foremost designed to protect individuals against the State, and particularly against a totalitarian regime. The right to the protection of family life, for example, was aimed at 'tackling and condemning the ruthless and savage way in which totalitarian regimes of the recent past had endeavoured to wipe out the concept of the family as the natural unit of society'.[76] Similarly, the reason for including a right to property in the first additional protocol to the Convention[77] was that the first acts of totalitarian States was to deprive political opponents of their property.[78]

3. LEGAL OBLIGATIONS IMPOSED BY THE CONVENTION

The previous section discussed the primary aim of the Convention as being to act as an 'alarm bell' for democratic Europe and to protect individuals against violations of fundamental rights by the State. To do so, the Convention imposes legal obligations on States, as clearly illustrated by Article 1 of the Convention, which provides that '[t]he High Contracting Parties shall secure to everyone within their jurisdiction the rights and freedoms defined in Section I of this Convention'. The specific use of the word *secure* is important here. First, it implies that Article 1 of the Convention involves an immediate obligation of both ends and means[79], rather than an obligation to merely promote the protection of human rights or to attempt to live up to the obligations under the Convention. Instead, after ratifying the Convention, States have a direct obligation under international law to ensure that their national laws are in conformity with the Convention. This means that States cannot avoid complying with obligations laid down in the Convention by claiming them to be inconsistent with national law.[80] The word *secure,* moreover, has been interpreted as imposing both negative and positive obligations on States and thus requiring them both to abstain from interfering with human rights and to take action to secure human rights.[81] Article 1 of the Convention

---

constitutionalisation of contract law, with emphasis on risky financial transactions, Sellier, European Law Publishers 2007, pp. 147–148.

76 Maxwell-Fyfe cited in Bates 2010 (n 45), p. 67.

77 Protocol No. 1 to the Convention entered into force in May 1954. The right to property was not part of the Convention text that was signed in 1950, but instead included in the First Protocol to the Convention. The reason for this is that it proved difficult to draft a provision that protected against arbitrary deprivation of property by totalitarian regimes and, at the same time, left room for nationalisation policies of socialist governments such as the British (Bates 2010 (n 45), p. 68).

78 Nicol 2005 (n 45), p. 162; Bates 2010 (n 45), p. 68.

79 I. Cameron, *An introduction to the European Convention on Human Rights*, iUSTUS 2018 (8th edition), p. 51. By way of comparison, according to the text of Article 2 (1) of the UN International Covenant on Civil and Political Rights (adopted by the UN General Assembly on 16 December 1966 and which entered into force on 23 March 1976), States must *undertake* action to *respect and to ensure* the rights recognised in the Convention. See also Bates 2010 (n 45), p. 111; Cameron 2018, p. 51.

80 Bates 2010 (n 45), pp. 111 and 129.

81 For a detailed discussion of positive obligations, see Chapter 5.

prescribes, furthermore, that States must *secure* the rights and freedoms laid down in the Convention to *everyone within their jurisdiction*. This represents a departure from the traditional international law concept of nationality.[82] Instead of only securing the rights and freedoms laid down in the Convention to their nationals, States must secure the rights and freedoms laid down in the Convention to every person within their jurisdiction, regardless of the person's nationality or status.[83]

It also clearly follows from the history of the Convention as explained in Section 2, as well as from the intentions of its drafters, and from Article 1 of the Convention, that the Convention imposes legal obligations on States only.[84] Accordingly, an application before the Court cannot be brought against another individual, as explained in more detail in Section 2.1 of Chapter 4. Moreover, the obligations imposed on States relate first and foremost to relations between individuals and the State, i.e. to vertical relationships.[85]

4. THE CONVENTION AND ITS ENFORCEMENT MECHANISMS: FROM INTER-STATE TO INDIVIDUAL APPLICATIONS

In the previous sections, it was shown that the Convention was the first regional human rights system to impose legal obligations on States to safeguard the fundamental rights of individuals. This section discusses how the Convention not only imposed legal obligations on States, but was also accompanied by a collective enforcement mechanism both to ensure protection of individual rights and to serve the 'alarm bell function' that the Convention system was intended to have. This, again, was revolutionary for its time.[86] The UDHR, for example, did not establish an institutional machinery to secure respect for its provisions.[87] Indeed, the revolutionary nature of a collective enforcement

---

82 Drzemczewski 2018 (n 64), p. 119.

83 In 1961 the European Commission on Human Rights already held that '[w]hereas, therefore, in becoming a Party to the Convention, a State undertakes, vis-à-vis the other High Contracting Parties, to secure the rights and freedoms defined in Section 1 to every person within its jurisdiction, regardless of his or her nationality or status; whereas, in short, it undertakes to secure these rights and freedoms not only to its own nationals and those of other High Contracting Parties, but also to nationals of States not parties to the Convention and to stateless persons' (*Austria v. Italy* App No 788/60 (EComHR 11 January 1961), paras. 18–19).

84 Occasionally, however, it has been argued that the Convention imposes obligations on private persons as well. See, for example, M.A. Eissen, 'The European Convention on Human Rights and the Duties of the Individual' (1962) *Nordisk Tidsskrift for International Ret* 230, 230.

85 However, this does not mean that infringements of the values, rights and liberties enshrined in the Convention by individuals are completely ignored in the Convention system. In Part II of this study (Chapter 5), it is explained that, through the concept of horizontal positive obligations, the Court has increasingly required States to protect Convention rights in relations between individuals (i.e. horizontal relations). By doing so, the Court has created a manner in which, albeit indirectly, the Convention may also impose obligations on individuals.

86 See also A. Kjeldgaard-Pedersen, *The international legal personality of the individual*, Oxford University Press 2018, pp. 167 and 176.

87 Brian Simpson 2001 (n 45), p. 11.

mechanism was witnessed by the great difficulties that the signatory States experienced in reaching agreement on the mechanism and its form.

The discussion on the enforcement mechanism accompanying the Convention focused on two issues: the creation of a Court and the right for individuals to petition. Two different viewpoints or groups were prominent in this discussion: one group of States – including Belgium, France, Ireland and Italy – subscribed to the idea of a European Commission and a European Court of Human Rights and a right for individuals to petition. Another group of States – including Greece, Norway, the Netherlands, and the United Kingdom – was hesitant regarding the setting-up of international institutions of control, in particular the creation of a European Court; these States were opposed to a right to petition for individuals.[88] These opposing views were linked to the underlying question of the nature of the Convention. Those who saw the Convention as a safeguard of democracy and regarded it as an 'alarm bell' were largely opposed to the instalment of a Court and the right to individual petition, while the proponents of a European Bill of Rights supported both of these issues.[89]

Given the prevailing notions and ideas in the 1940s, it was hardly surprising that some States were hesitant about establishing international enforcements mechanisms, including a right to petition for individuals. Indeed, the ideas of submitting to an international court and allowing a right to petition for individuals were opposite to the traditional dogmas and principles of international law[90], which regarded international law as being created by, between, and for States, and in which State sovereignty and State voluntarism were leading concepts.[91] By contrast, the envisaged enforcement mechanisms were about proclaiming and enforcing certain fundamental guarantees for individuals against the State.[92] Introducing them could have a direct effect on State sovereignty since an aspect of a State's control and authority over its activities within its territory would become subject to international legal review.[93] The revolutionary nature of this is well illustrated by a quote of Hersch Lauterpacht, one of the leading international lawyers of the twentieth century and author of several key publications on international (human rights) law. According to Lauterpacht, the transformation of relations between a State and its nationals into international legal obligations by which the international community could derive a respectable and meaningful level of control and censure would engender 'restrictions on sovereignty more far-reaching in their implications than any yet propounded in the annals of international utopias'.[94]

88 Bates 2010 (n 45), pp. 89–90.

89 Nicol 2005 (n 45), p. 164.

90 Bates 2010 (n 45), p. 85; Sweeney 2013 (n 60), pp. 12–13.

91 F. Mégret, 'Nature of obligations' in D. Moeckli, S. Shah, S. Sivakumaran (eds.), *International human rights law*, Oxford University Press 2014 (2nd edition), pp. 86–109, p. 87.

92 F. Mégret 2014 (n 91), p. 87; A. Moravcsik, 'The origins of Human Rights Regimes: Democratic Delegation in Postwar Europe' (2000) 54 *International Organisation* 217, pp. 217–218.

93 R. McCorquodale, 'The individual and the international legal system' in M. Evans (ed.), *International law*, Oxford University Press 2014 (4th edition), pp. 280–305, pp. 285 and 290.

94 H. Lauterpacht (1945) cited in Bates 2014 (n 55), p. 3.

In the end, the drafters of the Convention could not agree on the extent to which they wanted to break with the traditional dogmas and principles of international law. It was therefore decided to leave the creation of a Court and the granting of a right to petition to individuals up to the individual States. Consequently, the acceptance of the jurisdiction of the Court and the right to individual petition were not made compulsory in 1950, but were instead laid down in optional protocols. This did not mean, however, that the Convention did not provide a 'collective enforcement' mechanism from the start. Indeed, in the original Convention system, three institutions were made responsible for enforcing the Convention: the European Commission of Human Rights, the Committee of Ministers and the Court. Of these three bodies, the Commission and the Committee of Ministers were initially considered to be the most important. Illustrative in this regard is that although the Court came into being in 1959, until 1994 it was only possible for a case to be referred to the Court by the Commission or the States, and only if the respondent State had recognised the jurisdiction of the Court.[95]

From 1950, the Commission could receive applications from Convention States, while from 1955 it could also receive individual applications, but only if the State had accepted the optional protocol.[96] The Commission's main duties were to receive applications and assess their admissibility, to establish the facts of admissible cases, to reach a friendly settlement and, if such a settlement was not possible, to draft a full report stating its (non-binding) opinion as to whether the Convention had been breached.[97] This report was then sent to the Committee of Ministers (or to the Court if the respondent State had accepted its jurisdiction and the Commission or a State chose to refer the case to the Court) to make a final decision.

The Committee of Ministers already existed when the Convention entered into force. It was the standing executive organ of the Council of Europe and consisted of the political representatives of every Member State of the Council of Europe.[98] In the Convention system as originally designed, the Committee of Ministers exercised judicial powers. If a case was not referred to the Court, the Committee of Ministers would decide, by a two-thirds majority, whether the Convention had been violated. The decision of the Committee of Ministers (or the Court) was binding on the respondent State. The Committee of Ministers would subsequently monitor the respondent State's compliance with the final decision. The judicial role of a political body such as the Committee of Ministers is explained by several authors as being attributable to the revolutionary nature of the Convention system.[99] According to Sicilianos and Kostopoulou, for

95 This changed when Protocol No. 9 came into being as this allowed individuals to bring a case before the Court. This Protocol opened for signing in November 1990 and came into force in 1994 (see also Merrills and Robertson 2001 (n 45), p. 19; Dörr 2017 (n 61), p. 470.

96 Bates 2010 (n 45), p. 120.

97 Bates 2010 (n 45), p. 120. See also Cameron 2018 (n 79), pp. 45–46.

98 Under Article 13 of the Statute of the Council of Europe, the Committee of Ministers is the organ acting on behalf of the Council of Europe.

99 Bates 2010 (n 45), pp. 119 and 123; Cameron 2018 (n 79), pp. 45–46; L.A. Sicilianos and M.A. Kostopoulou, *The individual application under the European Convention on Human Rights*, Council of Europe 2019, p. 23.

example, the Committee of Ministers was given a judicial role in order to 'allay States' fears by affording them a degree of control over the way the system operated'.[100]

In the original procedure, as set out above, the individual had an 'inferior'[101] status. An individual could only bring an application before the Commission if the relevant State had accepted the optional protocol. And even when an individual was allowed to file a complaint, the individual applicant would not receive a copy of the Commission's report and would not have any contact with the Committee of Ministers.[102] More generally, the inclusion in optional protocols of the jurisdiction of the Court and the right to individual petition shows that in 1950 the collective enforcement of Convention rights was primarily concerned with ensuring that States fulfilled their basic obligations under the Convention, rather than with hearing personalised human rights cases and dispensing individual human rights justice.[103] Or, as Harris put it, '[t]he original purpose of the Convention was not primarily to offer a remedy for particular individuals who had suffered violations of the Convention but to provide a collective, inter-State guarantee that would benefit individuals generally by requiring the national law of the contracting parties to be kept within certain bound'.[104] Hence, an application was envisaged as a mechanism for bringing to light a breach of an obligation of one State to others, and not to provide a remedy for an individual victim.[105]

Over the years, however, the Convention system increasingly came to be viewed as a form of remedy that could help provide individual justice.[106] Two important developments in this regard were Protocol No. 9, which came into force in 1994 and allowed individuals to bring a case before the Court directly if their case had been decided by the Commission, and Protocol No. 11, which came into force in 1998 and was even more ground-breaking than Protocol No. 9. Protocol No. 11 completely restructured the Convention's enforcement mechanism by, first, abolishing the Commission and installing a new, single, permanent and full-time Court. Second, it resulted in the Committee of Ministers losing its judicial power to decide on cases, while nevertheless remaining the body responsible for supervising the execution of judgments. Third, Protocol No. 11 made the jurisdiction of the Court compulsory for all Convention States. Lastly, and most importantly, Protocol No. 11 gave individuals an automatic right to petition to the Court.[107] In other words, since Protocol No. 11 entered into force, the exercise of the individual right to petition has no longer been conditional on acceptance by the Convention States. Hence, Sicilianos and Kostopoulou speak of an 'unconditional' and 'procedural right in the true sense'.[108]

---

100 Sicilianos and Kostopoulou 2019 (n 99), p. 23.
101 Bates 2010 (n 45), p. 404.
102 Bates 2010 (n 45), pp. 122–123.
103 Bates 2010 (n 45), p. 131; Greer, Gerards, Slowe 2018 (n 64), pp. 12–13.
104 D. Harris et al., *Harris, O'Boyle and Warbrick: Law of the European Convention on Human Rights*, Oxford University Press 2018 (4th edition), p. 39.
105 Harris et al. 2018 (n 104), p. 39.
106 Bates 2010 (n 45), pp. 126 and 146. See also Wildhaber 2006 (n 69), p. 141.
107 Merrills and Robertson 2001 (n 45), pp. 20–22; Bates 2010 (n 45), p. 146.
108 Sicilianos and Kostopoulou 2019 (n 99), p. 13.

These reforms mean that the Convention system has become a fully fledged judicial regime, with a court of law as the single organ deciding exclusively whether the States have violated their obligations under the Convention.[109] The Convention's enforcement mechanism, moreover, has evolved from a system primarily focused on inter-State applications to a system dominated by individual applications. The current importance of the right to individual application is recognised by both the Court and the Convention States. In *Mamatkulov and Askarov* the Court held, for example, that:

> the provision concerning the right to individual application is one of the fundamental guarantees of the effectiveness of the Convention system of human rights protection. In interpreting such a key provision, the Court must have regard to the special character of the Convention as a treaty for the collective enforcement of human rights and fundamental freedoms. Unlike international treaties of a classic kind, the Convention comprises more than mere reciprocal engagements between Contracting States. It creates, over and above, a network of mutual, bilateral undertakings, objective obligations which, in the words of the Preamble, benefit from a "collective enforcement".[110]

In the Brighton Declaration of 2012, the Convention States reaffirmed that the right of individual petition is a cornerstone of the Convention system.[111]

The acceptance of a mandatory and unconditional right to petition for individuals and the acknowledgment of this right as a cornerstone of the Convention system would give the impression that it is widely accepted that providing individual justice is the primary task of the Convention system. Yet, there is an ongoing debate on whether this is indeed the Court's primary task.[112] More specifically, this debate concerns the question of whether the Convention should be seen primarily as a mechanism to provide individual justice, as a mechanism to provide constitutional justice, or as a mechanism to provide a combination of the two types of justice. According to proponents of the individual justice view, the Court's task is first and foremost to provide individuals with redress

---

109 Dörr 2017 (n 61), p. 470.

110 *Mamatkulov and Askarov v. Turkey* App Nos 46827/99 and 46951/99 (ECtHR (GC) 4 February 2005), para. 100.

111 Council of Europe April 2012, Brighton Declaration, paras. 2 and 13. Similar statements had been made in the Interlaken Declaration (Council of Europe 19 February 2010, Action Plan, para. 1) and the Izmir Declaration (Council of Europe 27 April 2011, Follow-up Plan, para. 1).

112 See, for example, L. Wildhaber, 'A constitutional future for the European Court on Human Rights?' (2002) 25 *Human Rights Law Journal* 161; P. Mahoney, 'New challenges for the European Court of Human Rights resulting from the expanding case load and membership' (2002) 21 *Penn State International Law Review* 101; W. Sadurski, 'Partnering with Strasbourg: constitutionalisation of the European Court of Human Rights, the accession of Central and East European States to the Council of Europe, and the idea of pilot judgments' (2009) 9 *Human Rights Law Review* 397; S. Greer and L. Wildhaber, 'Revisiting the debate about "constitutionalising" the European Court of Human Rights' (2012) 12 *Human Rights Law Review* 655; F. de Londras, 'Dual functionality and the persistent frailty of the European Court of Human Rights' (2013) 1 *European Human Rights Law Review* 38; K. Dzehtsiarou and A. Greene, 'Restructuring the European Court of Human Rights: preserving the right of individual petition and promoting constitutionalism' (2013) *Public Law* 710.

if one of their Convention rights is violated.[113] On the other hand, proponents of the constitutional justice view do not focus so much on the individual but on the Court's role in addressing systematic fundamental rights problems. Accordingly, they contend that the Court's primary responsibility is to select and to adjudicate on the most serious alleged violations of the Convention.[114]

Greer and Wildhaber, for example, argue that the idea that the systematic delivery of individual justice could and should be the Court's main function is untenable for three reasons.[115] Although they acknowledge that the principle of individual petition is likely to remain central to the Court's future, they hold, first, that the systematic delivery of individual justice was not what the Convention system was originally set up for, and that this applies even less so now. Referring to the 'alarm bell idea', they argue that the primary task of the Convention system is to defend the character and integrity of European political and legal orders, rather than to benefit individual applicants.[116] Second, they point out that there is no realistic prospect of justice being systematically delivered to every applicant with a legitimate complaint about a Convention violation. In this regard, they refer to the fact that the Court is only able to rule on about 10 per cent of the applications it receives.[117] Finally, they argue that even if a violation is found to have occurred, this may prove to be a hollow victory for applicants because the levels of compensation are generally not high and other rewards are few.[118] Similar to these two final arguments of Greer and Wildhaber, Christoffersen stated that '[t]he Crown jewel of the Convention is the right of individual petition, but the jewel does not shine as brightly as it used to'.[119] Reason for Christoffersen to make this point is the Court's lack of capacity and power to provide individual relief to the extent needed in the present-day Council of Europe.[120]

---

113 This view is represented, for example, by M.B. Dembour, '"Finishing off" cases: the radical solution to the problem of the expanding ECtHR caseload' (2002) 5 *European Human Rights Law Review* 604 and J. Wadham and T. Said, 'What price the right of individual petition: report of the evaluation group to the Committee of Ministers on the European Court of Human Rights' (2002) 2 *European Human Rights Law Review* 169. According to Dembour it is 'why the Court was created in the first place' (p. 622), while according to Wadham and Said it is the Court's 'crucial function' to provide individual justice (p. 174).

114 Greer, Gerards, Slowe 2018 (n 64), p. 112. On the constitutional justice view, see, for example, O.M. Arnardóttir, 'The Brighton aftermath and the changing role of the European Court of Human Rights' (2018) 9 *Journal of International Dispute Settlement* 223; Mahoney 2002 (n 112); Wildhaber 2002 (n 112); Greer and Wildhaber 2012 (n 112); De Londras 2013 (n 112).

115 Greer and Wildhaber 2012 (n 112), pp. 664–666. These reasons are also put forward and explained in Greer, Gerards, Slowe 2018 (n 64), pp. 111–112.

116 Greer and Wildhaber 2012 (n 112), pp. 664–665; Greer, Gerards, Slowe 2018 (n 64), p. 111. See also J.H. Gerards and L.R. Glas, 'Access to justice in the European Convention on Human Rights System (2017) 35:1 *Netherlands Quarterly of Human Rights* 11, 17.

117 Greer and Wildhaber 2012 (n 112), p. 665; Greer, Gerards, Slowe 2018 (n 64), p. 111.

118 Greer and Wildhaber 2012 (n 112), p. 666; Greer, Gerards, Slowe 2018 (n 64), p. 112.

119 J. Christoffersen, 'Individual and constitutional justice: can the power balance of adjudication be reversed?' in J. Christoffersen and M.R. Madsen (eds.), *The European Court of Human Rights: between law and politics*, Oxford University Press 2011, pp. 181–203, p. 182.

120 Christoffersen 2011 (n 119), p. 182.

The debate on the primary function of the Convention and its enforcement mechanism is inextricably intertwined with a discussion on whether the Convention and the Court are of a constitutional nature. Already around the time of the recognition of the unconditional right to individual petition in 1998, Cameron held that 'this ultimate recognition of the full procedural capacity of the individual makes it impossible to continue ignoring the quasi-constitutional character of the Convention'.[121] Cameron's qualification is grounded in the development of the Court's primary function into settling disputes between an individual and the State, i.e. his or her parliament, government, or administration. According to Cameron, the Court resembles national constitutional courts insofar as this task involves questioning the validity of national legislation.[122] Similarly, when identifying a number of reasons on which the idea of the constitutional character of the Convention and the Court is based, Bates mentioned that, in practice, the Court has obtained a certain power of review or control over the three branches of government at the national level. To illustrate this, Bates points out that the Court has interpreted and applied the Convention in such a way that it has a certain (albeit limited) capacity to question, or perhaps even indirectly invalidate, the policy choices of democratically elected parliaments.[123] Similarly, Sadurski refers to the Court increasingly seeking to identify structural defects in national laws and to States increasingly seeming to perceive the Court's judgments as a directive to change their laws.[124] At the same time, however, Sadurski acknowledges that the Court is not fully constitutional in the way that, for example, the US Supreme Court or the German Federal Constitutional Court are constitutional courts. According to Sadurski, the reason for this is that the State's duty to implement a Court's decision remains of an international law character, meaning that it is a treaty-based obligation, and that the mechanisms of enforcement for guaranteeing implementation are of a moral and political nature.[125] To further illustrate the constitutional character of the Convention and the Court, Bates also points out that the Convention reads like a European Bill of Rights that the Court has interpreted by using similar techniques to those employed by domestic Supreme Courts interpreting national Bills of Rights. Regarding the latter, Bates refers, for example, to the Court interpreting the Convention as a 'living instrument', meaning that the rights laid down in the Convention are interpreted evolutively, and that many concepts in the Convention have been interpreted autonomously.[126]

---

121 I. Cameron, 'Protocol 11 to the European Convention on Human Rights: the European Court of Human Rights as a Constitutional Court?' (1995) 15 *Yearbook of European Law* 219, 237.

122 Cameron 1995 (n 121), pp. 223–224.

123 Bates 2010 (n 45), pp. 155–157 and 358.

124 Sadurski 2009 (n 112), pp. 449–450.

125 Sadurski 2009 (n 112), pp. 448.

126 Bates 2010 (n 45), pp. 154 and 357. On constitutional reasoning and the ECtHR see also J.H. Gerards, 'The European Court of Human Rights' in A. Jakab, A. Dyevre, G. Itzcovich (eds.), *Comparative Constitutional reasoning*, Cambridge University Press 2017, pp. 237–276, pp. 255ff.

The pilot judgment procedure is an example of a relatively recent development that some scholars consider to be confirmation of the constitutional justice view and an indication of the Court's increasing constitutional nature.[127] Reason for this is that this procedure, which originated in the discussions of Protocol No. 14 in 2004, is intended to help the national authorities to eliminate systemic or structural problems highlighted by the Court.[128] In practice, this means that the Court selects one or several particular cases to provide the State with general recommendations on how to address the structural issue and then adjourns the examination of comparable cases awaiting the national measures.[129] Besides the pilot judgment procedure, the advisory opinion procedure may be viewed as another development contributing to the constitutional nature of the Court. Indeed, it was argued in the Wise Persons' Report of 2006 that an extended advisory jurisdiction would enhance the Court's 'constitutional role'.[130] The advisory opinion procedure was introduced in Protocol No. 16[131] and creates the opportunity for the highest courts and tribunals of a Convention State to request the Court for an advisory opinion on 'questions of principle relating to the interpretation or application of the rights and freedoms defined in the Convention or the Protocols

---

127 Sadurski 2009 (n 112), pp. 412ff; Greer and Wildhaber 2012 (n 112), p. 671; Gerards and Glas 2017 (n 116), p. 18. For an extensive analysis of the pilot-judgment procedure in the light of the function and nature of the Convention and its enforcement mechanisms see, for example, D. Kurban, 'Forsaking individual justice: the implications of the European Court of Human Rights' Pilot judgment procedure for victims of gross and systematic violations' (2016) 16 *Human Rights Law Review* 731.

128 For a detailed analysis of the pilot-judgment procedure see, for example, A. Buyse, 'The pilot judgment procedure at the European Court of Human Rights: possibilities and challenges' (2009) 57 *Nomiko Vina* 1913; P. Leach, H. Hardman, S. Stephenson, 'Can the European Court's pilot judgment help resolve systematic human rights violations? *Burdov* and the failure to implement domestic court decisions in Russia' (2010) 10 *Human Rights Law Review* 346; L.R. Glas, 'The functioning of the pilot-judgment procedure of the European Court of Human Rights in practice' (2016) 34 *Netherlands Quarterly of Human Rights* 41.

129 Rule 61 of the Rules of Court (ed. 18 October 2021). See also Gerards and Glas 2017 (n 116), p. 27.

130 Report of the Group of Wise Persons to the Committee of Ministers of 15 November 2006, doc. CM(2006)203, para. 81. In 1995, long before the introduction of the advisory opinion procedure, Cameron already said that 'the Court will not be a truly constitutional court unless either a preliminary reference procedure is introduced or an obligation of reopening becomes part of the Convention regime' (Cameron 1995 (n 121), p. 259).

131 Protocol No. 16 entered into force on 1 August 2018, after being ratified by ten Convention States (on 12 April 2018, France ratified the Protocol as the tenth Convention State). Protocol No. 16 is an optional protocol meaning that it is only in force for the countries that have ratified it (see https://conventions.coe.int for the current status of signatures and ratification). For a detailed discussion of the advisory opinion procedure see, for example, C. Giannopoulos, 'Considerations on Protocol No. 16: Can the New Advisory Competence of the European Court of Human Rights Breathe New Life into the European Convention on Human Rights?' (2015) 16 *German Law Journal* 337; A. Paprocka and M. Ziółkowski, 'Advisory opinions under Protocol No. 16 to the European Convention on Human Rights' (2015) 11 *European Constitutional Law Review* 274; T. Voland and B. Schiebel, 'Advisory opinions of the European Court of Human Rights: unbalancing the system of human rights protection in Europe?' (2017) 17 *Human Rights Law Review* 73; J.H. Gerards, 'Advisory Opinion: European Court of Human Rights (ECtHR)', *Max Planck Encyclopedia of International Procedural Law (MPEiPro)*, Oxford University Press 2019.

thereto'.[132] The procedure is regarded as enhancing the Court's constitutional role as it enables the Court to provide an opinion on the interpretation or application of the Convention, with the aim of giving the 'requesting court or tribunal guidance on Convention issues when determining the case before it' (instead of transferring the dispute to the Court).[133]

As noted above, a third stance in the debate on the primary task and nature of the Convention system comprises a combination of the two opposing views of individual and constitutional justice, with the Convention and the Court regarded as having a 'dual functionality'[134] and being of a 'dual nature'.[135, 136] In this view, the principle of individual petition is still central to the Convention system, but, at the same time, it is acknowledged that the Court provides constitutional justice. Similarly, and although the Court is not considered to be 'fully constitutional'[137], it is acknowledged that it has become 'much more constitutional than before'.[138] The view that the Convention and Court have a 'dual functionality' also seems to be held by the Convention States and the Court. In the above-mentioned Brighton Declaration, the Convention States not only reaffirmed the right of individual petition to be a cornerstone of the Convention system, but also emphasised that 'the Court should be in a position to focus its efforts on serious or widespread violations, systemic and structural problems, and important questions of interpretation and application of the Convention, and hence would need to remedy fewer violations itself and consequently deliver fewer judgments'.[139] In a similar vein, the Court has held as early as 1979 that its task is 'not only to decide those cases brought before the Court, but, more generally, to elucidate, safeguard and develop the rules instituted by the Convention'.[140] More recently, the Court held in *Karner* that:

> [a]lthough the primary purpose of the Convention system is to provide individual relief, its mission is also to determine issues on public-policy grounds in the common interest, thereby raising the general standards of protection of human rights and extending human rights jurisprudence throughout the community of Convention States.[141]

---

132 Article 1(1) Protocol No. 16 to the Convention. See also Rules of Court (ed. 18 October 2021), Chapter X.

133 *Advisory Opinion concerning the recognition in domestic law of a legal parent-child relationship between a child born through a gestational surrogacy arrangement abroad and the intended mother* App No P16-2018-001 (ECtHR (GC) 10 April 2019), para. 25.

134 This term is used by De Londras 2013 (n 112) and Dzehtsiarou and Greene 2013 (n 112).

135 Gerards 2017 (n 126), p. 239.

136 See also Drzemczewski 2018 (n 64), pp. 120–121; Gerards and Glas who conclude that 'increasingly, general and individual justice were proposed as equally important aspects of the system' (Gerards and Glas 2017 (n 116), p. 18) and Christoffersen who has said that 'there are severe restrictions on the Court's role as an institution granting individual relief, just as there are serious limits on the Court's scope for developing a constitutional role' (Christoffersen 2011 (n 119), p. 202).

137 Sadurski 2009 (n 112), p. 448.

138 Sadurski 2009 (n 112), p. 449.

139 Brighton Declaration 20 April 2012, para. 33.

140 *Ireland v. the United Kingdom* App No 5310/71 (ECtHR 18 January 1978), para. 154.

141 *Karner v. Austria*, App No 40016/98 (ECtHR 24 July 2003), para. 26.

In *Rantsev* the Court reiterated that:

> its judgments serve not only to decide those cases brought before it but, more generally, to elucidate, safeguard and develop the rules instituted by the Convention, thereby contributing to the observance by the States of the engagements undertaken by them as Contracting Parties.[142]

5. CONCLUSION

It follows from the preceding sections that, at the time the Convention was drafted and its enforcement mechanism was installed, the Convention was primarily seen as an inter-State pact against totalitarianism and an 'alarm bell' for democratic Europe.[143] In those early days, therefore, the primary objective of the Convention system thus was to deal with complaints by States against each other and to protect the democratic identity of Convention States, as well as to promote international cooperation between States.[144] However, at the time the Convention was drafted, some States also embraced a different objective, and specifically the objective of creating a European Bill of Rights and offering human rights justice to individuals. Indeed, over the years the Convention has been increasingly viewed as a remedy for individualised human rights justice, especially after the mandatory right to individual petition.[145] Nowadays, the Court's function is considered to be one of providing both individual and constitutional justice, and the Court's nature is regarded as having become more constitutional than before. This means that the Court not only provides individual redress if an individual's Convention rights are violated, but also addresses systematic problems pertaining to fundamental rights. The growing constitutional nature of the Court also results in the Court providing guidance on questions relating to the interpretation of Convention standards and that it has gained a certain power of review or control over the three branches of government in Convention States.

142 *Rantsev v. Cyprus and Russia* App No 25965/04 (ECtHR 7 January 2010), para. 197.
143 Bates 2010 (n 45), p. 104.
144 Greer, Gerards, Slowe 2018 (n 64), pp. 12–13.
145 Bates 2010 (n 45), p. 126.

CHAPTER 3
GUIDING CONVENTION PRINCIPLES

1. INTRODUCTION

In developing the introduction to the Convention system further, this chapter discusses two guiding Convention principles: the principle of effectiveness (Section 2) and the principle of subsidiarity (Section 3), which play an important role in the interpretation and application of the Convention and the functioning of the Convention system as a whole. This is further explained below by providing a general background to the effectiveness and subsidiarity principle and discussing different manifestations of these principles, including the no fourth-instance court doctrine, the margin of appreciation doctrine, and procedural review.

2. PRINCIPLE OF EFFECTIVENESS

In the *Belgian Linguistic* case of 1968 the Court held that the general aim of the Convention is 'to provide effective protection of fundamental rights'.[146] Eleven years later, in *Airey*, the Court articulated the principle of effectiveness for the first time, holding that 'the Convention is intended to guarantee not rights that are theoretical or illusory but rights that are practical and effective'.[147] Ever since, the Court has used this formula in its judgments. In *Scoppola (No. 2)* the Court even held that '[i]t is of crucial importance that the Convention is interpreted and applied in a manner which renders its rights practical and effective'.[148]

Thus, the effectiveness principle plays an important role in guiding the interpretation and application of the Convention.[149] In practice, this has resulted in a broad interpretation of Convention rights and a narrow interpretation of their exceptions and

---

146 *Belgian Linguistic Case* App No 1474/62 (ECtHR 23 July 1968), para. I.B.5.

147 *Airey v. Ireland* App No 6289/73 (ECtHR 9 October 1979), para. 24.

148 *Scoppola v. Italy (No. 2)* App No 10249/03 (ECtHR (GC) 17 September 2009), para. 104.

149 This was for the first time confirmed in *Soering* in which the Court held that 'the object and purpose of the Convention as an instrument for the protection of individual human beings require that its provisions be interpreted and applied so as to make its safeguards practical and effective' (*Soering v. the United Kingdom* (App No 14038/88 (ECtHR 7 July 1989), para. 87). See also J.H. Gerards, *General principles of the European Convention on Human Rights*, Oxford University Press 2019, p. 4.

restrictions.[150] The 'living instrument doctrine', which finds its basis in the effectiveness principle, plays an important role in this regard.[151] This doctrine entails that the Court interprets the Convention 'in the light of present-day conditions' and enables it to keep up with changing (technological or social) conditions in the Convention States.[152] As such, it is a tool for the Court to provide effective protection of Convention rights. By applying the living instrument doctrine, the Court has, for example, extended the scope of Article 4 ECHR to human trafficking[153] and the scope of Article 8 ECHR to gender identity[154] and environmental issues.[155] In addition to being a basis for a broad interpretation of Convention rights, the principle of effectiveness has been an important foundation for the development and recognition of positive obligations for States to protect Convention rights.[156] This is further explained in Part II (Chapter 5), in which the concept of (horizontal) positive obligations is discussed in detail.

The above examples are not the only manifestations of the principle of effectiveness. Illustrative in this regard is Judge Serghides' statement that 'the principle of effectiveness is one which must always follow the journey of an application from beginning to end, from the admissibility stage to the implementation stage'.[157] With regard to the admissibility stage, it should be noted that the effectiveness principle plays an important role in the application of the exhaustion of domestic remedies rule (Article 35(1) ECHR), even if this rule is mostly regarded as a manifestation of the subsidiarity principle.[158] However, the effectiveness principle here acts as a kind of 'check' on the subsidiarity principle. The exhaustion of domestic remedies rule requires States to have remedies in place that are effective and available, not only in theory, but also in practice.[159] In order to provide effective protection of Convention rights the Court may make an exception to the rule if the domestic remedies are 'inadequate or ineffective'.[160] It should also be noted, in relation to the admissibility stage, that the Court has interpreted the victim

150 D. Rietiker, 'The principle of "effectiveness" in the recent jurisprudence of the European Court of Human Rights: its different dimensions and its consistency with the public international law – No need for the concept of treaty sui generis' (2010) 79 *Nordic Journal of International Law* 245, 259.

151 Gerards 2019 (n 149), p. 52. See also L.R. Glas, *The Theory, Potential and Practice of Procedural Dialogue in the European Convention on Human Rights System*, Intersentia 2016, p. 32; G. Serghides, 'The Principle of Effectiveness in the European Convention on Human Rights. In Particular its Relationship to the other Convention Principles' in J. Vidmar (ed.) *Hague Yearbook of International Law* (Vol. 30), Brill Nijhoff 2017, pp. 1–16, pp. 3–4.

152 See, for example, *Christine Goodwin v. the United Kingdom* App No 28957/95 (ECtHR (GC) 11 July 2002), para. 74; *Scoppola v. Italy (No 2)* App No 10249/03 (ECtHR (GC) 17 September 2009), para. 104.

153 *Rantsev v. Cyprus and Russia* App No 25965/04 (ECtHR 7 January 2010).

154 *Christine Goodwin v. the United Kingdom* App No 28957/95 (ECtHR (GC) 11 July 2002).

155 *Hatton and Others v. the United Kingdom* App No 36022/97 (ECtHR (GC) 8 July 2003).

156 Gerards 2019 (n 149), pp. 4–5. See also Serghides 2017 (n 151), pp. 3–4.

157 Serghides 2017 (n 151), p. 15.

158 *Akdivar and Others v. Turkey* App No 21893/93 (ECtHR (GC) 16 September 1996), para. 65. See also Glas 2016 (n 151), pp. 30–31. For a discussion of the exhaustion of domestic remedies rule as a manifestation of the subsidiarity principle, see Section 3 in this chapter.

159 See, for example, *Akdivar and Others v. Turkey* App No 21893/93 (ECtHR (GC) 16 September 1996), para. 66.

160 See, for example, *Selmouni v. France* App No 25803/94 (ECtHR (GC) 28 July 1999), paras. 76–77.

requirement of Article 34 ECHR in the light of the principle of effectiveness; more specifically, by allowing a wider range of victims – indirect victims[161] and potential victims[162] – of a violation of the Convention to bring a complaint before the ECtHR. Finally, with regard to the execution of judgments, the effectiveness principle can manifest itself when the Court indicates individual or general measures, on the basis of Article 46 ECHR, that the respondent State should take to provide for redress for the violation of the Convention.[163]

The principle of effectiveness thus plays an important role in the interpretation and application of the Convention throughout the Court's proceedings. Indeed, as discussed with regard to the subsidiarity principle below, the Court sometimes uses the effectiveness principle as a 'safety net in situations where strict reliance on the subsidiarity principle may render the protection of the Convention rights practically ineffective'.[164]

3. PRINCIPLE OF SUBSIDIARITY

The principle of subsidiarity is another guiding Convention principle. The following discussion of the general background to this principle (Section 3.1) and its different manifestations (Section 3.2) explains how this principle relates to the relationship between the Court and the Convention States.

3.1. GENERAL BACKGROUND

Although Articles 1, 13, 19 and 35(1) of the Convention have been identified as the basis for the subsidiarity principle[165], the principle did not feature in the original text of the Convention until Protocol No. 15 to the Convention entered into force in 2021. In other words, the subsidiarity principle was first recognised in the Court's case law. In the *Belgian Linguistic* case the Court reasoned for the first time that:

> [i]n attempting to find out in a given case, whether or not there has been an arbitrary distinction, the Court cannot disregard those legal and factual features which characterise the life of the society in the State which, as a Contracting Party, has to answer for the measure in dispute. In so doing it cannot assume the rôle of the competent national authorities, for it

161 See, for example, *Sejdovic v. Italy* App No 56581/00 (ECtHR (GC) 1 March 2006), para. 45; *Selami and Others v. the former Yugoslavic Republic of Macedonia* App No 78241/13 (ECtHR 1 March 2018), para. 73.

162 See, for example, *Klass and others v. Germany* App No 5029/71 (ECtHR 6 September 1978), para. 34; *Roman Zakharov v. Russia* App No 47143/06 (ECtHR (GC) 4 December 2012), paras. 173–178.

163 Glas 2016 (n 151), p. 32.

164 Glas 2016 (n 151), pp. 28–29.

165 See, for example, *Scordino v. Italy (No 1)* App No 36813/97 (ECtHR (GC) 29 March 2006), para. 140. See also A. Mowbray, 'Subsidiarity and the European Convention on Human Rights' (2015) 15 *Human Rights Law Review* 313, 320.

> would thereby lose sight of the subsidiary nature of the international machinery of collective enforcement established by the Convention. The national authorities remain free to choose the measures which they consider appropriate in those matters which are governed by the Convention. Review by the Court concerns only the conformity of these measures with the requirements of the Convention.[166]

This reasoning was confirmed and further developed in *Handyside* in which the Court held that 'the machinery of protection established by the Convention is subsidiary to the national systems safeguarding human rights'[167], and that 'it is no way the Court's task to take the place of the competent national courts but rather to review … the decisions they delivered in the exercise of their power of appreciation'.[168] Since then, the Court has consistently referred to the subsidiarity principle in its case law, such as in *Scordino (No. 1),* when the Court held that:

> the primary responsibility for implementing and enforcing the rights and freedoms guaranteed by the Convention is laid on the national authorities. The machinery of complaint to the Court is thus subsidiary to national systems safeguarding human rights.[169]

These examples of the Court's case law clearly show that the principle of subsidiarity concerns the relationship between the Court and the Convention States. More specifically, it defines the role of the Court vis-à-vis the Convention States as a subsidiary and supervisory role. The Court's task is thus to review whether the measures chosen by the domestic authorities in matters governed by the Convention are consistent with the principles of the Convention, as interpreted in the Court's case law.[170]

The subsidiarity principle, as developed in the Court's case law, has featured in the Convention since Protocol No. 15 to the Convention entered into force.[171] Indeed, to 'enhance the transparency and the accessibility'[172] of characteristics of the Convention system such as the subsidiarity principle, the Convention States agreed to include an explicit reference to the subsidiarity principle in the Preamble to the Convention. The relevant recital reads as follows:

> [a]ffirming that the High Contracting Parties, in accordance with the principle of subsidiarity, have the primary responsibility to secure the rights and freedoms defined in this Convention and the Protocols thereto, and that in doing so they enjoy a margin of appreciation, subject to the supervisory jurisdiction of the European Court of Human Rights established by this Convention.[173]

---

166 *Belgian Linguistic Case* App No 1474/62 (ECtHR 23 July 1968), para. I.B.10.

167 *Handyside v. the United Kingdom* App No 5493/72 (ECtHR 7 December 1976), para. 48.

168 *Handyside v. the United Kingdom* App No 5493/72 (ECtHR 7 December 1976), para. 50.

169 *Scordino v. Italy (No 1)* App No 36813/97 (ECtHR (GC) 29 March 2006), para. 140.

170 See, for example, *Scordino v. Italy (No 1)* App No 36813/97 (ECtHR (GC) 29 March 2006), para. 191.

171 Protocol No. 15 to the Convention was adopted on 24 June 2013 and entered into force on 1 August 2021.

172 Explanatory report to Protocol No. 15 to the Convention, para. 7. See also Brighton Declaration 20 April 2012, para. 12.B.

173 Protocol No. 15 to the Convention, Article 1.

Protocol No. 15 was drafted to give effect to the Declaration adopted at the Brighton Conference in 2012.[174] This was one of five high-level conferences on the future of the Court, organised between 2010 and 2018.[175] These conferences must be seen against the background of growing domestic discontent with the Court.[176] National critics have alleged, inter alia, that the Court has become overly active and intrusive when interpreting the Convention and assessing decisions of domestic authorities and domestic policies in general.[177] According to political actors in some Convention States, this has undermined the structure of the Convention system by failing to acknowledge the primary role assigned to national authorities in securing the rights and freedoms defined in the Convention.[178] To address these concerns, the Brighton Declaration 'intended to rebalance national authorities relationships with the Strasbourg Court'[179] by stressing the importance of the subsidiarity principle. The Brighton Declaration states, for example, that 'the Convention system is subsidiary to the safeguarding of human rights at national level and that national authorities are in principle better placed than an international court to evaluate local needs and conditions'.[180] Hence, the Brighton Conference welcomed 'the development by the Court in its case law of principles such as subsidiarity and the margin of appreciation and encourages the Court to give great prominence to and apply consistently these principles in its judgments'.[181] Furthermore, it concluded that 'a reference to the principle of subsidiarity and the

174 Explanatory report to Protocol No. 15 to the Convention, para 4.

175 The first high-level conference on the future of the Court was organised in Interlaken on 18–19 February 2010. This was followed by the Izmir Conference (27–27 April 2011), the Brighton Conference (19–20 April 2012), the Brussels Conference (26–27 March 2015) and the Copenhagen Conference (12–13 April 2018). These conferences and their aftermath are extensively covered in the literature, see, for example, A. Mowbray, 'The Interlaken Declaration: The beginning of a new era for the European Court of Human Rights?' (2010) 10 *Human Rights Law Review* 519; R. Spano, 'Universality or diversity of human rights? Strasbourg in the age of subsidiarity' (2014) 14 *Human Rights Law Review* 487; D. Walton, 'Subsidiarity and the Brighton Declaration' in A. Seibert-Fohr and M. Villiger, *Judgments of the European Court of Human Rights: Effects and Implementation*, Nomos Verlagsgesellschaft 2014, pp. 193–206; P. Popelier and C. van de Heyning, 'Subsidiarity post-Brighton: procedural rationality an answer?' (2017) 30 *Leiden Journal of International Law* 5; O.M. Arnardóttir, 'The Brighton aftermath and the changing role of the European Court of Human Rights' (2018) 9 *Journal of International Dispute Settlement* 223; I. Cram, 'Protocol 15 and Articles 10 and 11 ECHR – The partial triumph of political incumbency post-Brighton?' (2018) 67 *International and Comparative Law Quarterly* 477; L.R. Glas, 'From Interlaken to Copenhagen: What has become of the proposals aiming to reform the functioning of the European Court of Human Rights?' (2020) 20 *Netherlands Quarterly of Human Rights* 121.

176 Glas 2020 (n 175), p. 134. See also O.M. Arnardóttir, 'Organised retreat? The move from "substantive" to "procedural" review in the ECtHR's case law on the margin of appreciation' (2015) *European Society of International Law Annual Conference*, p. 2.

177 The criticism was voiced particularly in the United Kingdom. Illustrative in this regard is a speech by Lord Hoffmann in 2009, entitled 'The universality of human rights' (Lord Hoffmann, 'The universality of human rights', Judicial Studies Board Annual Lecture 19 March 2009).

178 Cram 2018 (n 175), p. 478.

179 Cram 2018 (n 175), p. 478.

180 Brighton Declaration 20 April 2012, para. 11.

181 Brighton Declaration 20 April 2012, para. 12(a).

doctrine of the margin of appreciation as developed in the Court's case law should be included in the Preamble to the Convention'.[182]

The Copenhagen Conference, in 2018, was the fifth high-level conference on the future of the Court. In the declaration resulting from this conference it was claimed that the reform process started in 2010 had indeed led to the strengthening of subsidiarity.[183] In a similar vein, four years earlier, Judge Spano had argued that the adding of a direct reference to the concepts of subsidiarity and the margin of appreciation in the preamble:

> created an important incentive for the Court ... to develop a more robust and coherent concept of subsidiarity', and that 'in some very important recent judgments ... the Court has demonstrated its willingness to defer to the reasoned and thoughtful assessment by national authorities of their Convention obligations.[184]

At the same time, however, Spano stressed that this development did not 'introduce, in essence, any novel feature into Strasbourg jurisprudence, but constitutes rather a further refinement or reformulation of pre-existing doctrines'.[185] Glas drew a similar double-edged conclusion in an overview article on the five high-level conferences on the future of the Court, concluding that although 'the literature confirms cautiously that the Court has placed greater emphasis on the subsidiarity principle ... this change is neither widespread nor necessarily leads to more deference to domestic authorities'.[186] The foregoing shows that the meaning and function of the subsidiarity principle are highly complex[187], as further illustrated by the discussion of different manifestations of the subsidiarity principle below.

3.2. MANIFESTATIONS

The subsidiarity principle has different manifestations. The Court first distinguishes between procedural subsidiarity and substantive subsidiarity.[188] Procedural subsidiarity is explained as governing 'the working relationship between the Court and the national authorities and the division of responsibility for action and intervention'.[189] This procedural aspect of subsidiarity finds its manifestation mainly in the rules that the Court may deal with a case only after all domestic remedies have been exhausted (Article 35(1)) and that States are free to choose the means by which they comply

182 Brighton Declaration 20 April 2012, para. 12(b).
183 Copenhagen Declaration 13 April 2018, para. 4.
184 Spano 2014 (n 175), p. 491.
185 Spano 2014 (n 175), p. 491.
186 Glas 2020 (n 175), p. 149.
187 On the complexity of the principle of subsidiarity see also Mowbray 2015 (n 165).
188 European Court of Human Rights, *The principle of subsidiarity. Note by the Jurisconsult,* 8 July 2010, para. 17.
189 European Court of Human Rights, *The principle of subsidiarity. Note by the Jurisconsult,* 8 July 2010, para. 17.

with a judgment of the Court (Article 46(1)).[190] Substantive subsidiarity, on the other hand, is explained as 'governing relative responsibilities for decision-making and assessment'.[191] The Court identifies the no fourth-instance court and the margin of appreciation doctrine as the two manifestations of this particular type of subsidiarity. Because of their special relevance for the current study, the latter two manifestations of the subsidiarity principle are discussed in more detail below (Sections 3.2.1 and 3.2.2). In addition to the manifestations of the subsidiarity principle as distinguished by the Court, several other expressions of the subsidiarity principle have been identified in the literature. These include procedural review, whereby the Court examines the quality of national decision-making; that is, the domestic legislative process, decisions by administrative bodies or judicial decision-making. This particular manifestation of the subsidiarity principle is discussed in Section 3.2.3. Section 3.2.4 then provides a short overview of various other manifestations that have been identified in the literature.

3.2.1. No fourth-instance court doctrine

The no fourth-instance court doctrine makes clear what the Court is *not*. It prescribes that the Court is neither a court of appeal nor a court that can quash rulings given by the domestic courts or retry cases heard by them, and also that it cannot re-examine cases in the same way as a supreme court.[192] In the Action Plan of the Interlaken Declaration, for example, the Convention States invited the Court to 'avoid reconsidering questions of fact or national law that have been considered and decided by national authorities, in line with its case-law according to which it is not a fourth-instance court'.[193] It is for this reason, too, that, in the Convention system, 'fourth-instance complaints' (i.e., complaints inviting the Court to act as a fourth-instance court) are one of the four categories of complaints that will be held to be manifestly ill-founded within the meaning of Article 35(3a) ECHR.[194] More concretely, this means that applications asking the Court to deal with errors of fact or law allegedly committed by a national court will be declared inadmissible.

However, the no fourth-instance court doctrine does not play a role solely in the admissibility stage of the proceedings. If a complaint is declared admissible and assessed on its merits, the Court may not, as a general rule, question the findings and conclusions of the domestic courts regarding the establishment of the facts of the case, the interpretation and application of domestic law, the admissibility and assessment of evidence at the trial, the substantive fairness of the outcome of a civil dispute, or the

190 Article 46(1) ECHR is further discussed in Chapter 8 (Section 2).

191 European Court of Human Rights, *The principle of subsidiarity. Note by the Jurisconsult,* 8 July 2010, para. 17.

192 European Court of Human Rights, *The principle of subsidiarity. Note by the Jurisconsult,* 8 July 2010, para. 28.

193 Interlaken Declaration 19 February 2010, Action Plan, para. E.9(a). See similarly Izmir Declaration 27 April 2011, Follow-up Plan, para. F.2(c).

194 European Court of Human Rights, *Practical guide on the admissibility criteria* (last update: 1 August 2021), paras. 281ff. The other three categories are: complaints where there has clearly or apparently been no violation, unsubstantiated complaints and confused or far-fetched complaints.

guilt or innocence of the accused in criminal proceedings.[195] In *Perlala*, for example, the Court reasoned that:

> it is not for the Court to deal with errors of fact or law allegedly committed by a domestic court, unless they affected the rights and freedoms guaranteed in the Convention. The Court itself cannot assess the factual elements which led a national court to adopt a particular decision, otherwise it would be acting as a court of third or fourth instance and would disregard the limits of its task.[196]

This clearly illustrates the subsidiary, supervisory role of the Court. The Court does not have the authority to conduct a re-run of the proceedings at the domestic level as the domestic authorities are presumed to have greater expertise in the relevant facts of the case, as well as the contents of domestic law.[197] In other words, the role of the Court is not to 'replace the national courts in their tasks, but only to review their decision as a whole in the light of their Convention obligations'.[198]

It is important to note, however, that if a domestic court's alleged errors of fact or law may have led to an interference with rights and freedoms protected by the Convention, the Court may still examine the domestic decision on these points to provide effective protection of Convention rights. In, for example, *De Tommaso* the Court held that it should not act as a fourth-instance body unless the findings of the national courts can be regarded as 'arbitrary or manifestly unreasonable'.[199] Furthermore, in *Pla and Puncernau* the Court held that:

> it cannot remain passive where a national court's interpretation of a legal act, be it a testamentary disposition, a private contract, a public document, a statutory provision or an administrative practice appears unreasonable, arbitrary or, as in the present case, blatantly inconsistent with the prohibition of discrimination established by Article 14 and more broadly with the principles underlying the Convention.[200]

Thus, the application of the no fourth-instance court doctrine is not absolute and is partly determined by the effectiveness principle. As a result, it is not always easy to

---

195 See, for example, European Court of Human Rights, *The principle of subsidiarity. Note by the Jurisconsult*, 8 July 2010, para. 36; European Court of Human Rights, *Practical guide on the admissibility criteria* (last update: 1 August 2021), para. 290.

196 *Perlala v. Greece* App No 17721/04 (ECtHR 22 February 2007), para. 25 [author's translation of the French text].

197 See also G. Ulfstein, 'The European Court of Human Rights and national courts: a constitutional relationship?' in O.M. Arnardóttir and A. Buyse (eds.), *Shifting Centres of Gravity in Human Rights Protection: Rethinking relations between the ECHR, EU, and national legal orders'*, Routledge 2016, pp. 46–58, p. 50; L.A. Sicilianos and M.A. Kostopoulou, *The individual application under the European Convention on Human Rights*, Council of Europe 2019, p. 66.

198 Arnardóttir 2015 (n 176), p. 12.

199 *De Tommaso v. Italy* App No 43395/09 (ECtHR (GC) 23 February 2017) para. 170.

200 *Pla and Puncernau v. Andorra* App No 69498/01 (ECtHR 13 July 2007) para. 59. See also *Khurshid Mustafa and Tarzibachi v. Sweden* App No 23883/06 (ECtHR 16 December 2008), para. 33.

draw a clear line between fourth-instance cases and no fourth-instance cases. Indeed, the Court itself emphasised, in an information note by the Jurisconsult, that it proceeds on a case-by-case basis in this regard and that 'it will never be possible to establish a stable and immovable threshold defining where fourth-instance cases begin or end'.[201] This may explain why, in some cases, the Court seems to be very strict in applying the no fourth-instance doctrine, while in other cases it actually seems to act as a court of fourth instance.[202] Furthermore, judges also do not always agree on this point. In, for example, *Axel Springer AG*[203] the dissenting judges voiced the opinion that the majority had acted too much as a domestic court would have done. They argued that:

> [i]n order to exercise this Court's powers of review without becoming a fourth instance, our task in guaranteeing respect for Convention rights in this type of case is essentially to verify whether the domestic courts have duly balanced the conflicting rights and have taken into account the relevant criteria established in our case-law without any manifest error or omission of any important factor. Where these prerequisites have been met, that is, the domestic courts have expressly weighed the conflicting rights and interests and applied the pertinent criteria established in our above-cited case-law, an additional assessment of the competing interests by this Court, examining anew the facts and circumstances of the case, is tantamount to acting as a fourth instance (or, as now, a fifth instance).[204]

Regardless of the ambiguities related to the application of the no fourth-instance court doctrine, some aspects of it are fairly clear. In particular, the cases cited above illustrate that the no fourth-instance court doctrine extends to all substantive provisions of the Convention and thus applies irrespective of the legal sphere to which the proceedings belong at the domestic level.[205] In other words, although the no fourth-instance court doctrine was first articulated in relation to Article 6(1) ECHR and still usually concerns such cases[206], the doctrine is not limited to this particular provision. To illustrate, in the above-mentioned case of *Pla and Puncernau,* concerning the interpretation of a will, the Court reasoned that:

> [o]n many occasions, and in very different spheres, the Court has declared that it is in the first place for the national authorities, and in particular the courts of first instance and appeal, to construe and apply the domestic law. That principle, which by definition applies to domestic legislation, is all the more applicable when interpreting an eminently private instrument such as a clause in a person's will. In a situation such as the one here, the domestic courts

201 European Court of Human Rights, *The principle of subsidiarity. Note by the Jurisconsult,* 8 July 2010, para. 39.

202 M. Dahlberg, '"...It is not its task to act as a Court of fourth instance": the case of the European Court of Human Rights' (2014) 7 *European Journal of Legal Studies* 84, 116.

203 *Axel Springer AG v. Germany* App No 39954/08 (ECtHR (GC) 7 February 2012).

204 Dissenting opinion of Judge Lopez Guerra, joined by Judges Jungwiert, Jaeger, Villiger and Poalelunghi in *Axel Springer AG v. Germany* App No 39954/08 (ECtHR (GC) 7 February 2012).

205 European Court of Human Rights, *The principle of subsidiarity. Note by the Jurisconsult,* 8 July 2010, paras. 33–35.

206 For an extensive analysis of the no fourth-instance court doctrine in relation to Article 6 ECHR see, for example, Dahlberg 2014 (n 202).

> are evidently better placed than an international court to evaluate, in the light of local legal traditions, the particular context of the legal dispute submitted to them and the various competing rights and interests.[207]

To conclude, the no fourth-instance court doctrine is a manifestation of substantive subsidiarity because it governs relative responsibilities between the Court and domestic authorities for decision-making and assessment, in particular with regard to the establishment of the facts and the interpretation and application of domestic law.

3.2.2. Margin of appreciation doctrine

The margin of appreciation doctrine is another manifestation of substantive subsidiarity, governing the relative responsibilities for decision-making and assessment.[208] More specifically, the margin of appreciation can be regarded as 'an operational tool for the realization of the subsidiarity principle'[209], which allows the Court to 'vary the intensity of its review of the States' compliance with the negative and positive obligations following from the Convention'.[210] The margin of appreciation doctrine was introduced by the Court in the case of *Handyside,* concerning the right to freedom of expression and the prohibition and seizure of a book, in which it held that:

> … Article 10 para. 2 leaves to the Contracting States a margin of appreciation. This margin is given both to the domestic legislator ("prescribed by law") and to the bodies, judicial amongst others, that are called upon to interpret and apply the laws in force.[211]

---

207 *Pla and Puncernau v. Andorra* App No 69498/01 (ECtHR 13 July 2007), para. 46.

208 This section discusses some of the main features of the margin of appreciation doctrine. For a more detailed discussion see, for example, Y. Arai-Takahashi, *The margin of appreciation doctrine and the principle of proportionality in the jurisprudence of the ECHR*, Intersentia 2002; J. Christoffersen, *Fair balance: proportionality, subsidiarity and primarity in the European Convention on Human Rights*, Brill Nijhoff 2009; J.H. Gerards, 'Pluralism, Deference and the Margin of Appreciation Doctrine' (2011) 17 *European Law Journal* 80; D. Spielmann, 'Allowing the right margin: the European Court of Human Rights and the national margin of appreciation doctrine: waiver or subsidiarity of European review?' (2012) *Cambridge Yearbook of European Legal Studies 2011–2012*, pp. 381–418; Y. Arai-Takahashi, 'The margin of appreciation doctrine: a theoretical analysis of Strasbourg's variable geometry' in A. Føllesdal, B. Peters, G. Ulfstein (eds.) *Constituting Europe: The European Court of Human Rights in a National, European and Global Context,* Cambridge University Press 2013, pp. 62–105; O.M. Arnardóttir, 'Rethinking the two margins of appreciation' (2016) 12 *European Constitutional Law Review* 27; J.H. Gerards, 'Margin of Appreciation and Incrementalism in the Case Law of the European Court of Human Rights' (2018) 18 *Human Rights Law Review* 495; Gerards 2019 (n 149). The margin of appreciation doctrine is sometimes also considered to be a manifestation of the effectiveness principle, depending on how it is applied (see, for example, Glas 2016 (n 151), pp. 31–32).

209 Popelier and Van de Heyning 2017 (n 175), p. 9. See also Spano who refers to the 'functional tool' of the subsidiarity principle (R. Spano, 'Future of the European Court of Human Rights – Subsidiarity, process-based review and the rule of law' (2018) 18 *Human Rights Law Review* 473, 476). In a similar vein, the Court held in *A. and Others v the United Kingdom* that '[t]he doctrine of the margin of appreciation has always been meant as a tool to define relations between the domestic authorities and the Court (*A. and Others v. the United Kingdom* App No 3455/05 (ECtHR (GC) 19 February 2009), para. 184).

210 Gerards 2019 (n 149), p. 165.

211 *Handyside v the United Kingdom* App No 5493/72 (ECtHR 7 December 1976), para. 48.

The Court has since applied the margin of appreciation doctrine in its case law, primarily when it examines whether the interference with a Convention right was justified.[212] This is the final stage in the Court's review of a case on its merits.[213] In this last stage, the Court assesses whether the interference was prescribed by law, pursued a legitimate aim and met the proportionality requirement. Given that the Court uses the margin of appreciation doctrine mainly when it examines whether the interference was justified, the doctrine is especially relevant to relative rights with limitation clauses, notably Articles 8 to 11 ECHR.

One of the rationales for the margin of appreciation doctrine is that, in principle, the national authorities are better placed to assess the necessity and appropriateness of restrictions and the limitations of Convention rights.[214] In *Chapman*, for example, the Court held that:

> a margin of appreciation must, inevitably, be left to the national authorities, who by reason of their direct and continuous contact with the vital forces of their countries are in principle better placed than an international court to evaluate local needs and conditions.[215]

Thus, national authorities are considered to have better information about the need for specific restrictions and to be generally better-positioned to evaluate how a certain national measure or decision relates to national constitutional values and legal traditions.[216]

The scope of the margin of appreciation determines the extent of the Court's supervisory role. More specifically, 'the wider the margin, the more the role of the Court can be characterised as subsidiary'.[217] Indeed, when a wide margin is allowed to the domestic authorities, 'the Court will examine the choices made by the domestic authorities rather superficially to see whether the result is not (clearly) unreasonable or disproportionate'.[218] In other words, 'the Court will relatively easily accept the reasons and arguments advanced by the governments, except where they are clearly unconvincing or disclose arbitrary decision-making'.[219] Accordingly, the burden of

---

212 The Court has very rarely applied the margin of appreciation doctrine when determining the scope of Convention rights (Gerards 2019 (n 149), p. 170). In this regard, see, for example, *Vo v France* App No 53924/00 (ECtHR (GC) 8 July 2004) concerning the scope of the right to life. The Court has also applied the margin of appreciation doctrine in the context of Article 15 ECHR (L. Lavrysen, 'System of restrictions' in P. van Dijk, F. van Hoof, A. van Rijn, L. Zwaak (eds.), *Theory and practice of the European Convention on Human Rights*, Intersentia 2018 (5th edition), pp. 307–330, p. 327). See, for instance, *A. and Others v. the United Kingdom* App No 3455/05 (ECtHR (GC) 19 February 2009) concerning a 'public emergency' in the sense of Article 15(1) ECHR.

213 According to the structure of Convention rights review, as identified by Gerards (Gerards 2019 (n 149), pp. 11ff). In the first two stages the Court establishes whether the facts complained of fall within the scope of the Convention and whether there has been an interference with a Convention right.

214 Gerards 2018 (n 208), p. 498.

215 *Chapman v. the United Kingdom* App No 27238/95 (ECtHR (GC) 18 January 2001), para. 91.

216 Gerards 2018 (n 208), p. 498.

217 Glas 2016 (n 151), p. 27.

218 Gerards 2019 (n 149), p. 166.

219 Gerards 2018 (n 208), pp. 498–499.

proof to show that the restriction is unjustified is then often placed on the applicant.[220] A wide margin of appreciation may also result in the Court focusing on the decision-making process, applying a procedural rather than a substantive test.[221] To illustrate, in *Aksu,* the Court held that:

> if the assessment was made in the light of the principles resulting from its well-established case-law, the Court would require strong reasons to substitute its own view for that of the domestic courts, which consequently will enjoy a wider margin of appreciation.[222]

If, on the other hand, the margin of appreciation is narrow, the Court will 'closely consider the facts of the case, carefully identify and weigh the interests at stake and decide for itself where the appropriate balance between conflicting interests should have been struck'.[223] It is then up to the respondent State to show that the limitation of rights was based on a careful and objective assessment of facts and interests and supported by sufficiently weighty and important interests.

In reflection of the above, the scope of the State's margin of appreciation in a particular case will depend, according to the Court's case law, on various factors, including 'the nature of the Convention right in issue, its importance for the individual, the nature of the interference and the object pursued by the interference'.[224] More specifically, Gerards has distinguished three main factors, on the basis of the Court's case law, that have the most impact on the scope of the margin of appreciation.[225] These three factors are the 'common ground' factor, the 'better placed' factor, and the nature and importance of the Convention right at stake. The common ground factor concerns the question whether there is consensus on the issue in question between the Convention States. For example, the Court 'tends to leave a wider margin of appreciation to the States if there is little consensus between the Convention States on which modalities are best suited or most appropriate to serve a general interest'.[226] In *Hirst (No. 2),* for example, the Court held that States enjoy a wide margin of appreciation when it comes to the organisation of electoral systems because:

> '[t]here are numerous ways of organising and running electoral systems and a wealth of differences, *inter alia,* in historical development, cultural diversity and political thought within Europe which it is for each Contracting State to mould into their own democratic vision'.[227]

---

220 Gerards 2019 (n 149), p. 166.

221 Gerards 2019 (n 149), p. 167.

222 *Aksu v. Turkey* App Nos 4149/04 and 41029/04 (ECtHR (GC) 15 March 2012), para. 67.

223 Gerards 2019 (n 149), p. 167.

224 For example, *S. and Marper v. the United Kingdom* App Nos 30562/04 and 30566/04 (ECtHR 4 December 2008), para. 102.

225 Gerards 2019 (n 149), pp. 172ff.

226 Gerards 2019 (n 149), p. 175.

227 *Hirst v. the United Kingdom (No 2)* App No 74025/01 (ECtHR (GC) 6 October 2005), para. 61. The common ground factor already played an important role in *Handyside v. the United Kingdom,* in

The second factor – the better placed factor – entails that the Court may leave a wide margin of appreciation to the States 'because they are in a better position to assess the necessity, suitability or overall reasonableness of a limitation of a Convention right'.[228] This argument is applied, for example, in relation to moral and ethical issues, to political and operational policy choices in relation to socio-economic issues, and in cases involving a conflict between two Convention rights.[229] As the previous section on the no fourth-instance court doctrine showed, the Court has often emphasised that the domestic authorities are better placed when it comes to establishing the facts of the case and to interpreting and applying domestic law. In principle, therefore, States are granted a wide margin on these points. The no fourth-instance court and the margin of appreciation doctrines may consequently overlap and can be intertwined. To illustrate, in the case of *Pla and Puncernau,* in which the importance of the no fourth-instance court doctrine was emphasised in relation to Article 8 ECHR, and more specifically the interpretation of a will, the Court held that '[w]hen ruling on disputes of this type, the national authorities and, in particular, the courts of first instance and appeal have a wide margin of appreciation'.[230] Finally, the third factor, the nature and importance of the Convention right at stake, means that, in principle, the margin of appreciation will be narrow if the essence of one of the Convention rights is affected, whereas it will be wider if a less important aspect of a Convention right is at stake.[231]

Having set out the theory of the margin of appreciation doctrine, it should be noted that this doctrine has been criticised for not always meeting its theoretical function in practice.[232] In particular, the Court has been criticised for not being consistent in its application of the doctrine.[233] It has been claimed, for example, that the scope of the margin of appreciation is not always indicative for the strictness of the scrutiny applied; in other words, the Court may sometimes refer to a wide margin of appreciation, while actually carrying out a strict review.[234] Similarly, it has been argued that the Court does not clearly state the exact consequences of the margin of appreciation granted to the Convention States, or the standards of review that come with it.[235] This criticism notwithstanding, the margin of appreciation doctrine – like the no fourth-instance court doctrine – is a clear manifestation of the subsidiarity principle. As such it is important for the Convention system as a whole and the system of Convention supervision in particular.[236]

---

which the Court introduced the margin of appreciation doctrine (see *Handyside v. the United Kingdom* App No 5493/72 (ECtHR 7 December 1976), para. 48).

228 Gerards 2019 (n 149), p. 177.

229 Gerards 2019 (n 149), pp. 177ff.

230 *Pla and Puncernau v. Andorra* App No 69498/01 (ECtHR 13 July 2007), para. 46.

231 Gerards 2019 (n 149), p. 188.

232 See, for example, S. Greer, *The margin of appreciation: interpretation and discretion under the European Convention on Human Rights,* Council of Europe Publishing 2000; Gerards 2011 (n 208); J. Kratochvil, 'The inflation of the margin of appreciation doctrine by the European Court of Human Rights' (2011) 29 *Netherlands Quarterly of Human Rights* 324; Gerards 2018 (n 208).

233 Kratochvil 2011 (n 232), p. 357; Gerards 2011 (n 208), p. 114; Gerards 2018 (n 208), pp. 7ff.

234 Kratochvil 2011 (n 232), p. 330; Gerards 2011 (n 208), p. 106.

235 Kratochvil 2011 (n 232), pp. 325 and 335; Gerards 2018 (n 208), pp. 7ff.

236 See also J.H. Gerards, 'The European Court of Human Rights and the national courts – giving shape to the notion of 'shared responsibility' in J.H. Gerards and J.W.A. Fleuren (eds.), *Implementation of*

3.2.3. *Procedural review*

In addition to the manifestations of the subsidiarity principle distinguished by the Court, various other tools operationalising the subsidiarity principle – including procedural review – have been discussed in the literature.[237] This particular manifestation of the principle is discussed in this subsection in more detail.[238]

Article 32 of the Convention provides that 'the jurisdiction of the Court shall extend to all matters concerning the interpretation and application of the Convention and the Protocols'. According to Arnardóttir, this provision reflects the 'standard approach of full jurisdiction and own engagement by the Court on the merits of each case'.[239] In other words, it confirms that, in principle, the Court carries out a substantive review when deciding on individual complaints. Such a substantive review entails that the Court engages normatively with the merits of the case[240], and more specifically, that it carries out a reasonableness or proportionality review when deciding on an alleged interference with a Convention right. This requires the Court to examine the legitimate societal aims served by the relevant measure or decision, to assess the effectiveness and necessity of achieving these aims, and to decide whether a fair balance was struck between all interests concerned.[241] Illustrative in this regard is the Court's reasoning that 'it must look at the interference complained of in the light of the case as a whole and determine whether it was "proportionate to the legitimate aim pursued" and whether the reasons adduced by the national authorities to justify it are "relevant and sufficient"'.[242]

---

the European Convention on Human Rights and of the judgments of the ECtHR in national case law. A comparative analysis, Intersentia 2014, pp. 13–94, pp. 29 and 31.

237 See, for example, Gerards 2014 (n 236), p. 62; Spano 2014 (n 175), pp. 11–13; Popelier and Van de Heyning 2017 (n 175), pp. 8ff; E. Brems, 'The "Logics" of Procedural-Type Review by the European Court of Human Rights' in J.H. Gerards and E. Brems (eds.) *Procedural Review in European Fundamental Rights Cases*, Cambridge University Press 2017, pp. 17–39, p. 22. Spano 2018 (n 209), p. 481; T. Kleinlein, 'The procedural approach of the European Court of Human Rights: between subsidiarity and dynamic evolution' (2019) 68 *International and Comparative Law Quarterly* 91, 99ff; Glas 2020 (n 175), p. 136.

238 This subsection limits itself to a general introduction to procedural review, its relation to the subsidiarity principle in particular. For more detailed studies on procedural review by the Court see, for example, P. Popelier and C. van de Heyning, 'Procedural rationality: giving teeth to the proportionality analysis' (2013) 9 *European Constitutional Law Review* 230; O.M. Arnardóttir, 'The "procedural turn" under the European Convention on Human Rights and presumptions of Convention compliance' (2017) 15 *International Journal of Constitutional Law* 9; J.H. Gerards and E. Brems (eds.), *Procedural review in European fundamental rights cases*, Cambridge University Press 2017; L. Huijbers, 'Procedural-type review: a more neutral approach to human rights protection by the European Court of Human rights?' (2017) *European Society of International Law Conference Paper Series*; Popelier and Van de Heyning 2017 (n 175); Arnardóttir 2018 (n 175); Spano 2018 (n 209); L. Huijbers, *Process-based fundamental rights review. Practice, concept and theory*, Intersentia 2019; Kleinlein 2019 (n 237). The application of procedural review also features in the discussion on the Court's examination of verticalised cases (see Chapter 6).

239 Arnardóttir 2017 (n 238), p. 20.

240 See also Arnardóttir 2015 (n 176), p. 4.

241 See also Gerards and Brems (eds.) 2017 (n 238), p. 1.

242 See, for example, *Jehovah's Witnesses of Moscow and Others v. Russia* App No 302/02 (ECtHR 10 June 2010), para. 108.

In addition to substantive review, which is still the Court's main approach, another type of review has been detected in the Court's case law. In fact, the term 'procedural turn'[243] has been used to describe the development that the Court is increasingly performing a procedural review when examining cases coming before it.[244] Such procedural review means that the focus lies on the quality of the national decision-making process leading up to a decision, rather than on the contents or substance of a decision.[245] This review may relate to the legislative process, to decision-making by administrative bodies or to judicial decision-making.

The procedural turn taken by the Court is often placed in the context of the subsidiarity principle.[246] More specifically, the Court's application of procedural review has been considered a 'mechanism by which the Court implements the principle of subsidiarity in practice'.[247] This can be explained by procedural review being regarded as a way of showing deference to other decision-making authorities.[248] Indeed, the Court's procedural review is often deference-oriented – instead, for example, outcome-oriented – particularly in cases involving a conflict between two Convention rights.[249] As a result, procedural review does not directly determine whether the Court finds a violation, but instead influences the degree of deference given to the Convention State. The Court will be more deferential towards the substantive balance struck by the national authorities in the concrete case if those authorities have applied the Convention standards.[250] Put differently, States enjoy a wider margin of appreciation if their domestic courts have carefully assessed the case by, for example, assessing it in the light of the well-established Convention principles.[251] This illustrates that procedural review can be a way for the Court to supervise the review conducted by the domestic courts and thereby exercise its supervisory, subsidiary role rather than taking the place

243 See, for example, Arnardóttir 2017 (n 238), p. 9; Brems 2017 (n 237), p. 17; J.H. Gerards, 'Procedural Review by the ECtHR: a Typology' in J.H. Gerards and E. Brems (eds.) *Procedural Review in European Fundamental Rights Cases*, Cambridge University Press 2017, pp. 127–160, p. 127.

244 This is just one aspect of the procedural turn taken by the Court. The other aspect concerns the 'proceduralisation' of Convention rights; in other words, procedural positive obligations formulated by the Court in relation to different Convention rights, including, for example, the obligation under Article 2 ECHR to carry out an effective investigation when individuals have been killed as a result of the use of force by a State agent (see, for example, *McCannn and Others v. the United Kingdom* App No 18984/91 (ECtHR (GC) 27 September 1995), para. 161) (Gerards and Brems (eds.) 2017 (n 238), p. 3 and Gerards 2017 (n 243), pp. 127–128). On this, see also Arnardóttir 2015 (n 176), pp. 5–6; Arnardóttir 2017 (n 238), p. 14; Spano 2018 (n 209), p. 480.

245 See also Huijbers 2019 (n 238), pp. 101, 113.

246 Brems 2017 (n 237), p. 22 (with further references).

247 Spano 2018 (n 209), p. 481.

248 Huijbers 2019 (n 238), pp. 147ff, 214. The idea that procedural review demonstrates self-restraint by courts is also, however, contested (for this discussion, see Huijbers 2019 (n 238), pp. 215ff).

249 Huijbers 2017 (n 238), p. 15. See also Arnardóttir 2017 (n 238), p. 21.

250 Huijbers 2017 (n 238), pp. 16–17.

251 See also Arnardóttir 2017 (n 238), pp. 11, 21. It has also been argued that the ECtHR applies procedural review when States are granted a wide margin of appreciation (Gerards 2017 (n 243), pp. 146ff), or that procedural review should serve as a tool for scrutiny in the event of a wide margin of appreciation (Popelier and Van de Heyning 2013 (n 238), p. 243). On this, see also Huijbers 2019 (n 238), pp. 148ff.

of the domestic courts by substituting their decisions for its own substantive view on the reasonableness and proportionality of a certain limitation of a Convention right.[252] As such, it provides the Court with a mechanism to apply the subsidiarity principle in practice.

At the same time, procedural review by the Court does not 'necessarily smoothen the relationship between the Strasbourg Court and the national authorities'.[253] Former Judge Nussberger explained this observation by stating that procedural review 'may cause tensions in the so-called dialogue of judges, either because national judges feel personally offended or because they are of the opinion that the national system has not been understood and the Court has intruded into something which should be outside its reach'.[254] In a similar vein, Brems noted that 'negative interferences from blind application of a checklist may be unjustified to the extent that the domestic authorities may have performed a qualitative human rights scrutiny along different lines than the ECtHR had envisaged'.[255] Lastly, it has been suggested that the procedural standards developed by the Court are not necessarily neutral. Huijbers, for example, concluded that the more detailed and concrete the procedural standards are, the more the Court limits the choices of States and indirectly imposes its own perspective on the decision-making process.[256] In this regard, it should also be kept in mind that if the Court narrows down the margin of appreciation left to the Convention State on the basis of procedural review, it will look more closely into the substantive proportionality review by the national court.[257] Procedural review would then, in fact, facilitate a stricter review by the Court.[258]

It has also been noted that, in most cases, the Court's review is not fully procedural in nature.[259] In fact, the Court's approach has often been described as 'semi-procedural review'[260], with its review and reasoning thus containing elements of both substantive

252 See also Gerards 2014 (n 236), p. 62; Brems 2017 (n 237), p. 23; Gerards 2017 (n 243), p. 128; Arnardóttir 2018 (n 175), p. 229.

253 A. Nussberger, 'Procedural Review by the ECHR: View from the Court' in J.H. Gerards and E. Brems (eds.), *Procedural Review in European Fundamental Rights Cases*, Cambridge University Press 2017, pp. 161–176, p. 163; See also Popelier and Van de Heyning, who hold that 'if procedural rationality review serves as a reply to the Interlaken/Brighton process, it will not be able to tone down recent waves of criticism if the Court concludes that the decision-making procedure did not fulfil the requirements' (Popelier and Van de Heyning 2017 (n 175), p. 20).

254 Nussberger 2017 (n 253), p. 163.

255 Brems 2017 (n 237), p. 37.

256 Huijbers 2017 (n 238), p. 21. See also Nussberger, who holds that 'scrutinising the procedure on the national level can also be seen as a way of intensifying what is criticised as "micromanagement" of national legal systems' (Nussberger 2017 (n 253), p. 172).

257 See also Huijbers 2017 (n 238), p. 22.

258 See also Arnardóttir 2018 (n 175), p. 235. For a more extensive and general overview of arguments rejecting the idea that procedural review is a form of self-restraint on the side of the courts, see Huijbers 2019 (n 238), pp. 215ff.

259 See also Gerards 2017 (n 243), p. 153. In some instances, however, the Court does carry out a full procedural review (for examples see Arnardóttir 2017 (n 238)).

260 See, for example, I. Bar-Siman-Tov, 'Semi-procedural Judicial Review' (2012) 6 *Legisprudence* 271, 274; Arnardóttir 2017 (n 238), p. 21; Popelier and Van de Heyning 2017 (n 175), p. 10. In a similar

and procedural review. More specifically, procedural review of the decision-making process is often integrated into the Court's proportionality analysis.[261] Arnardóttir, for example, concluded that 'the Court to a certain extent relies on the quality of domestic procedures, but also engages in its own assessment of the merits of the case'.[262] Similarly, Gerards found that, in practice, the Court often still includes 'a number of more substantive arguments, complementing or comparing the national evaluation with one of its own'.[263] As a result, the procedural arguments 'form part of a "net" of arguments that, taken in their entirety, support the outcome reached by the Court'.[264]

The semi-procedural nature of the Court's approach is often explained by the Court's role within the Convention system. Arguably, even a seemingly full procedural review – for example, an examination of whether a balancing exercise has been duly conducted by the domestic courts – will always contain some substantive elements. Judge Spano stressed, for example, that the Court's review 'will always, at a minimum, include a substantive assessment of whether the outcome is within the parameters of reasonableness'.[265] Similarly, former Judge Nussberger held that even in cases in which the inclusiveness and transparency of the decision-making process is the most relevant element for the Court to review, 'procedural control cannot replace substantive control'.[266] It should also be noted in this respect that it is often difficult to make a sharp distinction between substantive and procedural reasoning.[267] In a detailed conceptual study on procedural review, Huijbers speaks of a 'spectrum of judicial review', ranging from 'purely substantive review, which is solely based on undeniably substantive considerations, and purely procedural review, which is solely based on undeniable procedural considerations'.[268] In between purely substantive review and purely procedural review, 'mixed forms of review can be found that encompass substantive and procedural considerations, and twilight-zone considerations'.[269] Such twilight-zone considerations refer to considerations that can be regarded as both procedural and substantive. Hence, Huijbers concludes that 'fundamental rights review is best perceived as less or more procedural or substantive in nature'.[270] But whatever the exact nature of the Court's procedural review, such review is a way for the Court to show deference to

vein, Kleinlein speaks of 'integrated procedural review', holding that the Court 'includes a focus on domestic procedures when determining the merits of a case' (Kleinlein 2019 (n 237), p. 93).

261 Bar-Siman-Tov 2012 (n 260), p. 274. See also Popelier and Van de Heyning, who hold that 'procedural rationality review is part of the substantive proportionality test, where scrutiny of the legislative or administrative records and the judicial reasoning serves to underpin the conclusion of whether or not a measure is the result of an informed balancing exercise' (Popelier and Van de Heyning 2017 (n 175), p. 10).

262 Arnardótttir 2017 (n 238), p. 34.

263 Gerards 2017 (n 243), p. 153. See also Nussberger 2017 (n 253), p. 174; Arnardóttir 2018 (n 175), p. 230.

264 Gerards 2017 (n 243), p. 159.

265 Spano 2018 (n 209), p. 488.

266 Nussberger 2017 (n 253), p. 174.

267 Huijbers 2019 (n 238), p. 365.

268 Huijbers 2019 (n 238), p. 113.

269 Huijbers 2019 (n 238), p. 113.

270 Huijbers 2019 (n 238), p. 365.

national decision-makers, and thus another manifestation of the subsidiarity principle, as illustrated above.

3.2.4. *Other manifestations*

To complete the discussion on the subsidiarity principle, this final subsection briefly examines several other manifestations of the subsidiarity principle, as identified in the literature. Gerards, for example, submitted that 'incrementalism' and 'judicial minimalism' can be regarded as another approach used by the Court to realise the subsidiarity principle in practice.[271] Put briefly, such an approach entails that the Court, when dealing with relatively new or sensitive cases, works from case-based and individualised judgments towards defining general principles (incrementalism). In such cases, the Court may also use 'shallow' judicial minimalist reasoning, based on precedent and references to external factors such as European consensus, instead of deep, moral and principled arguments.[272] More specifically, this means that the Court limits itself to 'superficial remarks on the general importance of a certain right in light of the underlying principles of the Convention or developments in Europe, while leaving fundamental issues undecided and trusting the general acceptance of a certain abstract definition'.[273]

Çali, meanwhile, used the term 'variable geometry' to describe another tool used by the Court to operationalise the subsidiarity principle in practice.[274] According to Çali, this is an approach in which the Court employs 'different treatment for different national institutional arrangements and national cultures of human rights in terms of their domestic ability and willingness to respect the Convention'.[275] More specifically, this means that the Court may 'operate under differentiated logics of trust'[276] by granting deference to States – domestic courts in particular – that respect the Convention and the Court's case law and by a tendency to identify bad faith attitudes towards the Convention protection by relying more often on Article 18 ECHR.[277]

---

271 Gerards 2014 (n 236); Gerards 2018 (n 208).

272 Gerards 2014 (n 236), p. 65.

273 Gerards 2014 (n 236), p. 63.

274 B. Çali, 'Coping with crisis: wither the variable geometry in the jurisprudence of the European Court of Human Rights' (2018) 35 *Wisconsin International Law Journal* 237. See also B. Çali, 'From flexible to variable standards of judicial review: the responsible courts doctrine at the European Court of Human Rights' in O.M. Arnardóttir and A. Buyse (eds.), *Shifting Centres of Gravity in Human Rights Protection: Rethinking relations between the ECHR, EU, and national legal orders'*, Routledge 2016, pp. 144–160. Similar to Çali, Dothan refers to a different approach towards 'high and low reputation States' (see S. Dothan, 'Judicial tactics in the European Court of Human Rights' (2011) 358 *University of Chicago Public Law & Legal Theory Working Paper* 115).

275 Çali 2018 (n 274), p. 254.

276 Çali 2018 (n 274), p. 269.

277 Çali 2018 (n 274), p. 269. See also Çali 2016 (n 274), p. 145.

4. CONCLUSION

This chapter discussed the principle of effectiveness and the principle of subsidiarity as two fundamental principles underpinning the Convention system. The general background provided on these two principles and the discussion of their different manifestations demonstrate how these principles guide the interpretation and application of the Convention and define the Court's position in the Convention system. The effectiveness principle, for example, requires Convention provisions to be interpreted and applied in a manner that makes the safeguards provided by the Convention both practical and effective. The subsidiarity principle, on the other hand, defines the Court's role vis-à-vis the Convention States as being a subsidiary, supervisory role. Accordingly, the Court's task is to review the measures chosen by domestic authorities in the light of the Convention.

Although these two principles have different functions and different manifestations, they are often interrelated. And while they will often be complementary, they may also be in tension with each other.[278] It was explained, for example, that to guarantee effective protection of Convention rights, the Court may make an exception to the exhaustion of domestic remedies rule, with this admissibility criterion having been introduced first and foremost as an operationalisation of the subsidiarity principle. In a similar vein, application of the no fourth-instance court doctrine, another manifestation of the subsidiarity principle, was shown not to be absolute, given that, in practice, this could render the protection afforded by Convention rights ineffective. Accordingly, the Court may have to act, in some cases, as a court of fourth instance in order to ensure effective protection of Convention rights.

[278] See also Glas 2016 (n 151), p. 30; L.R. Glas, 'Translating the Convention's Fairness Standards to the European Court of Human Rights: an exploration with a Case Study on Legal Aid and the Right to a Reasoned Judgment' (2018) 10 *European Journal of Legal Studies* 47, 63.

CHAPTER 4
CHARACTERISTICS OF ECtHR PROCEEDINGS

1. INTRODUCTION

As a final step in introducing the Convention system, this chapter explores the main characteristics – more specifically, the procedural rules and standards – of proceedings before the ECtHR. First, procedural rules and standards directly governing the Court's proceedings on the basis of certain Convention provisions and Rules of Court are explored (Section 2). Second, a short overview is provided of the procedural standards of Article 6 (the right to a fair trial) and Article 13 ECHR (the right to an effective remedy) (Section 3.1). At first sight, these standards seem less relevant for the characteristics of the ECtHR proceedings as they are directed to domestic authorities and, therefore, do not apply directly to the ECtHR proceedings.[279] However, they are discussed separately as it is often argued that the Court should adhere, in its own proceedings, to the procedural standards it has formulated for domestic courts. This argument is discussed in more detail in Section 3.2.

By discussing procedural rules and standards, this chapter serves as a basis for the subsequent analysis and evaluation of the Court's current approach to verticalised cases. Given that part of the main research question in this study concerns how the Court can deal with verticalised cases while taking due care of the procedural rights of private actors[280], this chapter focuses on aspects of the proceedings and procedural standards of most relevance to this question rather than on providing a detailed and comprehensive overview of ECtHR proceedings.[281]

---

279 See, for example, T. de Jong, *Procedurele waarborgen in materiële EVRM-rechten* [Procedural guarantees in substantive ECHR provisions], Wolters Kluwer 2017, p. 285; L.R. Glas, 'Translating the Convention's Fairness Standards to the European Court of Human Rights: an exploration with a Case Study on Legal Aid and the Right to a Reasoned Judgment' (2018) 10 *European Journal of Legal Studies* 47, 49; P. Pastor Vilanova, 'Le juge européen est-il tenu par les règles du procès equitable?' in R. Spano et al. (eds.), *Fair trial: regional and international perspectives (Liber amicorum Linos-Alexandre Sicilianos)*, Anthemis 2020, pp. 391–405, p. 392; G. Ravarani, 'The Fairness of Proceedings before the European Court of Human Rights' in R. Spano et al. (eds.), *Fair trial: regional and international perspectives (Liber amicorum Linos-Alexandre Sicilianos)*, Anthemis 2020, pp. 453–470, p. 454.

280 See Chapter 1 (Section 2).

281 For a complete overview, see, for example, N. Mole and C. Harby, *The right to a fair trial*, Council of Europe Human Rights Handbook No. 3, 2006 (2nd edition); P. Leach, *Taking a case to the European Court of Human Rights*, Oxford University Press 2017 (4th edition); B. Rainey (ed.), *Jacobs, White and*

2. PROCEDURAL RULES AND STANDARDS DIRECTLY GOVERNING ECtHR PROCEEDINGS

This section starts by discussing some procedural rules and standards that follow from the Convention and the Rules of Court[282] and that apply directly to the proceedings before the ECtHR. First, the question is discussed as to who has standing before the ECtHR. This relates to the right of access to a court (Section 2.1). Subsequently, a short overview is provided of the Court's procedural rules and standards for hearings, access to documents, third-party intervention, and giving reasons for judgments and decisions (Section 2.2).

2.1. WHO HAS STANDING BEFORE THE ECtHR?

The first question regarding the rules applying to proceedings before the ECtHR concerns the criteria to be met for an application to be declared admissible. The admissibility criteria are laid down in Article 35 ECHR.[283] First, an applicant must have exhausted all domestic remedies and file an application with the ECtHR within four months after the final decision on the matter by the domestic legal system.[284] Second, the Court cannot deal with an individual application that is anonymous or substantially the same as a matter that has already been examined by the Court or submitted to another procedure of international investigation or settlement and that contains no relevant new information.[285] Third, an application will be declared inadmissible if it is incompatible with the provisions of the Convention or the Protocols, if it is manifestly ill-founded or involves an abuse of the right of individual application, or if the applicant has not suffered a significant disadvantage.[286]

Even though Article 34 ECHR does not contain any admissibility criteria *stricto sensu*, it is equally relevant regarding the admissibility of applications in that it concerns the Court's competence (i.e. its jurisdiction) to decide on cases under the

---

Ovey: the European Convention on Human Rights, Oxford University Press 2017 (7th edition); P. van Dijk, F. van Hoof, A. van Rijn, L. Zwaak (eds.), *Theory and Practice of the European Convention on Human Rights*, Intersentia 2018 (5th edition).

282 The Rules of Court may be amended by the Plenary Court (Rule 116 Rules of Court). All the references in this study refer to the edition of the Rules of Court of 18 October 2021.

283 It is important to note that the Court may reject any application that it considers inadmissible under Articles 34 and 35 ECHR at any stage of the proceedings (Article 35(4) ECHR) (see, for example, *Sammut and Visa Investments Limited v. Malta* App No 27023/03 (ECtHR 16 October 2007 (dec.)), para. 56).

284 Article 35(1) ECHR.

285 Article 35(2) ECHR.

286 Article 35(3) ECHR. The 'significant disadvantage' criterion was added to the Convention by Protocol No. 14, which entered into force on 1 June 2010. For a critical review of the application of the significant disadvantage criterion, see D. Shelton, 'Significantly disadvantaged? Shrinking access to the European Court of Human Rights' (2016) 16 *Human Rights Law Review* 303.

Convention.[287] In practice, the Court usually rejects applications outside its competence *ratione personae* (i.e. the applicant cannot petition the Court, or the complaint is not directed against a Convention State), *ratione materiae* (i.e. the complaint does not relate to a right provided by the Convention), *ratione loci* (i.e. the Convention is not applicable in the place where the alleged events occurred) or *ratione temporis* (i.e. the right was not binding on the respondent State at the time of the alleged events occuring). Such applications are declared inadmissible.[288]

As regards the applicability of the Convention *ratione personae,* Article 34 ECHR provides that:

> The Court may receive applications from any person, non-governmental organisation or group of individuals claiming to be the victim of a violation by one of the High Contracting Parties of the rights set forth in the Convention or the Protocols thereto.

Because of this provision, the Court has systematically declined to examine complaints directed against private actors, finding that in such cases it lacks jurisdiction *ratione personae* and consequently declaring such complaints inadmissible.[289] In, for example, *Bogomolova,* the Court held that it 'has no jurisdiction to consider applications directed against private individuals or businesses'.[290] In this case, a photograph of the applicant's son was published on the cover page of a booklet entitled 'Children need a family', prepared by the Centre for Psychological, Medical and Social Support. Having brought civil proceedings against the publishing company that prepared and published the booklet, the applicant then complained before the ECtHR that the unauthorised publication of her son's photograph had infringed their private and family life and that the domestic authorities had failed to protect her and her son's right to respect

---

287 See, for example, S. Greer, *The European Convention on Human Rights: Achievements, Problems and Prospects,* Cambridge University Press 2006, p. 145 (fn. 46); Leach 2017 (n 281), p. 174; L. Zwaak, Y. Haeck, C. Burbano Herrera, 'Procedure before the Court' in P. van Dijk, F. van Hoof, A. van Rijn, L. Zwaak (eds.), *Theory and practice of the European Convention on Human Rights,* Intersentia 2018 (5th edition), pp. 79–271, p. 151.

288 Zwaak, Haeck, Burbano Herrera 2018 (n 287), p. 102.

289 See also D. Spielmann, 'The European Convention on Human Rights. The European Court of Human Rights' in J. Fedtke and D. Oliver (eds.) *Human rights and the private sphere: a comparative study,* Routledge-Cavendish 2007, pp. 427–464, p. 429. This is just one aspect of the ratione personae criterion. An application is also declared inadmissible ratione personae if applicants fail the victim status test (Leach 2017 (n 281), pp. 128ff).

290 *Bogomolova v. Russia* App No 13812/09 (ECtHR 20 June 2017), para. 38. See also *Reynbakh v. Russia* App No 23405/03 (ECtHR 29 September 2005), para. 18. The only instance in which the Court accepts complaints directed against a private actor is when this actor can be classified as a public authority or governmental organisation. A private actor enjoying sufficient institutional and operational independence from the State is not a public authority, according to the autonomous definition used by the Court (see, for example, *Mykhaylenky and Others v. Ukraine* App No 35091/02 (ECtHR 30 November 2004) and *Ališić and Others v. Bosnia and Herzegovina, Croatia, Serbia, Slovenia and the former Yugoslav Republic of Macedonia* App No 60642/08 (ECtHR (GC) 16 July 2014) (see also Spielmann 2007 (n 289), pp. 429–430 and J.H. Gerards, *General principles of the European Convention on Human Rights,* Oxford University Press 2019, pp. 138–141).

for private and family life. However, the Court declared the complaint concerning the publishing company (i.e. the first complaint) inadmissible, finding that it lacked jurisdiction *ratione personae* because the complaint was essentially directed at a private party, and not at the State.[291]

2.2. PROCEDURAL RULES AND STANDARDS

2.2.1. Hearings and access to documents

Article 38 ECHR provides that 'the Court shall examine the case together with the representatives of the parties and, if need be, undertake an investigation, for the effective conduct of which the High Contracting Parties concerned shall furnish all necessary facilities'.[292] This provision guarantees, inter alia, the transmission of documents between the parties. It obliges Convention States to provide the Court with all the necessary information for a proper and effective examination of the case, including information crucial for establishing the facts of the case.[293] It also requires applicants to adduce evidence or provide information requested by the Court.[294] Hence, this provision is often considered to be a reflection of the right to adversarial proceedings.[295] This follows even more clearly from the French text of Article 38, which states that 'la Cour examine l'affaire de façon contradictoire'.

With regard to the right to be heard, parties can request an oral hearing at any stage of the proceedings.[296] However, it is for the Court to decide whether such a hearing is necessary, and it is the Court's practice that decisions on admissibility or judgments on the merits of the case are made primarily on the basis of written submissions.[297] An amendment of the Rules of Court resulted, for example, in the deletion of the rule which provided that in general an oral hearing takes place.[298] However, an oral hearing, may still be arranged if further clarification is needed of the facts of the case or the relevant domestic law or practice[299], and most Grand Chamber cases continue to involve an oral hearing.[300] Oral hearings are held in public unless

291 *Bogomolova v. Russia* App No 13812/09 (ECtHR 20 June 2017), para. 40.

292 See also Rule 44A-D Rules of Court and Annex to the Rules of Court.

293 See, for example, *Janowiec and Others v. Russia* App No 55508/07 (ECtHR (GC) 21 October 2013), para. 202; *Petrov and X v. Russia* App No 23608/16 (ECtHR 23 October 2018), para. 78.

294 Rule 44C(1) Rules of Court.

295 See, for example, Pastor Vilanova 2020 (n 279), p. 396.

296 Rules 54(5) and Rule 59(3) Rules of Court.

297 De Jong 2017 (n 279), p. 283; Leach 2017 (n 281), p. 74; Zwaak, Haeck, Burbano Herrera 2018 (n 287), p. 188. Cases before the Grand Chamber are the exception as, in these cases, an oral hearing usually takes place.

298 Zwaak, Haeck, Burbano Herrera 2018 (n 287), p. 188. See new Rule 59(3) Rules of the Court.

299 Leach 2017 (n 281), p. 75.

300 D. Harris et al., *Harris, O'Boyle and Warbrick: Law of the European Convention on Human Rights*, Oxford University Press 2018 (4th edition), p. 145.

the Court decides otherwise.[301] Finally, with regard to third-party interveners, non-governmental organisations are not normally permitted to make oral submissions, whereas Convention States may sometimes make submissions at a hearing where they intervene as a third party.[302]

Although oral hearings take place in only a limited number of cases, it is important to point out that, under the Convention (Article 40(2)) and the Rules of Court (Rule 33)), all documents deposited with the Registry in connection with an application must be accessible to the public unless the President of the Chamber decides otherwise.[303] This should ensure that public access to information is provided even if no oral hearing is held.

2.2.2. Third-party interventions[304]

The first time that the Court allowed a third party to intervene in a case was in 1979.[305] In *Winterwerp*, the Court allowed the United Kingdom to submit observations, even though this State was not a party to the case. After the Court provided a legal basis, in its Rules of Court, for third-party interventions in 1983, Protocol No. 11, which entered into force in 1998, ensured that the right to third-party intervention was codified in the Convention itself. The third-party intervention procedure is now laid down in Article 36 ECHR and further elaborated in Rule 44.[306] Under Article 36 ECHR, third-party interventions are allowed in three situations. First, Convention States have the right to intervene in cases in which the applicant is one of its nationals.[307] Second, any person concerned (whether a State, an individual or an organisation) is allowed to intervene if this is considered to be 'in the interest of the proper administration of justice'.[308] Third, the Council of Europe Commissioner for Human Rights is allowed to intervene in a case.[309] The Court itself may also invite one of these stakeholders to intervene. In, for example, *Behrami and Saramati* the Court requested the United Nations to intervene because the case concerned the actions of a UN peacekeeping force.[310]

---

301 Article 40(1) ECHR. See also Rules of Court, Chapter VI.

302 Harris et al. 2018 (n 300), pp. 145 and 162.

303 See also Zwaak, Haeck, Burbano Herrera 2018 (n 287), pp. 90–91.

304 The third-party intervention procedure is discussed in more detail in Chapter 9 of this study.

305 *Winterwerp v. the Netherlands* App No 6301/73 (ECtHR 24 October 1979). See N. Bürli, *Third-party interventions before the European Court of Human Rights: Amicus Curiae, Member-State and Third-Party interventions*, Intersentia 2017 for an extensive study of third-party interventions before the Court.

306 See also L. van den Eynde, 'An empirical look at the amicus curiae practice of human rights NGOs before the European Court of Human Rights' (2013) 31 *Netherlands Quarterly of Human Rights* 271, 277; Bürli 2017 (n 305), pp. 4–5.

307 Article 36(1) ECHR.

308 Article 36(2) ECHR and Rule 44(3) Rules of Court.

309 Article 36(3) ECHR and Rule 44(2) Rules of Court.

310 *Behrami and Behrami v. France and Saramati v. France, Germany and Norway* App Nos 71412/01, 78166/01 (ECtHR (GC) 2 May 2007 (dec.)). For another example, see *Young, James and Webster v. the United Kingdom* App Nos 7601/76, 7806/77 (ECtHR 13 August 1981).

When the Court accepts a request for leave to intervene, it usually requests the intervening party not to directly address the facts, admissibility or merits of a case because the intervening party is not an actual party to the case.[311] More generally, third-party interventions can help by, for example, contributing legal expertise or by providing factual information or information on the broader consequences of the case, such as highlighting the potential implications of a decision or unintended consequences for people or groups not party to the legal action.[312]

2.2.3. Reasons for judgments and decisions

Article 45 ECHR requires the Court to give reasons for its judgments and decisions.[313] Accordingly, the obligation to state reasons applies both to judgments and to inadmissibility decisions issued by single judges.[314] Rule 74 of the Rules of Court stipulates, furthermore, the elements that a judgment of the Court must contain, including the facts of the case, a summary of the parties' submissions and the reasons in point of law. It does not, however, set minimum standards for the reasoning. This includes not requiring the Court to respond to all the complaints or arguments put forward by the applicant.[315]

3. PROCEDURAL STANDARDS INDIRECTLY GOVERNING ECtHR PROCEEDINGS

The previous section provided a short overview of procedural rules and standards directly governing ECtHR proceedings under certain Convention provisions and Rules of Court. The current section, by contrast, starts by discussing procedural standards that do not directly apply to these proceedings because of being directed to domestic authorities. These are the procedural standards set in Articles 6 and 13 ECHR and as explained in the Court's case law (Section 3.1). These standards are explored in addition to the rules and standards directly governing ECtHR proceedings as it is often argued that, in its proceedings, the Court should adhere to the procedural standards it has

---

311 L.R. Glas, 'State Third-Party Interventions before the European Court of Human Rights: the what and how of intervening' (2016) 5 *European Journal of Human Rights* 539, 542. Yet, there are still examples of interventions where interveners do precisely this (see Glas 2016, p. 548).

312 Van den Eynde 2013 (n 306), p. 274. See also Leach 2017 (n 281), p. 54.

313 Article 45(1) ECHR. See also Rules of Court, Chapter VIII.

314 In the past, however, single judge decisions have been criticised for a lack of reasoning. See, for example, J.H. Gerards, 'Inadmissibility Decisions of the European Court of Human Rights: A Critique of the Lack of Reasoning' (2014) 14 *Human Rights Law Review* 148; H. de Vylder, 'Stensholt v. Norway: Why single judge decisions undermine the Court's legitimacy' (2014) *Strasbourg Observers* 28 May 2014, <https://strasbourgobservers.com/2014/05/28/stensholt-v-norway-why-single-judge-decisions-undermine-the-courts-legitimacy-2/> accessed 31 January 2022. For a more general critique on the lack of reasoning of judgments see Pastor Vilanova 2020 (n 279), pp. 400ff.

315 See also Pastor Vilanova 2020 (n 279), p. 400.

defined for the Convention States. This argument is discussed in more detail in Section 3.2, including specific discussion of why and how proceedings before the Court should be assessed on the basis of standards similar to those used by the Court to assess the fairness of domestic legal proceedings.

3.1. PROCEDURAL STANDARDS SET BY THE ECHR

3.1.1. Main components of Article 6 ECHR

The fairness of domestic legal proceedings is assessed first and foremost on the basis of the standards set in Article 6 ECHR (the right to a fair trial) and the ECtHR's interpretation of these standards. Article 6(1) reads as follows:

> In the determination of his civil rights and obligations or of any criminal charge against him, everyone is entitled to a fair and public hearing within a reasonable time by an independent and impartial tribunal established by law. Judgment shall be pronounced publicly but the press and public may be excluded from all or part of the trial in the interests of morals, public order or national security in a democratic society, where the interests of juveniles or the protection of the private life of the parties so require, or to the extent strictly necessary in the opinion of the court in special circumstances where publicity would prejudice the interests of justice.

It follows from this that Article 6(1) applies to proceedings concerning civil rights and obligations and to proceedings concerning criminal charges. The terms 'civil rights and obligations' and 'criminal charge' have an autonomous meaning, such that their meaning does not depend on national law or national interpretations.[316] Instead, the ECtHR's own classification of domestic proceedings is decisive. When assessing, for example, whether proceedings concern 'civil rights and obligations' the Court has laid down three requirements: (1) a civil right or obligation is in issue; (2) there is a dispute concerning these rights or obligations, and (3) the result of this dispute is directly decisive for the right in question.[317] A 'civil right or obligation' generally amounts to a private law right[318]; that is, the rights of private persons in horizontal relationships in, for example, contract law, commercial law, tort law, family law, employment law or property law.[319] Over time, the notion has also come to encompass many areas frequently regarded in national legal systems as being part of public or administrative law[320], such as proceedings concerning objections to and the

316 See, for example, *Georgiadis v. Greece* App No 21522/93 (ECtHR 29 May 1997), para. 34. See also Leach 2017 (n 281), p. 191 and 335; Rainey 2017 (n 281), pp. 275–284.

317 See, for example, *Bochan v. Ukraine No. 2* App No 22251/08 (ECtHR (GC) 05 February 2015), paras. 42–43; *Naït Liman v. Switserland* App No 51357/07 (ECtHR (GC) 15 March 2018), para. 106.

318 Leach 2017 (n 281), p. 337.

319 Mole and Harby 2006 (n 281), p. 12.

320 Rainey 2017 (n 281), pp. 278–284. See also Leach 2017 (n 281), pp. 337–342.

enforcement of planning regulations and matters relating to the environment[321], the withdrawal of a restaurant's alcohol licence[322], or proceedings on entitlement to social security[323].[324] On the other hand, taxation proceedings[325] and matters of immigration and nationality[326], among other proceedings, have been found not to concern 'civil rights and obligations'.[327] For a case to fall within the ambit of Article 6(1), there is also required to be a *dispute* concerning these rights or obligations, and the result of this dispute must be directly *decisive* for the right in question.[328] To meet this requirement, the dispute must be 'genuine and serious'. The Court has consequently held that Article 6(1) is not applicable when, for example, actions in domestic courts proceedings are dismissed on procedural grounds, such as when a prior remedy has not been used.[329]

In assessing whether proceedings are criminal in nature the Court applies the 'Engel criteria'[330], whereby it considers how the offence is classified under national law, the nature of the proceedings in question, and the nature and degree of severity of the penalty.[331] In contrast to Article 6(1), Articles 6(2) and 6(3) contain specific provisions setting out standards applicable only in proceedings classified by the Convention as criminal. These specific criminal case standards do not apply to the cases central to this study, i.e. cases of a horizontal nature.[332] Therefore, the subsequent sections focus solely on the procedural standards flowing from Article 6(1) and on their scope and application in relation to proceedings concerning civil rights and obligations.

In dealing with a complaint under Article 6(1), the Court examines whether the proceedings, taken as a whole, were fair and complied with the specific safeguards stipulated by the Convention and in the Court's case law.[333] Looking at the proceedings as a whole means that the Court may accept minor infringements, provided that

---

321 See, for example, *Mats Jacobsen v. Sweden* App No 11309/84 (ECtHR 28 June 1990).

322 *Tre Traktörer AB v. Sweden* App No 10873/84 (ECtHR 7 July 1989).

323 See, for example, *Mennitto v. Italy* App No 33804/96 (ECtHR (GC) 3 October 2000).

324 For more examples, see Mole and Harby 2006 (n 281), pp. 12–14; Leach 2017 (n 281), pp. 337–338; Rainey 2017 (n 281), pp. 278–287.

325 See, for example, *Charalambos v. France* App No 49210/99 (ECtHR 8 February 2008 (dec.)).

326 See, for example, *V.P. v. the United Kingdom* App No 13162/87 (EComHR 9 November 1987 (dec.)).

327 For more examples, see Mole and Harby 2006 (n 281), pp. 14–16; Leach 2017 (n 281), pp. 338–339; Rainey 2017 (n 281), pp. 278–287.

328 See, for example, *Benthem v. the Netherlands* App No 5548/80 (ECtHR 23 October 1985), para. 32. See also Leach 2017 (n 281), pp. 337–340; Rainey 2017 (n 281), pp. 284–285.

329 See, for example, *Astikos Oikodomikos Synetairismos Nea Konstantinoupolis v. Greece* App No 37806/02 (ECtHR 20 January 2005 (dec.)); *Stavroulakis v. Greece* App No 22326/10 (ECtHR 28 January 2014 (dec.)); *Arvanitakis and Others v. Greece* App No 21898/10 (ECtHR 26 Augustus 2014 (dec.)).

330 *Engel and Others v. The Netherlands* App No 5100/71 (ECtHR 8 June 1976).

331 *Engel and Others v. The Netherlands* App No 5100/71 (ECtHR 8 June 1976), para. 82. For a more detailed discussion of these criteria see, for example, Leach 2017 (n 281), pp. 335–337; Harris et al. 2018 (n 300), pp. 377–379.

332 For the specific standards applying to criminal proceedings, see, for example, Rainey 2017 (n 281), pp. 309–339.

333 See, for example, *Khan v. the United Kingdom* App No 35394/97 (ECtHR 12 May 2000), paras. 34 and 38. See also Leach 2017 (n 281), p. 353; Rainey 2017 (n 281), pp. 275 and 291.

overall the proceedings were fair. Under certain conditions, any shortcomings in the proceedings may, moreover, be remedied at a later stage, either at the same level[334] or by a higher court.[335]

The wording of Article 6(1) ECHR is rather general and does not as such provide an extensive understanding of what a fair trial entails. This is illustrated by the open-ended nature of the right to a 'fair hearing', the central element of Article 6(1). This provides an opportunity to accept other specific rights that are not expressly listed in Article 6, but that are nevertheless considered to be essential to a 'fair hearing' and, more generally, a fair procedure.[336] Indeed, in its case law, the Court has recognised certain specific rights as being incorporated in the right to a 'fair hearing', including the right to be heard, the principle of equality of arms and the right to adversarial proceedings, and the right to a reasoned judgment. As these specific rights are the most relevant for this study, they are discussed in more detail below.[337] First, however, the right of access to a court is considered. Just like the specific rights that have been read into the right to a fair hearing, the right of access to a court is not explicitly provided for in Article 6.

3.1.1.1. Access to court

The right of access to a court is an inherent element of Article 6(1), albeit not explicitly mentioned in the text of Article 6(1). It was recognised for the first time by the Court in *Golder*.[338] In this case, the Court considered that '[t]he fair, public and expeditious characteristics of judicial proceedings are of no value at all if there are no judicial proceedings'.[339] Thus, the right of access to a court is essential in ensuring that the Convention guarantees rights that are practical and effective instead of theoretical or illusory.[340] The right of access to a court, however, is not an absolute right. States are free to determine the means of securing the right of access to a court, and this right may even be subject to restrictions, providing these restrictions do not impair the very essence of the right, are in pursuance of a legitimate aim, are proportionate and sufficiently foreseeable, and comply with the equality of arms principle.[341]

334 See, for example, *Helle v. Finland* App No 20772/92 (ECtHR 19 December 1997) paras. 46 and 54.

335 See, for example, *Schuler-Zgraggen v. Switzerland* App No 14518/89 (ECtHR 24 June 1993) para. 52.

336 Harris et al. 2018 (n 300), p. 410.

337 For a complete overview, see, for example, Mole and Harby 2006 (n 281); Leach 2017 (n 281); Rainey 2017 (n 281); Harris et al. 2018 (n 281); Van Dijk et al. (eds.) 2018 (n 281); P. Hirvelä and S. Heikkilä, *Right to a fair trial. A practical guide to the Article 6 case-law of the European Court of Human Rights*, Intersentia 2021.

338 *Golder v. the United Kingdom* App No 4451/70 (ECtHR 21 February 1975).

339 *Golder v. the United Kingdom* App No 4451/70 (ECtHR 21 February 1975), para. 35.

340 See also *Airey v. Ireland* App No 6289/73 (ECtHR 9 October 1979), para. 24.

341 See, for example, *Golder v. the United Kingdom* App No 4451/70 (ECtHR 21 February 1975), para. 37–40; *Ashingdane v. the United Kingdom* App No 8225/78 (ECtHR 28 May 1985), para. 57; *Ligue du monde islamique and Organisation islamique mondiale du secours islamique v. France* App Nos 36497/05, 37172/05 (ECtHR 15 January 2009), para. 58; *Bayar and Gürbüz v. Turkey* App No 37569/06 (ECtHR 27 November 2012), para. 48.

In order to guarantee effective exercise of the right of access to a court, the Court has created additional obligations for States. The right of access to a court includes, for example, the right to obtain determination of a dispute, and the requirement that the implementation of final and binding decisions will not remain inoperative to the detriment of one of the parties.[342] The right of access to a court is consequently not limited to the right to instigate proceedings.

3.1.1.2. Right to be heard

The right to a fair hearing, as guaranteed by Article 6(1) ECHR, includes the right of parties to the proceedings to submit any observations that they consider relevant to their case.[343] The Court has held that this right can be seen to be effective only 'if the observations are actually "heard", that is duly considered by the trial court'.[344] Accordingly, courts have a duty to conduct a proper examination of the submissions, arguments and evidence adduced by the parties.[345]

Under Article 6(1) ECHR, litigants also, in principle, have a right to a public oral hearing in at least one instance.[346] The obligation to hold a hearing, however, is not absolute.[347] Whether a hearing is required depends on the circumstances of the case.[348] For example, a hearing may not be required if there are no issues of credibility or contested facts necessitating a hearing and the courts may fairly and reasonably decide the case on the basis of the parties' submissions and other written material.[349] As regards the question of whether a party must attend the hearing, the Court has held that 'Article 6(1) does not guarantee the right to personal presence before a civil court, but rather a more general right to present one's case effectively before the court and to enjoy equality of arms with the opposing side'.[350]

---

342 See, for example, *Hornsby v. Greece* App No 18357/91 (ECtHR 19 March 1997), para. 40; *Burdov v. Russia* App No 59498/00 (ECtHR 7 May 2002), para. 34. See also Leach 2017 (n 281), p. 351. Effective access to a court may sometimes also require legal aid to be provided (see, for example, *Airey v. Ireland* App No 6289/73 (ECtHR 9 October 1979), para. 26; *Steel and Morris v. the United Kingdom* App No 68416/01 (ECtHR 15 February 2005), paras. 69–72).

343 See, for example, *Perez v. France* App No 47287/99 (ECtHR (GC) 12 February 2004), para. 80.

344 *Perez v. France* App No 47287/99 (ECtHR (GC) 12 February 2004), para. 80.

345 See, for example, *Van de Hurk v. the Netherlands* App No 16034/90 (ECtHR 19 April 1994), para. 59; *Perez v. France* App No 47287/99 (ECtHR (GC) 12 February 2004), para. 80.

346 See, for example, *Salomonsson v. Sweden* App No 38978/97 (ECtHR 12 November 2002) para. 36; *Yakovlev v. Russia* App No 72701/01 (ECtHR 15 March 2005), para. 19; *De Tommaso v. Italy* App No 43395/09 (ECtHR (GC) 23 February 2017), para. 163.

347 See, for example, *De Tommaso v. Italy* App No 43395/09 (ECtHR (GC) 23 February 2017), para. 163.

348 See, for example, *De Tommaso v. Italy* App No 43395/09 (ECtHR (GC) 23 February 2017), para. 163.

349 See, for example, *Döry v. Sweden* App No 28394/95 (ECtHR 12 November 2002), para. 37; *Mirovni Institut v. Slovenia* App No 32303/13 (ECtHR 13 March 2018), para. 37. In *Ramos Nunes de Carvalho e Sá v. Portugal* App No 55391/13 (ECtHR (GC) 6 November 2018), paras. 190–191) the Court provided an overview of situations in which a hearing is, or is not, necessary.

350 *Khuzhin and Others v. Russia* App No 13470/02 (ECtHR 23 October 2008), para. 104.

3.1.1.3. Equality of arms and the right to adversarial proceedings

The principle of equality of arms was recognised by the Court in *Neumeister*.[351] Since then, it has been regarded as a component of the right to a fair hearing, as enshrined in Article 6(1).[352] This principle requires a fair balance between the parties. In, for example, *Dombo Beheer B.V.* the Court found that, in the context of civil proceedings, 'each party must be afforded a reasonable opportunity to present his case – including his evidence – under conditions that do not place him at a substantial disadvantage vis-à-vis his opponent'.[353] This case involved a dispute over an agreement between a limited company and a bank. One person from each party had been present at the meeting where the agreement had allegedly been reached. However, the domestic court only allowed the person representing the bank to be heard as a witness. Accordingly, the Court found that the limited company had been put at a substantial disadvantage vis-à-vis the bank by the decision not to allow the company's witness to be heard.[354]

Thus, a breach of equality of arms can occur if one party may attend the hearing whereas the other may not[355], but it can also arise if parties are not treated equally when witnesses are called[356], or are not allowed to submit material evidence on an equal basis.[357]

The principle of equality of arms is closely related to the right to adversarial proceedings, which is also incorporated in the right to a fair hearing.[358] Under the right to adversarial proceedings, parties are entitled to have knowledge of and comment on all evidence adduced or observations filed.[359] Similarly, the principle of equality of arms requires the relevant material to be made available to both parties. Consequently, the Court often finds a simultaneous breach of equality of arms and of the right to adversarial proceedings.[360] If, however, a domestic constitutional court, for example, gathers additional evidence at its own initiative and does not communicate this to either party, only the right to adversarial proceedings is considered to be breached.[361]

3.1.1.4. Reasoned judgment

The right to a reasoned judgment is another element of the right to a fair trial that is not expressly required by Article 6(1). The right to a reasoned judgment has been

351 *Neumeister v. Austria* App No 1936/63 (ECtHR 27 June 1968). See also Rainey 2017 (n 281), pp. 291–292.
352 See for example *Avotiņš v. Latvia* App No 17502/07 (ECtHR 23 May 2016), para. 119.
353 *Dombo Beheer BV v. the Netherlands* App No 14448/88 (ECtHR 27 October 1993), para. 33.
354 *Dombo Beheer BV v. the Netherlands* App No 14448/88 (ECtHR 27 October 1993), para. 34.
355 *Komanický v. Slovakia* App No 32106/96 (ECtHR 4 June 2002).
356 *Dombo Beheer BV v. the Netherlands* App No 14448/88 (ECtHR 27 October 1993).
357 *De Haas and Gijsels v. Belgium* App No 19983/92 (ECtHR 24 February 1997).
358 See, for example, *Ruiz-Mateos v. Spain* App No 12952/87 (ECtHR 23 June 1993), para. 63.
359 See, for example, *Ruiz-Mateos v. Spain* App No 12952/87 (ECtHR 23 June 1993), para. 63; *K.S. v. Finland* App No 29346/95 (ECtHR 31 May 2001), para. 21.
360 See also Rainey 2017 (n 281), pp. 292–293.
361 *Krčmář v. Czech Republic* App No 35376/97 (ECtHR 3 March 2000).

recognised by the Court to be implicit in a fair hearing.[362] Although a duty is imposed on domestic courts to give reasons in both civil and criminal cases, the extent of the reasoning required depends on the nature of the decision.[363] For example, a lower court is expected to give reasons so as to enable parties to make effective use of the right of appeal, whereas an appellate body may endorse the reasoning of the lower court.[364] If, however, a submission is fundamental to the outcome of the case, the court must always deal with it specifically in its judgment.[365] More generally, it must be clear from the decision that the essential issues of the case have been addressed.[366] A reasoned judgment is required not only because it enables parties to make effective use of the right of appeal, but also because it serves to demonstrate to the parties that they have been heard.[367]

3.1.2. Right to an effective remedy

In addition to Article 6 ECHR, the right to an effective remedy under Article 13 is important with regard to the procedural standards set by the ECHR. Indeed, the right to a fair trial and the right to an effective remedy are considered the two main components of the right of access to justice.[368] Article 13 states that:

> Everyone whose rights and freedoms as set forth in this Convention are violated shall have an effective remedy before a national authority notwithstanding that the violation has been committed by persons acting in an official capacity.

It follows from the text of Article 13 that the right to an effective remedy as enshrined in the Convention requires only the availability of an effective remedy at the domestic level. This means that States have to guarantee, within their national legal order, a process by which a violation can be remedied at that level.[369] This remedy is required to be effective both in practice and in law.[370] The effectiveness of a remedy does not depend on the certainty of a favourable outcome for the applicant, and nor does the authority providing the effective remedy have to be a judicial authority. What is important is whether the remedy 'could have prevented the alleged violation occurring or continuing or could have afforded the applicant appropriate redress for any violation that had already occurred'.[371] What is considered to be 'appropriate redress' varies depending on the nature of the applicant's

---

362 *Van de Hurk v. the Netherlands* App No 16034/90 (ECtHR 19 April 1994), para. 61.
363 *Van de Hurk v. the Netherlands* App No 16034/90 (ECtHR 19 April 1994), para. 61.
364 *Garcia Ruiz v. Spain* App No 30544/96 (ECtHR 21 January 1999), para. 26.
365 *Hiro Balani v. Spain* App No 18064/91 (ECtHR 9 December 1994), paras. 27–28.
366 *Boldea v. Romania* App No 19997/02 (ECtHR 15 February 2007), paras. 33–34.
367 *Taxquet v. Belgium* App No 926/05 (ECtHR (GC) 16 November 2010), para. 91.
368 European Union Agency for Fundamental Rights and the Council of Europe, *Handbook on European Law relating to access to justice*, Luxembourg 2016, p. 20.
369 See, for example, *Klass and Others v. Germany* App No 5029/71 (ECtHR 6 September 1978), para. 64.
370 *Rotaru v. Romania* App No 28341/95 (ECtHR (GC) 4 May 2000), para. 67.
371 *Ramirez Sanchez v. France* App No 59450/00 (ECtHR (GC) 4 July 2006), para. 160.

complaint. Specifically, the Court has held that the 'nature of the right at stake has implications for the type of remedy which the State is required to provide'.[372] This implies, for example, that, as regards breaches of Articles 2 and 3 ECHR, compensation may be required for non-pecuniary damages flowing from the breach of the Convention.[373]

Article 13 ECHR only requires the availability of an effective remedy at the domestic level, which means that it does not grant potential applicants a comparable right at the Court.[374] This also follows from the fact that potential applicants do not have direct access to the Court, but must instead exhaust all the available domestic remedies before seeking recourse to the Court. This, in turn, can be explained by the subsidiary role of the Court. As explained in Section 3 of Chapter 3, primary responsibility for securing the Convention rights lies with the States, and the Court has a subsidiary, supervisory role vis-à-vis the Convention States.[375]

3.2. APPLYING STANDARDS DEVELOPED IN THE ECtHR CASE LAW TO PROCEEDINGS BEFORE THE ECtHR

Since the Court itself is not directly bound by the procedural standards of Articles 6 and 13 ECHR, as defined in its case law, the standards discussed in the previous section do not apply directly to the proceedings before the Court. At the same time, several scholars and judges at the Court have argued that the Court should not only oversee whether procedural standards are complied with at the domestic level, but should also ensure that the procedural standards are applied in its own proceedings and judgments.[376] This view, which clearly stresses the importance of procedural rights, is a view with which the Court, too, is not unfamiliar. Indeed, the Court has always emphasised that the right to a fair trial is 'one of the fundamental principles of any democratic society, within the meaning of the Convention'.[377] Hence, it has held that there can be 'no justification for interpreting Article 6(1) restrictively'.[378]

---

372 *Öneryildiz v. Turkey* App No 48939/99 (ECtHR (GC) 30 November 2004), para. 147. See also *Čonka v. Belgium* App No 51564/99 (ECtHR 5 February 2002), para. 75.

373 See, for example, *Z and Others v. UK* App No 29392/95 (ECtHR 10 May 2001).

374 J.H. Gerards and L.R. Glas, 'Access to justice in the European Convention on Human Rights System (2017) 35 *Netherlands Quarterly of Human Rights* 11, 15.

375 Gerards and Glas 2017 (n 374), p. 15.

376 See, for example, E. Brems and L. Lavrysen, 'Procedural justice in human rights adjudication: the European Court of Human Rights' (2013) 35 *Human Rights Quarterly* 176, 185; L. Lixinski, 'Procedural fairness in human rights systems' in A. Sarvarian, F. Fontanelli, R. Baker, V. Tsevelekos (eds.), *Procedural fairness in international courts and tribunals*, British Institute of International and Comparative Law 2015, pp. 325–342, pp. 325ff; Glas 2018 (n 279), pp. 51, 89; Pastor Vilanova 2020 (n 279), p. 391; Ravarani 2020 (n 279), p. 454; K. Wojtyczek, 'Procedural Justice and the Proceedings Before the European Court of Human Rights: Who Should Have the Right to be Heard?' in R. Spano et al (eds.), *Fair trial: regional and international perspectives (Liber amicorum Linos-Alexandre Sicilianos)*, Anthemis 2020, pp. 741–755, p. 741.

377 *Pretto and Others v. Italy* App No 7984/77 (ECtHR 8 December 1983), para. 21.

378 *Moreira de Azevedo v. Portugal* App No 11296/84 (ECtHR 23 October 1990), para. 66.

The importance of procedural rights is also confirmed by their being found in most UN and regional human rights treaties.[379] Under Article 14 of the International Convention on Civil and Political Rights (ICCPR), for example, which was used as a model by the drafters of Article 6 ECHR[380], all persons are equal before the courts and tribunals, and everyone is entitled to a fair and public hearing by a competent, independent and impartial tribunal established by law.[381] This includes being assured of equal access to justice and equality of arms, and requires the parties to the proceedings to be treated without discrimination.[382] In addition, and perhaps illustrating the importance of procedural rights even more clearly, the fundamental principles of a fair trial are considered by the UN Human Rights Committee to be peremptory norms of international law.[383]

In addition to the general fundamental importance of procedural rights, several authors have argued that procedural fairness is clearly relevant to the ECtHR proceedings, based on research in social psychology and criminology.[384] Empirical research in the field of social psychology, for example, has shown that the perception of procedural fairness can matter to individuals more than a procedure's outcome.[385] The perception of procedural fairness, moreover, influences the extent to which individuals are likely to accept the outcome of a decision and their perception of the legitimacy of the institution concerned, in particular in controversial or divisive cases.[386] As regards the ECtHR, guaranteeing the Court's legitimacy may be all the more important now that the Court itself is tasked with safeguarding procedural fairness. Indeed, the Court's legitimacy could be compromised if it did not adhere to the standards it has set for the Convention States.[387] Furthermore, the issue of legitimacy is particularly relevant for the ECtHR because it is elemental for the effective implementation of the

379 See, for example, Article 40 of the Convention on the Rights of the Child, Article 18 of the Migrant Workers Convention, Article 5(a) of the Convention on the Elimination of Racial Discrimination, Article 15 of the Convention against Torture, Article 13 of the Convention on the Rights of Persons with Disabilities. See also S. Shah, 'Detention and trial' in D. Moeckli, S. Shah, S. Sivakumaran (eds.), *International human rights law,* Oxford University Press 2014 (2nd edition), pp. 252–277, p. 264.

380 O. Sidhu, *The Concept of Equality of Arms in Criminal Proceedings under Article 6 of the European Convention on Human Rights,* Intersentia 2017, p. 52; T. Barkhuysen (et al.) 'Right to a fair trial' in P. van Dijk (et al.) (eds.), *Theory and practice of the European Convention on Human Rights,* Intersentia 2018 (5th edition), pp. 497–654, p. 501.

381 Article 14 (1) ICCPR.

382 HRC General Comment 32, para. 8.

383 HRC General Comment 29, para. 11. See also Shah 2014 (n 380), pp. 266ff.

384 See, for example, Brems and Lavrysen 2013 (n 376.), pp. 182–185; S. Ouald Chaib, 'Suku Phull v. France rewritten from a procedural justice perspective: taking religious minorities seriously' in E. Brems (ed.) *Diversity and European human rights. Rewriting judgments of the ECHR,* Cambridge University Press 2013, pp. 218–240, pp. 220ff; Glas 2018 (n 279), p. 49. For a similar view on human rights systems in general, see Lixinski 2015 (n 376), pp. 325ff.

385 J. Thibaut and L. Walker, *Procedural justice: a psychological analysis,* L. Erlbaum Associates 1975, pp. 1–3.

386 T. Tyler, *Why people obey the law,* Princeton University Press 2006, as cited and discussed in Brems and Lavrysen 2013 (n 376), p. 184.

387 See also De Vylder 2014 (n 314) and Pastor Vilanova 2020 (n 279), p. 401.

Court's judgments by States.[388] Finally, a fair procedure is also considered to be of value to those who decide cases. In order to carry out their task of deciding on the dispute in accordance with the law, judges need to be informed as comprehensively as possible of the relevant facts and need to be able to have the opportunity to test the material submitted by the parties.[389]

Owing to the importance of procedural rights and procedural fairness for the Court's proceedings, several authors have used the procedural standards set out in Articles 6 and 13 ECHR and developed in the Court's case law to evaluate the fairness of the Court's proceedings.[390] Direct application of these standards may, however, pose certain difficulties because of the difference between ECtHR proceedings and the domestic proceedings. Glas therefore developed a set of 'principles of translation' so that fairness standards as developed in the ECtHR case law could be applied in proceedings before the ECtHR.[391] These principles reflect features of the ECtHR's tasks and functioning and highlight the differences between the context of domestic authorities and that of the ECtHR.

Glas's first principle (Principe I) is 'subsidiary protection'. This refers to the different roles of the ECtHR and States, whereby the States are primarily responsible for securing Convention rights, while the ECtHR's role is subsidiary in nature.[392] Principle II is 'effective protection', which relates to the ECtHR's obligation to apply the Convention in a manner that renders its rights practical and effective, not theoretical and illusory.[393] Principles III and IV are 'individual' and 'general justice', respectively, and refer to the twofold task of the ECtHR: to render justice in individual cases, and to elucidate, safeguard and develop the rules instituted in the Convention.[394] Principle V is '*in concreto* review', and refers to the rule whereby applicants must prove that they are a victim of or directly affected by a specific measure.[395] Principle VI is 'autonomy' and refers to the ECtHR deciding autonomously on its jurisdiction, the scope of the facts that it examines and the evidence that it relies upon, and autonomously defining

388 T. Barkhuysen and M. van Emmerik, 'Legitimacy of European Court of Human Rights Judgments: Procedural Aspects' in N. Huls, M. Adams, J. Bomhoff (eds.), *The Legitimacy of Highest Courts' Rulings: Judicial Deliberations and Beyond*, TMC Asser Press 2009, pp. 437–449, p. 437. Brems and Lavrysen 2013 (n 376), pp. 182–184; Glas 2018 (n 279), p. 49.

389 K. Keith, 'Procedural fairness in the international legal tradition: the fundamentals of judicial procedure' in A. Sarvarian, F. Fontanelli, R. Baker, T. Vassilis (eds.), *Procedural fairness in international courts and tribunals*, British Institute of International and Comparative Law 2015, pp. 39–57, pp. 41–42.

390 See, for example, A. Butler, 'Legal aid before human rights treaty monitoring bodies' (2000) 49 *International and Comparative Law Quarterly* 360; De Vylder 2014 (n 314); Gerards 2014 (n 314); E. Gruodytė and S. Kirchner, 'Legal aid for intervenors in proceedings before the European Court of Human Rights' (2016) 2 *International Comparative Jurisprudence* 36; Glas 2018 (n 279), including further references (fn. 12).

391 Glas 2018 (n 279), pp. 52ff.

392 Glas 2018 (n 279), p. 53.

393 Glas 2018 (n 279), p. 54.

394 Glas 2018 (n 279), pp. 54–55.

395 Glas 2018 (n 279), p. 55.

Convention concepts.[396] Principle VII is 'deference to domestic authorities', which refers to the margin of appreciation enjoyed by States.[397] Principles VIII, IX and X refer to the ECtHR being 'no fourth-instance court', 'no first-instance court', and 'no criminal or civil court', respectively. These principles reflect that the ECtHR is not a court of appeal, that it does not adjudicate on large numbers of cases that require basic fact-finding or the calculation of monetary compensation, and that its role is not to rule on criminal guilt or civil liability, but instead on the responsibility of the Convention States under the Convention.[398] The final principle, Principle XI, is 'no involvement in execution matters' and refers to the discretion that States have regarding how they execute a judgment in which a violation was found.[399]

Applying these principles to the right to legal aid and the right to a reasoned judgment, Glas provides examples of standards of fairness that can be used in relation to the procedure before the ECtHR. Regarding the right to a reasoned judgment, for example, the translated standard would require the ECtHR to give adequate reasons.[400] Although the extent to which reason-giving is required could depend on the type of complaint and the content of the complaint and the judgment[401], Glas argued that, in the light of the translation principle of 'individual justice', the ECtHR's reasoning needs to demonstrate that it has heard the parties.[402] Similarly, in order to provide 'general justice', the Court's reasoning should be thorough since this is necessary in order to elucidate the Convention standards.[403] By contrast, the translation principle of 'no first-instance court' shows that reasoning in order to make an effective appeal possible is less relevant in an ECtHR context, even if this is another reason advanced by the ECtHR for requiring domestic courts to reason their judgments.[404]

The example of the right to a reasoned judgment shows that as well as helping translate the Convention standards to the ECtHR context, the principles formulated by Glas can provide justification for applying a particular Convention standard to the ECtHR proceedings. It also shows that translation does not necessarily mean adaptation or change. Sometimes the Article 6 or 13 standard can be applied directly to the Court's procedure, such as when the rationale for requiring a standard is equally relevant to the ECtHR context. This applies when, for example, the rationale is of a general nature, such as the requirement for reasoning in the interest of the proper administration of justice.[405]

In a manner different from Glas, but somewhat comparable in outcome, Brems and Lavrysen have identified four general procedural justice principles that should

---

396 Glas 2018 (n 279), pp. 56–57.
397 Glas 2018 (n 279), p. 57.
398 Glas 2018 (n 279), pp. 58–60.
399 Glas 2018 (n 279), p. 61.
400 Glas 2018 (n 279), p. 79.
401 Glas 2018 (n 279), p. 79.
402 Glas 2018 (n 279), p. 76.
403 Glas 2018 (n 279), p. 77.
404 Glas 2018 (n 279), p. 77.
405 Glas 2018 (n 279), pp. 80–81.

be observed by the Court in its proceedings.[406] These principles – participation, neutrality, respect and trustworthiness – derive from Tyler's work on procedural justice.[407] If applied to the Court's setting, the participation principle would require the Court not only to represent in its judgments the parties' different viewpoints and to carefully assess the merits of each argument, but also to pay attention to stakeholders who may not necessarily be formal parties in the case.[408] According to Brems and Lavrysen, it is important to address these views as they may represent widely held views or interests, and the Court's judgment can have authority beyond the parties and outside the State concerned.[409] The principle of neutrality, in these authors' view, requires the Court to abstain from expressing bias and to be transparent in its reasoning, such that the actual reasons behind an outcome are reflected in the judgment or decision.[410] The third principle, respect, requires the Court to show respect for people and their rights, such that people feel that they, and their concerns, are being taken seriously.[411] Lastly, Brems and Lavrysen hold, based on the principle of trustworthiness, that the Court should show that it cares about the applicant, even when finding against him.[412]

The four general procedural justice principles identified by Brems and Lavrysen are broadly similar to the procedural standards of Articles 6 and 13 ECHR. Different aspects of the principles of participation, neutrality, respect, and trust can be found, for example, in the right to be heard, the principle of equality of arms and the right to adversarial proceedings, and the right to a reasoned judgment. Indeed, in an article comparing Article 6(1) ECHR with procedural justice requirements, Van de Graaf found there to be a great deal of overlap between the guarantees offered by Article 6(1) and procedural justice requirements established in social psychology research on procedural justice.[413] Thus, the work of Brems and Lavrysen can be seen as another expression of the idea that the Court should adhere to the procedural standards it has set for domestic judicial proceedings, albeit sometimes in a slightly adapted manner to take account of the particular role and position of the Court; for instance, by requiring the Court to pay attention to stakeholders who may not be formal parties in the case, given that a judgment of the Court can have authority beyond the parties and outside the State concerned.

406 Brems and Lavrysen 2013 (n 376).

407 Brems and Lavrysen 2013 (n 376), pp. 180–182. Brems and Lavrysen use the four distinct principles as specified by T. Tyler (T. Tyler, 'Procedural justice and the courts' (2007) 44 *Court review: The journal of the American judges association* 26).

408 Brems and Lavrysen 2013 (n 376), p. 186.

409 Brems and Lavrysen 2013 (n 376), p. 186.

410 Brems and Lavrysen 2013 (n 376), p. 186.

411 Brems and Lavrysen 2013 (n 376), p. 188.

412 Brems and Lavrysen 2013 (n 376), pp. 188–189.

413 C. van de Graaf, 'Procedural fairness: between human rights law and social psychology' (2021) 39 *Netherlands Quarterly of Human Rights* 11, 29.

4. CONCLUSION

This chapter first discussed procedural rules and standards that apply directly to the ECtHR proceedings on the basis of certain Convention provisions and Rules of Court. Second, the procedural standards of Articles 6 and 13 ECHR, and as defined in the Court's case law, were discussed. These standards are directed to domestic authorities and, therefore, do not directly apply to ECtHR proceedings. In line, however, with commonly accepted principles, this study takes the view that the procedural standards of Articles 6 and 13 ECHR should also apply to proceedings before the ECtHR, albeit sometimes in a slightly adapted or 'translated' version to take account of the particular role and position of the Court. In practice, this would mean that the parties in the Court's proceedings would have the right to present their case effectively before the Court and to enjoy equality of arms with the opposing side. It would also mean that the observations would be duly considered by the Court and that the Court's judgment would show that the parties had been heard, and that submissions fundamental to the outcome of the case had been dealt with specifically. Although these procedural standards are broadly similar to the more general procedural justice principles of participation, neutrality, respect, and trustworthiness, they may need to be adapted to the Court's setting. Against this background, Brems and Lavrysen argued that the principle of participation requires the Court not only to represent in its judgments the parties' different viewpoints and to carefully assess the merits of each argument, but also to pay attention to stakeholders who may not be formal parties in the case.

PART II

VERTICALISED CASES UNRAVELLED

INTRODUCTION

The first part of this study explained that Article 34 ECHR stipulates that complaints about interferences with Convention rights have to be directed against a Convention State.[414] Hence, complaints directed against private actors are incompatible *ratione personae* with the provisions of the Convention. This does not mean, however, that no effect is given to the Convention in horizontal relationships. Indeed, over the years the Court has increasingly offered substantive protection of Convention rights in relations between private actors. It has done so by imposing horizontal positive obligations on Convention States, requiring the latter to take action to secure the rights and liberties guaranteed in the Convention in relations between private actors. Such obligations originate from the Convention States' responsibility for their own acts and omissions in relation to acts and omissions of private actors.[415]

The concept of horizontal positive obligations is the focus of the first chapter (Chapter 5) in this Part II, where it is explained that through the concept of horizontal positive obligations, the Court offers substantive protection of Convention rights in relation to a broad variety of relations between private actors and Convention rights. These obligations have in common that they are often imposed in cases originating from a conflict between two private actors (i.e. a horizontal conflict) at the domestic level. In other words, even if complaints have to be directed against a Convention State to be admissible *ratione personae* with the provisions of the Convention, this does not yet mean that the vertical proceedings before the Court cannot originate from a horizontal conflict at the domestic level. In cases, for example, concerning the right to reputation and respect for private life versus the right to freedom of expression, an individual may have brought proceedings at a domestic court to prevent a newspaper or magazine publisher from publishing (or continuing to publish) photos of the individual's private life. Because of Article 34, and in contrast to the domestic courts, the ECtHR cannot deal directly with such behaviour by a publisher. However, the individual victim of a breach of reputation by a private actor can complain before the ECtHR about the State's lack of compliance with its positive obligations to protect the individual's rights under Article 8 ECHR. If, therefore, the domestic courts decide not to grant an injunction preventing publication of the photos, the individual can lodge an application at the ECtHR to complain about the domestic courts' decision. The originally horizontal case

414 See Chapter 4 (Section 2.1).

415 See, for example, the Court's reasoning in *O'Keeffe v. Ireland* App No 35810/09 (ECtHR 28 January 2014), para. 168.

at the domestic level thus transforms into a vertical case before the ECtHR, and into what this study terms as a 'verticalised' case.

The notion of verticalised cases applies to a myriad of cases before the ECtHR. As these cases can originate from a wide range of horizontal conflicts and, therefore, involve many different issues and Convention rights, they have many different characteristics. To provide a better insight into and understanding of the notion of verticalised cases before the ECtHR, a detailed analysis of verticalised cases is provided in Chapter 6. On the basis of a case law analysis involving four case studies of different types of verticalised cases, the origins of such cases (i.e. the nature of and the parties involved in the conflict at the domestic level) are discussed in detail, as well as the Court's examination of verticalised cases.

The unravelling of the notion of verticalised cases provides a basis for analysing the problems that may arise in verticalised cases. This analysis is provided in Part III, where a more evaluative approach is taken by discussing problems that may arise during the Court's proceedings in such cases and also problems that can arise after the Court's judgment in a verticalised case.

CHAPTER 5
HORIZONTAL POSITIVE OBLIGATIONS

1. INTRODUCTION

Over the years, the Court has increasingly offered substantive protection of Convention rights in relations between private actors. Such horizontal positive obligations are a specific type of positive obligations: they govern the relations between private actors, whereas positive obligations are normally imposed in relations between the State and the individual.[416] To better understand horizontal positive obligations, this chapter starts with a general introduction to the concept of positive obligations (Section 2). This is followed by a discussion of various relations between private actors in which the Court has imposed horizontal positive obligations (Section 3)[417], thus illustrating the broad variety of such relations in which the Court has offered substantive protection of Convention rights. This detailed discussion of the concept of horizontal positive obligations is provided for two reasons. First, because such obligations are often imposed in verticalised cases: the different types of relations between private actors in which the Court has offered substantive protection of Convention rights through horizontal positive obligations thus provide a range of examples of verticalised cases before the Court. Second, gaining insight into the increased substantive protection of Convention rights in relations between private actors is important for understanding the consequences of verticalisation, since this substantive protection may influence the scope of possible procedural issues arising from such cases.[418]

---

416 For the distinction between horizontal and vertical positive obligations, see further L. Lavrysen, *Human rights in a positive state: rethinking the relationship between positive and negative obligations under the European Convention on Human Rights*, Intersentia 2016, pp. 78ff.

417 Parts of this section have also been published in C.M.S. Loven, '"Verticalised" cases before the European Court of Human Rights unravelled: an analysis of their characteristics and the Court's approach to them' (2020) 38 *Netherlands Quarterly of Human Rights* 246 and C.M.S. Loven, 'Horizontale positieve verplichtingen in de rechtspraak van het Europees Hof voor de Rechten van Mens' ['Horizontal positive obligations and the case law of the European Court of Human Rights'] (2020) 45 *Nederlands Tijdschrift voor de Mensenrechten* 479.

418 See also the Concurring Opinion of Judge Wojtyczek in *Bochan v. Ukraine (No. 2)* App No 2251/08 (ECtHR (GC) 5 February 2015), para. 6.

2. CONCEPT OF POSITIVE OBLIGATIONS

2.1. INTRODUCTION TO THE CONCEPT OF POSITIVE OBLIGATIONS

The *Belgian Linguistic* case and the cases of *Marckx, Airey,* and *X and Y* are generally considered to be the four landmark cases in relation to the concept of positive obligations.[419] Although in the *Belgian Linguistic* case, the Court did not specify the contents of any particular positive obligation that would have to be complied with under the Convention, this case was the first occasion on which that it introduced the concept of positive obligations in its reasoning.[420] In the subsequent cases of *Marckx, Airey,* and *X and Y* the Court did, however, impose specific positive obligations on Convention States. The case of *X and Y* is particularly relevant for this research since, in this case, the Court extended the concept of positive obligations to horizontal relations.[421] This case was about a girl who lived in a privately owned home for children with a mental disability, where she had been sexually assaulted at the age of sixteen. Under the Dutch Criminal Code of that time, only the girl herself could lodge a complaint about this – she was not permitted to have anyone act on her behalf. However, her mental condition meant the girl was incapable of protecting her own interests. There was thus a gap in Dutch criminal law for prosecuting the perpetrator of the crime. Reasoning that this seriously affected the applicant's Convention rights and the effectiveness of the protection offered by the Convention, the Court imposed a positive obligation on the Dutch State to amend the criminal law provisions.[422] In this respect, the Court expressly acknowledged that '[t]hese [positive] obligations may involve the adoption of measures designed to secure the respect for private life even in the sphere of the relations of individuals between themselves'.[423] Thus, the domestic authorities were required to give at least some effect to the Convention in a horizontal relationship.

The positive obligation imposed on the Dutch State in the *X and Y* case is illustrative for the different nature of positive and negative obligations. In general, three main differences between positive and negative obligations can be distinguished to promote a better understanding of the concept of positive obligations. First, positive obligations are mostly defined by the ECtHR, whereas negative obligations follow logically and directly from the text of the Convention. Positive obligations are sometimes, therefore,

---

419 *Belgian Linguistic case* App No 1474/62 (ECtHR 23 July 1968); *Marckx v. Belgium* App No 6833/74 (ECtHR 13 June 1979); *Airey v. Ireland* App No 6289/73 (ECtHR 9 October 1979); *X and Y v. the Netherlands* App No 8978/80 (ECtHR 26 March 1985).

420 *Belgian Linguistic case* App No 1474/62 (ECtHR 23 July 1968), para. 3. The Court held that '[i]t cannot be concluded from this [the negative formulation of the right to education] that the State has no positive obligation to ensure respect for such a right as is protected by Article 2 of the Protocol'. See further M. Beijer, *The limits of fundamental rights protection by the EU: the scope for the development of positive obligations*, Intersentia 2017, pp. 38–39. See also Lavrysen 2016 (n 416), p. 3.

421 See also Lavrysen 2016 (n 416), p. 4.

422 *X and Y v. the Netherlands* App No 8978/80 (ECtHR 26 March 1985), para. 27.

423 *X and Y v. the Netherlands* App No 8978/80 (ECtHR 26 March 1985), para. 23.

called 'implied' obligations'.[424] Second, positive obligations require States to take action, whereas negative obligations require States to abstain from interfering.[425] Finally, positive obligations generally leave open the exact measures that have to be taken by States to fulfil the positive obligation, whereas negative obligations leave less choice as to how they must be fulfilled.[426]

2.2. DEFINING POSITIVE OBLIGATIONS

Although it is clear from the Court's case law that positive obligations exist, the Court has not indicated a very clear and explicit legal basis for the recognition of positive obligations.[427] However, the main justification seems to be the need to guarantee an effective protection of fundamental rights and the general obligation of Article 1 ECHR, which requires States to secure the enjoyment of the Convention rights to everyone within their jurisdiction.[428] The Court has clarified the meaning of this obligation in its case law. In *Airey* it held, for example, that '[t]he Convention is intended to guarantee not rights that are theoretical or illusory but rights that are practical and effective'.[429]

Just like the question as to the legal basis for recognising positive obligations, the question as to how and to what degree positive obligations can be defined and imposed on States has not been clearly answered by the Court.[430] In *Plattform "Ärzte für das Leben"* the Court even held that '[t]he Court does not have to develop a general theory of the positive obligations which may flow from the Convention…'.[431] Several authors have nevertheless tried to systematise the Court's approach in this regard.[432] Gerards,

---

424 Beijer 2017 (n 420), pp. 42–43; J.H. Gerards, *General principles of the European Convention on Human Rights*, Oxford University Press 2019, p. 132.

425 Lavrysen 2016 (n 416), p. 11; Beijer 2017 (n 420), p. 44; Gerards 2019 (n 424), p. 132.

426 Beijer 2017 (n 420), p. 46. For this reason, the Court made it clear that a positive obligation is an obligation as to measures to be taken (obligation of means), and not as to results to be achieved (obligation to achieve) (see, for example, *Plattform "Ärzte für das Leben" v. Austria* App No 10126/82 (ECtHR 21 June 1988), para. 34) (see also S. van Drooghenbroeck, 'L'horizontalisation des droits de l'homme' in H. Dumont, F. Ost, S. van Drooghenbroeck (eds.), *La responsabilité, face cachée des droits de l'homme*, Bruylant 2005, pp. 355–390, p. 372). This is also why Stoyanova refers to the 'disjunctive structure of positive rights'. States have various options at their disposal for ensuring positive obligations, and, therefore, an omission has no definitive counterpart (see V. Stoyanova, 'The disjunctive juncture of positive rights under the European Convention on Human Rights' (2018) 87 *Nordic Journal of International Law* 344).

427 O. Cherednychenko, 'Towards the Control of Private Acts by the European Court of Human Rights?' (2006) 13 *Maastricht Journal of European and Comparative Law* 195, 200; Beijer 2017 (n 420), p. 46; Gerards 2019 (n 424), p. 109.

428 Lavrysen 2016 (n 416), p. 5; Beijer 2017 (n 420), p. 46; Gerards 2019 (n 424), p. 109.

429 *Airey v. Ireland* App No 6289/73 (ECtHR 9 October 1979), para. 24.

430 Gerards 2019 (n 424), p. 109. See also D. Spielmann, *L'effet potentiel de la Convention européenne des droits de l'homme entre personnes privées*, Bruylant 1995, pp. 83–84.

431 *Plattform "Ärzte für das Leben" v. Austria* App No 10126/82 (ECtHR 21 June 1988), para. 31.

432 For example, D. Xenos, *The positive obligations of the state under the European Convention of Human Rights*, Routledge 2012, pp. 57ff; Lavrysen 2016 (n 416), pp. 131ff; Gerards 2019 (n 424), pp. 110ff.

for example, has distinguished four methods used by the Court to define which positive obligations can reasonably be imposed on States.[433] First, the Court may rely on the general principle of effectiveness. Second, the Court may apply a 'fair balance test'.[434] Third, the Court may apply a 'reasonable knowledge and means' test. Finally, if the Court has already established the existence of a certain positive obligation in previous case law, it will reiterate the accepted positive obligations as general principles in its reasoning and apply these to the facts of the case (precedent-based method).[435] The first three methods are discussed in more detail below. Since the aim of this chapter is to illustrate how the Court gives effect to the Convention in relations between private actors, the methods are discussed by giving examples of cases originally involving a horizontal conflict.

2.2.1. Principle of effectiveness[436]

In the *Marckx* case the Court held that '...there may be positive obligations inherent in an effective "respect" for family life'.[437] Ever since, the notion of effectiveness has been used as a foundation for recognising many different positive obligations under the Convention.[438] In, for example, the above-mentioned case of *X and Y* the Court imposed a positive obligation on the State to introduce effectively deterring legislation to help protect the fundamental value of physical and mental integrity against interferences by third parties.[439] By imposing this positive obligation, the Court extended the idea that 'effectively' respecting Article 8(1) can entail positive obligations in relations between individuals.[440] Similarly, applying the effectiveness principle, the Court imposed a positive obligation under the right to freedom of assembly (Article 11 ECHR) in *Plattform "Ärzte für das Leben"*.[441] The applicant in this case, a pro-life campaign group, complained that the Austrian authorities had failed to protect its right to freedom of peaceful assembly from violent disruption by counterdemonstrators. The Court reasoned that:

> [t]he participants must ... be able to hold the demonstration without having to fear that they will be subjected to physical violence by their opponents ... Genuine, effective freedom of peaceful assembly cannot, therefore, be reduced to a mere duty on the part of the State not to interfere: a purely negative conception would not be compatible with the object and purpose of Article 11.[442]

433 Gerards 2019 (n 424), pp. 110ff.
434 Also referred to as a proportionality analysis.
435 See, for example, *Fernandes de Oliveira v. Portugal* App No 78103/14 (ECtHR 28 March 2017), paras. 65–81; *Sarishvili-Bolkvadze v. Georgia* App No 58240 (ECtHR 19 July 2018), paras. 67–98.
436 For a more general introduction to the principle of effectiveness, see also Chapter 3 (Section 2).
437 *Marckx v. Belgium* App No 6833/74 (ECtHR 13 June 1979), para. 31.
438 A. Mowbray, 'The creativity of the European Court of Human Rights' (2005) 5 *Human Rights Law Review* 57, 72; Lavrysen 2016 (n 416), p. 147.
439 *X and Y v. the Netherlands* App No 8978/80 (ECtHR 26 March 1985), paras. 23–30.
440 *X and Y v. the Netherlands* App No 8978/80 (ECtHR 26 March 1985), para. 23.
441 *Platfform "Ärzte für das Leben" v. Austria* App No 10126/82 (ECtHR 21 June 1988).
442 *Platfform "Ärzte für das Leben" v. Austria* App No 10126/82 (ECtHR 21 June 1988), para. 32.

Thus, to protect private actors against violence by third parties and to guarantee effective protection of Article 11 ECHR in relations between private actors, the Court imposed the positive obligation on the State 'to take reasonable and appropriate measures to enable lawful demonstrations to proceed peacefully'.[443]

2.2.2. *Fair balance test*

A fair balance test is mainly applied in relation to the right to private life, the right to freedom of religion, the right to freedom of expression, and the right to freedom of assembly and association (Articles 8–11 ECHR) and implies that the Court assesses which positive action is needed to strike a fair balance between the identified individual and general interests at play.[444] Examples of the application of this test can be found in *Hatton and Others* and *Moreno Gómez*.[445] The *Hatton and Others* case was about people living close to Heathrow International Airport in the United Kingdom who alleged that the right to respect for their private lives (Article 8 ECHR) was infringed by the government policy on night flights at Heathrow Airport. Their complaints related to the sleep disturbance caused by the many aircraft taking off and landing at night. Heathrow Airport and the aircraft were not owned, controlled or operated by the State or its agents. In this case, the application of the fair balance test meant that the Court examined whether in the implementation of the 1993 policy on night flights at Heathrow Airport, a fair balance had been struck between the competing interests of the individuals affected by the night noise and the community as a whole, in particular the economic interests of the country.[446] The Court concluded that the United Kingdom had sufficiently complied with its positive obligation to effectively protect the individual interests of the persons concerned.[447] In reaching this conclusion, the Court referred to several factors relevant to the balancing of the individual and general interests, such as the night flights' contribution to the economy, the availability of measures to mitigate the effects of aircraft noise (including the extent to which house prices had been affected by the noise and the individual's ability to leave the area), and the extent to which appropriate investigations and studies had been carried out by the State.[448]

Unlike in *Hatton and Others*, the Court concluded in *Moreno Gómez* that the State had not sufficiently complied with its positive obligation to effectively protect the

---

443 *Plattform "Ärzte für das Leben" v. Austria* App No 10126/82 (ECtHR 21 June 1988), para. 34. See also A. Clapham, *Human Rights in the Private Sphere*, Clarendon Press 1993, p. 238; Mowbray 2005 (n 439), p. 75; D. Spielmann, 'The European Convention on Human Rights. The European Court of Human Rights' in J. Fedtke and D. Oliver (eds.) *Human rights and the private sphere: a comparative study*, Routledge-Cavendish 2007, pp. 427–464, p. 448; Lavrysen 2016 (n 416), pp. 84 and 147.

444 On this test, see further Lavrysen 2016 (n 416), pp. 166ff; Gerards 2019 (n 424), pp. 111–116.

445 *Hatton and Others v. the United Kingdom* App No 36022/97 (ECtHR (GC) 8 July 2003); *Moreno Gómez v. Spain* App No 4143/02 (ECtHR 16 November 2004).

446 *Hatton and Others v. the United Kingdom* App No 36022/97 (ECtHR (GC) 8 July 2003), para. 119.

447 *Hatton and Others v. the United Kingdom* App No 36022/97 (ECtHR (GC) 8 July 2003), para. 129.

448 *Hatton and Others v. the United Kingdom* App No 36022/97 (ECtHR (GC) 8 July 2003), paras. 124–129.

individual interests concerned. This case was about night-time disturbances caused by bars and discotheques in the city centre of Valencia. As in *Hatton and Others*, therefore, the State was not the direct source of the noise pollution. The Court applied the fair balance test to determine whether the domestic authorities had undertaken sufficient action to put a stop to third-party breaches of Article 8 ECHR, and specifically whether they had struck a fair balance between the need to protect the applicant's Convention rights and the need to serve the general interest. Although the Valencia City Council had adopted noise regulations in order to secure respect of the applicant's private life, it had, according to the Court, tolerated, and thus contributed to, the repeated flouting of the rules that it had established itself.[449] Hence, it was the lack of enforcement of adopted rules, without a sound balancing exercise underlying that omission, that led to the finding that the State had not complied with its positive obligation under Article 8 ECHR.

In addition to balancing the individual and the general interests at play, the Court has also balanced interests of private parties in order to determine whether positive obligations existed. This can be see in, for example, the *Appleby* case[450], when three United Kingdom citizens and an environmental group argued that the State owed a positive obligation to secure the exercise of their rights in a privately owned shopping mall in the town centre. They had been prevented from imparting information and ideas about proposed local development plans in the shopping mall. The Court emphasised that the effective exercise of freedom of expression not only requires the State not to interfere with the freedom of expression, but also places a duty on the State to take positive measures of protection, even in the sphere of relations between individuals.[451] However, as a complicating factor, the interests of the other private party involved in this case, the shopping mall owner, were also protected by a fundamental right: the right to property (Article 1 of Protocol 1). Consequently, the Court had to consider the shopping mall owner's property rights in balancing the individual and the general interests.[452] The Court therefore took account of a variety of factors in its eventual balancing exercise: the physical layout and policies of shopping malls; changes in the demographic, social, economic and technical means of social interaction; and the availability of various alternative ways of communicating the applicants' views to the public.[453] Having considered and weighed all these factors and interests, the Court concluded that the applicants were not effectively prevented from communicating their views to their fellow citizens as a result of the refusal of the private company. Hence, the State had not failed to comply with any positive obligation to protect the applicants' freedom of expression.[454]

449 *Moreno Gómez v. Spain* App No 4143/02 (ECtHR 16 November 2004), para. 61.

450 *Appleby and Others v. the United Kingdom* App No 44306/98 (ECtHR 6 May 2003). See also Cherednychenko 2006 (n 427), pp. 201ff.

451 *Appleby and Others v. the United Kingdom* App No 44306/98 (ECtHR 6 May 2003), para. 39.

452 *Appleby and Others v. the United Kingdom* App No 44306/98 (ECtHR 6 May 2003), para. 43.

453 *Appleby and Others v. the United Kingdom* App No 44306/98 (ECtHR 6 May 2003), paras. 46–48.

454 *Appleby and Others v. the United Kingdom* App No 44306/98 (ECtHR 6 May 2003), paras. 48–49.

2.2.3. *Reasonable knowledge and means test*

The reasonable knowledge and means test involves examining whether the authorities knew or ought to have known of a real and immediate risk to the life of an identified individual or individuals from the criminal acts of a third party (reasonable knowledge) and whether the authorities failed to take measures, within the scope of their powers, that might have been expected to avoid that risk (reasonable means).[455] This test is mainly applied in relation to the right to life and the prohibition of torture and inhuman and degrading treatment or punishment (Articles 2–3 ECHR). In this regard, the test has been applied in a range of cases originating from horizontal conflicts, including cases on the risk of dangerous substances such as asbestos[456], industrial activities[457], human trafficking[458], sexual abuse of children in schools[459], and domestic violence.[460, 461]

The Court's application of the reasonable knowledge and means test can be illustrated by the case of *E. and Others*[462], which concerned the sexual and physical abuse of four siblings by their stepfather. The abuse continued despite the stepfather having been convicted of child abuse on an earlier occasion. The siblings complained before the Court that the local authority had failed to protect them from abuse by their stepfather and that they had had no access to an effective remedy in this respect. The Court held that:

> … [it] is satisfied that … the social services should have been aware that the situation in the family disclosed a history of past sexual and physical abuse from W.H. [the stepfather] and that, notwithstanding the probation order, he was continuing to have close contact with the family, including the children. Even if the social services were not aware he was inflicting abuse at this time, they should have been aware that the children remained at potential risk.[463]

According to the Court, the social services were 'under an obligation to monitor the offender's conduct in the aftermath of the conviction', but 'failed to take steps which would have enabled them to discover the exact extent of the problem and, potentially, to prevent further abuse taking place'.[464] The State was thus held to have a monitoring obligation in order to protect the children against abuse by their stepfather, and more generally to protect them against interference with Article 3 ECHR by their stepfather.

---

455 See, for example, *Osman v. the United Kingdom* App No 23452/94 (ECtHR 28 October 1998). See also Xenos 2012 (n 432), pp. 74ff; Lavrysen 2016 (n 416), pp. 131ff; Gerards 2019 (n 424), pp. 116ff.

456 *Brincat and Others v. Malta* App No 60908/11 (ECtHR 24 July 2014).

457 See, for example, *Öneryildiz v. Turkey* App No 48939/99 (ECtHR (GC) 30 November 2004).

458 See, for example, *Rantsev v. Cyprus and Croatia* App No 25965/04 (ECtHR 7 January 2010), paras. 286 and 289.

459 See, for example, *O'Keeffe v. Ireland* App No 35810/09 (ECtHR (GC) 28 January 2014), para. 149ff.

460 See, for example, *Opuz v. Turkey* App No 33401/02 (ECtHR 9 June 2009), para. 130ff.

461 See further Gerards 2019 (n 424), p. 118.

462 *E. and Others v. the United Kingdom* App No 33218/96 (ECtHR 26 November 2002). See also Lavrysen 2016, (n 416), pp. 134–135.

463 *E. and Others v. the United Kingdom* App No 33218/96 (ECtHR 26 November 2002), para. 96.

464 *E. and Others v. the United Kingdom* App No 33218/96 (ECtHR 26 November 2002), paras. 96–97.

2.3. LIMITS TO THE SCOPE OF POSITIVE OBLIGATIONS

The previous section discussed how the Court uses the effectiveness principle, the fair balance test, the reasonable knowledge and means test, and the precedent-based method to help define the positive obligations that can reasonably be imposed on States. The Court's application of all these tests illustrates that the scope of the positive obligations formulated in a specific case may be subject to some limitations. First, the Court's interpretation of what can reasonably be required to guarantee an effective protection may determine the scope of the imposed positive obligation.[465] Second, in applying the fair balance test, the Court has allowed significant leeway to States to decide if and how they want to intervene, providing the interference with a Convention right is not far-reaching and the essence of a right is not affected.[466] Finally, the extent of a State's knowledge is an important condition limiting the scope of a positive obligation. If, for example, the State did not know and could not reasonably have known of a violation of fundamental rights committed by private actors, a positive obligation is not imposed on the State.[467]

Another important limit to the scope of positive obligations is the 'impossible and disproportionate burden' test. In particular in cases involving social and economic obligations, the Court has held that positive obligations must not impose an impossible or disproportionate burden on States in terms of finances and organisation.[468] Accordingly, the impossible and disproportionate burden test refers to the choices that have to be made in terms of priorities and resources.[469] In, for example, *Öneryildiz*, a case about dangerous industrial activities, the Court reasoned that:

> ... it is not its task to substitute for the views of the local authorities its own view of the best policy to adopt in dealing with the social, economic and urban problems in this part of Istanbul. It therefore accepts the Government's argument that in this respect an impossible or disproportionate burden must not be imposed on the authorities without consideration being given, in particular, to the operational choices which they must make in terms of priorities and resources; this results from the wide margin of appreciation States enjoy, as the Court has previously held, in difficult social and technical spheres such as the one in issue in the instant case.[470]

---

465 *McCann and Others v. the United Kingdom* App No 18984/91 (ECtHR 27 September 1995). See also Lavrysen 2016 (n 416), pp. 150ff; Gerards 2019 (n 424), p. 120.

466 See, for example, *Remuszko v. Poland* App No 1562/10 (ECtHR 16 July 2013). See also Gerards 2019 (n 424), pp. 154–155.

467 Beijer 2017 (n 420), p. 65.

468 See, for example, *Osman v. the United Kingdom* App No 23452/94 (ECtHR 28 October 1998), para. 116; *Öneryildiz v. Turkey* App No 48939/99 (ECtHR (GC) 30 November 2004), para. 107; *Opuz v. Turkey* App No 33401/02 (ECtHR 9 June 2009), para. 129; *Verein gegen Tierfabriken Schweiz v. Switzerland no. 2* App No 32772/02 (ECtHR (GC) 30 June 2009), para. 81). See also Beijer 2017 (n 420), p. 68; Stoyanova 2018 (n 426), pp. 373ff.

469 Stoyanova 2018 (n 426), pp. 373–374.

470 *Öneryildiz v. Turkey* App No 48939/99 (ECtHR (GC) 30 November 2004), para. 107. Ultimately, however, the Court found the government's argument to be unconvincing. According to the Court,

3. HORIZONTAL POSITIVE OBLIGATIONS: AN OVERVIEW

The previous section provided a general introduction to the concept of positive obligations in order to provide a better understanding of horizontal positive obligations formulated by the Court and as discussed in the current section. More specifically, this section offers a more systematic overview of horizontal positive obligations by discussing various relations between private actors for which the Court has offered substantive protection of Convention rights through the concept of horizontal positive obligations. To this end, the horizontal positive obligations discussed relate to violence by private individuals (Section 3.1)[471], family relations (Section 3.2), defamatory publications (Section 3.3), one's surroundings (Section 3.4), one's property (Section 3.5), contractual relationships (Section 3.6) and employer-employee relations (Section 3.7).

3.1. PROTECTION AGAINST VIOLENCE BY PRIVATE INDIVIDUALS

The first example of horizontal positive obligations discussed here is the obligation for Convention States to protect individuals against violence by other individuals.[472] To illustrate, the Court held in the case of *Osman* that States have to secure the right to life by 'putting in place effective criminal-law provisions to deter the commission of offences against the person backed up by law-enforcement machinery for the

the timely installation of a gas-extraction system could have been an effective measure without diverting the State's resources to an excessive degree or giving rise to policy problems (see para. 107).

471 As explained in Chapter 1 (Section 3), cases arising from a conflict involving the use of violence by private individuals do not form part of the study of verticalised cases as conducted for the present research. Nevertheless, the category is included here to give a complete overview of the variety of relations between private actors for which the Court has offered substantive protection of Convention rights through the concept of horizontal positive obligations.

472 The Court has formulated this positive obligation under Articles 2 and 3 ECHR (for example, *Centre for Legal Resources on behalf of Valentin Câmpeanu v. Romania* App No 47848/08 (ECtHR (GC) 17 July 2014); *Talpis v. Italy* App No 41237/14 (ECtHR 2 March 2017), sometimes in conjunction with Article 8 ECHR (for example, *X and Y v. the Netherlands* App No 8978/80 (ECtHR 26 March 1985); *Costello-Roberts v. the United Kingdom* App No 13134/87 (ECtHR 25 March 1993); *Sandra Janković v. Croatia* App No 38478/05 (ECtHR 5 March 2009)). The Court has held, for example, that Article 3 requires States to take measures designed to ensure that individuals within their jurisdiction are not subjected to torture or inhuman or degrading treatment or punishment, even administered by private individuals (see, for example, *Talpis v. Italy* App No 41237/14 (ECtHR 2 March 2017), para. 102). For a more extensive discussion of the positive obligation to protect individuals against violence by other individuals, see, for example, L. Lazarus, 'Positive obligations and Criminal Justice: Duties to Protect or Coerce' in J. Roberts and L. Zedner (eds.), *Principled and values in Criminal Law and Criminal Justice: Essays in Honour of Professor Andrew Ashworth*, Oxford University Press 2012, pp. 135–155; L. Lavrysen and N. Mavronicola (eds.), *Coercive Human Rights: Positive Duties to Mobilise the Criminal Law under the ECHR*, Hart Publishing 2020.

prevention, suppression and sanctioning of breaches of such provisions'.[473] In addition, the Court reasoned that, in certain situations, the obligation to protect individuals against violence by other individuals may extend to the obligation to 'take preventive operational measures to protect an individual whose life is at risk from the criminal acts of another individual'.[474] Relying on this case law, the Court formulated positive obligations for domestic violence cases in *Kurt*[475], which concerned a situation where a man had killed his son. In this specific context, the Court held that, securing the right to life requires, first, 'an immediate response to allegations of domestic violence'.[476] Second, national authorities must carry out 'an autonomous, proactive and comprehensive risk assessment' to establish whether there exists a real and immediate risk to the life of one or more identified victims of domestic violence.[477] Finally, if the risk assessment reveals a real and immediate risk to life, States have the obligation to take preventive operational measures. These measures must be 'adequate and proportionate to the level of the risk assessed'.[478]

The States' obligation to protect individuals against violence by other individuals also applies in other situations, such as those in which persons exercising their freedom to manifest their religion are physically, verbally or symbolically attacked by other individuals[479] or when individuals are subjected to homophobic ill-treatment.[480] Similarly, the Court has held in relation to the freedom of assembly that protestors must be able to hold a demonstration without having to fear being subjected to physical violence by their opponents.[481]

3.2. PROTECTION OF CONVENTION RIGHTS IN FAMILY RELATIONS

The example of domestic violence already touched upon the protection of Convention rights in relations between family members. The protection of Convention rights in such relations between individuals extends to the establishment of family ties and legal

473 *Osman v. the United Kingdom* App No 23452/94 (ECtHR (GC) 28 October 1998), para. 115.
474 *Osman v. the United Kingdom* App No 23452/94 (ECtHR (GC) 28 October 1998), para. 115.
475 *Kurt v. Austria* App No 62903/15 (ECtHR (GC) 15 June 2021). In *Kurt* the Court clarified, for the first time, the general principles applicable in domestic violence cases under Article 2 ECHR. Other illustrative cases include *Opuz v. Turkey* App No 33401/02 (ECtHR 9 June 2009); *E and Others v. the United Kingdom* App No 33218/96 (ECtHR 26 November 2002).
476 *Kurt v. Austria* App No 62903/15 (ECtHR (GC) 15 June 2021), para. 190.
477 *Kurt v. Austria* App No 62903/15 (ECtHR (GC) 15 June 2021), para. 190.
478 *Kurt v. Austria* App No 62903/15 (ECtHR (GC) 15 June 2021), para. 190.
479 See, for example, *Karaahmed v. Bulgaria* App No 30587/13 (ECtHR 24 February 2015) and *Members of the Gldani Congregation of Jehovah's Witnesses and Others v. Georgia* App No 71156/01 (ECtHR 3 May 2007).
480 See, for example, *Sabalić v. Croatia* App No 50231/13 (ECtHR 14 January 2021); *Association ACCEPT and Others v. Romania* App No 19237/16 (ECtHR 1 June 2021).
481 *Plattform "Ärzte für das Leben" v. Austria* App No 10126/82 (ECtHR 21 June 1988), para. 32. For a more recent case, see, for example, *Berkman v. Russia* App No 46712/15 (ECtHR 1 December 2020).

relationships and the granting and enforcing of custody and access rights.[482] Regarding the former, the Court has held that respect for private life as enshrined in Article 8 of the Convention requires that everyone should be able to obtain details of their identity, such as information about the identity of their parents or the circumstances in which they were born.[483] In practice, for example, this entails that when a child starts civil judicial proceedings to establish whether someone who denies paternity is his or her biological father, the alleged father may be obliged to provide a genetic sample.[484] In relation to the granting and enforcing of custody and access rights, Article 8 ECHR also requires States to take all necessary steps that could be reasonably demanded in the special circumstances of the case to facilitate reunion between a parent and a child.[485] This obligation may even apply to situations in which difficulties in arranging access for a parent to his or her child are largely due to animosity between the parents.[486]

3.3. POSITIVE OBLIGATIONS IN RELATION TO DEFAMATORY PUBLICATIONS

Horizontal positive obligations have also been imposed in cases involving a conflict between the right to reputation and private life of one individual (Article 8 ECHR) and the right to freedom of expression of another (Article 10).[487] In these cases, the

---

482 For a detailed study see, for example, A. Büchler and H. Keller (eds.) *Family forms and parenthood: theory and practice of Article 8 ECHR in Europe*, Intersentia 2016; N. Ismaïli, *Who cares for the child?: regulating custody and access in family and migration law in the Netherlands, the European Union and the Council of Europe*, VU Amsterdam (diss.) 2018.

483 See, for example, *Odièvre v. France* App No 42326/98 (ECtHR (GC) 13 February 2002), para. 29; *Mikulić v. Croatia* App No 53176/99 (ECtHR 7 February 2002), paras. 54, 65; *Mifsud v. Malta* App No 62257/15 (ECtHR 29 January 2019), para. 56.

484 *Mifsud v. Malta* App No 62257/15 (ECtHR 29 January 2019), paras. 74, 77. It should be noted, however, that it is not compulsory for States to put in place a system that compels an alleged father to undergo a DNA test. In this regard, the Court has held that the protection of third persons may preclude their being compelled to make themselves available for medical testing of any kind, including DNA testing (see, for example, *Mikulić v. Croatia* App No 53176/99 (ECtHR 7 February 2002), para. 64).

485 *Hokkanen v. Finland* App No 19823/92 (ECtHR 23 September 1994), para. 58; *Ignaccolo-Zenide v. Romania* App No 31679/96 (ECtHR 25 January 2000), para. 94; *Pisică v. the Republic of Moldova* App No 23641/17 (ECtHR 29 October 2019), para. 63.

486 See, for example, *Hokkanen v. Finland* App No 19823/92 (ECtHR 23 September 1994) (animosity between parent and grandparents); *Pisică v. the Republic of Moldova* App No 23641/17 (ECtHR 29 October 2019) (animosity between parents).

487 For a thorough analysis of conflicts between human rights, including the right to reputation and private life versus the right to freedom of expression see, for example, S. Smet, *Resolving conflicts between human rights: a legal theoretical analysis in the context of the ECHR*, Ghent University (diss.) 2014; S. Smet, *Resolving conflicts between human rights: the judge's dilemma*, Routledge 2017. For a specific analysis of conflicts between the right to reputation and private life and the right to freedom of expression see, for example, A. Ieven, 'Privacy rights in conflict: in search of the theoretical framework behind the European Court of Human Rights' balancing of private life against other rights' in E. Brems (ed.) *Conflicts between fundamental rights*, Intersentia 2008, pp. 39–67; S. Smet, 'Freedom of expression and the right to reputation: human rights in conflict' (2010) 26 *American University International Law Review* 183.

Court has interpreted the 'obligation to adopt measures designed to secure respect for private life even in the sphere of the relations of individuals between themselves' as one requiring Convention States to strike a fair balance between the right to reputation and private life and the right to freedom of expression. The Court has, moreover, identified and listed criteria that must be taken into account by the domestic courts when they engage in an exercise of balancing the two competing rights and interests of the private actors involved. These criteria are: the contribution to a debate of general interest; how well-known is the person concerned; the content, form and consequences of the publication; the circumstances in which the photos were taken or the information was obtained; and the severity of the sanction imposed.[488]

3.4. PROTECTION OF ONE'S SURROUNDINGS

Horizontal positive obligations have also been imposed in relation to the protection of one's surroundings, i.e. in relation to acts or omissions that have an impact on an individual's home or physical or non-physical surroundings.[489] This includes disturbance caused by airports[490], industrial emissions[491], noise pollution caused by bars or clubs[492], or acts of harassment by third parties causing nuisance such as the dumping of several cartloads of manure or the setting off fireworks.[493] To illustrate, the Court has held that Article 8 may apply when State responsibility arises from the failure to regulate private-sector activities properly.[494] Hence, authorities may have

488 The Court first identified these criteria in *Von Hannover v. Germany (No. 2)* App Nos 40660/08 and 60641/08 (ECtHR (GC) 7 February 2012), paras. 108–113, in which the applicant invoked Article 8 ECHR. On the same day the Court issued the judgment in *Axel Springer AG v. Germany* App No 39954/08 (ECtHR (GC) 7 February 2012), in which the applicant invoked Article 10 ECHR. In this case, the Court formulated the following broadly similar criteria: the contribution to a debate of general interest; how well known is the person concerned and what is the subject of the report; the prior conduct of the person concerned; the method of obtaining the information and its veracity; the content, form and consequences of the publication; and the severity of the sanction imposed (paras 89–95),

489 For a detailed study of cases related to one's surroundings see, for example, D. Sanderink, *Het EVRM en het materiële omgevingsrecht* [The relationship between the ECHR and substantive environmental and planning law], Kluwer 2015.

490 See, for example, *Powell and Rayner v. the United Kingdom* App No 9310/81 (ECtHR 21 February 1990); *Hatton and Others v. the United Kingdom* App No 36022/97 (ECtHR (GC) 8 July 2003).

491 See, for example, *López Ostra v. Spain* App No 16798/90 (ECtHR 9 December 1994); *Guerra and Others v. Italy* App No 14967/89 (ECtHR (GC) 19 February 1998); *Taşkin and Others v. Turkey* App No 46117/99 (ECtHR 10 November 2004); *Giacomelli v. Italy* App No 59909/00 (ECtHR 2 November 2006); *Băcilă v. Romania* App No 19234/04 (ECtHR 30 March 2010).

492 See, for example, *Moreno Gómez v. Spain* App No 4143/02 (ECtHR 16 November 2004); *Oluić v. Croatia* App No 61260/08 (ECtHR 20 May 2010); *Mileva and Others v. Bulgaria* App Nos. 43449/02 and 21475/04 (ECtHR 25 November 2010).

493 See, for example, *Surugiu v. Romania* App No 48995/99 (ECtHR 20 April 2004); *Zammit Maempel v. Malta* App No 24202/10 (ECtHR 22 November 2011).

494 See, for example, *Hatton and Others v. the United Kingdom* App No 36022/97 (ECtHR (GC) 8 July 2003), para. 98; *Fadeyeva v. Russia* App No 55723/00 (ECtHR 9 June 2005), para. 89.

to take reasonable and adequate action, even where they are not directly responsible for, for example, the pollution caused by a factory.[495] This may include introducing a regulatory system that governs the licensing, setting-up, operating, security and supervision of the activity, and the obligation to make it compulsory for all those concerned to take practical measures to ensure the effective protection of citizens whose lives may be endangered by inherent risks.[496] To illustrate, in the case of *Băcilă*[497], the Court found a violation of Article 8 ECHR since the domestic authorities had omitted to oblige a factory to reduce its emissions, while these emissions had a severe impact on the health of citizens living close to the factory. In relation to industrial, pollutant or dangerous activities the Court has also formulated procedural positive obligations relating to the decision-making process. In *Tătar*, for example, it held that the decision-making process had to involve appropriate investigations and studies to assess the environmentally damaging effects of the impugned activities.[498] In addition, the Court stressed the importance of public access to these studies[499] and the public's involvement in the decision-making process.[500]

3.5. PROTECTION OF ONE'S PROPERTY

Closely related to the protection of one's surrounding is the protection of one's property. In relation to the right to property, as protected by Article 1 of Protocol 1 to the Convention, the Court has held that:

> when an interference with the peaceful enjoyment of "possessions" is perpetrated by a private individual, a positive obligation arises for States to ensure in its domestic legal system that property rights are sufficiently protected by law and that adequate remedies are provided whereby the victim can vindicate his rights, including, where appropriate, by claiming damages in respect of any loss sustained.[501]

This obligation means, for example, that States are required to 'afford judicial procedures that offer the necessary procedural guarantees and therefore enable the domestic courts and tribunals to adjudicate effectively and fairly any disputes between private persons'.[502]

---

495 This was for example the case in *Băcilă v. Romania* App No 19234/04 (ECtHR 30 March 2010).

496 See, for example, *Tătar v. Romania* App No 67021/01 (ECtHR 27 January 2009), para. 88; *Cordella and Others v. Italy* App Nos 54414/13 and 54264/14 (ECtHR 24 January 2019), para. 159.

497 *Băcilă v. Romania* App No 19234/04 (ECtHR 30 March 2010).

498 *Tătar v. Romania* App No 67021/01 (ECtHR 27 January 2009), para. 88.

499 See, for example, *Giacomelli v. Italy* App No 59909/00 (ECtHR 2 November 2006), para. 83.

500 See, for example, *Tătar v. Romania* App No 67021/01 (ECtHR 27 January 2009), paras. 113–118.

501 See, for example, *Blumberg v Latvia* App No 70930/01 (ECtHR 14 October 2008), para. 67; *Kotov v Russia* App No 54522/00 (ECtHR (GC) 3 April 2012), para. 113.

502 See, for example, *Sovtransavto Holding v. Ukraine* App No 48553/99 (ECtHR 25 July 2002), para. 96; *Anheuser-Busch Inc. v. Portugal* App No 73049/01 (ECtHR (GC) 11 January 2007), para. 83.

3.6. PROTECTION OF CONVENTION RIGHTS IN CONTRACTUAL RELATIONSHIPS

Contractual relationships are yet another example of relations between private actors for which the Court has formulated horizontal positive obligations for Convention States. In general, the Court can be said to require domestic courts to interpret private law contracts in line with the Convention. In the case, for example, of *Van Kück*[503], which concerned a conflict between a transsexual and a private health insurance company over the interpretation of a health insurance agreement, the Court examined whether the domestic courts' interpretation of the provision in the insurance contract was in line with Article 8 ECHR. Similarly, in *Pla and Puncernau*[504], concerning a dispute over a will, the Court examined whether the domestic courts' interpretation of a testamentary provision interfered with a Convention right. Another example is provided by the case of *Khurshid Mustafa and Tarzibachi*[505], which concerned a dispute between tenants and their landlord over the landlord's termination of a tenancy agreement. The landlord had terminated the tenancy agreement and successfully initiated judicial proceedings to execute the termination because, in violation of a provision in the tenancy agreement, the tenants had mounted a satellite dish in order to receive television programmes in Arabic and Farsi. The Court concluded that the interpretation of the tenancy agreement by the Swedish courts was incompatible with the Convention as they had not attached sufficient weight to the applicants' interest in receiving television broadcasts in Arabic and Farsi.[506]

3.7. PROTECTION OF CONVENTION RIGHTS IN EMPLOYER-EMPLOYEE RELATIONS

Finally, horizontal positive obligations have been formulated in cases involving employer-employee relations, which are a specific type of contractual relationship.[507] The Court's case law shows that various Convention rights may be at stake in this type of relations between private actors. The Court has imposed horizontal positive obligations in relation to slavery, servitude and forced labour (Article 4)[508], surveillance in the workplace (Article 8)[509], and dismissal on grounds of religion or political opinion

503 *Van Kück v. Germany* App No 35968/97 (ECtHR 12 June 2003).

504 *Pla and Puncernau v. Andorra* App No 69498/01 (ECtHR 13 July 2004).

505 *Khurshid Mustafa and Tarzibachi v. Sweden* App No 23883/06 (ECtHR 16 December 2008).

506 *Khurshid Mustafa and Tarzibachi v. Sweden* App No 23883/06 (ECtHR 16 December 2008), paras. 36–50.

507 For an extensive analysis see, for example, F. Dorssemont, K. Lörcher, I. Schömann (eds.), *The European Convention on Human Rights and the Employment Relation*, Hart Publishing 2013; P.M. Collins, *Putting human rights to work. Labour law, the ECHR, and the employment relation*, Oxford University Press 2021.

508 See, for example, *Siladin v. France* App No 73316/01 (ECtHR 26 July 2005); *Rantsev v. Cyprus and Russia* App No 25965/04 (ECtHR 7 January 2010); *C.N. v. the United Kingdom* App No 4239/08 (ECtHR 13 November 2012); *S.M. v. Croatia* App No 60561/14 (ECtHR (GC) 25 June 2020).

509 See, for example, *Bărbulescu v. Romania* App No 61496/08 (ECtHR (GC) 5 September 2017); *López Ribalda and Others v. Spain* App Nos. 1874/13 and 8567/13 (ECtHR (GC) 17 October 2019).

or affiliation (Articles 9–11).[510] States have an obligation, for example, to ensure that employers respect their employees' freedom of religion. More specifically, if an employer interferes with the right to freedom of religion of its employees, domestic courts have to examine whether a fair balance was struck between the employee's right to freedom of religion and the rights and interests of the employer.[511] Regarding surveillance in the workplace, the Court has held that States have a positive obligation to ensure that an employer's monitoring of employees' correspondence and other communication is adequately and sufficiently safeguarded against abuse.[512] Furthermore, employees must have access to a judicial remedy to determine whether the relevant requirements for monitoring measures in the workplace are met.[513] Finally, in order to ensure the proportionality of surveillance measures in the workplace, domestic courts should take account of the following factors when examining the proportionality of a measure and assessing the various competing interests: (i) whether the employee has been notified clearly and in advance of the possibility that the employer might monitor correspondence and other communications, and of the implementation of such measures; (ii) the extent of the monitoring by the employer and the degree of intrusion into the employee's privacy (traffic and content); (iii) whether the employer has provided legitimate reasons to justify monitoring the communications and accessing their actual content; (iv) whether there is a possibility of establishing a monitoring system based on less intrusive methods and measures; (v) the seriousness of the consequences of the monitoring for the employee subjected to it, as well as the use made of the results of monitoring; and (vi) whether the employee has been provided with adequate safeguards including, in particular, prior notification of the possibility of accessing the content of communication.[514]

4. CONCLUSION

The case law examples discussed in Section 3 illustrate that, over the years, the Court has imposed horizontal positive obligations in all sorts of relations between private actors, including relations between family members and employer-employee relations, and

[510] See, for example, *Redfearn v. the United Kingdom* App No 47335/06 (ECtHR 6 November 2012) (dismissal on grounds of political affiliation); *Eweida and Others v. the United Kingdom* App No 48420/10 (ECtHR 15 January 2013) (dismissal on grounds of religion).

[511] *Eweida and Others v. the United Kingdom* App No 48420/10 (ECtHR 15 January 2013), paras. 84 and 91. See also *Schüth v. Germany* App No 1620/03 (ECtHR 23 September 2010).

[512] *Bărbulescu v. Romania* App No 61496/08 (ECtHR (GC) 5 September 2017), paras. 119–120.

[513] *Bărbulescu v. Romania* App No 61496/08 (ECtHR (GC) 5 September 2017), paras. 121–122; *López Ribalda and Others v. Spain* App Nos. 1874/13 and 8567/13 (ECtHR (GC) 17 October 2019), para. 115.

[514] The Court first formulated these criteria in *Bărbulescu v. Romania* App No 61496/08 (ECtHR (GC) 5 September 2017) (para. 121) in relation to the monitoring of employees' correspondence and communications. In *López Ribalda and Others v. Spain* App Nos. 1874/13 and 8567/13 (ECtHR (GC) 17 October 2019) the Court held that these criteria also apply to situations in which an employer implements video-surveillance measures in the workplace (para. 116).

cases where the behaviour of one private actor impacts on the rights or surroundings of another, as in cases concerning defamatory publications or noise pollution. In other words, it has offered substantive protection of Convention rights in relation to a broad variety of relations between private actors and Convention rights. In addition, the examples show that the Court has formulated various means by which this protection can be effectuated by the Convention States: criminal law or other types of legislation, effective law enforcement, operational measures, and effective legal remedies.[515]

The horizontal positive obligations discussed in this chapter have in common that they are often imposed in cases originating from a conflict between two private actors at the domestic level. As such, they provide a range of examples of verticalised cases that have come before the ECtHR. The next chapter examines these verticalised cases in more detail by focusing on four of the seven categories discussed above: cases related to one's surroundings, cases involving a conflict between the right to reputation and private life and the right to freedom of expression, family life cases, and employer-employee cases.

515 Gerards 2019 (n 424), pp. 147ff.

CHAPTER 6

DETAILED ANALYSIS OF VERTICALISED CASES BEFORE THE ECtHR

1. INTRODUCTION

The previous chapter showed that the Court can offer substantive protection of Convention rights in relations between private actors through the concept of horizontal positive obligations. To reiterate, this is explained by the fact that Article 34 of the Convention requires complaints to be directed against a Convention State in order to be admissible *ratione personae*. It is thus inherent in the Convention system that proceedings before the Court are of a vertical nature; that is, they involve a private actor (an individual, a group of individuals, or a company) who has lodged an application against a Convention State. Yet, this does not mean that these vertical proceedings cannot originate from a conflict between two private actors at the domestic level. A complaint stemming from a horizontal conflict at the domestic level can be successfully brought before the ECtHR, where it is transformed into a vertical – and thus 'verticalised' – case.

As discussed in the previous chapter, many cases coming before the ECtHR are, in fact, verticalised cases. They can originate from a wide range of horizontal conflicts and so can involve many different issues and Convention rights, including, for example, defamation cases, but also cases between an employer and an employee about wearing religious symbols at work.

The very fact that so many cases before the ECtHR are verticalised and originate from such manifold horizontal relationships implies that they have different characteristics and that the Court may need to take account of their variety by dealing with them differently. For example, the private actors involved may be different, just like the manner in which their relationship is regulated in domestic law, the types of procedures available for redress at the national level, and so on. To provide an insight into and a better understanding of the various characteristics of verticalised cases and the approach the Court takes in dealing with them, this chapter offers an in-depth analysis of the Court's reasoning in ruling on such verticalised cases.[516] First, the

516 Parts of this section have also been published in C.M.S. Loven, '"Verticalised" cases before the European Court of Human Rights unravelled: an analysis of their characteristics and the Court's approach to them' (2020) 38 *Netherlands Quarterly of Human Rights* 246.

origins of verticalised cases are described by discussing differences in the nature of, and the parties involved in, the conflict at the domestic level (Section 2) so as to provide insight into the characteristics of the conflict giving rise to the case before the Court. Second, the Court's approach to verticalised cases is explored (Section 3), with specific attention being paid to the Court's type of review (procedural, substantive, or a combination of the two), the rights and interests that are taken into account by the Court when examining a verticalised case, and the question of whether the private party involved in the conflict at the domestic level, not being the applicant, is involved in the Court's proceedings by way of a third-party intervention.

The discussion of these topics here is based on an in-depth, qualitative case law analysis of four types of verticalised cases: cases related to one's surroundings, cases involving a conflict between the right to reputation and private life and the right to freedom of expression, family life cases, and employer-employee cases.[517] These four types of verticalised cases form relatively homogenous groups and represent a good variety of the horizontal conflicts from which verticalised cases can originate, as listed in Chapter 5. They also relate to four areas forming an important part of the Court's standard case law. At the same time, it should be recalled that the previous chapter showed that other cases, too, can originate from a conflict between private actors at the domestic level. The present discussion, therefore, does not offer a full and exhaustive account of how the ECtHR deals with verticalised cases, but instead aims to present the four categories as illustrative case studies to help to unravel the notion of verticalised cases and the Court's approach to them.

2. ORIGINS OF VERTICALISED CASES: UNDERLYING CONFLICTS AND INVOLVED PARTIES

As stated earlied, verticalised cases before the ECtHR originate from a horizontal conflict at the domestic level. An examination of the characteristics of and the private actors involved in the conflict at the domestic level is therefore an important first step towards understanding the nature of verticalised cases and the particular problems and issues related to the Court's dealing with such cases. This will provide insight into the horizontal conflict from which verticalised cases before the ECtHR originate, by, for example, shedding light on the private actor not involved in the proceedings before the ECtHR. This is important for understanding procedural issues that may arise in verticalised cases. This section consequently discusses these characteristics for each of the four types of verticalised cases selected for this study.

[517] For a detailed discussion of the methodology, including the selection of cases, see Chapter 1 (Section 4). A complete overview of the case law sample can be found in Appendix I.

2.1. CASES RELATED TO ONE'S SURROUNDINGS

At first glance, cases relating to the impact of private individuals' behaviour on one's surroundings would seem to be clear examples of cases originating from a horizontal conflict at the domestic level. To illustrate, the case of *Hatton and Others*[518] related to noise disturbance caused by private flight operators at Heathrow Airport. In *Moreno Gómez*[519], another case about noise disturbance, the nuisance complained of was caused by privately owned bars and discotheques. However, a closer examination of the domestic proceedings shows that these cases are not always such clear examples of cases originating from a horizontal conflict, given that the contested activity is caused by two connected sets of activities: that is, activities (or omissions) of a private actor and activities (or omissions) of the State. In cases, for example, of noise disturbance caused by airplane operators or a privately owned bar, health problems caused by industrial emissions, or damage caused to one's property by third parties, the two connected sets of activities are the actual activities of the private actor involved, on the one hand, and the granting of a permit for operating a dangerous installation, the lack of monitoring of the noise or emission levels, or the lack of enforcement by domestic authorities, on the other hand. Thus, both the State and a private actor may be responsible for the alleged harm to an individual's rights. The Court recognised this expressly in *Hatton and Others,* holding that:

> [i]t is clear that in the present case the noise disturbances complained of were not caused by the State or by State organs, but that they emanated from the activities of private operators. It may be argued that the changes brought about by the 1993 Scheme are to be seen as a direct interference by the State with the Article 8 rights of the persons concerned. On the other hand, the State's responsibility in environmental cases may also arise from a failure to regulate private industry in a manner securing proper respect for the rights enshrined in Article 8 of the Convention.[520]

Another example of such combined or shared responsibility is provided by the case of *Zammit Maempel*[521], which concerned annual firework displays in a village that took place close to the applicants' residence. The applicants alleged that the fireworks exposed them to grave risk and peril to their life, physical health and personal security, and also alleged that the fireworks caused damage to their residence. The Court reasoned that:

> the Government considered the case as one regarding positive obligations, in that the letting off fireworks was carried out by third parties, but it was the State which issued the relevant conditions, regulations and permits. Such measures regulated interference by third parties

518 *Hatton and Others v. the United Kingdom* App No 36022/97 (ECtHR (GC) 8 July 2003).
519 *Moreno Gómez v. Spain* App No 4143/02 (ECtHR 16 November 2004).
520 *Hatton and Others v. the United Kingdom* App No 36022/97 (ECtHR (GC) 8 July 2003), para. 119.
521 *Zammit Maempel v. Malta* App No 24202/10 (ECtHR 22 November 2011).

> with a person's private rights, and required a balance to be reached between the religious and social expression of village communities and the interests of the applicants.[522]

Owing to this combined or shared responsibility of both the State and a private actor, the case at the domestic level may be of a vertical as much as of a horizontal nature. To illustrate, in *Olujić*[523], a case about excessive noise coming from a bar, the Court noted that:

> the applicant ... had a choice between, on the one hand, a civil action against the owner of the F. bar whereby she could have sought the removal of the source of the excessive noise, cease of all further exposure to excessive noise as well as damages in relation to the exposure of her flat to excessive noise and, on the other hand, the administrative remedies before the relevant administrative bodies.[524]

In such cases, therefore, the question of whether the case before the ECtHR originates from a civil procedure (i.e., a horizontal case) or administrative proceedings (i.e., a vertical case) at the domestic level may depend on the choice of the applicant. Regardless, however, of the nature of the domestic proceedings, the shared responsibility construction clearly shows that, at least at some point, two private actors – such as an individual and a company or factory owner – were involved in the conflict at the domestic level, with one of these parties no longer being involved in the proceedings when the case comes before the ECtHR.

2.2. RIGHT TO REPUTATION AND PRIVATE LIFE VERSUS FREEDOM OF EXPRESSION CASES

In contrast to cases related to one's surroundings, cases involving a conflict between the right to reputation and private life of one individual and the right to freedom of expression of another individual clearly originate from a horizontal conflict; that is, a conflict between private actors at the domestic level. This can be illustrated by recalling the example given in the introduction to Part II. This example, based on the *Von Hannover (No. 2)* case[525], described how an individual brought domestic court proceedings to prevent the publisher of a newspaper or magazine from publishing (or continuing to publish) photos of the individual's private life. In the *Von Hannover* case, this individual was Princess Caroline von Hannover and her husband, who had tried to prevent publication of photos about their private life in the tabloid press. These legal actions had no effect, however, as the domestic courts had not granted an injunction against any further publication of the photos. For this reason, the princess and her

522 *Zammit Maempel v. Malta* App No 24202/10 (ECtHR 22 November 2011), para. 51.
523 *Olujić v. Croatia* App No 61260/08 (ECtHR 20 May 2010).
524 *Olujić v. Croatia* App No 61260/08 (ECtHR 20 May 2010), para. 36.
525 *Von Hannover v. Germany (No. 2)* App Nos 40660/08 and 60641/08 (ECtHR (GC) 7 February 2012).

husband sought redress at the ECtHR. As the ECtHR could not deal directly with the publisher's behaviour, the applicants complained before the ECtHR about the lack of adequate State protection of their right to respect for private life (Article 8 ECHR). As a result, therefore, of the vertical nature of the Court's proceedings, the publishing company directly responsible for the alleged infringement was not formally involved as a party in the ECtHR proceedings following the conflict at the domestic level.[526]

Conversely, had the injunction been granted, the journalist or media company responsible for publication could have invoked the right to freedom of expression (Article 10) before the ECtHR. That would have meant that the alleged victim of the publication would not have had any formal position in the proceedings before the Court. To illustrate this in terms of the Court's case law, in *Axel Springer AG*[527], a well-known actor had initiated proceedings against Axel Springer AG at the domestic level. Axel Springer AG is a publishing company that owns, inter alia, the German newspaper *Bild*. This newspaper had published a front-page article about the actor's arrest for the possession of cocaine, supplemented by a more detailed article on another page. This was followed by a second article on the actor's conviction for unlawful possession of drugs. In the proceedings initiated by the actor, the German courts had imposed an injunction against reporting on the arrest and conviction of the actor for a drug-related offence and ordered the publishing company to pay a penalty. The publishing company then brought a case before the ECtHR, stating that the injunction had infringed its right to freedom of expression. As a result of the verticalisation of the case when it came before the ECtHR, formally, the actor who had alleged an infringement of his right to reputation and private life and who had initiated the proceedings at the domestic level in the first place could no longer play a role.

These examples show that two scenarios are possible in cases involving a conflict between the right to reputation and private life of one individual and the right to freedom of expression of another individual, depending on the outcome of the domestic proceedings. If, on the one hand, the domestic courts decide not to grant an injunction or not to offer redress in any other way, an individual who has experienced harm to his private life from a publication can invoke his right to reputation and private life before the ECtHR; in that situation, the private party directly responsible for the interference (and who could claim the right to freedom of expression) is not formally involved in the proceedings. If, on the other hand, the domestic courts decide to grant an injunction or impose a fine, the journalist or media company responsible for the publication can invoke their right to freedom of expression before the ECtHR; in that case, the person who allegedly suffered a breach of his or her right to reputation and private life cannot formally claim these rights in the proceedings before the Court.

526 A publishing company responsible for publishing one of the photos in question was, however, granted leave to intervene as a third party in the proceedings before the Court. This is discussed in more detail in Section 3.2 below and the subsequent chapters.

527 *Axel Springer AG v. Germany* App No 39954/08 (ECtHR (GC) 7 February 2012).

2.3. FAMILY LIFE CASES

Applications concerning relations between family members are another example of cases originating from clear horizontal conflicts at the domestic level.[528] In such applications, a distinction can be made between cases involving custody and access to a child, and cases involving access to information about one's origins.[529] Custody and access to a child cases arise primarily from a conflict between separated or divorced parents. At the domestic level, a mother or father (or presumed mother or father) can initiate proceedings in order to receive custody or access rights or to seek the enforcement of these rights. Depending on the outcome of the domestic case, the mother, father or child can subsequently seek redress by lodging an application with the ECtHR, claiming that the decision or approach of the domestic authorities violated his or her right to private and family life (Article 8 ECHR). In, for example, *Ignaccolo-Zenide*[530], after several civil custody and access proceedings at the domestic level, a mother of two children complained about the inadequacy of the measures taken by the domestic authorities to enforce court decisions ordering the return of her children. The other parent involved in the custody and access proceedings in such cases at the domestic level does not then play a role in the ECtHR proceedings.

Most cases concerning access to information about one's origins involve applicants claiming a right to information about their descent or the circumstances surrounding their birth and early life.[531] This claim can interfere with the rights of another private actor in three ways.[532] First, access to such information may constitute interference with the private lives of those who have provided the information subject to confidentiality.[533] Second, it may constitute an interference with the private life of a mother who gave birth anonymously.[534] Third, it may constitute interference with the right to bodily integrity of a presumed father who is unwilling to undergo a paternity test.[535] Of these three types of interferences, the third type of interference is most likely to result in a verticalised case before the ECtHR. This is because if, for example, a mother gave birth anonymously, the individual seeking information about his or her

528 Family life cases can also, however, result from a clearly vertical conflict at the domestic level; if, for example, the State interferes with the right to family life by taking a child into public care (see for example *K. and T. v. Finland* App No 25702/94 (ECtHR (GC) 12 July 2001).

529 Cases involving relations between family members may also concern domestic violence. However, as explained in Chapter 1 (Section 3), such cases are not discussed here since they involve the use of violence by private individuals and therefore fall outside the scope of this research.

530 *Ignaccolo-Zenide v. Romania* App No 31679/96 (ECtHR 25 January 2000).

531 On this type of conflict, see also, for example, S. Besson, 'Enforcing the child's right to know her origins: contrasting approaches under the Convention on the Rights of the Child and the European Convention on Human Rights' (2007) 21 *International Journal of Law, Policy and the Family* 137.

532 These three situations are distinguished by Ieven (A. Ieven, 'Privacy rights in conflict: in search of the theoretical framework behind the European Court of Human Rights' balancing of private life against other rights' in E. Brems (ed.) *Conflicts between fundamental rights*, Intersentia 2008, pp. 39–67, p. 44).

533 See, for example, *Gaskin v. the United Kingdom* App No 10454/83 (ECtHR 7 July 1989).

534 See, for example, *Odièvre v. France* App No 42326/98 (ECtHR (GC) 13 February 2002).

535 See, for example, *Mikulić v. Croatia* App No 53176/99 (ECtHR 7 February 2002).

descent cannot initiate civil proceedings against the mother, but instead has to initiate proceedings against the institution (often a public institution) where the baby was given up for adoption.[536] In that situation, verticalisation is not necessary for the case to be admissible, as the case is already vertical at the national level. By contrast, a case about an interference with the right to bodily integrity of a presumed father clearly arises from a horizontal conflict, governed by private law, at the domestic level. In, for example, *Mikulić*[537], a child born out of wedlock had started civil judicial proceedings to establish whether a man, who denied paternity, was her biological father. The child lost the case and then turned to the ECtHR, claiming that the domestic courts had been inefficient in deciding her paternity claim and had therefore left her uncertain as to her identity. In this verticalised case before the ECtHR, the man alleged to be her biological father was no longer involved as a party. Somewhat similarly, the case of *Mifsud*[538] is an example where it was the child who was not involved in the Court's proceedings. At the domestic level, X. had initiated civil proceedings requesting the court to declare the applicant to be her biological father and to order this to be reflected on her birth certificate. The domestic courts had then ordered the applicant, as the presumed biological father, to provide a genetic sample. Subsequently, the presumed father brought a complaint before the ECtHR, claiming that the imposition of a mandatory order to provide a genetic sample violated his right to private and family life. In the procedure before the Court, the child no longer played a role.

It follows from these two examples that in cases where the child brings the complaint before the ECtHR the presumed father or mother is not involved in the Court's proceedings, whereas in cases where the complaint is brought before the ECtHR by the presumed father or mother, the child is not involved. The examples also illustrate that, unlike in cases concerning a conflict between the right to reputation and private life and the right to freedom of expression (where two different Convention provisions, Articles 8 and 10, conflict), the rights of two different private parties that are in conflict derive from the very same Convention provision (Article 8).

2.4. EMPLOYER-EMPLOYEE CASES

Cases concerning employer-employee relations are a final example of purely horizontal conflicts that have to be verticalised in order to be decided by the Court. Such cases generally originate from civil cases at the domestic level in which employees challenge their dismissal or other sanctions taken by their employer. In, for example, *Eweida and Others*[539], Ms Eweida started civil proceedings after her employer – a private company, British Airways – had sanctioned her for wearing a cross visibly around her neck.

536 This was the situation in the case of *Odièvre v. France* App No 42326/98 (ECtHR (GC) 13 February 2002).

537 *Mikulić v. Croatia* App No 53176/99 (ECtHR 7 February 2002).

538 *Mifsud v. Malta* App No 62257/15 (ECtHR 29 January 2019).

539 *Eweida and Others v. the United Kingdom* App No 48420/10 (ECtHR 15 January 2013).

After the UK employment tribunals dismissed her claim that British Airways' uniform code constituted indirect discrimination based on religion, Ms Eweida complained before the ECtHR that these judgments constituted a violation of her right to freedom of religion (Article 9) taken in conjunction with the right to non-discrimination (Article 14). Similarly, in *Schüth*[540], a church employee had brought a case before the German employment tribunals when his contract was terminated after his divorce and second marriage. When the employment tribunals refused to annul his dismissal by the Catholic Church, Mr Schüth alleged before the ECtHR that this decision had breached his right to private and family life (Article 8). Finally, in *Bărbulescu*[541], an employee had challenged his dismissal before the domestic courts on the grounds that this decision was based on the monitoring of his correspondence by his employer. After the dismissal had been upheld by the domestic courts, the employee complained before the ECtHR that the domestic courts had failed in their obligation to ensure effective protection of his right to private life. In all three cases, therefore, it was the employee who brought a complaint before the ECtHR, based on different provisions of the Convention. Consequently, it was the employer who could not be a party to the ECtHR proceedings.

2.5. CONCLUSION

The examples discussed above show that verticalised cases before the ECtHR can originate from different types of horizontal conflicts at the domestic level, and that different types of private actors may consequently be involved. Indeed, some of the cases discussed involved two individuals – for example two parents, or a parent (or alleged parent) and a child (or adult child), while others concerned relations between individuals and companies, such as an individual and a publishing house, or an employee and a company. In yet other cases, the actual involvement of the State authorities was so strong that, even at the domestic level, there is a shared or combined responsibility and the conflict can be qualified as a vertical conflict as much as a horizontal one. Finally, the examples demonstrate that the verticalised cases before the ECtHR can relate to different Convention rights, and involve a conflict between the same Convention provision equally much as a conflict between two different Convention provisions.

3. THE COURT'S EXAMINATION OF VERTICALISED CASES

The previous sections have shown that rather than just one type of verticalised cases, the notion can refer to several different types of cases. While these cases are rooted in different types of horizontal conflicts at the domestic level and relate to different

540 *Schüth v. Germany* App No 1620/03 (ECtHR 23 September 2010).

541 *Bărbulescu v. Romania* App No 61496/08 (ECtHR (GC) 5 September 2017).

relations between private actors, and to different Convention rights, they all have in common that one of the private actors involved in the horizontal conflict at the domestic level is not part of the ECtHR proceedings.

The differences between verticalised cases, and the feature they have in common, prompt the question of how these cases are approached by the Court; more specifically, whether and how the differences discussed in Section 2 are reflected in the Court's approach and how the Court deals with the rights and interests of the party not involved in the ECtHR proceedings. The current subsection seeks to answer these questions by analysing the Court's approach in the four categories of cases discussed above. Particular attention is paid to the Court's type of review (procedural, substantive, or a combination of the two), the rights and interests that are taken into account by the Court when examining a verticalised case, and whether the private party involved in the conflict at the domestic level, not being the applicant, is involved in the Court's proceedings by way of third-party intervention.[542]

3.1. CASES RELATED TO ONE'S SURROUNDINGS

Section 2.1 explained that, in cases relating to one's surroundings, it is relatively easy to distinguish a harmful activity or omission by the State. In other words, although a private actor might be directly responsible for the alleged harmful activity, this activity often depends on, or is legitimised by, domestic regulations or concrete decisions by national authorities. This shared or combined responsibility may explain why, in cases related to one's surroundings, the Court usually examines whether a fair balance was struck between the competing interests of the individual and those of the community as a whole, taking account of the margin of appreciation that has to be granted to the States.[543] In, for example, *Hatton and Others*, the Court examined whether a fair balance was struck between the competing interests of, on the one hand, the individuals

---

542 The possibility for third-party intervention is provided by Article 36 ECHR. For a detailed discussion of the rules regarding third-party intervention, see Chapter 9.

543 See, for example, *Powell and Rayner v. the United Kingdom* App No 9310/81 (ECtHR 21 February 1990), para. 41; *López Ostra v. Spain* App No 16798/90 (ECtHR 9 December 1994), para. 51; *Hatton and Others v. the United Kingdom* App No 36022/97 (ECtHR (GC) 8 July 2003), para. 98; *Moreno Gómez v. Spain* App No 4143/02 (ECtHR 16 November 2004), para. 55; *Giacomelli v. Italy* App No 59909/00 (ECtHR 2 November 2006), para. 78; *Tătar v. Romania* App No 67021/01 (ECtHR 27 January 2009), para. 87; *Băcilă v. Romania* App No 19234/04 (ECtHR 30 March 2010), para. 60; *Oluić v. Croatia* App No 61260/08 (ECtHR 20 May 2010), para. 46; *Zammit Maempel v. Malta* App No 24202/10 (ECtHR 22 November 2011), para. 61. A similar approach can be seen in verticalised cases relating to property issues (Article 1 Protocol No. 1) that are examined by the Court under the third rule of Article 1 Protocol No. 1, that is, control of the use of property. In such cases the Court examines whether a fair balance was struck between the demands of the general interest and the requirements of the protection of the individual's fundamental rights (see, for example, *Immobiliare Saffi v. Italy* App No 22774/93 (ECtHR (GC) 28 July 1999); *Schirmer v. Poland* App No 68880/01 (ECtHR 21 September 2004); *J.A. PYE (Oxford) LTD and J.A. PYE (Oxford) Land LTD v. the United Kingdom* App No 44302/02 (ECtHR (GC) 30 August 2007).

affected by the noise of airplanes taking off and landing during the night and, on the other hand, the community as a whole, in particular the economic interests of the country.[544] In *Moreno Gómez,* meanwhile, the Court examined whether the domestic authorities had struck a fair balance between the need to protect the applicant's Convention rights and the need to serve the general interest.[545] In both cases it was not the State, but private actors who were the direct source of the noise disturbances complained of. However, the activities and interests of these private actors did not, as such, play a role in the Court's reasoning and judgment.[546]

In two of the seventeen cases related to one's surroundings examined for this study, the private party involved in the conflict at the domestic level was granted leave to intervene as a third party in the Court's proceedings. A closer look at the nature of these submissions and how the Court dealt with them further illustrates that the activities and interests of the private actor directly responsible for the alleged harmful activity did not, as such, play a role in the Court's reasoning and judgment. In *Hatton and Others,* one of the companies (British Airways) responsible for operating and controlling the aircraft causing the noise disturbance was involved in the Court's proceedings as a third party. Supported by the British Air Transport Association (BATA) and the International Air Transport Association (IATA), the company submitted that 'night flights at Heathrow play a vital role in the United Kingdom's transport infrastructure, and contribute significantly to the productivity of the United Kingdom economy and the living standards of United Kingdom citizens'.[547] Hence, the airline argued that 'the loss of night flights would cause significant damage to the United Kingdom economy'.[548] This shows that British Airways primarily referred to general interests rather than to its own private interests. This is further illustrated by the fact that British Airways' third-party submission was rather similar to the submissions made by the government. The government, too, referred to the economic interests of airline operators and other enterprises and their clients and the economic interests of the country as a whole.[549] When examining the case, the Court focused on the substantive merits of the government's decision; that is, whether the government had struck a fair balance, and also scrutinised the fairness of the decision-making process.[550] Regarding the former, the Court paid considerable attention to the economic interests involved, in

544 *Hatton and Others v. the United Kingdom* App No 36022/97 (ECtHR (GC) 8 July 2003), para. 119.

545 *Moreno Gómez v. Spain* App No 4143/02 (ECtHR 16 November 2004), para. 55.

546 See also the judgments cited in n 543.

547 *Hatton and Others v. the United Kingdom* App No 36022/97 (ECtHR (GC) 8 July 2003), para. 115.

548 *Hatton and Others v. the United Kingdom* App No 36022/97 (ECtHR (GC) 8 July 2003), para. 115.

549 *Hatton and Others v. the United Kingdom* App No 36022/97 (ECtHR (GC) 8 July 2003), paras. 106–110.

550 *Hatton and Others v. the United Kingdom* App No 36022/97 (ECtHR (GC) 8 July 2003), para. 99. Since *Hatton and Others* the Court has used this formula ('there are two aspects to the inquiry which may be carried out by the Court. First, the Court may assess the substantive merits of the government's decision, to ensure that it is compatible with Article 8. Secondly, it may scrutinise the decision-making process to ensure that due weight has been accorded to the interests of the individual') in cases concerning environmental issues (see, for example, *Giacomelli v. Italy* App No 59909/00 (ECtHR 2 November 2006), para. 79; *Taşkin and Others v. Turkey* App No 46117/99 (ECtHR 10 November 2004), para. 115; *Fadeyeva v. Russia* App No 55723/00 (ECtHR 9 June 2005), paras. 104–105).

particular the economic interests of the country as a whole, as British Airways and the government had emphasised in their submissions. The Court, for example, held that:

> one can readily accept that there is an economic interest in maintaining a full service to London from distant airports, and it is difficult, if not impossible, to draw a clear line between the interests of the aviation industry and the economic interests of the country as a whole.[551]

This suggests that it was easier for British Airways to have its interests acknowledged and considered by the Court because it had translated them, in its third-party intervention, into a more general interest.

The other case in which the private party in the domestic conflict intervened as a third party in the ECtHR case is that of *Taşkin and Others*.[552] The applicants in this case alleged that the domestic authorities' decision to issue a permit to use a cyanidation operating process in a gold mine and the related decision-making process had given rise to a violation of their rights guaranteed by Article 8 ECHR. The receiver of the permit, the Normandy Madencilik A.S. Company, was granted leave to intervene in the Court's proceedings. As a third-party intervener, the company stressed that it had received the necessary permits for operating the gold mine in question and referred to several reports that concluded that the risks involved were negligible.[553] Hence, and in contrast to the submissions by British Airways in *Hatton and Others*, the company focused on its own private interests. Although the responsible private party thus intervened in the Court's proceedings, the Court's reasoning suggests that its activities and interests did not, as such, appear to have played any role in the Court's eventual judgment. The main issue discussed by the Court was not the lawfulness of the activities as such, but the question of whether the State authorities' defiance of final judicial decisions infringed the applicants' rights. More specifically, as in *Hatton and Others*, the Court held that its assessment concerned the substantive merits of the national authorities' decision as well as the fairness of the decision-making process. In its reasoning, it also focused strongly on whether the decision-making process complied with the procedural guarantees of Article 8.[554]

It was mentioned above that the Court's approach in cases related to one's surroundings may be explained by the shared or combined responsibility in these cases. The Court's apparent lack of attention for the acts and interests of one of the private actors in the underlying domestic conflict may also be explained by the fact that the relevance of these cases often goes beyond the particular private conflict, given that

---

551 *Hatton and Others v. the United Kingdom* App No 36022/97 (ECtHR (GC) 8 July 2003), para. 126.

552 *Taşkin and Others v. Turkey* App No 46117/99 (ECtHR 10 November 2004).

553 *Taşkin and Others v. Turkey* App No 46117/99 (ECtHR 10 November 2004), paras. 82–88.

554 *Taşkin and Others v. Turkey* App No 46117/99 (ECtHR 10 November 2004), paras. 115ff. The Court found a detailed examination of the material aspect of the case not to be necessary, given that the Supreme Administrative Court had annulled the authorities' decision to issue an operating permit for the gold mine (see para. 117).

in such cases – such as cases on noise disturbance or pollution – there is not only an impact on the individual directly involved in the private conflict, but also a much broader impact.[555] Dangerous emissions or the noise of night flights, for example, may affect the health of everyone living in a specific area, and measures taken to reduce the dangers of pollution may have important economic consequences for the country as a whole. This is different for verticalised cases involving a conflict between the right to reputation and private life and the right to freedom of expression, family life cases, and employer-employee cases, as is illustrated in more detail below.

3.2. RIGHT TO REPUTATION AND PRIVATE LIFE VERSUS FREEDOM OF EXPRESSION CASES

As well as examining how the national authorities balanced the competing interests of one individual and of the community as a whole, the Court may approach verticalised cases by examining whether a fair balance was struck between the competing rights and interests of two private actors, i.e. the applicant and the private actor involved in the conflict at the domestic level. The Court takes this approach in the remaining three types of verticalised cases discussed here: verticalised cases involving a conflict between the right to reputation and private life and the right to freedom of expression, verticalised family life cases, and verticalised cases involving employer-employee relations.

Section 3.3 of Chapter 5 explained that, in cases involving a conflict between the right to reputation and private life and the right to freedom of expression, the Court has required Convention States to strike a fair balance between those competing rights by taking into account the criteria listed by the Court.[556] To reiterate, these criteria are: the contribution to a debate of general interest; how well-known is the person concerned; the content, form and consequences of the publication; the circumstances in which the photos were taken or the information was obtained; and the severity of the sanction imposed.[557] In principle, the Court examines whether the domestic courts weighed the

555 I am indebted to Professor Smet for drawing my attention to this point.

556 The Court has held that the examination and outcome of the application should not differ depending on whether the application has been brought under Article 8 or Article 10 because these rights deserve, as a matter of principle, equal respect (see, for example, *Axel Springer AG v. Germany* App No 39954/08 (ECtHR (GC) 7 February 2012), para. 87; *Von Hannover v. Germany (No. 2)* App Nos 40660/08 and 60641/08 (ECtHR (GC) 7 February 2012), para. 106). Some authors have argued, however, that, looking at the Court's case law, this is not always true (see, for example, Smet who refers in this regard to 'preferential framing' (S. Smet, *Resolving conflicts between human rights: a legal theoretical analysis in the context of the ECHR*, Ghent University (diss.) 2014; S. Smet, *Resolving conflicts between human rights: the judge's dilemma*, Routledge 2017)). The issue of 'preferential framing' is discussed in more detail in Chapter 7 (Section 2.2).

557 As explained in Section 3.1 of Chapter 5, the Court first identified these criteria in *Von Hannover v. Germany (No. 2)* App Nos 40660/08 and 60641/08 (ECtHR (GC) 7 February 2012), paras. 108–113, in which Article 8 was invoked. On the same day, the Court formulated the relevant, and largely the same, criteria in a case in which Article 10 was invoked (*Axel Springer AG v. Germany* App No 39954/08 (ECtHR (GC) 7 February 2012) (see n 488).

right to reputation and private life and the right to freedom of expression in conformity with these criteria laid down by the Court. This amounts to a semi-procedural review as described in Chapter 3. In, for example, the case of *Von Hannover (No. 2),* the Court held that:

> [w]here the balancing exercise has been undertaken by the national authorities in conformity with the criteria laid down in the Court's case-law, the Court would require strong reasons to substitute its view for that of the domestic courts.[558]

In *Aksu* the Court further specified this by holding that:

> if the balance struck by the national judicial authorities is unsatisfactory, in particular because the importance or the scope of one of the fundamental rights at stake was not duly considered, the margin of appreciation accorded to the decisions of the national courts will be a narrow one. However, if the assessment was made in the light of the principles resulting from its well-established case-law, the Court would require strong reasons to substitute its own view for that of the domestic courts, which consequently will enjoy a wider margin of appreciation.[559]

This suggests that the Court, first and foremost, reviews the national judicial decision-making process by focusing on the balancing exercise conducted by the domestic courts, without performing a substantive balancing exercise of its own. In, for example, *Von Hannover (No. 2)* the Court reasoned that the domestic courts had 'carefully balanced the right of the publishing companies to freedom of expression against the right of the applicants for their private life'.[560] In doing so, they had, moreover, explicitly taken account of the Court's relevant case law.[561] Accordingly, the Court did not find a violation of Article 8 ECHR. A similar approach is visible in *Gheorghe-Florin Popescu*[562], in which the domestic courts had ordered a journalist to pay damages (approximately EUR 1,100) to the editor-in-chief of a newspaper and a television producer for a local channel (L.B). The journalist was ordered to pay this sum as compensation for non-pecuniary damage caused by the publication of several blogposts in which he had accused L.B. of being morally responsible for a murder-suicide (*meurtre-suicide*) without any supportive evidence. Before the ECtHR, the journalist complained that this decision had violated his right to freedom of expression.

558 *Von Hannover v. Germany (No. 2)* App No 40660/08 (ECtHR (GC) 7 February 2012), para. 107.

559 *Aksu v. Turkey* App No 4149/04 (ECtHR (GC) 15 March 2012), para. 67. The former President of the Court, Dean Spielmann, called this reasoning a demonstration of the 'systemic objective' of the margin of appreciation. According to Spielmann, it 'devolves to the domestic level a measure of responsibility for ensuring observance of human rights' (D. Spielmann, 'Whither the margin of appreciation?' (2014) 67 *Current Legal Problems* 49, 63).

560 *Von Hannover v. Germany (No. 2)* App Nos 40660/08 and 60641/08 (ECtHR (GC) 7 February 2012), para. 124.

561 *Von Hannover v. Germany (No. 2)* App Nos 40660/08 and 60641/08 (ECtHR (GC) 7 February 2012), para. 125.

562 *Gheorghe-Florin Popescu v. Romania* App No 79671/13 (ECtHR 12 January 2021).

When examining the complaint, the Court held, inter alia, that the domestic courts had failed to 'analyse certain elements'[563], and to 'take explicit account of the relevant criteria set out in the Court's case law and to note that the dispute concerned a conflict between the right to freedom of expression and the right to protection of reputation'.[564] Thus, without conducting a substantive balancing exercise of its own, the Court found a violation of Article 10 ECHR.

The Court also used the approach set out in *Von Hannover (No. 2)*, but with a different outcome, in *Petro Carbo Chem S.E.*[565] Here, the domestic courts had ordered a company to pay symbolic compensation to the CEO of a company in which it held shares for publicly criticising the CEO's management. The company ordered to pay damages complained before the ECtHR that its right to freedom of expression had been violated. The Court held that 'there are serious reasons for it to substitute its opinion for that of the domestic courts'.[566] According to the Court, the domestic courts had failed to take into account the criteria emerging from the Court's case law and had, moreover, failed to acknowledge that the dispute involved a conflict between the right to freedom of expression and the right to reputation.[567] Consequently, the Court itself examined what a fair balance would have been between the right to freedom of expression of the applicant company and the right to reputation and private life of the CEO. It found that the applicant company's comments did not relate to aspects of the CEO's private life, but to his performance as a CEO. Accordingly, the Court considered the statements to concern a matter of general interest relating to the activities of powerful companies and to holding managers of such companies accountable for the long-term interests of their business.[568] The Court also reasoned that the statements were not devoid of any factual basis or based on false or misleading information.[569] Hence, it considered the applicant company's intention to have been to open a debate on the management of the company in which it held shares rather than to endanger the commercial success and viability of that company for its shareholders and employees and the economy in general.[570] This led the Court to conclude that the domestic courts had failed to strike a fair balance between the CEO's right to reputation and the applicant company's right to freedom of expression.[571]

However, this is not the only approach visible in the Court's case law on verticalised cases involving a conflict between the right to reputation and private life and the

563 *Gheorghe-Florin Popescu v. Romania* App No 79671/13 (ECtHR 12 January 2021), para. 33 [author's translation of the original French text].

564 *Gheorghe-Florin Popescu v. Romania* App No 79671/13 (ECtHR 12 January 2021), para. 34 [author's translation of the original French text].

565 *Petro Carbo Chem S.E. v. Romania* App No 21768/12 (ECtHR 30 June 2020).

566 *Petro Carbo Chem S.E. v. Romania* App No 21768/12 (ECtHR 30 June 2020), para. 46 [author's translation of the original French text].

567 *Petro Carbo Chem S.E. v. Romania* App No 21768/12 (ECtHR 30 June 2020), para. 45.

568 *Petro Carbo Chem S.E. v. Romania* App No 21768/12 (ECtHR 30 June 2020), para. 43.

569 *Petro Carbo Chem S.E. v. Romania* App No 21768/12 (ECtHR 30 June 2020), paras. 49–51.

570 *Petro Carbo Chem S.E. v. Romania* App No 21768/12 (ECtHR 30 June 2020), para. 52.

571 *Petro Carbo Chem S.E. v. Romania* App No 21768/12 (ECtHR 30 June 2020), paras. 55–56.

right to freedom of expression. Although it almost always reiterates the standard *Von Hannover (No. 2)* formula discussed above, the exact features of the Court's review vary and the Court is not necessarily fully consistent in its approach.[572] There are also, for example, cases in which the Court has taken a substantive approach by re-doing the balancing exercise conducted by the domestic courts and by adopting an independent stance of its own as to where the balance should be struck, even if there did not seem to have been much reason for it to do so.[573] This differs, therefore, from the case of *Petro Carbo Chem S.E.* discussed above, in which it was evident from the Court's reasoning that it had cause to perform a substantive balancing exercise of its own.

Even more often, the Court's approach concerns a combination of procedural and substantive review in which it is sometimes difficult to clearly distinguish between the two.[574] More specifically, the Court may include substantive elements in its reasoning when examining whether the domestic courts took all the criteria into account when engaging in the balancing exercise. Indeed, in many cases it was only after having made at least some substantive comments that the Court concluded that the examination by the domestic courts was, or was not, carried out in conformity with the Court's case law. Illustrative in this regard is the Court's reasoning in the case of *Dupate*[575], in which the applicant claimed that her right to private and family life had been infringed by the domestic courts' dismissal of her complaint about the publication of covertly taken photographs, with captions, depicting her leaving the hospital with her new-born baby. At the time of the impugned article, the applicant's partner was the chairman of a political party that did not have a seat in parliament. Previously, the applicant's partner had been the director-general of a state-owned joint-stock company and had participated in a nationwide advertising campaign in a weekly celebrity-focused magazine – the magazine that had published the article. When examining the merits of the case, the Court started its reasoning by holding that:

572 See also A. Nussberger, 'Subsidiarity in the Control of Decisions Based on Proportionality: An Analysis of the Basis of the Implementation of ECtHR judgments into German Law' in A. Seibert-Fohr and M. Villiger, *Judgments of the European Court of Human Rights: Effects and Implementation*, Nomos Verlagsgesellschaft 2014, pp. 165–185, p. 181;.H. Gerards, 'Procedural Review by the ECtHR: a Typology' in J.H. Gerards and E. Brems (eds.) *Procedural Review in European Fundamental Rights Cases*, Cambridge University Press 2017, pp. 127–160, p. 153ff; O.M. Arnardóttir, 'Organised retreat? The move from "substantive" to "procedural" review in the ECtHR's case law on the margin of appreciation' (2015) *European Society of International Law Annual Conference*, p. 13; O.M. Arnardóttir, 'The Brighton aftermath and the changing role of the European Court of Human Rights' (2018) 9 *Journal of International Dispute Settlement* 223, 230.

573 See, for example, *Axel Springer AG v. Germany* App No 39954/08 (ECtHR (GC) 7 February 2012) (in this case, five dissenting judges disagreed with the substantive approach of the majority (Dissenting opinion of Judge López Guerra joined by Judges Jungwiert, Jaeger, Villiger and Poalelungi)); *Medžlis Islamske Zajednice Brčko and Others v. Bosnia and Herzegovina* App No 17224/11 (ECtHR (GC) 27 June 2017). See also Gerards (n 572), pp. 155ff.

574 See, for example, *Ageyevy v. Russia* App No 7075/10 (ECtHR 18 April 2013); *Rubio Dosamantes v. Spain* App No 20996/10 (ECtHR 21 February 2017); *Rodina v. Latvia* App No 48543/10 (ECtHR 14 May 2020); *Dupate v. Latvia* App No 18068/11 (ECtHR 19 November 2020); *Société Editrice de Mediapart and Others v. France* App No 281/15 (ECtHR 14 January 2021).

575 *Dupate v. Latvia* App No 18068/11 (ECtHR 19 November 2020).

> in exercising its supervisory function, the Court's task is to review, in the light of the case as a whole, whether the decisions the domestic courts have taken pursuant to their power of appreciation are in conformity with the criteria laid down in the Court's case-law. Accordingly, the Court will analyse in turn the elements identified as relevant in this regard in its case-law and the domestic courts' assessment thereof.[576]

Subsequently, the Court compared the domestic courts' assessment with its own assessment for each standard laid down in the Court's case law. The Court then concluded that:

> while the domestic courts did engage in the balancing exercise between the right to private life and freedom of expression, this exercise was not carried out in conformity with the criteria laid down in the Court's case-law. Most importantly, sufficient attention was not paid to the limited contribution the article had made to issues of public importance and the sensitive nature of the subject matter shown in the photographs. No distinction was made between factual information partially falling within the public sphere and the publication of covertly taken photographs depicting an essentially private moment of the applicant's life. The assessment of the applicant's prior conduct was flawed and the intrusive manner of taking the photographs – which had been the focus of the article – was not taken into account.[577]

The Court's tendency to include substantive elements in its reasoning may be explained by the fact that the criteria it wants the domestic courts to take account of are of a substantive nature. In other words, the particular nature of the criteria may make it difficult for the Court to clearly distinguish between a procedural and substantive review, and so it may have to include some substantive considerations of its own in order to evaluate the domestic court's assessment of the case.[578]

The Court's choice for a mixed procedural and substantive (or semi-procedural) approach is important in relation to the verticalised nature of this category of cases. Some of the standards identified and listed by the Court as relevant for the balancing exercise may relate directly to the acts and interests of the private actor involved in the conflict at the domestic level. In cases, for example, in which Article 8 is invoked, the Court can consider the question of whether a journalist who has harmed someone's reputation acted in good faith or properly verified the facts. To illustrate, the Court held in *Ageyevy*[579] that:

> [e]ven though nothing in the case-file suggests that the journalists responsible for the material were not acting in "good faith", they obviously failed to take the necessary steps to

576 *Dupate v. Latvia* App No 18068/11 (ECtHR 19 November 2020), para. 49.

577 *Dupate v. Latvia* App No 18068/11 (ECtHR 19 November 2020), para. 74.

578 In this regard, see also the remarks made by Judge Spano and former Judge Nussberger, as cited in Section 3.2.3 of Chapter 3.

579 *Ageyevy v. Russia* App No 7075/10 (ECtHR 18 April 2013).

> report the incident in an objective and rigorous manner, trying instead either to exaggerate or oversimplify the underlying reality.[580]

In this case, the applicant complained, inter alia, that the domestic courts had failed to protect her reputation in defamation proceedings she had instituted in respect of media reports describing her alleged ill-treatment of her son. Similarly, in cases in which Article 10 is invoked the Court may sometimes examine the role or function of the person concerned, the person's prior conduct or the impact of a publication on a person's private life.[581] In the case of *Axel Springer AG*, for example, the Court held in relation to the prior conduct of the person who had initiated the proceedings at the domestic level that:

> [a]nother factor is X's prior conduct *vis-à-vis* the media. He had himself revealed details about his private life in a number of interviews ... In the Court's view, he had therefore actively sought the limelight, so that, having regard to the degree to which he was known to the public, his "legitimate expectation" that his private life would be effectively protected was henceforth reduced.[582]

Thus, when the Court itself examines where the balance should be struck between the right to reputation and private life and the right to freedom of expression, or includes some substantive comments in its reasoning, it may scrutinise the acts and interests of the private actor not involved in the Court's proceedings on the basis of the standards it has laid down for the balancing exercise in its own precedents. To exercise such scrutiny, the Court seems to rely primarily on the case file and the submissions made by the government and the applicant. Indeed, the private actor involved in the conflict at the domestic level was granted leave to intervene in the Court's proceedings in only two of the twenty-four cases examined for this study. More specifically, one of the publishing companies responsible for the publication of one of the relevant photos in *Von Hannover (No. 1)* and *Von Hannover (No. 2)* was granted leave to intervene in the Court's proceedings. In both cases, the publishing company primarily referred in its submission to the importance of the freedom of the press in Germany.[583] In other words, they put more focus on the general interest than on their own specific interests, such as the circumstances in which the photos were taken or the reasons for publishing the photos. It is also important to reiterate that, in *Von Hannover (No. 2)*, the Court

580 *Ageyevy v. Russia* App No 7075/10 (ECtHR 18 April 2013), para. 237. See also *White v. Sweden* App No 42435/02 (ECtHR 19 September 2006), paras. 23–24; *Polanco Torres and Movilla Polanco v. Spain* App No 34147/06 (ECtHR 21 September 2010), para. 49ff; *Rodina v. Latvia* App Nos 48534/10 and 19532/15 (ECtHR 14 May 2020), para. 110ff.

581 See, for example *Axel Springer AG v. Germany* App No 39954/08 (ECtHR (GC) 7 February 2012), paras. 97–101; *Medžlis Islamske Zajednice Brčko and Others v. Bosnia and Herzegovina* App No 17224/11 (ECtHR (GC) 27 June 2017), paras. 98–106.

582 *Axel Springer AG v. Germany* App No 39954/08 (ECtHR (GC) 7 February 2012), para. 101.

583 *Von Hannover v. Germany (No. 1)* App No 59320/00 (ECtHR 24 June 2004), para. 47; *Von Hannover v. Germany (No. 2)* App No 40660/08 (ECtHR (GC) 7 February 2012), para. 91.

primarily focused on the balancing exercise conducted by the domestic courts, while in the cases in which a substantive balancing exercise, or substantive comments, formed part of the Court's reasoning, not all private parties to the conflict at the domestic level were involved in the Court's proceedings, not even by way of a third-party intervention. Consequently, the Court could only assess their acts and interests based on information provided by the case file and on the submissions of the government and the applicant(s).

3.3. FAMILY LIFE CASES

In Section 2.3 of this chapter, cases involving custody and access to a child and cases involving access to information about one's origins were identified as verticalised cases involving family relations. Such applications are another type of verticalised cases in which the Court typically examines whether a fair balance was struck between the competing rights and interests of two private actors, i.e. the applicant and the private actor involved in the conflict at the domestic level. In cases involving custody and access to a child, however, the Court's examination tends not to focus on the conflict between the rights and interests of the parents as such, but instead on whether the interests of the child prevailed in the decision-making process. This can be illustrated by the Court's reasoning in the case of *Petrov and X*[584], which concerned the refusal by the domestic courts to make a residence order in favour of the father and his son. In this case, the Court held that it must:

> ascertain whether the domestic courts conducted an in-depth examination of the entire family situation ... and made a balanced and reasonable assessment of the respective interests of each person, with a constant concern for determining what the best solution would be for the child.[585]

Furthermore, the Court held that:

> Article 8 requires that the domestic authorities should strike a fair balance between the interests of the child and those of the parents and that, in the balancing process, particular importance should be attached to the best interests of the child, which, depending on their nature and seriousness, may override those of the parents.[586]

Similarly, in the studied cases concerning the enforcement of custody and access rights, the Court examined whether the domestic authorities had taken all the necessary steps to facilitate a reunion between a parent and child that could reasonably be demanded in the special circumstances of the case and whether the domestic courts had complied

---

584 *Petrov and X v. Russia* App No 23608/16 (ECtHR 23 October 2018).

585 *Petrov and X v. Russia* App No 23608/16 (ECtHR 23 October 2018), para. 98.

586 *Petrov and X v. Russia* App No 23608/16 (ECtHR 23 October 2018), para. 100. See similarly *Sahin v. Germany* App No 30943/96 (ECtHR (GC) 8 July 2003), para. 66.

with their duty to strike a fair balance between the rights and interests of all persons concerned, whereby the interests of the child should prevail.[587]

This also shows that the Court's examination of verticalised cases involving custody and access to a child is primarily concerned with the decision-making process at the domestic level.[588] Indeed, the Court has held that it is not its role to substitute its own assessment for that made by the competent domestic authorities in regulating custody and access issues.[589] Similarly, it has reasoned that it is not its task to take the place of the domestic authorities in deciding in whose favour a residence order should be given in respect of a child of divorced parents.[590] States are also granted a wide margin of appreciation in custody cases, although the Court has called for stricter scrutiny in cases that entail further limitations to the right to respect for one's family life, such as the restriction of access rights.[591] Having in mind this generally wide margin of appreciation, the Court has held in cases involving the enforcement of custody and access rights that '[w]hat is decisive is whether the national authorities have taken all necessary steps to facilitate the execution that can reasonably be demanded in the specific circumstances of each case'.[592] Similarly, in cases concerning a request for custody or access rights, the Court examines whether the reasons adduced by the domestic courts to justify the decision were relevant and sufficient and whether the decision-making process as a whole was fair.[593] If the domestic courts examined the question at issue with care and in line with the principles laid down in the Court's case law, the Court requires very strong reasons to substitute its own assessment for that of the domestic courts. By contrast, a failure to make a sufficiently thorough examination

---

587 See, for example, *Hokkanen v. Finland* App No 19823/92 (ECtHR 23 September 1994), para. 58; *Ignaccolo-Zenide v. Romania* App No 31679/96 (ECtHR 25 January 2000), para. 94; *Mijuskovic v. Montenegro* App No 49337/07 (ECtHR 21 September 2010), para. 82; *Milovanović v. Serbia* App No 56065/10 (ECtHR 8 October 2019), para. 118. See also Ieven 2008 (n 532), p. 49; N. Koffeman, *Morally sensitive issues and cross-border movement in the EU. The cases of reproductive matter and legal recognition of same-sex relationships*, Intersentia 2015, p. 22; B. Rainey (ed.), *Jacobs, White and Ovey: the European Convention on Human Rights*, Oxford University Press 2017 (7th edition), p. 376.

588 See also Popelier and Van de Heyning who held that '[f]or some time, the Court has accentuated the importance of procedural guarantees in judicial and administrative decisions. In particular if the interest of the child is at stake...' (P. Popelier and C. van de Heyning, 'Subsidiarity post-Brighton: procedural rationality an answer?' (2017) 30 *Leiden Journal of International Law* 5, 13).

589 See, for example, *Sahin v. Germany* App No 30943/96 (ECtHR (GC) 8 July 2003), para. 64; *Hokkanen v. Finland* App No 19823/92 (ECtHR 23 September 1994), para 55.

590 *Petrov and X v. Russia* App No 23608/16 (ECtHR 23 October 2018), para. 106.

591 See, for example, *Sahin v. Germany* App No 30943/96 (ECtHR (GC) 8 July 2003), para. 65; *Görgülü v. Germany* App No 74969/01 (ECtHR 26 February 2004), para. 42; *Fröhlich v. Germany* App No 16112/15 (ECtHR 26 July 2018), para. 41. In cases concerning access rights the Court grants States a narrower margin of appreciation, because limiting access rights would entail the risk of the family relations between a child and one of its parents effectively being curtailed. For a more general discussion of the margin of appreciation doctrine and the subsidiarity principle, see Chapter 3 (Section 3).

592 *Gluhakovic v. Croatia* App No 21188/09 (ECtHR 12 April 2011), para. 58. See also *Hokkanen v. Finland* App No 19823/92 (ECtHR 23 September 1994), para. 58; *Ignaccolo-Zenide v. Romania* App No 31679/96 (ECtHR 25 January 2000), para. 96; *Milovanovic v. Servia* App No 56065/10 (ECtHR 8 October 2019), para. 118.

593 See, for example, *Sahin v. Germany* App No 30943/96 (ECtHR (GC) 8 July 2003), para. 68.

will amount to a violation of Article 8 ECHR.[594] To illustrate, the Court did not find a violation of Article 8 in the case of *Sahin*[595] which concerned the refusal to grant a biological father access to a child born out of wedlock. The Court showed itself satisfied that 'the German courts procedural approach was reasonable in the circumstances and provided sufficient material to reach a reasoned decision on the question of access in the particular case'.[596] Similarly, in the case of *Fröhlich*[597], concerning the refusal to grant a biological father contact rights, the Court reasoned, inter alia, that the domestic courts had adduced relevant reasons to justify their decision, that the applicant was directly involved in the proceedings, the child and the child's legal parents had also been heard by the domestic courts, and the courts had taken account of the entire family situation.[598] In these cases, the private actor involved in the conflict at the domestic level was not part of the Court's proceedings by way of third-party intervention. In fact, it was only in one of the verticalised cases involving custody and access rights examined for this study that the private party involved in the conflict at the domestic level was granted leave to intervene as a third party in the case before the ECtHR.[599]

It follows from the above that, in the custody and access cases examined for this study, the Court mostly applies a strongly procedural type of review. This is true even in cases on access rights, in which States are, in principle, granted a narrower margin of appreciation and the Court's scrutiny is therefore rather strict.[600] The Court's approach, moreover, is characterised by a procedural type of review that focuses on procedural safeguards in relation to the decision-making process as a whole. This may be explained by the fact that the Court has read a number of procedural obligations into Article 8 ECHR. These obligations imply that the decision-making process must be fair and, as such, ensure due respect of the interests safeguarded by Article 8, meaning that the applicant has been adequately involved in the decision-making process.[601]

In the other type of verticalised family life cases identified in this study – cases concerning access to information about one's origins – the Court may examine whether a fair balance was struck between the rights and interests of the individual seeking information about his or her origins and the rights and interests of the mother or father (or presumed mother or father), possibly relating to their wish for confidentiality or

594 *Petrov and X v. Russia* App No 23608/16 (ECtHR 23 October 2018), para. 106.
595 *Sahin v. Germany* App No 30943/96 (ECtHR (GC) 8 July 2003).
596 *Sahin v. Germany* App No 30943/96 (ECtHR (GC) 8 July 2003), para. 77.
597 *Fröhlich v. Germany* App No 16112/15 (ECtHR 26 July 2018).
598 *Fröhlich v. Germany* App No 16112/15 (ECtHR 26 July 2018), paras. 42–43.
599 This was the case of *Hokkanen v. Finland* App No 19823/92 (ECtHR 23 September 1994). The Court's judgment does not, however, include a summary of the third-party submissions, and nor did the Court refer to them in its reasoning.
600 See, for example, *Sahin v. Germany* App No 30943/96 (ECtHR (GC) 8 July 2003); *Fröhlich v. Germany* App No 16112/15 (ECtHR 26 July 2018); *Petrov and X v. Russia* App No 23608/16 (ECtHR 23 October 2018); *Honner v. France* App No 19511/16 (ECtHR 12 November 2020).
601 See, for example, *Görgülü v. Germany* App No 74969/01 (ECtHR 26 February 2004), para. 52; *Petrov and X v. Russia* App No 23608/16 (ECtHR 23 October 2018), para. 101.

secrecy. In doing so, again, the Court's review appears to focus on the fairness of the domestic decision-making process.[602] In, for example, *Mifsud,* a case concerning the imposition of a mandatory order to provide a genetic sample, the Court reiterated that 'even in paternity cases, the Court must assess whether the decision-making process, seen as a whole, was fair and provided the applicant with the requisite protection of his interests safeguarded by Article 8'.[603] In this case the Court found that the 'domestic courts struck a fair balance between the interests of X to have paternity established and that of the applicant not to undergo the DNA test'.[604] In reaching this conclusion, the Court attached special weight to the fact that the DNA test was only ordered after 'fully fledged constitutional proceedings – undertaken at the applicant's request'.[605] In the national proceedings in *Mifsud,* the domestic courts had, moreover, duly balanced the two competing rights and interests and had provided the applicant with the opportunity to participate in a way that respected his defence rights.[606] Similarly, in *Mikulić,* in which the applicant had complained that the domestic courts had been inefficient in deciding her paternity claim and had therefore left her uncertain as to her identity, the Court focused on the available procedural means. In this case the Court found a violation of Article 8, reasoning that the available procedure had not struck a fair balance between, on the one hand, the interests of the applicant to have her uncertainty as to her personal identity eliminated without unnecessary delay and, on the other hand, the interest of her supposed father in not having to undergo a DNA test.[607] The Court mentioned, as the main reason for this, that the lack of any measure to compel the alleged father to comply with the court order to undergo a DNA test had not been compensated for by ordering any alternative way of determining the paternity claim speedily.[608]

In the above-mentioned case of *Mikulić* the Court reiterated that it is not its task to substitute itself for the domestic authorities in determining the most appropriate methods for establishing paternity, but to review under the Convention the decisions taken by the domestic authorities.[609] At the same time, in other verticalised cases on access to information about one's origins the Court has pointed out that 'particularly rigorous scrutiny is called for when weighing up the competing interests' since the right to know one's parentage forms 'an integral part of the notion of private life'.[610]

602 See, for example, *Mandet v. France* App No 30955/12 (ECtHR 14 January 2016); *Mifsud v. Malta* App No 62257/15 (ECtHR 29 January 2019); *Koychev v. Bulgaria* App No 32495/15 (ECtHR 13 October 2020).

603 *Mifsud v. Malta* App No 62257/15 (ECtHR 29 January 2019), para. 59.

604 *Mifsud v. Malta* App No 62257/15 (ECtHR 29 January 2019), para. 77.

605 *Mifsud v. Malta* App No 62257/15 (ECtHR 29 January 2019), para. 74.

606 *Mifsud v. Malta* App No 62257/15 (ECtHR 29 January 2019), paras. 74–77.

607 *Mikulić v. Croatia* App No 53176/99 (ECtHR 7 February 2002), paras. 65–66.

608 *Mikulić v. Croatia* App No 53176/99 (ECtHR 7 February 2002), para. 64.

609 *Mikulić v. Croatia* App No 53176/99 (ECtHR 7 February 2002), para. 59. See also *A.M.M. v. Romania* App No 2151/10 (ECtHR 14 February 2012), para. 54.

610 See, for example, *Jäggi v. Switzerland* App No 58757/00 (ECtHR 13 July 2006), para. 37; *Godelli v. Italy* App No 33783/09 (ECtHR 25 September 2009), para. 52.

Accordingly, the Court may also carry out a more substantive review by closely examining the balancing exercise conducted by the domestic courts and reaching its own conclusions as to where the balance should have been struck. Such an approach can be found in the case of *Jäggi*[611], in which the applicant complained that he had been unable to have a DNA test carried out on a deceased person in order to ascertain whether that person was his biological father. Having considered the conflicting interests, the domestic courts had concluded that the rights of the deceased and his close relatives and the principle of legal certainty outweighed the rights and interests of the applicant. In examining whether a fair balance was struck the Court, first, reasoned that:

> [i]n weighing up the different interests at stake, consideration should be given, on the one hand, to the applicant's right to establish his parentage and, on the other hand, to the right of third parties to the inviolability of the deceased's body, the right to respect for the dead, and the public interest in preserving legal certainty.[612]

Thus, the Court showed its awareness of the rights and interests of the private person involved in the conflict at the domestic level. Subsequently, however, the Court re-balanced these interests to arrive at a different conclusion from that reached by the domestic courts. In contrast to the domestic courts, the Court held that an individual's interest in discovering his parentage did not disappear with age.[613] The Court also attached weight to the fact that the deceased family had not cited any religious or philosophical grounds for opposing the taking of a DNA sample, and mentioned that the measure was relatively unintrusive.[614] Accordingly, based on this substantive examination of the case, the Court found a violation of Article 8, holding that the domestic courts had not secured the applicant's right to private life. The dissenting opinion of Judge Hedigan, joined by Judge Gyulumyan, however, shows that the Court's judges may have different opinions on whether the Court should conduct such a substantive review in this type of cases. According to Judge Hedigan, the Court had insufficient reason to justify a violation as the domestic courts had made a careful and well-reasoned analysis of the conflicting interests at stake, had relied upon relevant and sufficient reasons and had arrived at a reasonable conclusion.[615] Judge Hedigan thereby attached particular weight to the subsidiarity principle by stressing that, in cases such as these, the decisions by domestic courts frequently rely heavily on the ability to hear witnesses or otherwise assess evidence, and involve delicate and complex interpersonal issues, and that national authorities have the benefit of direct contact with all the persons concerned.[616] The reasons adduced by Judge Hedigan may explain why, in the

611 *Jäggi v. Switzerland* App No 58757/00 (ECtHR 13 July 2006).
612 *Jäggi v. Switzerland* App No 58757/00 (ECtHR 13 July 2006), para. 39.
613 *Jäggi v. Switzerland* App No 58757/00 (ECtHR 13 July 2006), para. 40.
614 *Jäggi v. Switzerland* App No 58757/00 (ECtHR 13 July 2006), para. 41.
615 Dissenting opinion of Judge Hedigan joined by Judge Gyulumyan in *Jäggi v. Switzerland* App No 58757/00 (ECtHR 13 July 2006).
616 Regarding the latter Hedigan referred to the Court's reasoning, in cases on custody and access to a child, on the Court's task in the light of the subsidiarity principle (Dissenting opinion Judge Hedigan

cases on access to information about one's origins examined for this study, a substantive review as described above appears to be the exception rather than the rule.

This is further illustrated by the one verticalised family life case concerning access to information about one's origins in which the private person involved in the conflict at the domestic level was part of the Court's proceedings by way of third-party intervention. In this case, *Mandet*[617], the domestic courts had decided that it was in the child's best interests to know the truth about his origins. More specifically, the courts had recognised, against the will of the child, the legal paternity of his biological father. Before the Court, the legal parents and the child claimed that this decision violated their right to respect for their private and family life. The biological father, who had initiated the proceedings at the domestic level, was granted leave to intervene as a third party in the Court's proceedings. In his third-party submissions, he provided the Court with a different reading of the facts. He submitted that the mother had obstructed any contact between him and the child, and that this had been the circumstance leading him to initiate proceedings in order to have his paternity legally established.[618] The biological father held, furthermore, that the domestic courts had judged his case fairly and that he was pleased with the outcome. However, he had been unable to exercise the right of access and accommodation, which had also been granted to him, because the legal father and mother and the child had moved to Dubai before the domestic proceedings ended.[619] When reviewing the case, the Court examined the judicial decision-making process and the reasons adduced by the domestic courts to justify their decision. Eventually, the Court did not find a violation of the right to private and family life of the legal parents and the child. In reaching this decision, the Court considered it important that the domestic courts had tried to include the child in the decision-making process and that the interests of the child had been placed at the heart of the reasoning.[620] Thus, the Court focused on the best interests of the child. In its reasoning, the Court, moreover, did not refer to the third-party submissions by the biological father, the private actor who had initiated the proceedings at the domestic level. This makes it difficult to observe whether and how the third-party submissions influenced the Court's reasoning, even though the Court's decision can be seen to be in the biological father's favour.

In conclusion it can be said that the Court approaches verticalised family life cases by carrying out a procedural type of review that focuses on the decision-making process as a whole. In particular, the Court pays attention to whether all persons concerned have been involved in the decision-making process, whether the domestic courts adduced relevant reasons to justify their decision, and whether the best interests of the child prevailed in the decision-making process. In only two of the twenty-one verticalised family cases examined for this study was the private party involved in the conflict at the

joined by Judge Gyulumyan in *Jäggi v. Switzerland* App No 58757/00 (ECtHR 13 July 2006).

617 *Mandet v. France* App No 30955/12 (ECtHR 14 January 2016).

618 *Mandet v. France* App No 30955/12 (ECtHR 14 January 2016), para. 42.

619 *Mandet v. France* App No 30955/12 (ECtHR 14 January 2016), para. 43.

620 *Mandet v. France* App No 30955/12 (ECtHR 14 January 2016), paras. 53–60.

domestic level granted leave to intervene in the Court's proceedings. Accordingly, the Court bases its examination of the case primarily on the case file and the submissions made by the government and the applicant(s).

3.4. EMPLOYER-EMPLOYEE CASES

Verticalised employer-employee cases are the final example of verticalised cases to be discussed here. As in the two types of verticalised cases discussed above, in all the verticalised employer-employee cases analysed for the present study the Court examined whether a fair balance was struck between the competing rights and interests of two private actors; that is, the applicant (usually the employee) and the other private actor involved in the conflict at the domestic level (usually the employer). The Court can be seen to have taken either a substantive or a mixed substantive and procedural review approach in assessing these cases. It chose the former approach in the case of *Eweida and Others,* concerning the wearing of religious symbols at work, in that it carried out a substantive review of its own, rather than reviewing the reasonableness and procedural fairness of the national balancing exercise. In relation to Ms Eweida's application, the Court held, for example, that:

> [o]n one side of the scales was Ms Eweida's desire to manifest her religious belief. ... On the other side of the scales was the employer's wish to project a certain corporate image. The Court considers that, while this aim was undoubtedly legitimate, the domestic courts accorded it too much weight. Ms Eweida's cross was discreet and could not have detracted from her professional appearance. There was no evidence that the wearing of other, previously authorised, items of religious clothing, such as turbans and hijabs, by other employees, had any negative impact on British Airways' brand or image.[621]

Although, therefore, the Court also reasoned that 'it is clear that the legitimacy of the uniform code and the proportionality of the measures taken by British Airways in respect of Ms Eweida were examined in detail'[622], it found a violation of the Convention as it did not agree with the domestic courts' conclusion on where the balance must be struck. The reasoning cited above shows, furthermore, that the Court explicitly considered the interests of Ms Eweida's employer, British Airways, which was involved in the domestic proceedings before the employment tribunals initiated by Ms Eweida, but did not intervene as a third party in the Court's proceedings. Accordingly, the Court must have based its reasoning on the information provided by the case file and the submissions by the government and the applicant.

In other verticalised cases involving employer-employee relations, the Court has taken a rather mixed substantive and procedural approach. This is well illustrated by

621 *Eweida and Others v. the United Kingdom* App No 48420/10 (ECtHR 15 January 2013), para. 94.
622 *Eweida and Others v. the United Kingdom* App No 48420/10 (ECtHR 15 January 2013), para. 92.

three cases against Germany, all of which involved a conflict between an employee and a church, acting as an employer, concerning the termination of an employment relationship.[623] In these cases the Court examined whether the domestic courts had struck a fair balance between the rights of the applicant[624] and the rights of the church in question under Articles 9 and 11 ECHR.[625] In doing so, it carried out a mixed substantive and procedural review of the judicial decision-making process. To illustrate, the Court held, in *Schüth,* that 'the interests of the employing Church were ... not balanced against the applicant's right to respect for his private and family life guaranteed by Article 8 of the Convention, but only against his interest in keeping his post'.[626] This then led the Court to conclude that:

> the employment tribunals did not sufficiently explain the reasons why, according to the findings of the Employment Appeal Tribunal, the interests of the Church far outweighed those of the applicant, and that they failed to weigh the rights of the applicant against those of the employing Church in a manner compatible with the Convention.[627]

Besides these rather procedural considerations, the Court included some substantive elements in its reasoning by holding, for example, that '[i]n the Court's opinion, the fact that an employee who has been dismissed by a Church has limited opportunities of finding another job is of particular importance'.[628] When reviewing the judicial decision-making process, the Court also considered the rights and interests of the employer. In *Schüth,* for example, it reasoned that 'it is true that, under the Convention, an employer whose ethos is based on religion or on a philosophical belief may impose specific duties of loyalty on its employees'.[629] Interestingly, all three churches were granted leave to intervene in the Court's proceedings, with the Catholic Diocese of Essen intervening as a third party in the case of *Schüth.* This Diocese could be regarded

---

623 *Schüth v. Germany* App No 1620/03 (ECtHR 23 September 2010); *Obst v. Germany* App No 425/03 (ECtHR 23 September 2010; *Siebenhaar v. Germany* App No 18136/02 (ECtHR 3 February 2011).

624 In *Schüth v. Germany* App No 1620/03 (ECtHR 23 September 2010) and *Obst v. Germany* App No 425/03 (ECtHR 23 September 2010) the applicant relied on the right to private life (Article 8 ECHR), while in *Siebenhaar v. Germany* App No 18136/02 (ECtHR 3 February 2011) the applicant invoked his right to freedom of religion (Article 9 ECHR).

625 *Schüth v. Germany* App No 1620/03 (ECtHR 23 September 2010), para. 57; *Obst v. Germany* App No 425/03 (ECtHR 23 September 2010), para. 43; *Siebenhaar v. Germany* App No 18136/02 (ECtHR 3 February 2011), para. 40.

626 *Schüth v. Germany* App No 1620/03 (ECtHR 23 September 2010), para. 67.

627 *Schüth v. Germany* App No 1620/03 (ECtHR 23 September 2010), para. 74. Cf. *Obst v. Germany* App No 425/03 (ECtHR 23 September 2010) and *Siebenhaar v. Germany* App No 18136/02 (ECtHR 3 February 2011) in which the Court did not find a violation of the Convention, on the grounds that the domestic courts were found to have taken account of all relevant factors and conducted a detailed and thorough balancing exercise.

628 *Schüth v. Germany* App No 1620/03 (ECtHR 23 September 2010), para. 73.

629 *Schüth v. Germany* App No 1620/03 (ECtHR 23 September 2010) para. 69. In a similar vein, albeit more generally, see *Obst v. Germany* App No 425/03 (ECtHR 23 September 2010), para. 44 and *Siebenhaar v. Germany* App No 18136/02 (ECtHR 3 February 2011), para. 41.

as the employer's representative because the applicant worked for a church of which it was part. In its submission, the Diocese argued that:

> the finding of a violation of the Convention would be seen as a serious interference with consequences not only for the Diocese, but also for all the contracts of employment of the Catholic and Protestant Churches. In the Diocese's opinion, the employing Churches would then find themselves unable to require their employees to comply with particular occupational duties corresponding to their specific missions.[630]

Although the Court did not refer explicitly to the Diocese's submission, the Court's reasoning shows that it did indeed consider the church's interests, as reflected both in the Court's reasoning cited above and, for example, in the Court's consideration that 'in signing his employment contract, the applicant accepted a duty of loyalty towards the Catholic Church, which limited his right to respect for his private life to a certain degree'.[631]

As a final example illustrating the Court's approach, mention should be made of employer-employee cases involving surveillance measures.[632] Section 3.7 of Chapter 5 explained that, as in cases involving a conflict between the right to reputation and private life and the right to freedom of expression, the Court has listed substantive criteria that have to be taken into account by the domestic courts examining the proportionality of surveillance measures and balancing the competing rights and interests at stake. The Court first formulated these criteria in the case of *Bărbulescu*, in which it held that its task is to 'determine whether, in the light of all the circumstances of the case, the competent national authorities struck a fair balance between the competing interests at stake when accepting the monitoring measures to which the applicant was subjected'.[633] In making this assessment the Court acknowledged that:

> the employer has a legitimate interest in ensuring the smooth running of the company, and that this can be done by establishing mechanisms for checking that its employees are performing their professional duties adequately and with the necessary diligence.[634]

Subsequently the Court went on to examine whether the domestic courts took the substantive criteria into account in their reasoning when they weighed the competing

---

630 *Schüth v. Germany* App No 1620/03 (ECtHR 23 September 2010), para. 52. The submissions of the respective churches in the case of *Obst v. Germany* App No 425/03 (ECtHR 23 September 2010) and *Siebenhaar v. Germany* App No 18136/02 (ECtHR 3 February 2011) are very similar (see paras, 37–38 (*Obst*) and paras. 34–35 (*Siebenhaar*).

631 *Schüth v. Germany* App No 1620/03 (ECtHR 23 September 2010), para. 71.

632 It should be mentioned, however, that the cases of *Bărbulescu v. Romania* (App No 61496/08 (ECtHR (GC) 5 September 2017)) and *López Ribalda and Others v. Spain* (App Nos. 1874/13 and 8567/13 (ECtHR (GC) 17 October 2019)) are two Grand Chamber cases in which the Court, for the first time, defined the applicable standards for the particular issue of surveillance measures deployed by private employers. Hence, future case law has to be awaited to further define the application of these standards and the Court's approach to such cases.

633 *Bărbulescu v. Romania* App No 61496/08 (ECtHR (GC) 5 September 2017), para. 127.

634 *Bărbulescu v. Romania* App No 61496/08 (ECtHR (GC) 5 September 2017), para. 127.

rights and interests. With regard to the balancing exercise conducted by the domestic courts, the Court concluded as follows:

> it appears that the domestic courts failed to determine, in particular, whether the applicant had received prior notice from his employer of the possibility that his communications on Yahoo Messenger might be monitored; nor did they have regard either to the fact that he had not been informed of the nature or the extent of the monitoring, or to the degree of intrusion into his private life and correspondence. In addition, they failed to determine, firstly, the specific reasons justifying the introduction of the monitoring measures; secondly, whether the employer could have used measures entailing less intrusion into the applicant's private life and correspondence; and thirdly, whether the communications might have been accessed without his knowledge.[635]

Six dissenting judges did not agree with the reasoning of the majority. In contrast to the majority, they reasoned, inter alia, that the domestic courts had considered the question of prior notification[636] and, more generally, had carried out a careful balancing exercise between the interests at stake.[637] They concluded that 'the choice of the national authorities to give the employer's interests precedence over those of the employee is not capable in itself of raising an issue under the Convention'[638], in particular in the light of the discretion enjoyed by States when required to strike a balance between several competing interests.[639] It can be seen from this that the Court's judges may have differing opinions on the balancing exercise conducted by the domestic courts and on the extent to which the Court should replace the substantive assessment of the domestic courts by one of its own. It should be noted in this regard that the private actor involved in the conflict at the domestic level, the employer, did not intervene as a third party in the Court's proceedings.

In *López Ribalda and Others,* concerning the covert video surveillance of supermarket cashiers and sales assistants by their employer, the Court held that the criteria formulated in *Bărbulescu* also apply to situations where an employer implements video surveillance measures in the workplace. As in *Bărbulescu,* the Court conducted a semi-procedural review, examining whether, in line with the criteria identified in the Court's case law, the domestic courts had struck a fair balance between respect for the applicants' private life and the possibility for the employer to ensure the protection of its property and the smooth operation of its company. In this regard, the Court held that:

> the employment courts identified the various interests at stake, referring expressly to the applicants' right to respect for their private life and the balance to be struck between

635 *Bărbulescu v. Romania* App No 61496/08 (ECtHR (GC) 5 September 2017), para. 140.

636 Joint dissenting opinion of Judges Raimondi, Dedov, Kjølbro, Mits, Mourou-Vikström and Eicke in *Bărbulescu v. Romania* App No 61496/08 (ECtHR (GC) 5 September 2017), paras. 19–20.

637 Joint dissenting opinion of Judges Raimondi, Dedov, Kjølbro, Mits, Mourou-Vikström and Eicke in *Bărbulescu v. Romania* App No 61496/08 (ECtHR (GC) 5 September 2017), para. 21.

638 Joint dissenting opinion of Judges Raimondi, Dedov, Kjølbro, Mits, Mourou-Vikström and Eicke in *Bărbulescu v. Romania* App No 61496/08 (ECtHR (GC) 5 September 2017), para. 23.

639 Joint dissenting opinion of Judges Raimondi, Dedov, Kjølbro, Mits, Mourou-Vikström and Eicke in *Bărbulescu v. Romania* App No 61496/08 (ECtHR (GC) 5 September 2017), para. 23.

> that right and the employer's interest in ensuring the smooth running of the company by exercising its management powers. It will thus ascertain how those courts took into account the factors listed above when they weighed up these interests.[640]

Again, the Court included some substantive considerations in its reasoning by holding, for example, that 'the length of the monitoring does not … appear excessive in itself'[641] and that 'only the supermarket manager, the company's legal representative and the union representative viewed the recordings obtained … before the applicants themselves had been informed'.[642] On the basis of these and other factors, it took the view that 'the intrusion into the applicants' privacy did not attain a high degree of seriousness'.[643] After evaluating the various criteria, the Court held that the domestic courts 'carried out a detailed balancing exercise between, on the one hand, their right to respect for their private life, and on the other the employer's interest in ensuring the protection of its property and the smooth operation of the company' and noted that the 'proportionality criteria established by the Constitutional Court's case-law and followed in the present case are close to those which it has developed in its own case-law'.[644] As in *Bărbulescu*, the employer was not involved in the Court's proceedings by way of a third-party intervention.

The foregoing shows that, in verticalised employer-employee cases, the Court's review may involve a substantive review or a combination of substantive and procedural review. The Court can do this by, for example, including substantive findings in its reasoning when examining whether the domestic courts took all the relevant criteria into account. The examples of verticalised employer-employee cases also show that the Court sometimes explicitly considered the interests, and sometimes the rights, of the employer even though the employer was not always formally involved in the proceedings before the Court. The interests taken into account by the Court were primarily business-related interests, but sometimes coincided with the right to property.[645]

3.5. CONCLUSION

It has been shown above that not only do verticalised cases have different characteristics, but the Court's approach to them differs as well. The Court generally approaches

640 *López Ribalda and Others v. Spain* App Nos. 1874/13 and 8567/13 (ECtHR (GC) 17 October 2019), para. 122.
641 *López Ribalda and Others v. Spain* App Nos. 1874/13 and 8567/13 (ECtHR (GC) 17 October 2019), para. 126.
642 *López Ribalda and Others v. Spain* App Nos. 1874/13 and 8567/13 (ECtHR (GC) 17 October 2019), para. 126.
643 *López Ribalda and Others v. Spain* App Nos. 1874/13 and 8567/13 (ECtHR (GC) 17 October 2019), para. 126.
644 *López Ribalda and Others v. Spain* App Nos. 1874/13 and 8567/13 (ECtHR (GC) 17 October 2019), para. 132.
645 Or the right to freedom of religion (Article 9 ECHR) or assembly (Article 11 ECHR) in cases in which the employer was a religious organisation.

verticalised cases, with the exception of cases related to one's surroundings, by examining whether the domestic courts struck a fair balance between the competing rights and interests of two private actors. In doing so, it carries out different types of review. These may be more or less procedural or substantive in nature, semi-procedural or a combination of the two. The Court's substantive approach implies re-doing the balancing exercise conducted by the domestic courts and adopting an independent stance of its own as to where the balance should be struck. In other cases, the Court has chosen to rely on a combination of procedural and substantive reasoning, by, for example, examining whether the domestic courts conducted a balancing exercise in line with the substantive criteria laid down in the Court's case law. Finally, the Court may rely on a procedural review of the national judicial decision-making process by focusing on the balancing exercise conducted by the domestic courts, without performing a balancing exercise of its own, or by examining the procedural fairness of the decision-making process as a whole.

It also follows from the above that verticalised family life cases stand out in the sense that the Court approaches these cases primarily by conducting a procedural review. More specifically, the Court focuses in such cases on the fairness of the decision-making process by paying attention to whether all relevant persons have been involved in this process, whether the domestic courts adduced relevant reasons to justify their decision, and whether the best interests of the child duly prevailed in the decision-making process. In the other types of verticalised cases, the Court's type of review is more varied: sometimes it approaches cases by conducting a substantive review, while in other cases it opts for a procedural review, or a combination of the two.

The cases discussed in this section also show that there are differences in the extent to which the Court takes into account the rights and interests of the private actor who was involved in the conflict at the domestic level, but who does not play a formal role in the Court's proceedings. The Court pays little attention, for example, to the interests of this private party in verticalised cases involving a conflict between the right to reputation and private life and the right to freedom of expression (even though it may scrutinise the acts of this private party), whereas in verticalised employer-employee cases the Court sometimes explicitly considers the rights or interests of the party not formally involved in the ECtHR proceedings. These differences do not seem to be influenced by whether the private party involved in the conflict at the domestic level submits a third-party intervention in the Court's proceedings. Indeed, relatively few of the cases examined for this study involved the private actor, not being the applicant, intervening as a third party in the case before the ECtHR. Furthermore, in the rare case of a third-party intervention, the Court did not expressly refer to the submissions in its reasoning, thus making it difficult to examine whether and to what extent these influenced the Court's reasoning. More generally, the relatively low level of third-party submissions by the private party involved in the conflict at the domestic level, not being the applicant, suggests that the Court primarily relies on the information provided by the case file and the submissions by the government and the applicant(s) for its examination of the case, including its assessment of the rights, interests and acts of the private actor not formally involved in the case before the Court.

CONCLUSION

This part of the research has provided a detailed analysis of verticalised cases before the ECtHR by looking at the origins of such cases, i.e. the characteristics of and the private actors involved in the case at the domestic level, and the Court's subsequent examination of these verticalised cases.

To qualify as a verticalised case as defined in this study, a case must originate from a horizontal conflict at the domestic level; in other words, a private actor has initiated proceedings against another private actor before the domestic courts, and, subsequently, one of these two private actors complains about State action or inaction in relation to this case before the ECtHR. This situation arises in a broad range of cases, as is clear from the case law analysis presented in the previous chapters. Verticalised cases can be rooted in different horizontal conflicts at the domestic level, involving different relations between private actors, and relating to different Convention rights. They can involve, for example, a conflict between an individual and a journalist about the right to reputation and private life and the right to freedom of expression, or a conflict between a child and an alleged father about access to information about one's origins. They can also relate to a conflict between separated or divorced parents on custody and access rights, or a conflict between an employer and an employee about religion in the workplace. In yet other verticalised cases, such as those relating to one's surroundings, the involvement of State authorities can be so strong that, on the domestic level, there is a shared or combined responsibility, resulting in a case involving both a Convention State and two private actors.

The wide variety of verticalised cases and the differences between them are reflected in the approach the Court takes to assessing these cases. In verticalised cases related to one's surroundings the Court examines whether a fair balance was struck between the interests of the individual and of the community as a whole, while in the other types of verticalised cases it examines how competing rights and interests of two private actors – the rights and interests of the applicant and those of the private actor involved in the conflict at the domestic level – were balanced. When examining whether a fair balance was struck, the Court's review may be less or more procedural, or substantive, in nature. In some cases, for example, it focuses on the quality of the decision-making process by examining whether the domestic courts took account of the relevant substantive criteria set out in the Court's case law when engaging in the balancing exercise or by examining whether the decision-making process as a whole was fair and ensured the interests safeguarded by the Convention. In other cases, it may adopt a semi-procedural or combined approach, whereby it relies on both procedural and substantive reasoning when examining the balancing exercise conducted by the domestic courts.

Finally, it is clear from the analysis that an important aspect of verticalised cases is that one of the private actors involved in the conflict at the domestic level is not formally part of the proceedings before the ECtHR. In only a few cases was this private party involved in the Court's proceedings by way of third-party intervention. Regardless, however, of whether the private party involved in the conflict at the domestic level submits a third-party intervention in the Court's proceedings, differences exist in the way the Court deals with the rights and interests of this party. The next part of this study examines in more detail the extent to which this situation presents specific challenges for the Convention system.

PART III

PROBLEMS IN VERTICALISED CASES

INTRODUCTION

In the previous part of this study, it was shown, first, that the Court offers substantive protection of Convention rights in a wide variety of horizontal relations through the concept of horizontal positive obligations. Second, the notion of verticalised cases was unravelled by looking into the origins of verticalised cases; that is, the characteristics of, and the private actors involved in the case at the domestic level, and the Court's approach to them. From this analysis it became clear that an important aspect of verticalised cases is the fact that one of the original parties to the conflict at the domestic level is not involved in the proceedings before the ECtHR. In other words, one of the original parties 'disappears' from the conflict when the case comes before the ECtHR. As shown in the previous part, this 'disappeared party' can have different characteristics, depending on the nature of the conflict. In verticalised cases related to one's surroundings, for example, it is often the private actor directly responsible for the act that had an impact on the individual's physical or non-physical surroundings who is not involved in the Court's proceedings. Meanwhile, in verticalised cases on a conflict involving the right to reputation and private life and the right to freedom of expression, it is the journalist, the media company or the person who allegedly suffered as a result of the right to freedom of expression being exercised who is not involved in the Court's proceedings. In verticalised family life cases concerning custody and access rights, one of the parents is not involved in the Court's proceedings, whereas in the other type of verticalised family life cases – concerning access to information about one's origins – it is the mother or father (or presumed mother or father), or, if one of the latter complains before the ECtHR, the child, who is not part of the Court's proceedings. Finally, in verticalised employer-employee cases, the employer is the party most likely not to be involved in the Court's proceedings.

In addition to the different characteristics of the disappeared party, there are differences with regard to the Court's approach to verticalised cases. More specifically, it follows from the analysis presented in Chapter 6 that, with the exception of cases related to one's surroundings, the Court generally approaches verticalised cases by examining whether a fair balance was struck between the competing rights and interests of two private actors; that is, the applicant and the disappeared party. In doing so, the Court carries out different types of review, which may be either more or less procedural or substantive in nature, or semi-procedural or mixed/combined. The extent to which the Court takes account of the rights and interests of the disappeared party also differs. In some cases, the Court pays little attention to the interests of the disappeared party, but still scrutinises the acts of this party, whereas in other cases it sometimes explicitly considers the rights and interests of the party that is not involved in the proceedings before it.

This important aspect of verticalised cases – that one of the original parties to the conflict at the domestic level is not involved in the Court's proceedings – can present some specific challenges to the Convention system, as has been pointed out both by scholars and judges of the Court.[646] The disappeared party, for example, is not able to defend his acts, interests and rights, while these aspects still may be part of the Court's examination, and the Court's judgment may affect this private actor. This situation also creates difficulties for Convention States during and after the Court's proceedings as it may result in Convention States being asked to defend the acts of private actors. Similarly, it may pose problems for domestic courts when they have to apply and enforce a judgment of the Court in a verticalised case. Finally, there is the potentially problematic issue for the Court that it receives only the version of facts and arguments presented by the applicant(s) and the Convention States, while it often examines whether a fair balance was struck between the rights and interests of two private actors.

These questions are further examined in this Part III, where the implications of verticalisation for private actors, Convention States and the Court itself are discussed in a rather more evaluative fashion. This is done, first, by looking into problems that may arise *during* the Court's proceedings (Chapter 7) and, second, by examining problems that may arise *after* the Court's proceedings (Chapter 8).

646 See, for example, A. Nussberger, 'Subsidiarity in the Control of Decisions Based on Proportionality: An Analysis of the Basis of the Implementation of ECtHR judgments into German Law' in A. Seibert-Fohr and M. Villiger, *Judgments of the European Court of Human Rights: Effects and Implementation,* Nomos Verlagsgesellschaft 2014, pp. 165–185; N. Bürli, *Third-party interventions before the European Court of Human Rights: Amicus Curiae, Member-State and Third-Party interventions,* Intersentia 2017; P. Pastor Vilanova, 'Third parties involved in international litigation proceedings. What are the challenges for the ECHR?' in P. Pinto de Albuquerque and K. Wojtyczek (eds.), *Judical power in a globalized world (Liber amicorum Vincent de Gaetano),* Springer 2019, pp. 377–393; C.M.S. Loven, 'A and B v. Croatia and the concurring opinion of Judge Wojtyczek: the procedural status of the "disappearing party"' (2019) *Strasbourg Observers* 16 July 2019 <www.strasbourgobservers.com/2019/07/16/a-and-b-v-croatia-and-the-concurring-opinion-of-judge-wojtyczek-the-procedural-status-of-the-disappearing-party/> accessed 31 January 2022; A. Nussberger, '"Second-hand justice" and the rule of law. Dilemmas in implementing the judgments of the European Court of Human Rights' in R. Spano et al (eds.) *Fair trial: regional and international perspectives (Liber amicorum Linos-Alexandre Sicilianos),* Anthemis 2020, pp. 349–363; K. Wojtyczek, 'Procedural Justice and the Proceedings Before the European Court of Human Rights: Who Should Have the Right to be Heard?' in R. Spano et al (eds.), *Fair trial: regional and international perspectives (Liber amicorum Linos-Alexandre Sicilianos),* Anthemis 2020, pp. 741–755; Concurring Opinion of Judge Wojtyczek in *Bochan v. Ukraine (No. 2)* App No 22251/08 (ECtHR (GC) 5 February 2015) (Judge Wojtyczek expressed similar criticism in his Concurring Opinion in *A and B v. Croatia* App No 7144/15 (ECtHR 20 June 2019) which originated from a criminal vertical case on (alleged) sexual abuse); Dissenting Opinion of Judge Koskelo in *Kosmas and Others v. Greece* App No 20086/13 (ECtHR 29 June 2017); Partly Dissenting Opinion of Judge Kjølbro in *Orlović and Others v. Bosnia and Herzegovina* App No 16332/18 (ECtHR 1 October 2019); Joint Concurring Opinion of Judges Ravarani and Elósegui in *A.M. and Others v. Russia* App No 47720/19 (ECtHR 6 July 2021).

CHAPTER 7
PROBLEMS THAT MAY ARISE DURING THE COURT'S PROCEEDINGS

1. INTRODUCTION

This chapter discusses the implications of verticalisation by examining problems that can manifest themselves *during* the Court's proceedings and, more specifically, by examining the extent to which the important aspect of verticalised cases – the fact that one of the original parties to the conflict is not involved in the Court's proceedings – presents challenges for the Convention system. Attention is paid to the perspectives of private actors (Section 2), Convention States (Section 3.1) and the Court (Section 3.2), with the extent to which problems arise during the Court's proceedings being assessed for each different actor in turn. The discussion regarding private actors concerns whether it is problematic that the private actor involved in the conflict at the domestic level, not being the applicant, is not formally involved in the Court's proceedings unless he intervenes as a third party. The implications of this situation for the position of Convention States are also examined. Finally, and in relation to the Court's perspective, the question of whether the Court is provided with a full and balanced account of the facts and the rights and interests involved in verticalised cases is considered.

2. PRIVATE ACTORS

The notion of the 'disappeared party', referring to the private party who is involved in the conflict at the domestic level, but who 'disappears' from the conflict when the case comes before the ECtHR, was mentioned in the introduction to this part of the research. Despite being one of the original parties to the conflict, the disappeared party will be unable to defend his acts, interests or rights in the ECtHR procedure unless he intervenes as a third party.[647] This holds true for all four types of verticalised cases examined in this study; i.e. to cases related to one's surroundings, to the right to

---

647 See also O. Cherednychenko, 'Towards the Control of Private Acts by the European Court of Human Rights?' (2006) 13 *Maastricht Journal of European and Comparative Law* 195, 207; N. van Leuven, *Contracten en mensenrechten: een mensenrechtelijke lezing van het contractenrecht* [Contract law and human rights], Intersentia 2009, p. 59; S. Smet, *Resolving conflicts between human rights: a legal theoretical analysis in the context of the ECHR*, Ghent University (diss.) 2014, pp. 64 and 66–67; S.

reputation and respect for private live versus the right to freedom of expression cases, to family life and to employer-employee cases. The extent to which problems may arise in this regard depends, however, on the nature of the Court's approach, as explained in more detail below (Section 2.1). How the Court's approach to verticalised cases may give rise to problems for private actors is subsequently discussed more generally (Section 2.2).

2.1. DEFENDING ACTS, INTERESTS AND RIGHTS: AN ANALYSIS OF THE FOUR CASE STUDIES

2.1.1. *Cases related to one's surroundings*

It was explained in Part II (Chapter 6) that it is relatively easy in cases related to one's surroundings to distinguish a harmful activity or an omission to act by the State. Because of the State already having such a strong involvement at the domestic level, such cases were characterised as concerning a shared or combined responsibility. It was further discussed that this shared or combined responsibility may explain why, in cases related to one's surroundings, the Court usually examines whether a fair balance was struck between the competing interests of the individual and those of the community as a whole. In other words, in cases related to one's surroundings, the acts, interests and rights of the disappeared party are not the object of the case before the ECtHR, not even indirectly. Instead, the case before the Court concerns the acts and interests of the applicant and those of the respondent State. For this reason, the fact that one of the private actors who played an important role in the conflict at the domestic level is not involved in the Court's proceedings does not, as such, lead to substantial problems during the Court's proceedings.

This is different, however, for other types of verticalised cases, such as those involving a conflict between the right to reputation and private life and the right to freedom of expression, family life cases, and cases involving employer-employee relations. In those cases, the Court examines whether a fair balance was struck between the competing rights and interests of two private actors; that is, the applicant and the disappeared party.

2.1.2. *Right to reputation and private life versus freedom of expression cases*

First, with regard to verticalised cases involving a conflict between the right to reputation and private life and the right to freedom of expression, it was explained that the Court approaches such cases by examining whether the domestic courts weighed the right to reputation and private life and the right to freedom of expression

Smet, *Resolving conflicts between human rights: the judge's dilemma*, Routledge 2017, p. 36. See Chapter 9 for a discussion of the procedural rules regarding third-party interventions.

in conformity with the criteria laid down in the Court's case law.[648] When doing so, the Court may review the national judicial decision-making process with or without performing a substantive balancing exercise of its own. It may also include substantive elements in its reasoning when examining whether the domestic courts took all the criteria into account in the balancing exercise. Finally, when the Court itself examines where the balance should be struck between the right to reputation and private life and the right to freedom of expression, or includes some substantive comments in its reasoning, it may scrutinise the acts and interests of the private actor not involved in the Court's proceedings, based on the standards it has laid down for the balancing exercise in its own precedents. To recall, in cases in which Article 8 is invoked, the Court can consider whether the journalist, whom the domestic courts found to have violated someone's reputation acted in good faith or properly verified the facts. Similarly, in cases in which Article 10 is invoked, the Court sometimes examines the role or function of the person concerned, the person's prior conduct or the impact of a publication on a person's private life.[649] However, the disappeared party – the journalist, media company or individual – is not a direct party to the Court's proceedings and so cannot explain or defend his acts and interests, while questions on whether, for example, the journalist acted in good faith or verified the facts properly touch upon the core of a journalist's work. Indeed, in exercising this scrutiny the Court seems to rely primarily on the case file and the submissions made by the applicant(s) and the government, as shown in Chapter 6. In other words, information on the acts and interests of the disappeared party is not provided by this party itself, but by the case file and the submissions made by the applicant(s) and the government.

2.1.3. Family life cases

Unlike the Court's approach in verticalised cases involving a conflict between the right to reputation and private life and the right to freedom of expression, the Court mostly applies a strong procedural type of review in verticalised family life cases. Its approach in such cases is also characterised by a procedural type of review focusing on procedural safeguards in relation to the decision-making process as a whole.[650] In particular, it considers whether all persons concerned were involved in the decision-making process, whether the domestic courts adduced relevant reasons to justify their decision, and whether the best interests of the child prevailed in the decision-making process. In general, therefore, the Court does not conduct a substantive balancing exercise of its own and, for example, substantively assess what is in the best interests of the child without hearing the other parent involved in the conflict at the domestic level. Accordingly, it can be seen as less problematic that the disappeared party in verticalised family life cases is not involved in the Court's proceedings. Irrespective

648 See Chapter 6 (Section 3.2).
649 See Chapter 6 (Section 3.2).
650 See Chapter 6 (Section 3.3).

of the Court's approach, however, a Court's judgment in a verticalised family life case may still indirectly affect the disappeared party, as discussed in the next chapter.[651] This may be an important reason to claim that although the Court's review is predominantly procedural in nature, the disappeared party should be involved in the Court's proceedings. Furthermore, hearing the disappeared party in the Court's proceedings could also be of importance when the Court carries out a procedural review focusing on the fairness of the decision-making process as a whole. To be fully equipped to carry out a such a review, the Court needs sufficient and adequate information on the judicial decision-making process. Such information may be found in domestic judicial decisions and is often brought forward by the respondent State, but may also be provided by the parties involved in the conflict at the domestic level, particularly in cases from judicial systems where it is less common for a judgment to provide detailed information on how the judgment was arrived at and the balancing exercise conducted.[652] Hearing the disappeared party in the Court's proceedings consequently allows this party to provide the Court with an additional perspective on the balancing exercise conducted by the domestic courts, the rights and interests at stake, and important elements relating to how the national proceedings were conducted. An illustrative case in this regard is that of *Mandet* discussed in Chapter 6 and concerning the establishing of legal paternity. In this case, the biological father, who had initiated the domestic proceedings, was granted leave to intervene as a third party in the Court's proceedings and, in this intervention, submitted, inter alia, that the domestic courts had judged his case fairly and that he was pleased with the outcome.[653]

2.1.4. Employer-employee cases

In verticalised employer-employee cases, the Court conducts either a substantive review or a mixture of a substantive and procedural review when assessing whether a fair balance was struck between the competing rights and interests of the employee and the employer.[654] As the analysis in the previous chapter showed, the Court sometimes explicitly considers the interests, and sometimes the rights, of the employer (the disappeared party), even though the employer is not always formally involved in the proceedings before the Court. This differs, therefore, from verticalised cases involving a conflict between the right to reputation and private life and the right to freedom of expression. That the Court sometimes explicitly considers the rights and interests

651 See Chapter 8 (Section 2).

652 Lasser, for example, explained that in the French system the main judicial debate and deliberations take place behind closed doors and are not in detail reflected in the final judgment, while judgments of German courts provide quite a detailed reasoning and information on the balancing exercise (De S.-O.l'E Lasser, *Judicial Deliberations: A Comparative Analysis of Judicial Transparency and Legitimacy*, Oxford University Press 2004, p. 324 cited in L. Huijbers, *Process-based fundamental rights review. Practice, concept and theory*, Intersentia 2019, p. 324).

653 *Mandet v. France* App No 30955/12 (ECtHR 14 January 2016), para. 43.

654 See Chapter 6 (Section 3.4).

of the disappeared party makes it even more important for this party to be heard in the Court's proceedings. Otherwise, the disappeared party will not be able to explain or defend his rights and/or interests himself, thus making it difficult for the Court to have a full account of all the rights and interests at stake and the exact meaning and importance of these interests for this party. This can be further illustrated by cases in which the disappeared party intervened as a third party in the Court's proceedings. In three cases against Germany, for example, the employers were granted leave to intervene in these proceedings. These cases all involved a conflict between an employee and a church, acting as the employer, concerning the termination of an employment relationship. Their third-party intervention enabled the employers to provide the Court with additional information. In *Schüth*, for example, the employer's representative submitted that 'the finding of a violation of the Convention would be seen as a serious interference with consequences not only for the Diocese, but also for all the contracts of employment of the Catholic and Protestant Churches'.[655] In the Diocese's opinion, 'the employing Churches would then find themselves unable to require their employees to comply with particular occupational duties corresponding to their specific missions'.[656] Although the Court did not refer explicitly to this submission, it was shown in Chapter 6 that the Court took the church's interests into account.[657] This submission also shows that the third-party intervention procedure offered the disappeared party the opportunity to provide the Court with a better account of all the rights and interests at stake and the exact meaning and importance of these rights and interests for this party.

2.1.5. Concluding observations: consequences for procedural rights

The issues raised above all concern the fact that the disappeared party does not play a formal role in the Court's proceedings and, consequently, does not have the opportunity to explain and defend his acts, interests and rights, while these aspects may be part of the Court's examination. In other words, the disappeared party is not heard in the Court's proceedings. And although the above illustrates that the existing instrument of third-party intervention is a way for the disappeared party to become involved in the Court's proceedings and to have his voice heard, it was concluded in Chapter 6 that such an intervention by the disappeared party is the exception rather than the rule and, moreover, that even if the disappeared party intervenes, the Court does not generally refer to this party's submissions.[658]

---

655 *Schüth v. Germany* App No 1620/03 (ECtHR 23 September 2010), para. 52.

656 *Schüth v. Germany* App No 1620/03 (ECtHR 23 September 2010), para. 52.

657 See Chapter 6 (Section 3.4).

658 Glas drew a similar conclusion in relation to third-party submissions by States, concluding that the Court does not generally refer to the State intervener's arguments in its reasoning (L.R. Glas, 'State Third-Party Interventions before the European Court of Human Rights: the what and how of intervening' (2016) 5 *European Journal of Human Rights* 539, 555).

These issues can be seen as problematic in the light of the procedural standards discussed in Part I of this study[659], where it was explained that it is both necessary and important for the Court to adhere to the procedural standards it has set for domestic judicial proceedings, as well as to more general principles of procedural justice, which are broadly similar. Although these procedural standards may need some adaptation or translation to take account of the particular role and position of the Court, this would generally mean the parties involved in the Court's proceedings having the right to present their case effectively before the Court and to enjoy equality of arms with the opposing side. The Court should also duly consider observations, while its judgment should reflect that the parties have been heard, and submissions fundamental to the outcome of the case should be specifically dealt with. Finally, it can be derived from the more general procedural justice principle of participation that the Court's judgment should not only represent the different viewpoints of the parties and carefully assesses the merits of each argument, but also pay attention to stakeholders who may not be among the formal parties in the case.[660] Looking at the issues described above, the Court's current approach does not seem to correspond with these procedural standards. The disappeared party is rarely involved in the Court's proceedings, and even if this is the case, it is not clear whether and how the third-party submissions are taken into account. In other words, although the fact that the instrument of third-party intervention is an existing way of addressing the problem of the disappeared party not being a formal party to the Court's proceedings, it does not seem to provide a real solution in its current form. For this reason, this instrument is discussed separately and extensively in Part IV of this study, in which suggestions are made for improving the Court's approach to verticalised cases and, more specifically, a proposal is made for redesigning the third-party intervention procedure so that it more effectively addresses the problems arising in verticalised cases.

2.2. POSSIBLE PROBLEMS FURTHER EXPLORED

The fact that the disappeared party does not play a formal role in the Court's proceedings and consequently has no opportunity to explain and defend his acts, interests and rights, while these aspects may be part of the Court's examination was criticised by Judge Wojtyczek in his concurring opinion in *A and B*.[661] This case has, so far, not been discussed in this research because it concerns individuals' (alleged) use of violence and was thus not included in the sample of cases examined for this study. However, the criticism expressed by Wojtyczek in his concurring opinion also applies to the verticalised cases examined for this study and, as such, provides a further illustration of problems that may arise for private actors during the Court's proceedings.

---

659 See Chapter 4 in particular.

660 This was discussed in detail in Section 3.2 of Chapter 4.

661 Concurring Opinion of Judge Wojtyczek in *A and B v. Croatia* App No 7144/15 (ECtHR 20 June 2019).

A and B concerned a mother (A) who accused the father (C) of sexually abusing their four-year-old daughter (B). After the Croatian State Attorney's Office decided not to prosecute the father, finding that it could not conclude that he had committed any prosecutable offence, A and B lodged a complaint at the Court, complaining that the Croatian authorities had failed to provide a proper response to allegations of child sexual abuse. The father did not intervene as a third party and was thus not a party to the Court's proceedings, meaning that he did not claim his rights before the Court nor assert his interests. His rights and interests were clearly, however, involved in the case before the ECtHR because of his role as a father and legal representative of his daughter, and because of his role as the accused in the domestic proceedings.

In his concurring opinion, Judge Wojtyczek criticised the issue of the father not having a role in the Court's proceedings. According to Wojtyczek, the fact that the father neither claimed his rights before the Court nor asserted his interests constituted a 'fundamental flaw of the proceedings before the Court'.[662] In the Judge's view this was deeply problematic because it meant that the Court would only get a fragmentary account of the relevant facts; after all, in cases such as this, the Court hears only the version of the facts and the arguments presented by the applicant(s) and the Convention State.[663] Similarly, he pointed out, there was a risk of the Court being presented with a one-sided image of the rights and interests at stake, while it had to examine whether the domestic authorities had struck a fair balance between the various rights and interests. Consequently, the balancing exercise might be 'flawed'.[664] Lastly, Wojtyczek argued that the party not involved in the Court's proceedings may eventually be affected, albeit indirectly, by the Court's judgment, as this may have consequences for this party in the national process of execution and implementation.[665] This latter argument is further discussed in the next chapter (Chapter 8), in which possible problems that may arise after the Court's proceedings are discussed.

The concurring opinion of Judge Wojtyczek highlights that the characteristic of verticalised cases whereby one of the original parties in the domestic conflict is not involved in the Court's proceedings may present the Convention system with some specific challenges. These essentially boil down to the problem that the private actor who is not involved in the Court's proceedings is not able to defend his acts, interests and rights, while these aspects may be part of the Court's examination. This issue is closely related to the risk of 'preferential framing'; in other words, that the Court addresses solely the right(s) invoked by the applicant and, to a certain extent, disregards

---

662 Concurring Opinion of Judge Wojtyczek in *A and B v. Croatia* App No 7144/15 (ECtHR 20 June 2019), para. 9.

663 Concurring Opinion of Judge Wojtyczek in *A and B v. Croatia* App No 7144/15 (ECtHR 20 June 2019), para. 3.

664 Concurring Opinion of Judge Wojtyczek in *A and B v. Croatia* App No 7144/15 (ECtHR 20 June 2019), para. 3.

665 Concurring Opinion of Judge Wojtyczek in *A and B v. Croatia* App No 7144/15 (ECtHR 20 June 2019), para. 4.

the other Convention right(s) at stake.[666] As Smet has explained, this is problematic as an overemphasis on the right invoked may cause the Court to decide the conflict in favour of that right, while the possible damage done to the other Convention rights at stake remains invisible.[667] In cases, for example, on the right to reputation and private life versus the right to freedom of expression, the Court is likely to focus on the possible damage done to the Convention right invoked, thereby possibly paying less attention to potential damage to the other Convention right at stake.[668] This problem of preferential framing, in turn, is related to the situation in which recognising a positive obligation for the State to protect the rights of one individual may imply restricting another individual's rights.[669] If the State, for example, refuses to condemn a journalist, it respects its negative obligation not to interfere with the journalist's right to freedom of expression, whereas the holder of the right to reputation and private life may consider the State to have failed to protect his rights, and vice versa.[670] For such cases, Beijer has stressed that the ECtHR must recognise that it needs to take into account that fundamental rights or interests of third parties can be affected by horizontal positive obligations. If such obligations are imposed on States, the Court should ensure, therefore, that these do not conflict with States' obligation to respect and protect the fundamental rights of all individuals under the Convention.[671] This confirms the importance of taking the acts, interests and rights of the disappeared party into account in the Court's proceedings.

The above discussion showed that, in verticalised cases, problems may arise for private actors *during* the Court's proceedings, particularly because of one of the original parties in the domestic conflict not being involved in the Court's proceedings. First, procedural problems may manifest themselves because, unless he intervenes as a third party, the disappeared party is not formally involved in the Court's proceedings and is therefore unable to defend or explain his acts, interests or rights, while these aspects may be part of the Court's examination. Second, problems may arise for private actors because the fact that they are not a party to the Court's proceedings may have an impact on the Court's reasoning and the final outcome in a case. In Chapter 8 (Section 2), problems that may arise for private actors are further examined by examining the stage *after* the Court's proceedings. First, however, attention is paid to problems that can manifest themselves during the proceedings for the Convention States and the Court itself.

---

666 The concept of 'preferential framing' was introduced by Stijn Smet (See S. Smet, 'Freedom of expression and the right to reputation: human rights in conflict' (2010) 26 *American University International Law Review* 183; Smet 2014 (n 647); Smet 2017 (n 647).

667 Smet 2010 (n 666), p. 185; Smet 2014 (n 647), for example, pp. 64, 161 and 166; Smet 2017 (n 647), p. 35ff. See also more generally E. Brems, 'Introduction' in E. Brems (ed.), *Conflicts between fundamental rights*, Intersentia 2008, pp. 1–16, p. 3.

668 See also Smet 2010 (n 666).

669 See, for example, the discussion of the *Appleby* case in Section 2.2 of Chapter 5.

670 See also P. Ducoulombier, 'Conflicts between fundamental rights and the ECHR: an overview' in E. Brems (ed.) *Conflicts between fundamental rights*, Intersentia 2008, pp. 217–247, pp. 221–222.

671 M. Beijer, *The limits of fundamental rights protection by the EU: the scope for the development of positive obligations*, Intersentia 2017, pp. 78–79.

3. CONVENTION STATES AND THE ECtHR

In addition to the problems that can arise from the Court's current approach to verticalised cases for private actors, issues may also arise for Convention States, as well as for the Court itself. This section therefore focuses on the impact of verticalisation on Convention States (Section 3.1) and, second, on the Court itself (Section 3.2).

3.1. CONVENTION STATES

With regard to Convention States, the problems that can manifest themselves during the proceedings are twofold. These concern: (1) situations in which States are asked to defend the acts of private actors before the Court, and (2) the extent to which States can reasonably be held accountable for the acts of private actors, both of which are discussed below. A third problem that may arise from the perspective of Convention States occurs when a Court judgment in a binary applicant-State relationship has to be enforced by domestic courts in a multi-dimensional and multi-subject case. As this relates to problems that can manifest themselves *after* the Court's proceedings, this is discussed in the next chapter.

In the previous section it was explained that the disappeared party does not have the opportunity to explain and defend his acts, interests and rights in the Court's proceedings and is consequently dependent on the State for this. Indeed, States' submissions in verticalised cases clearly illustrate that governments are sometimes under the impression that they are actually being asked to defend the acts of a private actor and that, in some cases, they clearly object to this. In, for example, *Ignaccolo-Zenide*[672], a case about custody and access rights, the government argued that:

> the failure to execute the decision was due firstly to non-compliance by the father, for whose behaviour the Government could not be held responsible, and secondly to the children's refusal to go and live with the applicant, again a matter for which the Government could not be blamed.[673]

Similarly, in *Khurshid Mustafa and Tarzibachi*[674], a case concerning the termination of a private tenancy agreement, the respondent government emphasised in its observations that the case concerned a dispute between two private actors about a contractual obligation and should therefore have been declared inadmissible.[675] This clearly shows a lack of willingness by the State to defend the disappearing party's case with full force.

---

672 *Ignaccolo-Zenide v. Romania* App No 31679/96 (ECtHR 25 January 2000).

673 *Ignaccolo- Zenide v. Romania* App No 31679/96 (ECtHR 25 January 2000), para. 91.

674 *Khurshid Mustafa and Tarzibachi v. Sweden* App No 23883/06 (ECtHR 16 December 2008). This case was briefly discussed in Chapter 5 (Section 3.6), but is not included in the case law sample since it does not fall within the scope of the four types of verticalised cases examined for this study.

675 *Khurshid Mustafa and Tarzibachi v. Sweden* App No 23883/06 (ECtHR 16 December 2008), paras. 26–30.

Leaving aside the question of whether a State is willing to defend the acts and interests of the disappeared party, it can also be questioned whether States are sufficiently capable of defending the acts and interests of the disappeared party as part of their role in defending the national position in the Court's proceedings. In this regard, Smet, emphasised that:

> the government's agent will arguably be primarily concerned with defending the process and outcome of domestic legislative deliberations and/or judicial proceedings, instead of directly protecting the Convention rights of the "disappeared party".[676]

In a similar vein, Judge Wojtyczek put forward that the absence of the disappeared party is not

> compensated for by the Government, who are not able either to see all the relevant factual or legal elements or to articulate fully all their rights and interests. Moreover, the interests of the Government and the private parties not represented in the proceedings are not identical.[677]

Related to the question of whether States are willing to defend the acts of the disappeared party, and capable of doing so, is the more fundamental question of the extent to which States can reasonably be held accountable for the acts of private actors, i.e. the disappeared party. The acceptance of horizontal positive obligations[678], means the State is no longer solely a possible violator of fundamental rights, but also an important protector of these rights: States have to protect individuals from violations caused both by State agents and by private parties.[679] From the State's perspective, however, it may not be possible to predict when, for what kind of private interferences and for what reasons States have to take positive measures to protect individuals from fundamental rights violations caused by other individuals.[680] This reflects a more general criticism of positive obligations, and one relating to the Court's expansive interpretation of the responsibilities States incur under the Convention.[681] As the question of how, and to what degree, positive obligations can be defined and imposed on States has not been clearly answered by the ECtHR[682], the scope of positive obligations

---

676 Smet 2014 (n 647), pp. 66–67.

677 Concurring Opinion of Judge Wojtyczek in *A and B v. Croatia* App No 7144/15 (ECtHR 20 June 2019), para. 3. See also Bürli who held that 'third-party interests are not invariably represented or protected by the respondent State (N. Bürli, *Third-party interventions before the European Court of Human Rights: Amicus Curiae, Member-State and Third-Party interventions*, Intersentia 2017, p. 179).

678 See Chapter 5.

679 Brems 2008 (n 667), p. 2; Beijer 2017 (n 671), p. 61.

680 Beijer 2017 (n 671), pp. 61 and 79.

681 For an overview of this criticism, see, for example, L. Lavrysen, *Human rights in a positive state: rethinking the relationship between positive and negative obligations under the European Convention on Human Rights*, Intersentia 2016, pp. 7ff; Beijer 2017 (n 671), pp. 86ff.

682 Discussed in Section 2.2 of Chapter 5.

is unclear, and seems almost unlimited.[683] This creates legal uncertainty for State authorities by frustrating the ability of State authorities to foresee the obligations they will incur under the Convention.[684] More specifically, in relation to horizontal positive obligations, it may be difficult for States to foresee the kinds of acts of private actors for which they may potentially be held responsible in the future.

The above shows that the Court's current approach to verticalised cases poses several problems for Convention States. Just like the problems for private actors, these problems arise from the fact that, in a verticalised case, the disappeared party is not part of the Court's proceedings and is not able to defend or explain his acts, interests or rights. Problems also arise in relation to the horizontal positive obligations that are often imposed in verticalised cases. Since the Court has not been particularly clear in its reasoning for defining and imposing horizontal positive obligations, it is difficult for States to foresee the horizontal positive obligations they may incur under the Convention.

3.2. THE ECtHR

Besides private actors and Convention States, the Court itself is another relevant actor for whom verticalised cases may have some implications and challenges. Again, as shown below, these originate from the fact that an important aspect of verticalised cases is that one of the original parties in the domestic conflict is not involved in the Court's proceedings.

It was explained in Chapter 6 that the Court generally relies on the information provided by the case file and the submissions by the government and the applicant(s) when examining a verticalised case. This is because third-party intervention submissions by the disappeared party are the exception rather than the rule and no other mechanism exists for involving the disappeared party in the Court's proceedings. In most cases, therefore, the Court receives solely the version of the facts and arguments presented by the applicant(s) and the Convention States, as also illustrated earlier. As a result, it is difficult for the Court to have a full account of all the rights and interests at stake and the exact meaning and importance of the disappeared party's interests. That this creates some specific challenges for the Court is illustrated by the concerns expressed by Judges Ravarani and Elósegui in their joint concurring opinion in the case of *A.M. and Others,* a verticalised family life case concerning custody and access rights. They commenced their concurring opinion by stating that:

> [i]t is not without some difficulties that we found ourselves able to agree with the finding of a violation in the present case. Our doubts do not stem from the legal analysis itself but merely

683 D. Xenos, *The positive obligations of the state under the European Convention of Human Rights,* Routledge 2012, p. 91; Beijer 2017 (n 671), pp. 86–87; V. Stoyanova, 'Common law tort of negligence as a tool for deconstructing positive obligations under the European Convention on Human Rights' (2020) 24 *The International Journal of Human Rights* 632, 634ff.

684 Beijer 2017 (n 671), pp. 86–87; Stoyanova 2020 (n 683), pp. 634ff.

> from the impression that the Court lacked some essential factual information enabling it to have a fully-fledged and balanced view of the underlying facts of the case. This, to our mind, originates in the general issue … of the adequate representation of the interests (and even rights) of persons concerned by the proceedings before the Court but not directly represented therein.[685]

They also raised the question of whether it could be said that the Court

> had a *complete picture* of the various interests at stake – which could be seen as a precondition for a proper assessment of the domestic courts' examination of the case – since it did not hear either the explanations and arguments of the mother or those of the children?[686]

Lastly, they argued that:

> [w]hile the Court increasingly deals with cases originating in disputes between civil parties, as in the case at hand …, the vertical structure of proceedings before the Court, that is to say, where individuals are opposed to States, sometimes does not perfectly reflect the various interests at stake. This partial reflection can turn into a blind spot in cases, such as the present one, where the party who won the case at domestic level (in this case, the natural mother) and those who are concerned first and foremost by the outcome of the proceedings before the Court (that is, the children themselves and the applicant) had no opportunity to put forward their respective standpoints.[687]

Similar to Judges Ravarani and Elósegui, Judge Wojtyczek referred to the balancing exercise as potentially being "flawed"[688] as a result of the private actor involved in the original conflict not being heard by the Court. To stress the importance of the Court having full account of all rights and interests at stake, Wojtyczek, moreover, held that:

> [t]he involvement of third parties may … bring relevant evidence concerning the facts of the case and relevant arguments concerning the interests at stake and their weight, which are indispensable to reach a just judicial decision at the end of the proceedings.[689]

It can be argued that the issues raised above do not create a particularly problematic situation for the Court since the disappeared party's arguments should be embodied by the State and that the Court can always put additional questions to the applicant or

685 Joint Concurring Opinion of Judges Ravarani and Elósegui in *A.M. and Others v. Russia*, App No 47220/19 (ECtHR 6 July 2021), para. 1.

686 Joint Concurring Opinion of Judges Ravarani and Elósegui in *A.M. and Others v. Russia*, App No 47220/19 (ECtHR 6 July 2021), para. 3.

687 Joint Concurring Opinion of Judges Ravarani and Elósegui in *A.M. and Others v. Russia*, App No 47220/19 (ECtHR 6 July 2021), para. 6.

688 Concurring Opinion of Judge Wojtyczek in *A and B v. Croatia* App No 7144/15 (ECtHR 20 June 2019), para. 3.

689 K. Wojtyczek, 'Procedural Justice and the Proceedings Before the European Court of Human Rights: Who Should Have the Right to be Heard?' in R. Spano et al (eds.), *Fair trial: regional and international perspectives (Liber amicorum Linos-Alexandre Sicilianos)*, Anthemis 2020, pp. 741–755, p. 751.

the respondent State. The previous section, however, raised the question of whether a State is actually willing to defend the acts and interests of the disappeared party and is also capable of doing so. Indeed, the respondent State and the disappeared party have different interests and the State may have no desire to reflect the disappeared party's interests in addition to (or even in conflict with) those of its own. Moreover, the respondent State may not have the information needed to provide the Court with a full and correct account of the rights and interests of the disappeared party.

Another argument that could be used to claim that it is not problematic for the Court not to have a complete description of the disappeared party's interests is that the Court is not a fourth-instance court.[690] Since its task is merely to scrutinise whether Convention rights have been sufficiently protected and respected in a particular case, and not to decide the case as presented at the domestic level, it does not need to have a full account of the underlying facts and rights and interests at stake. In this regard, however, Judges Ravarani and Elósegui stressed that:

> it must be recognised that despite the fact that the Court does not in the first place re-examine the underlying facts but rather assesses the soundness of the domestic authorities' handling of the legal issues and their assessment of the established facts, it precisely turns into a fourth-instance body once it finds that the outcome of the domestic proceedings appears to be arbitrary or manifestly unreasonable. The Court delivers individual justice and it necessarily has to deal with the underlying facts of a case.[691]

In other words, and although it is true that the Court does not act as a court of fourth instance, it will always have to deal with the facts of the case, at least to some extent. This can be compared to the discussion about procedural review, which, just like the no fourth-instance court doctrine, is a manifestation of the subsidiarity principle.[692] In relation to procedural review, several judges at the Court have submitted that such a review cannot replace a substantive review as the Court's review will always include some degree of substantive review when assessing whether the outcome is reasonable.[693] To carry out such substantive review, the Court has to deal with the facts of the case, at least to some extent. This, too, then confirms the importance of the Court being provided with a full account of the facts and the rights and interests involved.

Finally, the fact that the Court receives solely the version of facts and arguments presented by the applicant(s) and the Convention State could give rise to a situation in which not all the parties to the original conflict feel they have been heard by the Court. This situation can affect the Court's authority[694], as shown in Part I of this study, which

690 For a discussion of the no fourth-instance court doctrine, see Chapter 3 (Section 3.2.1).

691 Joint Concurring Opinion of Judges Ravarani and Elósegui in *A.M. and Others v. Russia*, App No 47220/19 (ECtHR 6 July 2021), para. 7.

692 The subsidiarity principle and its various manifestations are discussed in Chapter 3 (Section 3).

693 See the discussion on procedural review in Chapter 3 (Section 3.2.3).

694 See also Judge Ravarani and Elósegui who held in their joint concurring opinion in the case of *A.M. and Others v Russia* that '[t]he case at hand clearly shows that what is at stake is not only the procedural legitimacy of the Court's decisions, but also the well-informed nature of its decision-making process'

discusses research showing how the perception of procedural fairness can influence the perception of the relevant institution's legitimacy.[695] As regards the ECtHR, the risk of procedural limitations affecting the Court's perceived legitimacy is even higher, given that the Court itself is tasked with safeguarding procedural fairness. If the Court itself does not adhere to the standards it has set for the Convention States, this may adversely impact on the image individual applicants have of the Court.[696] The issue of authority and legitimacy is, moreover, particularly relevant for the ECtHR because it is elemental in States' effective implementation of the Court's judgments.[697]

4. CONCLUSION

This chapter focused on the implications of verticalised cases by examining problems that can manifest themselves *during* the Court's proceedings, with attention being paid to implications for private actors, Convention States and the Court itself. The discussion showed that the Court's approach to verticalised cases does not have implications only for private actors, but also for the Convention States and the Court itself. These implications all relate to the fact that one of the original parties to the conflict at the domestic level is not involved in the Court's proceedings and thus disappears from the conflict. In practice, this means that the disappeared party is not represented in the Court's proceedings unless he intervenes as a third party, and is therefore not able to defend or explain his acts, interests or rights, while these may be part of the Court's examination. This may also result in a situation in which Convention States are asked to defend the rights and interests of the disappeared party, while they may, in practice, be unwilling to do so or incapable of such. Lastly, it also means that the Court receives solely the version of facts and arguments presented by the applicant(s) and the Convention States, which may mean the Court has to examine a verticalised case without having a full and balanced account of the facts of the case and the rights and interests at stake.

(Joint Concurring Opinion of Judges Ravarani and Elósegui in *A.M. and Others v. Russia,* App No 47220/19 (ECtHR 6 July 2021), para. 9).

695 J. Thibaut and L. Walker, *Procedural justice: a psychological analysis,* L. Erlbaum Associates 1975, pp. 1–3. See also Chapter 4 (Section 3).

696 H. de Vylder, 'Stensholt v. Norway: Why single judge decisions undermine the Court's legitimacy' (2014) *Strasbourg Observers* 28 May 2014, <https://strasbourgobservers.com/2014/05/28/stensholt-v-norway-why-single-judge-decisions-undermine-the-courts-legitimacy-2/> accessed 31 January 2022.

697 T. Barkhuysen and M. van Emmerik, 'Legitimacy of European Court of Human Rights Judgments: Procedural Aspects' in N. Huls, M. Adams, J. Bomhoff (eds.), *The Legitimacy of Highest Courts' Rulings: Judicial Deliberations and Beyond,* TMC Asser Press 2009, pp. 437–449, p. 436; E. Brems and L. Lavrysen, 'Procedural justice in human rights adjudication: the European Court of Human Rights' (2013) 35 *Human Rights Quarterly* 176, 182–184; L.R. Glas, 'Translating the Convention's Fairness Standards to the European Court of Human Rights: an exploration with a Case Study on Legal Aid and the Right to a Reasoned Judgment' (2018) 10 *European Journal of Legal Studies* 47, 49. See also Chapter 4 (Section 3).

CHAPTER 8

PROBLEMS THAT MAY ARISE AFTER THE COURT'S PROCEEDINGS

1. INTRODUCTION

The previous chapter focused on problems arising from the Court's approach to verticalised cases that can manifest themselves *during* the Court's proceedings. To take the analysis a step further, this chapter focuses on problems that can manifest themselves *after* the Court's proceedings; that is, during the national follow-up and executing of the Court's judgment in a verticalised case and that can result, for example, in domestic proceedings being reopened. First, the effects of a Court judgment for the disappeared party are discussed. These are examined in some detail, given that the extent to which a third party is affected by a judgment is often considered an important factor in determining whether to involve this party in the proceedings, i.e. whether this party should be heard.[698] Second, attention is paid to the perspectives of Convention States and the Court in relation to possible problems that can manifest themselves after the Court has handed down a judgment in a verticalised case (Section 3).

2. EFFECTS OF A JUDGMENT FOR THE DISAPPEARED PARTY

When discussing the effects of a Court judgment for the disappeared party, it must be kept in mind that the Court does not issue judgments imposing any legal effects on, or granting rights to, private actors, but instead finds for or against the respondent State. The Court's judgments are, moreover, essentially declaratory in nature. Yet this does not mean that such judgments do not affect the rights and interests of the disappeared party. The effect of a judgment of the Court on the disappeared party may be indirect. In their joint concurring opinion in the case of *A.M. and Others*[699], concerning the restriction of parental rights, Judges Ravarani and Elósegui held, for example, that '[i]t should not be forgotten that its [the Court's] judgments can lead to the final deprivation

---

698 See also Concurring Opinion Judge Wojtyczek in *Bochan v. Ukraine (No. 2)* App No 22251/08 (ECtHR (GC) 5 February 2015), para. 7.

699 *A.M. and Others v. Russia* App No 47220/19 (ECtHR 6 July 2021).

of rights previously acquired by third parties, or at least have serious consequences in practice…'.[700] In his concurring opinion in *Bochan (No. 2)*[701] and *A and B*[702], Judge Wojtyczek also described how the indirect effect of a Court judgment can manifest itself. In *Bochan (No. 2)*, which concerned the fairness of civil proceedings about a dispute over a title to land, Wojtyczek stated that:

> … the Court's finding of a violation of the Convention on account of a judicial decision in a civil case may have practical and legal consequences for the other parties to the civil proceedings and for the implementation of their rights. This problem is particularly acute in the case of applications against States whose legal systems allow the reopening of civil proceedings following a judgment of the Court.[703]

Similarly, Wojtyczek argued in his concurring opinion in *A and B* that the finding of a violation may be a strong argument for the applicant to request the reopening of the domestic proceedings or to initiate new domestic proceedings in respect of a certain aspect of the case.[704] According to Wojtyczek, the views expressed by the Court may be a determinative argument in these follow-up proceedings at the domestic level because of the Court's authority and the weight attributed to its judgments. As he put it, '[a] favourable dictum, let alone a favourable judgment, may be a valuable asset in future legal battles against the same litigants'.[705] Similarly, former Judge and Vice-President of the Court Nussberger wrote in a scholarly publication that in cases concerning the right to family life, '[t]he reopening of civil procedures as well as new decisions in continuing situations can turn those who have won their case on national level – unexpectedly – into losers'.[706] For similar reasons, Bürli even speaks of a third party being *directly* affected by a judgment of the Court when this party has a legal, as opposed to merely

700 Joint Concurring Opinion Judges Ravarani and Elósegui in *A.M. and Others v. Russia* App No 47220/19 (ECtHR 6 July 2021), para. 7. See similarly A. Nussberger, '"Second-hand justice" and the rule of law. Dilemmas in implementing the judgments of the European Court of Human Rights' in R. Spano et al (eds.) *Fair trial: regional and international perspectives (Liber amicorum Linos-Alexandre Sicilianos)*, Anthemis 2020, pp. 349–363, pp. 357ff; G. Ravarani, 'Third parties – poor relations in proceedings before the European Court of Human Rights' (2021) (on file with the author), section on 'the practical consequences of the Court's judgments on third parties'.

701 *Bochan v. Ukraine (No. 2)* App No 22251/08 (ECtHR (GC) 5 February 2015).

702 *A and B v. Croatia* App No 7144/15 (ECtHR 20 June 2019). This case and the Concurring Opinion of Judge Wojtyczek have also been discussed in Section 2.2 of the previous chapter.

703 Concurring Opinion Judge Wojtyczek in *Bochan v. Ukraine (No. 2)* App No 22251/08 (ECtHR (GC) 5 February 2015), para. 8. See also K. Wojtyczek, 'Procedural Justice and the Proceedings Before the European Court of Human Rights: Who Should Have the Right to be Heard?' in R. Spano et al (eds.), *Fair trial: regional and international perspectives (Liber amicorum Linos-Alexandre Sicilianos)*, Anthemis 2020, pp. 741–755, pp. 744ff.

704 Concurring Opinion Judge Wojtyczek in *A and B v. Croatia* App No 7144/15 (ECtHR 20 June 2019), para. 4.

705 Concurring Opinion Judge Wojtyczek in *A and B v. Croatia* App No 7144/15 (ECtHR 20 June 2019), para. 4.

706 Nussberger 2020 (n 700), p. 358.

virtual, interest in the case.[707] Bürli thereby defines 'having a legal interest' as being affected in one's human rights by individual measures, such as the reopening of domestic proceedings, taken by the respondent State in order to comply with the Court's judgment.[708]

Clearly, thus, a judgment of the Court can have an impact on the disappeared party. To examine this potential impact in more detail, the next subsections discuss, first, the extent to which the Court indicates, or even prescribes, the taking of individual measures, such as the reopening of domestic proceedings, in its judgments and, in this event, what the consequences of this approach are for the rights and interests of the disappeared party (Section 2.1). Second, attention is paid to the execution of judgments in verticalised cases, i.e. to the practice at the domestic level, and the potential problems that may arise in this regard for the disappeared party (Section 2.2).

2.1. ARTICLE 46 ECHR AND THE NATURE OF THE COURT'S JUDGMENTS

2.1.1. The indication of general or individual measures by the Court

Article 46 (1) ECHR requires Convention States 'to abide by the final judgment of the Court in any case to which they are parties'. The Court has clarified that, on the basis of this provision, a Convention State is:

> under an obligation not just to pay those concerned the sums awarded by way of just satisfaction, but also to take individual and/or, if appropriate, general measures in its domestic legal order to put an end to the violation found by the Court and to redress the effects, the aim being to put the applicant, as far as possible, in the position he would have been in had the requirements of the Convention not been disregarded.[709]

Individual measures concern the applicant's personal situation and can include, for example, reopening domestic proceedings, striking out an unjustified criminal conviction from the criminal records or granting a residence permit.[710] General measures, on the other hand, primarily aim to prevent violations similar to those found

---

707 N. Bürli, *Third-party interventions before the European Court of Human Rights: Amicus Curiae, Member-State and Third-Party interventions*, Intersentia 2017, pp. 160–161. See also P. Pastor Vilanova, 'Third parties involved in international litigation proceedings. What are the challenges for the ECHR?' in P. Pinto de Albuquerque and K. Wojtyczek (eds.), *Judical power in a globalized world (Liber amicorum Vincent de Gaetano)*, Springer 2019, pp. 377–393.

708 Bürli 2017 (n 707), p. 161.

709 *Verein gegen Tierfabriken Schweiz v. Switzerland (No 2)* App No 32772/02 (ECtHR (GC) 30 June 2009), para. 85. See also *Scozzari and Giunta v. Italy* App Nos 39221/98 and 41963/98 (ECtHR (GC) 13 July 2000), para. 249; *Assanidze v. Georgia* App No 71503/01 (ECtHR (GC) 8 April 2004), para. 198; *V.A.M. v. Serbia* App No 39177/05 (ECtHR 13 March 2007), para. 166.

710 Rule 6(2)(b) for the supervision of the execution of judgments and of the terms of friendly settlements. On individual and general measures, see also, for example, L.R. Glas, *The Theory, Potential and*

or to end continuing violations, and can involve, for example, changes to legislation and regulations, or judicial practice.[711]

States remain free to choose the means by which to achieve *restitutio in integrum*, i.e. they may decide for themselves which individual or general measures they wish to take. Ever since the *Marckx*[712] case the Court has repeatedly held that its judgments are essentially declaratory in nature and that, in general, it is primarily for the State concerned to choose the means to be used in its domestic legal order to discharge the State's obligation under Article 46 ECHR.[713] In principle, therefore, the Court abstains from indicating or prescribing specific measures in its judgments.[714] Over the past few decades, however, the Court has become increasingly willing to move away from a purely declaratory approach by indicating in its reasoning, and sometimes even prescribing in the operative provisions of its judgments, which execution measures the respondent State should take.[715] It first took this approach in 1995 in the case of *Papamichalopoulos*[716], which concerned land expropriation in Greece contrary to Article 1 of Protocol No. 1 to the Convention. Although the Court held in its judgment in this case that '[t]he Contracting States that are parties to a case are in principle free to choose the means whereby they will comply with a judgment in which the Court has

Practice of Procedural Dialogue in the European Convention on Human Rights System, Intersentia 2016, p. 209.

711 Rule 6(2)(b) for the supervision of the execution of judgments and of the terms of friendly settlements.

712 *Marckx v. Belgium* App No 6833/74 (ECtHR 13 June 1979), para. 58.

713 See, for example, *Scozzari and Giunta v. Italy* App Nos 39221/98 and 41963/98 (ECtHR (GC) 13 July 2000), para. 249.

714 H. Keller and C. Marti, 'Reconceptualizing implementation: the judicialization of the execution of the European Court of Human Rights' judgments' (2016) 25 *European Journal of International Law* 829, 835. See also V. Colandrea, 'On the power of the European Court of Human Rights to order specific non-monetary measures: some remarks in light of the Assanidze, Broniowski and Sejdovic cases' (2007) 7 *Human Rights Law Review* 396, 397; J. Jahn, 'Ruling (in)directly through individual measures? Effect and legitimacy of the ECtHR's new remedial power' (2014) 74 *ZaöRV* 1, 4; Glas 2016 (n 711), p. 385. This approach is rooted in the subsidiarity principle (see also E. Abdelgawad, 'The execution of the judgments of the European Court of Human Rights: towards a non-coercive and participatory model of accountability' (2009) 69 *ZaöRV* 2009 471, 474; Glas 2016 (n 710), pp. 48, 348; Keller and Marti 2016 (n 714), p. 835.

715 On this development, see also G. Ress, 'The effect of decisions and judgments of the European Court of Human Rights in the domestic legal order' (2005) 40 *Texas International Law Journal* 359; L. Caflisch, 'New practice regarding the implementation of the judgments of the Strasbourg Court' (2005) 15 *Italian Yearbook of International Law* 3; Colandrea 2007 (n 714); Abdelgawad 2009 (n 714); L.A. Sicilianos, 'The involvement of the European Court of Human Rights in the implementation of its judgments: recent developments under Article 46 ECHR' (2014) 32 *Netherlands Quarterly of Human Rights* 235; Keller and Marti 2016 (n 714); L.R. Glas, 'The European Court of Human Rights supervising the execution of its judgments' (2019) 37 *Netherlands Quarterly of Human Rights* 228. Cf. Donald and Speck who found that the use of specifying remedial measures 'has – contrary to some perceptions – not increased in recent years but rather fluctuates year-by-year' (A. Donald and A.K. Speck, 'The European Court of Human Rights' remedial practice and its impact on the execution of judgments' (2019) 19 *Human Rights Law Review* 83, 87ff).

716 *Papamichalopoulos and Others v. Greece* (just satisfaction) App No 14556/89 (ECtHR 31 October 1995).

found a breach'[717], it indicated in its reasoning, and repeated in the operative provisions of the judgment, that the respondent State should return the property to the applicants or, failing such restitution, should pay compensation.[718] That the Court repeated the individual measures to be taken by the respondent State in the operative provisions meant that these measures were not merely a recommendation. This is because, unlike measures indicated in the reasoning, measures indicated in the operative provisions of a Court judgment create legal obligations for and bind the respondent State.[719] Research has shown, however, that, for the Execution Department and the Committee of Ministers, there is no major material difference between specific measures indicated in the Court's reasoning and specific measures indicated in the operative provisions. Consequently, the Committee of Ministers is likely to close its supervision of a certain case only when the State has taken not only the prescribed measures, but also the indicated or recommended measures.[720] For the follow-up at the national level, therefore, the Court's recommendations and findings always matter, regardless of whether they form part of the official obligations imposed through the dictum or are merely concrete recommendations made by the Court based on Article 46 ECHR or as part of its reasoning in the case.

Verticalised cases, in particular family life cases concerning custody and access rights, provide some examples of cases in which the Court has indicated such specific measures. In *Görgülü*, for example, the Court held that, in order to discharge its legal obligation under Article 46, the respondent State should make it 'possible for the applicant to at least have access to his child'.[721] Meanwhile in *V.A.M.* the Court held that '[t]he government shall …, by appropriate means, enforce the interim access order of 23 July 1999 and bring to a conclusion, with particular diligence, the ongoing civil proceedings'.[722] However, the Court did not repeat these measures in the operative provisions of the judgment. The case of *Gluhaković*[723], on the other hand, is an example of a case in which the Court did include the specific measures in the operative provisions. This case concerned the complaint of a divorced father who was unable to

717 *Papamichalopoulos and Others v. Greece* (just satisfaction) App No 14556/89 (ECtHR 31 October 1995), para. 34.

718 *Papamichalopoulos and Others v. Greece* (just satisfaction) App No 14556/89 (ECtHR 31 October 1995), paras. 38–39 merits and paras. 2–3 operative provisions. See also *Brumărescu v. Romania* (just satisfaction) App No 28342/95 (ECtHR (GC) 23 January 2001), paras. 1–2 operative provisions; *Vasiliu v. Romania* App No 29407/95 (ECtHR 21 May 2002), paras. 4–5 operative provisions. On restitution as a remedy for human rights violations, including the *Papamichalopoulos* and *Brumărescu* cases, see also A. Buyse, *Post-conflict housing restitution: the European human rights perspective, with a case study on Bosnia and Herzegovina*, Intersentia 2008.

719 Sicilianos 2014 (n 715), p. 246; Glas 2016 (n 710), p. 392; D. Harris, M. O'Boyle, E. Bates, C. Buckley, *Harris, O'Boyle and Warbrick: Law of the European Convention on Human Rights*, Oxford University Press 2018 (4th edition), p. 171. Judges, however, sometimes disagree on the precise legal effect of measures indicated in the reasoning versus measures indicated in the operative part (see also Donald and Speck 2019 (n 715), p. 85).

720 Glas 2016 (n 710), p. 392. See also Sicilianos 2014 (n 715), p. 245.

721 *Görgülü v. Germany* App No 74969/01 (ECtHR 26 February 2004), para. 64.

722 *V.A.M. v. Serbia* App No 39177/05 (ECtHR 13 March 2007), para. 166.

723 *Gluhaković v. Croatia* App No 21188/09 (ECtHR 12 April 2011).

exercise his right to contact with his daughter. Given the particular circumstances of the case and the urgent need to end the violation, the Court included as an operative provision that the respondent State 'shall secure effective contact between the applicant and his daughter'.[724] The Court's prescribing of this specific measure in the operative provisions meant the respondent State was legally bound to enforce it. In *Görgülü* and *V.A.M.*, the respondent State had more freedom, at least in theory, to decide how to execute the Court's judgment. As mentioned above, however, the Committee of Ministers is still likely to take account of the particular phrasing of the Court's finding regarding Article 46 when monitoring the national measures and decisions.

In addition to these family life cases, the case of *Orlović and Others*[725] provides an example of another type of verticalised case in which the Court indicated specific measures in its reasoning and, like in *Gluhaković*, repeated the specific measures in the operative provisions. The applicants in this case had been forced to flee their home during the 1992–1995 Bosnian war. After the war, at the request of the Drinjača Serbian Orthodox Parish, a part of the applicants' land had been expropriated and allocated to the parish for building a church. Although it was established that the applicants were entitled to repossess the land, their efforts to regain full possession had been unsuccessful and the church continued to stand on their land. Reasoning that the violation found in the applicants' case did not leave any real choice as to the measures required to remedy it, the Court ordered, in the operative provisions, that the church should be removed from the applicants' land within three months from the date on which the judgment became final.[726]

Finally, having regard to the arguments put forward by Wojtyczek and Bürli, it should be mentioned that the Court has not yet prescribed the reopening of domestic civil proceedings in the operative provisions of a judgment in a verticalised case.[727] In the case of *Jäggi*, for example, the applicant asked the Court to find that he was entitled to a reopening of the proceedings in the relevant Swiss courts in order to secure his right to establish his parentage.[728] The Court, however, did not follow the applicant's request, but held instead that 'the respondent State remains free to choose the means by which it will discharge its legal obligation under Article 46'.[729] In the case of *Verein gegen Tierfabriken Schweiz (No. 2)* the Court also reasoned that it did

---

724 *Gluhaković v. Croatia* App No 21188/09 (ECtHR 12 April 2011), para. 89 merits and para. 3 operative provisions.

725 *Orlović and Others v. Bosnia and Herzegovina* App No 16332/18 (ECtHR 1 October 2019).

726 *Orlović and Others v. Bosnia and Herzegovina* App No 16332/18 (ECtHR 1 October 2019), para. 4(a) operative provisions. See also paras. 70–71 of the reasoning. Judge Kjølbro voted against this specific point of the operative provisions, arguing that it should be left to the domestic authorities to choose the appropriate measures. This is discussed further in Section 2.1.2 below.

727 Incidentally, however, the Court has prescribed the reopening of criminal proceedings in the operative provisions of its judgment (see, for example, *Maksimov v. Azerbaijan* App No 38288/05 (ECtHR 8 October 2009), para. 3 operative provisions) or the reopening of civil proceedings in the operative provisions of a judgment in a non-verticalised case (see, for example, *Lungoci v. Romania* App No 62710/00 (ECtHR January 2006), para. 3(a) operative provisions).

728 *Jäggi v. Switzerland* App No 58757/00 (ECtHR 13 July 2006), para. 59.

729 *Jäggi v. Switzerland* App No 58757/00 (ECtHR 13 July 2006), para. 60.

not have jurisdiction to order measures such as the reopening of proceedings[730], but at the same time acknowledged the importance of such an individual measure by holding that 'the reopening of proceedings ... is simply a means – albeit a key means – that may be used for a particular purpose, namely the full and proper execution of the Court's judgments'.[731] The importance of the individual measure of reopening domestic proceedings after a judgment of the Court is further illustrated by a recommendation of the Committee of Ministers of the Council of Europe, in which it advises Convention States to adopt provisions in their national legal systems for reopening civil and criminal proceedings after a judgment of the Court.[732] According to the Committee of Ministers, reopening proceedings after a judgment of the Court is sometimes the most efficient, if not the only, means of achieving *restitutio in integrum*.[733]

Although the cases described clearly show that, on some occasions, the Court indicates specific measures in its reasoning, and sometimes even repeats these measures in the operative provisions, it should be noted that this approach remains the exception to the rule.[734] In by far the majority of cases, it is left up to the respondent State to choose the appropriate measures to remove the consequences of the wrongful act and to ensure that the domestic legal order is consistent with the Convention. Generally, the Court will formulate a specific measure only if the violation is such that it excludes any choice as to the means of reparation open to the State.[735] In practice, this means that specific measures are mainly applied in cases concerning unlawful expropriating of property, unfair trials and unlawful detentions of individuals by the State.[736]

---

730 *Verein gegen Tierfabriken Schweiz v. Switzerland (No 2)* App No 32772/02 (ECtHR (GC) 30 June 2009), para. 89.

731 *Verein gegen Tierfabriken Schweiz v. Switzerland (No 2)* App No 32772/02 (ECtHR (GC) 30 June 2009), para. 90.

732 Committee of Ministers 19 January 2000, Recommendation No. R. 2000 (2) of the Committee of Ministers to member states on the re-examination or reopening of certain cases at the domestic level following judgments of the European Court of Human Rights. The ECtHR explicitly subscribed to this recommendation in *Bochan v. Ukraine (No. 2)* App No 22252/08 (ECtHR (GC) 5 February 2015), para. 58.

733 Committee of Ministers 19 January 2000, Recommendation No. R. 2000 (2), Explanatory Memorandum, para. 3. Achieving *restitutio in integrum* is about putting the applicant, as far as possible, in the position he would have been in had the requirements of the Convention not been disregarded. For a discussion of this recommendation see also L.A. Sicilianos, 'La tierce intervention devant la Cour Européenne des Droits de l'Homme' in H. Ruiz Fabri and J.M. Sorel (eds.), *La tiers à l'instance devant les juridictions internationales,* Pedone 2005, pp. 123–150, pp. 133–134. According to Sicilianos, it is reasonable to expect that, eventually, the recommendation will result in an increase of requests for third-party intervention by persons who were involved in the conflict at the domestic level.

734 Colandrea 2007 (n 714), p. 411; Jahn 2014 (n 714), p. 15; Glas 2016 (n 710), p. 385; Sicilianos 2014 (n 715), p. 243; Donald and Speck 2019 (n 715), p. 92.

735 Coloandrea 2007 (n 714), p. 411. See also *Guerra and Others v. Italy* App No 14967/89 (ECtHR (GC) 19 February 1998); *Fadeyeva v. Russia* App No 55723/00 (ECtHR 9 June 2005); *Giacomelli v. Italy* App No 59909/00 (ECtHR 2 November 2006) in which the Court rejected the applicant's request to indicate specific measures.

736 P. Leach, 'No longer offering fine mantras to a parched child? The European Court's developing approach to remedies' in A. Føllesdal, B. Peters, G. Ulfstein (eds.), *Constituting Europe: the European*

2.1.2. *Impact of the indication of specific measures on the disappeared party*

Although the Court does not directly adjudicate on the rights of the disappeared party, the examples of cases discussed in the previous section illustrate that a judgment of the Court may have an impact on the disappeared party, depending on the extent to which, and the way in which, the Court indicates or even prescribes specific measures in its judgment. In other words, the extent to which an indirect effect may manifest itself for the disappeared party does not depend only on the execution measures taken by the respondent State, but may already be determined by the approach taken by the Court in indicating specific measures, as explained in more detail below.

In the previous section, it was shown that the Court may indicate specific measures in its reasoning, and sometimes even repeat these in the operative part of the judgment. It can also formulate these measures in different ways, leaving little or much freedom to the respondent State. If, for example, the Court indicates in the operative provisions of the judgment that the respondent State shall ensure effective contact between the applicant and his daughter, or that property should be returned to the applicant within a certain period, little freedom is left to the respondent State in the execution process. More specifically, the respondent State must act accordingly and has little room to act otherwise by, for example, taking account of the interests of the third party involved in the domestic proceedings. If, on the other hand, the Court suggests only in its reasoning that reopening the domestic proceedings may be the best way to execute the Court's judgment, the respondent State remains free to choose the appropriate measures and, as a result, the domestic authorities will have more room to consider the rights and interests of the relevant third party when executing the judgment. This was also emphasised in the partly dissenting opinion of Judge Kjølbro in the case of *Orlović and Others*. As explained in the previous section, the Court ordered, in the operative provisions of this judgment, that the church was to be removed from the applicants' land within three months after the judgment became final. Kjølbro voted against this specific point in the operative provisions[737], arguing that, by ordering this specific measure, the Court had *de facto* ruled on a dispute between two private parties; that is, the applicants and the parish. Since the parish was not a party to the proceedings before the Court and had not had a chance to express its views and defend its interests, Kjølbro argued that it should have been left to the domestic courts to decide how to resolve the dispute between the applicants and the parish. The balancing of the applicants' rights and interests could have taken place in these domestic proceedings.[738] According to Kjølbro, therefore, the Court should only have suggested that the best way to execute the Court's judgment was either to remove the church and return the property or to pay

---

Court of Human Rights in a national, European and global context, Cambridge University Press 2013, pp. 142–180, p. 149.

737 Partly Dissenting Opinion Judge Kjølbro in *Orlović and Others v. Bosnia and Herzegovina* App No 16332/18 (ECtHR 1 October 2019), para. 1.

738 Partly Dissenting Opinion Judge Kjølbro in *Orlović and Others v. Bosnia and Herzegovina* App No 16332/18 (ECtHR 1 October 2019), paras. 2–6.

compensation representing the actual value of the land, with the domestic authorities being left to choose the appropriate measure.[739]

2.2. EXECUTION PROCESS: PRACTICE AT THE DOMESTIC LEVEL

Moving beyond the Court's judgment, this section examines the execution of verticalised cases, i.e. the practice at the domestic level, and potential problems that may arise in this regard for the disappeared party. This is done by analysing the execution process in the verticalised cases that were originally analysed to gain insight into the characteristics of verticalised cases and the Court's approach to them. As explained in Chapter 1, this sample comprises cases related to one's surroundings, right to reputation and private life versus freedom of expression cases, family life cases, and employer-employee cases. Between 15 and 25 judgments were analysed for each type of case, amounting to an overall sample of nearly 80 judgments.[740] For these cases, documents of the Committee of Ministers of the Council of Europe on the execution of judgments – more specifically, resolutions, action plans and action reports – were studied to obtain insight into the specific measures taken by Convention States when executing judgments of the Court in verticalised cases.[741] This analysis focused on whether proceedings were reopened or new proceedings were initiated, given the above-mentioned argument put forward by Bürli, Nussberger and Wojtyczek on the effects for the disappeared party of reopening or initiating new domestic proceedings after a judgment of the Court. The information provided by the Committee of Ministers allows for providing more clarity on the use made of this opportunity in practice and its effects on the disappeared party.

Before the results of the analysis are presented, it should be mentioned that not all Convention States allow civil proceedings to be reopened after a judgment of the Court. Information from 2015 shows that around half of the Convention States allow proceedings to be reopened following a Court judgment[742], based either on general or on specific provisions governing the reopening of civil proceedings following a judgment of the Court.[743] Convention States that do not allow civil proceedings to be

739 Partly Dissenting Opinion Judge Kjølbro in *Orlović and Others v. Bosnia and Herzegovina* App No 16332/18 (ECtHR 1 October 2019), para. 13.

740 For a more detailed description of the methodology, in particular the selection of the cases, see Chapter 1 (Section 4).

741 These documents can be accessed at: www.hudoc.exec.coe.int.

742 Council of Europe (Committee of Experts on the Reform of the Court (DH-GDR), Overview of the exchange of views held at the 8th meeting (27–29 May 2015 of DH-GDR on the provision in the domestic legal order for the re-examination or reopening of cases following judgments of the Court (DH-GDR (2015)008 Rev), para. 14.

743 Council of Europe (Committee of Experts on the Reform of the Court (DH-GDR), Overview of the exchange of views held at the 8th meeting (27–29 May 2015 of DH-GDR on the provision in the domestic legal order for the re-examination or reopening of cases following judgments of the Court (DH-GDR (2015)008 Rev), para. 15.

reopened after a judgment of the Court have expressed concerns regarding *res judicata*, legal certainty, and third-party protection.[744] Austria, for example, stated that 'bearing in mind the effects a reopening of civil proceedings might have on third parties, there are no specific provisions providing for a reopening of civil proceedings'.[745] Similarly, Poland argued against amending the law so as to allow reopening of civil proceedings by stating that 'civil proceedings are of a particular nature as compared to criminal or administrative court proceedings; a departure from the principle of *res judicata* in such proceedings could affect relations between the parties and the burden of such departure would be shifted to third parties' and that 'third parties do not participate in proceedings before the ECtHR and are deprived of a possibility to defend their interests in these proceedings'.[746] Similarly, the Netherlands submitted that:

> if provisions were made for overturning judgments in cases in which judgments of the Court have found a breach of the Convention, the effect would be to produce a lack of legal certainty for the parties to the proceedings and any third parties until the moment at which the Court decides whether or not to overturn the judgments.[747]

It should be stressed that the concerns described above are expressed in relation to the *reopening* of domestic proceedings, and that it may still be possible to initiate new proceedings in these Convention States, given that concerns relating, for example, to *res judicata* and legal certainty do not apply in newly initiated cases, such as civil proceedings in which the State is held liable for the damages suffered by the victim of the Convention violation. Indeed, in some States that have expressed concerns about reopening domestic proceedings because of third-party interests, initiating such tort proceedings is considered an alternative remedy.[748] However, the results presented

---

[744] Council of Europe (Committee of Experts on the Reform of the Court (DH-GDR), Overview of the exchange of views held at the 8th meeting (27–29 May 2015) of DH-GDR on the provision in the domestic legal order for the re-examination or reopening of cases following judgments of the Court, DH-GDR (2015)008 Rev, para. 15.

[745] Council of Europe (Committee on Experts on the Reform of the Court (DH-GDR)), Compilation of written contributions on the provision in the domestic legal order for re-examination or reopening of cases following judgments of the Court, DH-GDR(2015)002Rev (last update 31 March 2016), p. 8.

[746] Council of Europe (Committee on Experts on the Reform of the Court (DH-GDR)), Compilation of written contributions on the provision in the domestic legal order for re-examination or reopening of cases following judgments of the Court, DH-GDR(2015)002Rev (last update 31 March 2016), p. 74.

[747] Council of Europe (Committee on Experts on the Reform of the Court (DH-GDR)), Compilation of written contributions on the provision in the domestic legal order for re-examination or reopening of cases following judgments of the Court, DH-GDR(2015)002Rev (last update 31 March 2016), p. 68.

[748] This possibility exists, for example, in the Netherlands, which submitted this option as an alternative for providing a judicial remedy in civil cases (Council of Europe (Committee on Experts on the Reform of the Court (DH-GDR)), Compilation of written contributions on the provision in the domestic legal order for re-examination or reopening of cases following judgments of the Court, DH-GDR(2015)002Rev (last update 31 March 2016), p. 68). On initiating tort proceedings against the State as an alternative remedy in cases that cannot be reopened because of third-party interests see also T. Barkhuysen and M. van Emmerik, 'A comparative view on the execution of judgments of the European Court of Human Rights' in T. Christou and J.P. Raymond (eds.), *European Court of Human*

below illustrate that newly initiated proceedings may also be brought against the party to the original proceedings.

2.2.1. *Cases related to one's surroundings*

In fourteen of the cases related to one's surroundings examined for this study the Court found a violation of the Convention. In none of these cases was the Court's judgment followed by civil domestic proceedings.[749] Instead, it appears that in these cases the respondent State took general rather than specific measures to discharge its legal obligation under Article 46 ECHR. In cases, for example, on pollution by a privately operated plant, the breach was usually ended by introducing and enforcing stricter legislation. Indeed, in the case of *Cordella and Others*, which concerned air pollution by a steel plant, the Committee of Ministers noted that:

> individual measures in this case are strictly linked to and dependent on the adoption of the general measures which are necessary for the protection of the population from the environmental pollution caused by the steel plant.[750]

This need for such general measures to remedy the violation explains why the reopening of domestic proceedings may be less useful in such cases. In this regard, it should also be noted that although general measures are primarily about the obligation to prevent future violations, they may also be necessary and used to end an individual continuing violation.[751]

2.2.2. *Right to reputation and private life versus freedom of expression cases*

In fourteen of the cases analysed for this study and involving a conflict between the right to reputation and private life versus the right to freedom of expression, the Court found a violation. Although the respondent government in four of these cases submitted that the proceedings could have been reopened after the Court's judgment, the applicant(s) did not make use of this opportunity.[752] This suggests that they were satisfied with the award of just satisfaction.

Rights. Remedies and execution of judgments, British Institute of International and Comparative Law 2005, pp. 1–23, p. 7.

749 In three of the cases examined for this study in which the Court found a violation, the execution procedure was still pending at the time of writing (December 2021) (*Fadeyeva v. Russia* App No 55723/00; *Cevrioglu v. Turkey* App No 69546/12; *Cordella and Others v. Italy* App No 54414/13).

750 *Cordella and Others v. Italy* App No 54414/13, Committee of Ministers, Notes 1369th DH meeting (03–05 March 2020). See also *Giacomelli v. Italy* App No 59909/00, Committee of Ministers, Action report submitted by the Italian government (DH-DD(2014)898, 2 July 2014). Execution of this judgment is still pending. The Committee of Ministers has expressed concerns that a dangerous situation continues to persist.

751 Glas 2016 (n 710), p. 209 with reference to Rule 6(2)(b) for the supervision of the execution of judgments and of the terms of friendly settlements.

752 *Von Hannover v. Germany (No. 1)* App No 59320/00, Committee of Ministers, ResDH(2007)124, adopted on 31 October 2007; *Axel Springer AG v. Germany* App No 39954/08, Committee of

2.2.3. *Family life cases*

The Court also found a violation in sixteen of the family life cases analysed for this study. In two of these cases, the children had reached the age of majority by the time the Court's judgment was executed, thus making it no longer necessary to reopen domestic proceedings.[753] This also applied in three other cases, in which the matter had already been settled during the Court's proceedings.[754] In four of the cases in which the Court had found a violation of the Convention, however, the Court's judgment was followed by domestic proceedings.[755] In *Salgueiro da Silva Mouta*[756] and *Godelli*[757] the applicants lodged a new application before the domestic courts to enforce the Court's judgment. In both cases, this proved successful, with the applicants in the new domestic proceedings being granted custody and access rights[758] and access to information about the applicant's biological mother[759], respectively. In the case of *Görgülü,* which is discussed in more detail in Section 3.1, the applicant attempted to

---

Ministers, Action report submitted by the German government (DH-DD(2017)17, 9 January 2017), ResDH(2017)137, adopted on 10 May 2017; *Ageyevy v. Russia* App No 7075/10, Committee of Ministers, Communication by the Russian government (DH-DD(2014)1002, 28 Augustus 2014); *Rubio Dosamantes v. Spain* App No 20996/10, Committee of Ministers, Communication from the Spanish government (DH-DD(2018)284, 20 March 2018). In three cases the execution proceedings were still pending at the time of writing (December 2021) (*Petro Carbo Chem S.E. v. Romania* App No 21768/12; *Gheorghe-Florin Popescu v. Romania* App No 79671/13; *Budinova and Chaprazov v. Bulgaria* App No 12567/13).

753 *Ignaccolo-Zenide v. Romania* App No 31679/96, Committee of Ministers, Action report submitted by the Romanian government (DH-DD(2015)1001, 2 October 2015), ResDH(2015)185, adopted on 4 November 2015; *Milovanovic v. Serbia* App No 56065/10, Committee of Ministers, Action report submitted by the Serbian government (DH-DD(2020)1153, 11 December 2020), ResDH(2021)20, adopted on 3 February 2021. In *Ignaccolo-Zenide* one of the two children had turned eighteen by the time of the Court's judgment, while the other child reached the age of majority twenty months after the judgment.

754 *Mikulić v. Croatia* App No 53176/99, Committee of Ministers, Appendix to Resolution ResDH(2006)69, adopted on 20 December 2006 (Information about the measures to comply with the judgment in the case of Mikulić against Croatia); *Bevacqua and S. v. Bulgaria* App No 71127/01, Committee of Ministers, Action report submitted by the Bulgarian government (DH-DD(2012)922, 8 October 2012); *Mijušković v. Montenegro* App No 49337/07, Committee of Ministers, Action report submitted by the government of Montenegro (DH-DD(2016)805, 6 July 2016).

755 In *A.M.M. v. Romania* App No 2151/10 (concerning paternity proceedings) the government submitted that the Code of Civil Procedure allowed for proceedings to be reopened following an ECtHR judgment finding a violation. Yet no further information is provided as to whether proceedings were indeed reopened (Committee of Ministers, Action report submitted by the Romanian government (DH-DD(2013)55)). In three of the cases examined in which the Court found a violation, the execution of the Court's judgment was still pending at the time of writing (December 2021) (*Petrov and X v. Russia* App No 23608/16 (ECtHR 23 October 2018); *Koychev v. Bulgaria* App No 32495/15 (ECtHR 13 October 2020); *A.M. and Others v. Russia* App No 47220/19 (ECtHR 6 July 2021).

756 *Salgueiro da Silva Mouta v. Portugal* App No 33290/96 (ECtHR 21 December 1999).

757 *Godelli v. Italy* App No 33783/09 (ECtHR 25 September 2012).

758 *Salgueiro da Silva Mouta v. Portugal* App No 33290/96, Committee of Ministers, Appendix to ResDH(2007)89, adopted on 20 June 2007.

759 *Godelli v. Italy* App No 33783/09, Committee of Ministers, Action report submitted by the Italian government (DH-DD(2015)999, 2 October 2015) and ResDH(2015)176, adopted on 4 November 2015.

enforce the Court's judgment by invoking this judgment in the domestic custody and access proceedings that had continued during the Court's proceedings. The Court had held in its reasoning in this case that in order to discharge its legal obligation under Article 46, the respondent State should make it possible for the applicant to at least have access to his child and, after lengthy proceedings at the domestic level, the applicant was granted custody and access rights.[760] Finally, in the case of *Jäggi*[761], the applicant lodged an application for revision with the Federal Court, followed by proceedings at a first-instance court in which the applicant asked for authorisation to proceed with a DNA test to establish paternity.[762] Although Swiss law allows for domestic civil proceedings to be reopened after a judgment of the Court, it is not clear from the documents provided by the Committee of Ministers whether the procedure before the first-instance court concerned the reopening of proceedings or the initiation of new proceedings. In any event, these domestic proceedings proved to be successful for the applicant as they led to the ordering of a DNA test, followed by the establishing of paternity.[763] In *Gluhaković*, in which the Court had prescribed in the operative provisions that the respondent State should secure effective contact between the applicant and his daughter, the Court's judgment was not followed by domestic proceedings. Instead, the local welfare centre worked intensively to secure contacts between the applicant and his daughter, resulting in significant progress in this regard.[764] Finally, mention can be made of the case of *Petrov and X*, in which the Court found a violation of the Convention regarding the domestic courts' refusal to make a residence order in favour of a father and his son. Although the execution of the Court's judgment was still pending at the time of writing, it follows from information submitted to the Committee of Ministers by the applicant that the domestic courts have so far refused his request to reopen the domestic proceedings.[765] The domestic courts justified this decision by holding that 'the Convention violation[s] found … are not crucial for correct handling the civil case because these violations are of a pure procedural character and do not influence the essence of the family case', 'legal certainty presupposes respect for the principle of *res judicata*, that is the principle of the finality of judgments', and the applicant 'has a right to open new proceedings and to ask for a residence order in respect of his child in a

760 *Görgülü v. Germany* App No 74969/01, Committee of Ministers, Appendix to ResDH(2009)4, adopted on 9 January 2009.

761 *Jäggi v. Switzerland* App No 58757/00 (ECtHR 13 July 2006).

762 *Jäggi v. Switzerland* App No 58757/00, Committee of Ministers, Appendix to ResDH(2010)114, adopted on 15 September 2010.

763 *Jäggi v. Switzerland* App No 58757/00, Committee of Ministers, Appendix to ResDH(2010)114, adopted on 15 September 2010.

764 *Gluhakovic v. Croatia* App No 21188/09, Committee of Ministers, Action plan and report submitted by the Croatian government (DH-DD(2011)955) and ResDH(2013)225, adopted on 20 November 2013.

765 *Petrov and X v. Russia* App No 23608/16, Committee of Ministers, Communication from the applicant, DH-DD(2019)388 (June 2019); DH-DD(2019)776 (September 2019). Article 392 of the Russian Code of Civil Procedure allows for a case to be reopened following a Court judgment in which a violation of the Convention was found.

new case'.[766] Following this decision, the applicant asked the Committee of Ministers to provide an opinion on the question as to whether the Court's judgment implied that the domestic proceedings should be reopened. In his opinion, the decision by the domestic courts violated Article 46 ECHR.[767] The applicant, submitted, inter alia, that 'the opening of a new procedure regarding the residence order … without quashing the domestic judgment of 2014 is not a restoration of a *status quo* breached by the domestic court in 2014'.[768] In this regard, the applicant claimed that:

> [t]he domestic judgment of 2014 has a prejudicial influence on the parties, i.e. it has a binding effect to all possible future procedures regarding facts found by the domestic court … and according to Russian case-law regarding the scope of the case and the best interest of the child interpretation.[769]

This illustrates the importance for the applicant of reopening domestic proceedings after the Court's judgment in a verticalised family life case and the possible effects of such reopening for the original party to the conflict at the domestic level; that is, for the disappeared party.

2.2.4. Employer-employee cases

Lastly, the Court found a violation in nine of the employer-employee cases examined for this study.[770] In two of these cases, individual follow-up measures were not considered necessary as the applicants had either stopped working for the same employer or were no longer obliged to join a trade union[771], or had settled the matter with the employer and returned to employment during the Court's proceedings.[772] In one of the cases in which the Court found a violation, the domestic proceedings were reopened at the request of the applicant. This was the *Heinisch* case[773], concerning an applicant who had been dismissed by her employer after she had acted as a whistle-blower. In this case, the Court had found a violation of Article 10 ECHR on the grounds that the dismissal

766 *Petrov and X v. Russia* App No 23608/16, Committee of Ministers, Communication from the applicant, DH-DD(2019)776 (September 2019).

767 *Petrov and X v. Russia* App No 23608/16, Committee of Ministers, Communication from the applicant, DH-DD(2019)388 (June 2019); DH-DD(2019)776 (September 2019).

768 *Petrov and X v. Russia* App No 23608/16, Committee of Ministers, Communication from the applicant, DH-DD(2019)776 (September 2019), p. 2.

769 *Petrov and X v. Russia* App No 23608/16, Committee of Ministers, Communication from the applicant, DH-DD(2019)776 (September 2019), p. 2.

770 In one of the cases examined, the execution was still pending at the time of writing (December 2021) (*Herbai v. Hungary* App No 11608/5 (ECtHR 5 November 2019)). Another case has been referred to the Grand Chamber (*Halet v. Luxembourg* App No 21884/18 (ECtHR 11 May 2021)).

771 *Sørensen and Rasmussen v. Denmark* App Nos 52562/99 and 52620/99, Committee of Ministers, Appendix to Resolution CM/ResDH(2007)6, adopted on 28 February 2007 (Information about the measures to comply with the judgment in the case of Sørensen and Rasmussen against Denmark).

772 *Eweida and Others v. the United Kingdom,* App No 48420/10, Committee of Ministers, (Revised) Action report submitted by the UK government (DH-DD(2013)1360, 18 December 2013).

773 *Heinisch v. Germany* App No 28274/08 (ECtHR 21 July 2011).

without notice had been disproportionate and the domestic courts had failed to strike a fair balance between the employer's right to reputation and the employee's right to freedom of expression. Hence, the Court ordered the respondent State to pay the applicant just satisfaction, but did not indicate or prescribe a specific measure such as the reopening of domestic proceedings. The subsequent reopening of the proceedings at the applicant's request resulted in a judicial settlement in which the employer agreed to pay the employee pecuniary compensation in the amount of 90,000 euros and to give the employee a work reference.[774] In another case in which the Court had found a violation – the case of *Schüth*, concerning the dismissal of a church employee – the applicant requested the reopening of the domestic proceedings after the Court's judgment.[775] Interestingly, the Court had suggested in this case that reopening the domestic proceedings would be an appropriate way of offering redress.[776] The request, however, was refused by the domestic courts on the grounds that a new law allowing proceedings to be reopened applied only to proceedings that had been concluded with final and binding effect since September 2006.[777] Finally, in the case of *Bărbulescu*, which concerned an employer's monitoring of an employee's communications, the Court held that the finding of a violation constituted just satisfaction in itself.[778] In this case, the government submitted to the Committee of Ministers that the applicant had the opportunity to request a review of the final domestic decision in the light of the Court's judgment.[779] However, no further information was provided on whether the applicants actually made use of the opportunity to reopen proceedings.

2.3. CONCLUSION

It follows from the above that in only one of the verticalised cases examined for this study were domestic proceedings reopened after the Court's judgment, while in two cases a request to reopen proceedings was refused by the domestic courts. A judgment of the Court in a verticalised case can also be followed by domestic proceedings being continued or new proceedings being initiated, examples of which can be found in the family life cases examined for this study. Regardless of whether the domestic proceedings were reopened, continued or newly initiated after the Court's judgment,

---

774 *Heinisch v. Germany* App No 28274/08, Committee of Ministers, Action report submitted by the German government (DH-DD(2013)813, 11 July 2013) and ResDH(2017)62, adopted on 22 February 2017.

775 *Schüth v. Germany* App No 30668/96, Committee of Ministers, Communication from the German government (DH-DD(2014)1412, 19 November 2014); ResDH(2014)264, adopted on 4 December 2014.

776 *Schüth v. Germany* App No 30668/96 (ECtHR 28 June 2012) (judgment on just satisfaction), para. 17.

777 *Schüth v. Germany* App No 30668/96, Committee of Ministers, Communication from the German government (DH-DD(2014)1412, 19 November 2014); ResDH(2014)264, adopted on 4 December 2014.

778 *Bărbulescu v. Romania* App No 61496/08 (ECtHR (GC) 5 September 2017), para. 2 operative provisions.

779 *Bărbulescu v. Romania* App No 61496/08, Committee of Ministers, Action report submitted by the Romanian government (DH-DD(2018)644, 22 June 2018); ResDH(2019)124, adopted on 6 June 2019.

these subsequent proceedings all proved to be very successful for the applicants in the cases examined: they led to a financial settlement between an employer and an employee, to the granting of custody and access rights, to the ordering of a DNA test followed by the establishing of paternity, or to access to information about one's biological mother. Accordingly, these examples can be seen as supporting the above-mentioned views of Judge Wojtyczek and former Judge Nussberger. To reiterate briefly, Wojtyczek argued that a favourable judgment may be a valuable asset in future legal battles against the same litigants, while Nussberger wrote that reopening civil procedures, as well as new decisions in continuing situations, can – unexpectedly – turn those who won their case on the national level into losers. This also illustrates that a judgment of the Court may have an indirect effect on the rights and interests of the disappeared party. If, for example, custody or access rights are granted, or a DNA test is ordered and results in the establishing of paternity, based on the judgment of the Court, this necessarily affects the rights and interests of the disappeared party. This is important because the extent to which a third party is affected by a judgment is often considered an important factor in determining whether this party should be involved in the Court's proceedings.

3. IMPLICATIONS OF A JUDGMENT FOR CONVENTION STATES AND THE COURT ITSELF

So far, attention has been paid to possible problems that can manifest themselves after the Court's proceedings for the disappeared party. The current section moves on to look at the position of Convention States and the Court itself by subjecting the case of *Görgülü* to a detailed examination. This case is of special interest because it involved the German Federal Constitutional Court indicating problems that may arise for domestic courts having to apply and enforce a Court judgment in cases in which the original parties to the domestic proceedings are a party. In other words, it sheds light on problems that may manifest themselves for Convention States and the Court after the Court has handed down a judgment in a verticalised case.

The specific case discussed here concerns Mr Görgülü, who was the biological father of a child born out of wedlock. The biological mother had ended their relationship while she was pregnant and had given up their son for adoption immediately after giving birth. Görgülü had learned about his son's birth and the mother's decision to give the child up for adoption two months later. Since then, he had attempted to obtain custody of the child and to be granted access rights. These attempts, however, had proved to be unsuccessful: the domestic courts found that granting the father custody would not be in the child's best interests because of the deep social and emotional bond that had since evolved between the child and his foster family.[780] At the ECtHR the father had complained that the domestic court's decision to refuse him access to and custody

[780] For a summary of the domestic courts' reasoning see the judgment of the ECtHR (*Görgülü v. Germany*, App No 74969/01 (ECtHR 26 February 2004), paras. 8ff).

of his son violated his right to respect for his family life under Article 8 ECHR. The Court found a violation of the father's right to family life by holding that the domestic courts had not fulfilled their positive obligation to unite father and son. The Court also indicated in its reasoning that the respondent State should make it 'possible for the applicant to at least have access to his child'[781], as explained in Section 2.1.1.

The father subsequently attempted to enforce the Court's judgment by invoking it in the domestic custody and access proceedings that had continued during the Court's proceedings. Since one of the courts did not give effect to the ECtHR judgment[782], the case eventually came before the German Federal Constitutional Court (*Bundesverfassungsgericht*)[783], which focused on the question of whether the German domestic courts were bound by ECtHR judgments and, if so, what legal effects would this have. It concluded that, in principle and subject to certain conditions, the domestic courts are obliged to take ECtHR judgments into account.[784] In this regard, the *Bundesverfassungsgericht* reasoned as follows:

> [p]recisely in cases in which national courts, as in private law, have to structure multipolar fundamental rights situations, it is always important that various subjective legal positions are sensitively weighed against each other, and if there is a change in the persons involved in the dispute or a change in the actual or legal circumstances, this weighing up may lead to a different result. There may be constitutional problems if one of the subjects of fundamental rights in conflict with another obtains an ECHR judgment in his or her favour against the Federal Republic of Germany and German courts schematically apply this decision to the private law relationship, with the result that the holder of fundamental rights who has lost in this case and was possibly not involved in the proceedings at the ECHR would no longer be able to take an effective part in the proceedings as a party.[785]

This brought it to conclude that:

> [i]t is necessary for the national courts to evaluate the ECtHR decision when taking it into account; in this process, account may also be taken of the fact that the individual application proceedings before the ECHR, in particular where the original proceedings were in civil law,

---

781 ECtHR *Görgülü v. Germany* App No 74969/01 (ECtHR 26 February 2004), para. 64.

782 For a summary of the second instance court's reasoning see paras. 17–18 of BVerfGE, Order of the Second Senate of 14 October 2004, 2 BvR 1481/04 (*Görgülü*) (official English translation).

783 BVerfGE, Order of the Second Senate of 14 October 2004, 2 BvR 1481/04 (*Görgülü*) (official English translation). For an extensive analysis of this judgment see, for example, H.J. Cremer, 'Zur Bindungswirkung von EGMR-Urteilen – Anmerkung zum Görgülü-Beschluss des BVerfG vom 14.10.2004' (2004) 31 *Europäische Grundrechte-Zeitschrift* 683; S. Beljin, 'Bundesverfassungsgericht on the Status of the European Convention of Human Rights and ECHR Decisions in the German Legal Order. Decision of 14 October 2004' (2005) 1 *European Constitutional Law Review* 553; M. Hartwig, 'Much ado about human rights: the Federal Constitutional Court confronts the European Court of Human rights' (2005) 6 *German Law Journal* 869.

784 BVerfGE, Order of the Second Senate of 14 October 2004, 2 BvR 1481/04 (*Görgülü*) (official English translation), para. 29.

785 BVerfGE, Order of the Second Senate of 14 October 2004, 2 BvR 1481/04 (*Görgülü*) (official English translation), para. 50.

> possibly does not give a complete picture of the legal positions and interests involved. The only party to the proceeding before the ECHR apart from the complainant is the State party affected; the possibility for third parties to take part in the applications proceedings is not an institutional equivalent to the rights and duties as a party to proceedings or another party involved in the original national proceedings.[786]

Thus, the *Bundesverfassungsgericht* found it necessary for the domestic courts to evaluate the ECtHR judgment when taking it into account in a reopened or continued case between the original parties to the case. This means that, when reaching a decision, the domestic courts must make sure that all the relevant interests are taken into account, including the interests of the disappeared party in the case before the ECtHR – the foster parents in the case of *Görgülü*. The reason for this is that the ECtHR proceedings involved an applicant-State relationship, whereas the original proceedings and continued or reopened proceedings may involve different parties and may even be a multi-dimensional and multi-subject case. According, therefore, to the *Bundesverfassungsgericht*, the Court's judgments may not necessarily provide a complete picture of the legal positions and interests involved.

The reasoning of the *Bundesverfassungsgericht* illustrates that problems arising after the Court's proceedings do not manifest themselves solely for private actors, but also for Convention States[787], and that this can happen particularly in situations in which domestic courts have to apply and enforce an ECtHR judgment in a multi-dimensional and multi-subject case. To this day, the reasoning of the *Bundesverfassungsgericht* is often recalled.[788] In 2021, for example, two ECtHR judges referred in a joint concurring opinion to the judgment of the *Bundesverfassungsgericht*. They held that it should be kept in mind that the Court's judgments can have 'serious consequences in practice – both for third parties and for the authority of the Court's judgments, since this issue relates to the potential difficulties that national authorities may encounter at the stage of execution of the Court's decisions'. When making this point, they stated that this concern has been 'expressed in a straightforward manner by the German Federal Constitutional Court'.[789]

The concurring judges' reference to the 'authority of the Court's judgments' suggests that the difficulties for Convention States in enforcing and applying a judgment of the Court in a verticalised case may also affect the Court itself as part of the broader Convention system. In particular, it is problematic for the Court if domestic courts

786 BVerfGE, Order of the Second Senate of 14 October 2004, 2 BvR 1481/04 (*Görgülü*) (official English translation), para. 59.

787 See also Bürli 2017 (n 707), p. 180. Bürli held that 'the disregard of third-party interests might cause problems for respondent states in implementing the Court's judgment'.

788 See, for example, A. Nussberger, 'Subsidiarity in the Control of Decisions Based on Proportionality: An Analysis of the Basis of the Implementation of ECtHR judgments into German Law' in A. Seibert-Fohr and M. Villiger, *Judgments of the European Court of Human Rights: Effects and Implementation*, Nomos Verlagsgesellschaft 2014, pp. 165–185, p. 171; Bürli 2017 (n 707), p. 180; Pastor Vilanova 2019 (n 707), pp. 388–389; Nussberger 2020 (n 700), pp. 358ff.

789 Joint Concurring Opinion of Judges Ravarani and Elósegui in *A.M. and Others v. Russia*, App No 47220/19 (ECtHR 6 July 2021), para. 7.

become more hesitant about, or even refrain from, enforcing and applying a judgment of the Court in a verticalised case because of the Court's judgment not giving a complete picture of the legal positions and interests involved. Such reluctance not only has a negative impact on the effective implementation of Court judgments, but also affects the relationship between the Court and the domestic courts, even though this relationship is important for the functioning of the Convention system as a whole. In this regard, it is worth recalling the subsidiarity principle as one of the guiding Convention principles discussed in Chapter 3 (Section 3). According to this principle, the primary responsibility for implementing and enforcing the Convention lies with national authorities. The Court's role vis-à-vis the Convention States is a subsidiary, supervisory one. In the light of this, the Court and domestic courts have been said to have a 'shared responsibility' in protecting the Convention.[790] Gerards, for example, explained that although domestic courts 'have to make sure that the Court's case-law is implemented and respected in their own judgments and decisions and they have to make full use of their competences to secure compliance with the Convention', the Court also depends on 'constructive collaboration with the national courts and on the persuasiveness and quality of its interpretations'.[791] Having in mind this shared responsibility, it is important for the Court and the Convention States alike that domestic courts do not encounter difficulties when enforcing and applying a judgment of the Court in a verticalised case.

4. CONCLUSION

The above analysis presents a mixed picture. While the importance of the reopening of civil proceedings to offer redress for violations has clearly been stressed by the Court and the Committee of Ministers, and almost half of the Convention States actually offer this possibility in verticalised cases, the cases analysed also show that, in practice, domestic proceedings are not often reopened after a Court judgment in a verticalised case, although in some cases, particularly family life cases, a Court judgment is followed by continued or newly initiated domestic proceedings. Regardless of whether the domestic

790 On the notion of a 'shared responsibility', see further J.H. Gerards, 'The European Court of Human Rights and the national courts – giving shape to the notion of 'shared responsibility' in J.H. Gerards and J.W.A. Fleuren (eds.), *Implementation of the European Convention on Human Rights and of the judgments of the ECtHR in national case law. A comparative analysis*, Intersentia 2014, pp. 13–94. In the *Preliminary opinion of the Court in preparation of the Brighton Conference,* the Court held that '[a] key element in the process initiated at Interlaken has been increased recognition that responsibility for the effective operation of the Convention has to be shared' (*Preliminary opinion of the Court in preparation of the Brighton Conference,* adopted by the Plenary Court on 20 February 2012, para. 4). For an explicit reference to the notion of 'shared responsibility' in the Court's case law, see, for example, *Burmych and Others v. Ukraine* App No 46852/12 (ECtHR (GC) 12 October 2017), para. 218. According to Judge Raimondi (former President of the Court), the notion of a 'shared responsibility' lay at the heart of this judgment, and this made this case one of the leading judgments of 2017 (Annual report ECtHR 2018, p. 15). The notion of a 'shared responsibility' has also been endorsed by the Convention States, see, for example, Brussels Declaration 27 March 2015, p. 2; Copenhagen Declaration 13 April 2018, paras. 6ff.

791 Gerards 2014 (n 790), pp. 33–34.

proceedings after the Court's judgment are reopened, continued or newly initiated, the domestic proceedings examined proved to be very successful for the applicants at the Court, given that the national courts duly considered the Court's findings. Even if account is taken of the small size of the sample, a judgment of the Court would seem to be able to impact on the rights and interests of the disappeared party and result, for example, in custody or access rights being granted, or paternity being established.

The reasoning of the *Bundesverfassungsgericht* in the *Görgülü* case also shows that problems may arise when domestic courts have to apply and enforce a judgment of the Court in a case that has been verticalised so that it can be judged by the Court. As explained earlier, the reason for this is that the ECtHR proceedings involve an applicant-State relationship, whereas the original proceedings and any continued, reopened or newly initiated proceedings may involve different parties and may even be a multi-dimensional and multi-subject case. According, therefore, to the *Bundesverfassungsgericht,* it is possible that the Court's judgments do not give a complete picture of the legal positions and interests involved, and this may be unfair to the parties in the original case. This is also why Spain, for example, submitted that in cases where a possible reopening may affect third parties, the ECtHR should invite the parties to the proceedings to act as third-party interveners in accordance with Article 36(2) ECHR.[792] For the same reason, Germany now has legislation in place that prescribes that third parties must be informed by the government agent if it becomes apparent that their interests will be affected in the proceedings before the Court and that legal aid can be provided if this party wishes to appear before the Court.[793] Finally, Switzerland and the Republic of Moldova have both introduced legislation to enable the federal tribunal to invite each and every party to the original proceedings that have led to the application to the Court to give their written observations or oral pleadings when proceedings are reopened.[794] These examples show that some Convention States have taken measures to address problems that may arise after a judgment of the Court in a verticalised case, and specifically problems caused by the fact that the disappeared party was not involved in the Court's proceedings, and that the judgment of the Court may eventually have a strong impact on the legal situation at the domestic level.

---

792 Council of Europe (Committee on Experts on the Reform of the Court (DH-GDR)), Compilation of written contributions on the provision in the domestic legal order for re-examination or reopening of cases following judgments of the Court, DH-GDR(2015)002Rev (last update 31 March 2016), p. 108.

793 Council of Europe (Committee of Experts on the Reform of the Court (DH-GDR), Overview of the exchange of views held at the 8th meeting (27–29 May 2015) of DH-GDR on the provision in the domestic legal order for the re-examination or reopening of cases following judgments of the Court, DH-GDR (2015)008 Rev, para. 17(c). See the Assistance with Costs for Third Parties in Proceedings before the European Court of Human Rights Act of 20 April 2013.

794 Council of Europe (Committee of Experts on the Reform of the Court (DH-GDR), Overview of the exchange of views held at the 8th meeting (27–29 May 2015) of DH-GDR on the provision in the domestic legal order for the re-examination or reopening of cases following judgments of the Court, DH-GDR (2015)008 Rev, para. 17(c). With regard to Switzerland, see Article 127 Loi sur le tribunal fédéral which provides that '[p]our autant que le Tribunal fédéral ne considère pas la demande de révision comme irrecevable ou infondée, il la communique à l'autorité précédente ainsi qu'aux éventuels autres parties ou participants à la procédure, ou aux autorités qui ont qualité pour recourir; ce faisant, il leur impartit un délai pour se déterminer'.

CONCLUSION

The implications of verticalisation have been examined here in detail so as to establish the extent to which verticalised cases pose challenges to the Convention system. The previous two chapters focused on possible problems that may arise *during* the Court's proceedings with respect to verticalised cases, and possible problems that may arise *after* these proceedings, with attention being paid to implications of the Court's current approach to verticalised cases for private actors, for Convention States and for the Court itself. This conclusion summarises these findings, showing that verticalised cases do indeed have implications for all actors involved and therefore pose challenges to the Convention system.

Starting with possible problems manifesting themselves during the Court's proceedings, it is important, first, to point out that the implications for private actors, Convention States and the Court itself, all relate to the fact that, in verticalised cases, one of the original parties in the conflict at the domestic level is not involved in the Court's proceedings and thus disappears from the conflict. For private actors, this results in a situation in which the disappeared party is not able to defend or explain his acts, interests or rights unless he intervenes as a third party in the Court proceedings. This poses challenges to the Convention system because, with the exception of cases related to one's surroundings, these acts, interests or rights may be part of the Court's examination in a verticalised case. For example, the Court may scrutinise the acts of the disappeared party or explicitly consider that party's interests, without having any information provided by the disappeared party. This also implies that the Court may be confronted with a situation in which it has to examine a verticalised case without having a full and balanced account of the facts of the case and all the rights and interests at stake. This is not only problematic for private actors, but also for the Court itself. Furthermore, it may result in a situation in which Convention States are asked to defend the rights and interests of the disappeared party, while they may be unwilling to do so or incapable of such.

Second, it was shown that the fact that the disappeared party is not involved in the Court's proceedings not only gives rise to problems during the proceedings, but also to problems afterwards. This is because a Court judgment in a verticalised case may strongly impact on the legal situation at the domestic level. It was illustrated, for example, that reopening, continuing or initiating new domestic proceedings after a judgment of the Court in a verticalised case sometimes proved to be very successful for the applicant at the Court, such as when such applicant was granted custody or access rights, or able to establish paternity. The reasoning of the *Bundesverfassungsgericht* in the *Görgülü* case also showed that problems may arise when domestic courts have to apply and enforce a judgment of the Court in a case that has been verticalised so that it can be judged by the Court. As explained, this is because proceedings at the ECtHR involve an applicant-State relationship, whereas the original proceedings and any continued, reopened or newly initiated proceedings may involve different parties and may even be multi-dimensional and multi-subject. According, therefore, to the *Bundesverfassungsgericht,* the Court's judgments may not necessarily give a complete picture of the legal positions and interests involved, and this may make it difficult for domestic courts to apply and enforce a judgment of the Court in a verticalised case. This also affects the Court itself as part of the broader Convention system since it impacts on the relationship between the Court and domestic courts, while this relationship plays an important role in the functioning of the Convention system as a whole.

Clearly, thus, verticalised cases pose challenges to the Convention system. The final part of this study, therefore, considers measures that could be taken by the Court to address these challenges. In particular, attention is paid to the third-party intervention procedure and to possible ways to optimise this procedure so as to address the issues arising from verticalised cases. Based, however, on the findings in this current part of the research, it is taken into account that, besides private actors, the Convention States and the Court itself should be the focus of any solutions formulated for addressing the challenges arising from verticalised cases.

PART IV

TOWARDS A NEW APPROACH TO VERTICALISED CASES

INTRODUCTION

Building on the analyses provided in the first parts of this study, this final part contains a proposal for a new approach to verticalised cases. This aims to address the problems arising in such cases, as identified in Part III. To reiterate, these problems find their origins in the main characteristic of verticalised cases, whereby one of the original parties in the domestic conflict is not involved in the Court's proceedings and thus disappears. For private actors, this results in the 'disappeared party' not being able to defend or explain his acts, interests or rights, even though these may be part of the Court's examination and while this party may be affected by a judgment of the Court. This situation is not only problematic for private actors, but also for the Court and the Convention States: the Court may have to examine a case without having a full and balanced account of the facts and the rights and interests at stake, while Convention States may be asked to defend the rights and interests of the disappeared party even though they may be unwilling to do so or incapable of such. Domestic courts, moreover, may encounter problems when applying and enforcing a judgment of the Court in a verticalised case since this judgment may not necessarily give a complete picture of the legal positions and interests involved.

To address these problems in verticalised cases, it is proposed redesigning the third-party intervention procedure of Article 36 ECHR by granting third parties with a legal interest in the case ('actual third parties') a right to intervene in the Court's proceedings. The proposed procedural change will create a genuine and effective opportunity for the original party in the conflict at the domestic level to defend or explain his acts, interests or rights in the Court's proceedings. Although this suggests a focus on private actors' perspective, attention is also paid to the perspectives of Convention States and the Court, with an explanation of how redesigning the third-party intervention procedure will benefit these parties too. At the same time, practical aspects of the proposed new approach for Convention States and the Court are considered, including the implications for the Court's workload.

It follows from the above that the prime focus of the proposal for a new approach to verticalised cases is not the Court's review of verticalised cases as such, but rather the procedural framework. It is not proposed making one particular type of review (substantive, procedural, or a combination of the two) the standard in verticalised cases. A harmonised and uniform approach could admittedly seem an ideal solution in that it would acknowledge that verticalised cases are a specific and unique type of case brought before the Court and would give Convention States and applicants more clarity on how such cases are decided by the Court. In view, however, of the findings in the previous chapters – essentially, that the notion of verticalised cases covers a wide variety of cases, rooted in a variety of different horizontal conflicts at the domestic level, involving different relations between private actors, and relating to different Convention rights – a one-size-fits-all approach directed at the Court's review would be difficult to design, let alone apply in practice. It would also give the Court less room to tailor its review to the particular nature of the case before it. For these reasons, therefore, it has been chosen to propose a change in procedure only.

This part of the study starts with a description of the form and features of the current third-party intervention procedure of Article 36 ECHR (Chapter 9), followed by the proposal for redesigning this procedure (Chapter 10).

CHAPTER 9
CURRENT THIRD-PARTY INTERVENTION PROCEDURE

1. INTRODUCTION

As explained above, the proposal for a new approach to verticalised cases presented here is directed at the third-party intervention procedure. However, a proposal to redesign this procedure cannot be made without taking full account of the features of the current procedure. Hence, this chapter introduces the rules governing the procedure, the various forms of third-party intervention allowed under the Convention, and the current third-party intervention practice before the Court.[795] An overview of the current procedural requirements is presented in Section 2, followed by a discussion of the various forms of third-party intervention allowed under the Convention (Section 3), and, finally, a discussion of how third-party interventions influence the Court's case law (Section 4).

2. PROCEDURAL REQUIREMENTS

Before Protocol No. 11 to the Convention entered into force in 1998, the Convention did not contain a provision on third-party intervention, even though the Court had allowed a third party to intervene as early as 1979. This was in the case of *Winterwerp*[796], which concerned the compulsory confinement of a psychiatric patient. In this case against the Netherlands, the Court granted the United Kingdom leave to intervene on the basis of

795 For a detailed study of third-party interventions before the Court, see, for example, L. Bartholomeusz, 'The *Amicus Curiae* before International Courts and Tribunals' (2005) 5 *Non-State Actors and International Law* 209; L.A. Sicilianos, 'La tierce intervention devant la Cour Européenne des Droits de l'Homme' in H. Ruiz Fabri and J.M. Sorel (eds.), *La tiers à l'instance devant les juridictions internationales*, Pedone 2005, pp. 123–150; N. Bürli, *Third-party interventions before the European Court of Human Rights: Amicus Curiae, Member-State and Third-Party interventions*, Intersentia 2017. Bartholomeusz does not only provide a discussion of the third-party intervention procedure before the Court, but also of third-party intervention procedures before other international courts and tribunals.

796 *Winterwerp v. the Netherlands* App No 6301/73 (ECtHR 24 October 1979). See also *Young, James and Webster v. the United Kingdom* App Nos 7601/76 and 7806/77 (ECtHR 13 August 1981), concerning closed-shop agreements, in which the Court agreed to hear a representative of the British Trade Union Congress.

the Court's competence to 'hear as a witness or expert in any other capacity any person whose evidence or statements seem likely to assist in the carrying out of its task'.[797] In 1983, the Court provided a separate legal basis for third-party interventions in its Rules of Court. This was followed by the entering into force of Protocol No. 11 in 1998, which ensured that the third-party intervention procedure was codified in the Convention. The procedure is now laid down in Article 36 ECHR, which reads as follows:

1. In all cases before a Chamber or the Grand Chamber, a High Contracting Party one of whose nationals is an applicant shall have the right to submit written comments and to take part in hearings.
2. The President of the Court may, in the interest of the proper administration of justice, invite any High Contracting Party which is not a party to the proceedings or any person concerned who is not the applicant to submit written comments or take part in hearings.
3. In all cases before a Chamber or the Grand Chamber, the Council of Europe Commissioner for Human Rights may submit written comments and take part in hearings.[798]

It follows from Article 36 ECHR that the Convention allows three types of third-party intervention. First, Convention States have the right to intervene in cases in which the applicant is one of their nationals.[799] Second, any person concerned (whether it is a State, an individual or an organisation) is allowed to intervene if this is considered to be 'in the interest of the proper administration of justice'.[800] Third, the Council of Europe Commissioner for Human Rights may submit written comments and take part in hearings.[801] With regard to these different types of third-party intervention, it is important, first, to point out that, in contrast to the second type of third-party intervention, the first and third types of such interventions encompass a *right* to intervene. Third-party interveners in the second category, on the other hand, are not granted a right to intervene. Instead, this type of third-party intervention is permitted at the Court's discretion. It also follows from the text of Article 36 that third-party interventions are possible only in Chamber or Grand Chamber proceedings and not in Committee or single judge proceedings.[802] This was confirmed by the Explanatory Report to Protocol No. 14, which states that 'it was decided not to provide for a

797 *Winterwerp v. the Netherlands* App No 6301/73 (ECtHR 24 October 1979), para. 7. Rule 38 of the Rules of Court in effect at that time gave the Court this capacity.

798 The third paragraph was added when Protocol No. 14 to the Convention entered into force in 2010. The rationale for this was that 'the Commissioner's experience may help enlighten the Court on certain questions, particularly in cases which highlight structural or systemic weaknesses in the respondent or other High Contracting Parties' (Explanatory Report to Protocol No. 14 to the Convention (Strasbourg 2004), para. 87).

799 Article 36(1) ECHR.

800 Article 36(2) ECHR and Rule 44(3).

801 Article 36(3) ECHR and Rule 44(2) Rules of Court.

802 See also L. Zwaak, Y. Haeck, C. Burbano Herrera, 'Procedure before the Court' in P. van Dijk, F. van Hoof, A. van Rijn, L. Zwaak (eds.), *Theory and practice of the European Convention on Human Rights*, Intersentia 2018 (5th edition), pp. 79–271, p. 177.

possibility of third-party intervention in the new committee procedure under the new Article 28, paragraph 1.b, given the straightforward nature of cases to be decided under that procedure'.[803]

The various types of third-party intervention allowed under Article 36 ECHR are discussed in more detail in Section 3. First, however, some remarks are made with regard to the procedural requirements for such interventions.

Any party wanting to intervene in a Chamber or Grand Chamber case on the basis of Article 36(2) ECHR has to submit a written request for leave to intervene no later than twelve weeks after notice of the application has been given to the respondent State.[804] Such a request for leave must be 'duly reasoned'[805] so that it can be established that the intervention is 'in the interest of the proper administration of justice'. The Court's case law does not provide much guidance on whether an intervention is in the interest of a proper administration of justice as the Court's judgments rarely make reference to unsuccessful requests for intervention.[806] It follows, however, from the Explanatory Report to Protocol No. 11 that the person concerned must have an interest in the result of the case brought before the Court.[807] This does not have to be a direct or personal interest: parties defending a general interest or interest of a specific group of people can be granted leave to intervene.[808] More generally, it has to be established that the third party is directly or indirectly affected by, or connected to the case, or has an interest in the interpretation of a specific issue.[809] This liberal approach is also reflected in the broad interpretation of the term 'any person concerned'.[810] This may be a natural or a legal person,

---

803 Explanatory Report to Protocol No. 14 to the Convention (Strasbourg 2004), para. 89. The Court's case law does, however, include some examples of judgments by a Committee in which a third party was granted leave to intervene (see, for example, *Majidli and Others v. Azerbaijan* App No 56317/11 (ECtHR 26 September 2019), para. 2; *Rana v. Hungary* App No 40888/17 (ECtHR 16 July 2020) text above para. 1).

804 Rule 44(3b) Rules of Court. Similarly, when a Convention State wishes to exercise its right to intervene under Article 36(1) ECHR or when the Council of Europe Commissioner for Human Rights wishes to exercise its right to intervene under Article 36(3) ECHR, they should inform the Court no later than twelve weeks after communication of the case to the respondent State (See Rule 44(1b-2)).

805 Rule 44(3b) Rules of Court.

806 Bürli 2017 (n 795), p. 10.

807 Explanatory Report to Protocol No. 11 to the Convention (Strasbourg 1994), para. 48. See also Zwaak, Haeck, Burbano Herrera 2018 (n 802), p. 177. This requirement does not apply to Convention States; they do not have to show that they have an interest in the outcome of the case as Convention States are considered to have an interest in all the cases before the Court (see also P. Mahoney, 'Commentaire' in H. Ruiz Fabri and J.M. Sorel (eds.), *La tiers à l'instance devant les juridictions internationales,* Pedone 2005, pp. 151–161, p. 158).

808 L. Hennebel, 'Le role des amici curiae devant la Cour Européenne des Droits de l'Homme', (2007) 71 *Revue Trimestrielle des droits de l'homme* 641, 641–642.

809 A. Wiik, *Amicus curiae before international courts and tribunals,* Nomos Verlagsgesellschaft 2018, p. 236.

810 See, for example, Sicilianos 2005 (n 795), p. 143; D. Harris, M. O'Boyle, E. Bates, C. Buckley, *Harris, O'Boyle and Warbrick: Law of the European Convention on Human Rights,* Oxford University Press 2018 (4th edition), p. 160; Wiick 2018 (n 809), p. 236.

including intergovernmental organisations such as the European Commission[811] and the Office of the United Nations High Commissioner for Refugees[812], monitoring bodies of the Council of Europe[813], non-governmental local and international human rights interests groups[814], private individuals[815], trade unions[816] and academic institutions.[817]

The Court itself may also invite a State, an individual or an organisation to intervene. In, for example, *Behrami and Saramati*[818], the Court requested the United Nations to intervene as the case concerned the actions of a UN peacekeeping force.[819] More recently, in the case of *Strand Lobben and Others*[820], which concerned the decision-making process in adoption proceedings, the Court invited the adoptive parents of the second applicant to intervene in the written proceedings.[821] Finally, in the case of *Y.S. and O.S.*[822], concerning the abduction of a child by the mother, the Court invited the father to intervene in the Court's proceedings.[823] These examples, however, are exceptions, as it is generally rather unusual for the Court to invite interventions of its own motion.[824]

---

811 See, for example, *Bosphorus v. Ireland* App No 45036/98 (ECtHR (GC) 30 June 2005).

812 See, for example, *M.S.S. v. Belgium and Greece* App No 30696/09 (ECtHR (GC) 21 January 2011).

813 See, for example, the Council of Europe Group of Experts on Action against Violence against Women and Domestic Violence (GREVIO) in *Kurt v. Austria* App No 62903/15 (ECtHR (GC) 15 June 2021).

814 See, for example, Interights in *Kiyutin v. Russia* App No 2700/10 (ECtHR 10 March 2011). See also Section 3.1 on amicus curiae interventions.

815 For example, the parents of the boy who was killed by the applicant in *Gäfgen v. Germany* App No 22978/05 (ECtHR (GC) 1 June 2010). See also Section 3.2 on actual third-party interventions.

816 For example, the European Trade Union Confederation and the Trades Union Congress in *National Union of Rail, Maritime and Transport Workers v. the United Kingdom* App No 31045/10 (ECtHR 8 April 2014).

817 For example, the Human Rights Centre of Ghent University in *S.A.S. v. France* App No 43835/11 (ECtHR (GC) 1 July 2014).

818 *Behrami and Behrami v. France and Saramati v. France, Germany and Norway* App Nos 71412/01, 78166/01 (ECtHR (GC) 2 May 2007 (dec.)).

819 *Behrami and Behrami v. France and Saramati v.. France, Germany and Norway* App Nos 71412/01, 78166/01 (ECtHR (GC) 2 May 2007 (dec.)).

820 *Strand Lobben and Others v. Norway* App No 37283/12 (ECtHR (GC) 10 September 2019).

821 This is not made explicit in the information provided in the judgment, but follows from a scholarly publication by one of the judges in the case (P. Pastor Vilanova, 'Third parties involved in international litigation proceedings. What are the challenges for the ECHR?' in P. Pinto de Albuquerque and K. Wojtyczek (eds.), *Judical power in a globalized world (Liber amicorum Vincent de Gaetano)*, Springer 2019, pp. 377–393, p. 388). See also the case of *Omorefe v. Spain* App No 69339/16 (ECtHR 23 June 2020) in which the President of the Chamber informed the adoptive parents about the application brought before the Court and the possibility of third-party intervention. It seems, however, that the adoptive parents did not make use of this opportunity as no summary of third-party submissions is provided in the judgment, and nor is any reference made to third-party submissions in the Court's reasoning.

822 *Y.S. and O.S. v. Russia* App No 17665/17 (ECtHR 15 June 2021).

823 As in *Strand Lobben and Others v. Norway*, this is not made explicit in the information provided in the judgment, but follows from a concurring opinion in another case by one of the judges in the case of *Y.S. and O.S. v. Russia* (Concurring Opinion Judge Elósegui in *A.M. and Others v. Russia* App No 47220/19 (ECtHR 6 July 2021), para. 9).

824 Harris et al. 2018 (n 810), p. 162.

When a request for leave is granted under Article 36(2) ECHR, the President of the Chamber or Grand Chamber may set certain conditions[825], including, for example, a maximum length for the written submission, a specified time limit for lodging the submission, and conditions as to the matters able to be covered by the intervention.[826] Regarding the latter, the Court, usually requests the intervening party not to directly address the facts, admissibility or merits of a case, but instead to provide information based on the expertise or experience of the intervener.[827] Third-party submissions are then forwarded to the parties of the case by the Registrar. The parties to the case are entitled, subject to any conditions set by the Court, to file written observations in reply or, where appropriate, to state them at a hearing.[828] In theory, 'any person concerned' may be invited to take part in hearings.[829] In practice, however, such participation is limited to 'exceptional cases'[830], thus making written submissions the norm.[831]

3. DIFFERENT TYPES OF THIRD-PARTY INTERVENTION

The previous section explained that the Convention allows three types of third-party intervention: (1) intervention by the State of which the applicant is a national if the case is brought against another Convention State; (2) intervention by any other Convention State or any other person concerned whose intervention furthers the proper administration of justice; (3) intervention by the Council of Europe Commissioner for Human Rights. Although these three forms of third-party intervention are laid down in a single provision, the reasons why they are included in the Convention differ. The first possibility for intervening reflects the right to diplomatic protection[832], which is about a State's entitlement to invoke the responsibility of another State when the rights and interests of one of the former's citizens are breached by the latter.[833] The third possibility – the right for the Council of Europe Commissioner for Human Rights to intervene – is so that the Court can be informed of structural or systematic weaknesses

825 Rule 44(5) Rules of Court.

826 P. Leach, *Taking a case to the European Court of Human Rights*, Oxford University Press 2017 (4th edition), p. 53.

827 Leach 2017 (n 826), p. 53; L.R. Glas, 'State Third-Party Interventions before the European Court of Human Rights: the what and how of intervening' (2016) 5 *European Journal of Human Rights* 539, 542; Harris et al. 2018 (n 810), p. 161. However, there are examples of interventions where interveners do directly address the admissibility or merits of the case (see Glas 2016 (n 827), p. 548).

828 Rule 44(6) Rules of Court.

829 Article 36(2) ECHR.

830 Rule 44(3) Rules of Court.

831 See also Wiick 2018 (n 809), p. 320.

832 Sicilianos 2005 (n 795), pp. 125ff; Hennebel 2007 (n 808), p. 646; Harris et al. 2018 (n 810), p. 159.

833 For an introduction to the right to diplomatic protection see, for example, J. Dugard, 'Diplomatic Protection', *Max Planck Encyclopedias of International Law*, Oxford University Press 2009. See also the ILC Draft Articles on Diplomatic Protection (2006).

in the Convention States.[834] Meanwhile there are various reasons for the second type of third-party intervention – intervention by any other Convention State or any other person concerned – as this is a broad category covering various different types of third-party intervention. As shown in the previous section, the Court interprets the term 'any person concerned' broadly to mean a private individual, a group of individuals or an organisation. To bring some structure to this broad and relatively unordered category of third-party interventions, legal scholars have identified certain sub-categories. Hennebel, for example, distinguishes two types of interveners able to be classified as 'any person concerned': amicus curiae in the strict sense, and persons who have a direct and personal interest in the case because of their involvement in the case at the domestic level.[835] Similarly, Bürli distinguishes between amicus curiae and actual third-party interventions.[836] The notion of amicus curiae interventions refers to organisations with no direct legal interest in the case, but with a specific expertise or authority regarding the issue before the Court.[837] Actual third-party interventions, on the other hand, in Bürli's view, encompass interventions by natural and legal persons implicated in the facts of the case and who were usually a party to the case at the domestic level.[838]

The remainder of this section is based on Bürli's further categorisation of the second type of third-party interventions. As explained in the next two subsections, these two subtypes of third-party intervention serve different aims and, therefore, play different roles in the Court's proceedings.[839] The other types of interventions mentioned above, being interventions by Convention States or the Commissioner for Human Rights, are not discussed separately since they are less relevant for this study.[840]

3.1. AMICUS CURIAE INTERVENTIONS

The majority of third-party interventions before the Court are amicus curiae interventions and so involve organisations that have no direct legal interest in the case, but have a specific expertise or authority regarding the issue before the Court.[841] They can include NGOs, interest groups, research institutions, national human rights

834 Explanatory Report to Protocol No. 14 to the Convention (Strasbourg 2004), para 87.

835 Hennebel 2007 (n 808), p. 653.

836 Bürli 2017 (n 795). For another, although quite similar, distinction see, for example, Bartholomeusz 2005 (n 795). Bartholomeusz distinguishes between persons other than the applicant with a clear interest in the domestic proceedings to which an application before the ECtHR relates; entities, groups or individuals with relevant specialist legal expertise or factual knowledge; and industry interest groups with views closely aligned to the applicant (p. 36).

837 Bürli 2017 (n 795), p. 6.

838 Bürli 2017 (n 795), p. 9.

839 See also Bürli 2017 (n 795), p. 2.

840 For an analysis of State third-party interventions before the ECtHR, see, for example, Glas 2016 (n 827).

841 Bürli 2017 (n 795), p. 6. See also L. van den Eynde, 'An empirical look at the amicus curiae practice of human rights NGOs before the European Court of Human Rights' (2013) 31 *Netherlands Quarterly of Human Rights* 271, 273.

institutions, or international organisations and their bodies that may want to intervene in a case[842] to inform the Court on factual or legal issues central to the case and, by doing so, influence the Court's case law and serve the interests they represent.[843]

Amicus curiae interventions can provide the Court with various types of information, including, for example, factual information that can help the Court to decide on the case before it, as illustrated in *D.H. and Others*.[844] In this case on discrimination of Roma children, nine different organisations intervened to provide the Court with statistical and other information on the historical and systemic discrimination of Roma children in the education system.[845] Examples of factual third-party interventions can also be found in non-refoulement cases, in which the Court has to establish whether the extradition or reparation of an applicant to a third state may lead to a violation of Article 3 ECHR. In such cases, amicus curiae interventions can provide the Court with information on the situation in the third state.[846]

Amicus curiae interventions can also provide information on the broader domestic policy or legislation involved, or information on European or international law.[847] In the case, for example, of *Aydin*[848], concerning the rape and ill-treatment of a female detainee by a State agent, Amnesty International provided the Court with information on the case law of the Inter-American Commission on Human Rights and the reports of the United Nations Special Rapporteur on Torture, the International Criminal Tribunal for Former Yugoslavia, and the United Nations Convention against Torture and other Cruel, Inhuman or Degrading Treatment or Punishment to determine the content and scope of the prohibition of torture and inhuman or degrading treatment or punishment as laid down in the Convention.[849] Such information can help the Court to determine the existence of European or international consensus on a certain issue or to draw inspiration from legal solutions adopted in other systems.[850] This is also illustrated by third-party comments in the more recent case of *Kurt*[851], concerning the positive obligation to take protective measures in situations of domestic violence. In their third-party comments, several interveners informed the Court about the importance

842 Bürli 2017 (n 795), pp. 7–8. On this type of third-party intervention, see also Sicilianos 2005 (n 795), pp. 135ff.

843 Hennebel 2007 (n 808), p. 653.

844 *D.H. and Others v. the Czech Republic* App No 57325/00 (ECtHR (GC) 13 November 2007).

845 *D.H. and Others v. the Czech Republic* App No 57325/00 (ECtHR (GC) 13 November 2007), para. 161ff. See also Bürli 2017 (n 795), p. 105. Similarly, see Sicilianos 2005 (n 795), p. 137 on the factual information provided by the European Roma Rights Centre in several cases against the United Kingdom.

846 For example, *Hirsi Jamaa and Others v. Italy* App No 27765/09 (ECtHR (GC) 23 February 2012), paras 101–109; *M.A. v. Belgium* App No 19656/18 (ECtHR 27 October 2020), paras 75–76. See also Wiik 2018 (n 809), pp. 353–354.

847 Bürli 2017 (n 795), pp. 30ff. See also Van den Eynde 2013 (n 841), p. 274.

848 *Aydin v. Turkey* App No 23178/94 (ECtHR (GC) 25 September 1997). On this case, see also Sicilianos 2005 (n 795), p. 139.

849 *Aydin v. Turkey* App No 23178/94 (ECtHR (GC) 25 September 1997), para. 51.

850 Hennebel 2007 (n 808), p. 658.

851 *Kurt v. Austria* App No 62903/15 (ECtHR (GC) 15 June 2021).

of standardised risk assessments in protecting victims of domestic violence.[852] For instance, the Council of Europe Group of Experts on Action against Violence against Women and Domestic Violence (GREVIO) submitted that Article 51 of the Istanbul Convention requires authorities to carry out a risk assessment[853], while also providing the Court with information on internationally recognised tools for carrying out such risk assessments.[854]

Finally, amicus curiae interventions can help the Court to appreciate the different interests at play and thus, where necessary, to balance various public and private interests.[855] In such cases, amicus curiae interventions can provide the Court with more information on the societal, political, ethical and moral aspects of the different interests at stake[856], as is illustrated in the case of *A, B and C*.[857] This concerned the right to abortion and the question of whether the right to life, as provided for in Article 2 ECHR, could be seen to extend to the foetus. Several amicus curiae interveners provided the Court with their views on the different interests at stake in this case. Whereas the joint intervention by the European Centre for Law and Justice, the Family Research Council, and the Society for the Protection of Unborn Children and the intervention by Pro-Life Campaign defended the right to life of the unborn and argued that this right outweighed any putative conflict with the interests of the woman to health, privacy and bodily integrity[858], the Doctors for Choice, the British Pregnancy Advisory Service, the Center for Reproductive Rights, and the International Reproductive and Sexual Health Law Programme defended the rights and interests of women and the right to abortion.[859] The fact that amicus curiae interventions can help the Court to appreciate the different interests at play is further illustrated by cases involving a conflict between the right to reputation and private life and the right to freedom of expression. In, for example, *MGN Limited*[860], amicus curiae interveners provided the Court with information on the consequences for the media of the high costs of defamation proceedings in the United Kingdom. In particular, they submitted that the case raised an important issue regarding the chilling effect of high costs in defamation proceedings involving NGOs and small media organisations with

852 *Kurt v. Austria* App No 62903/15 (ECtHR (GC) 15 June 2021), paras. 137–145 (submissions by GREVIO), para. 149 (submission by the Federal Association of Austrian Centres for Protection from Violence), para. 151 (submission by Women's Popular Initiative 2.0), paras. 152–153 (submission by Association of Autonomous Austrian Women's Shelters), para. 154 (submission by Women Against Violence Europe).

853 The Istanbul Convention is the Council of Europe Convention on preventing and combating violence against women and domestic violence which entered into force on 1 August 2014. GREVIO is the body responsible for monitoring the implementation of this Convention.

854 *Kurt v. Austria* App No 62903/15 (ECtHR (GC) 15 June 2021), paras. 140ff.

855 Hennebel 2007 (n 808), p. 658.

856 Bürli 2017 (n 795), p. 74. See also Hennebel 2007 (n 808), p. 664.

857 *A,B and C v. Ireland* App No 25579/05 (ECtHR (GC) 16 December 2010).

858 *A,B and C v. Ireland* App No 25579/05 (ECtHR (GC) 16 December 2010), paras. 196–205.

859 *A,B and C v. Ireland* App No 25579/05 (ECtHR (GC) 16 December 2010), paras. 206–211.

860 *MGN Limited v. the United Kingdom* App No 39401/04 (ECtHR 18 January 2011).

limited budgets and stressed the importance of investigative reporting for the public interest.[861]

In conclusion, it follows from the above that amicus curiae interventions serve to protect the public interest.[862] They allow members of the public and civil society to present both information and also their own ideas and views. It is consequently argued that amicus curiae interventions strengthen the Court's legitimacy in its democratic environment.[863] It also follows from the above that although amicus curiae interveners do not have a direct legal interest in the case, they are often not neutral or impartial either. They may defend a certain interest and, by doing so, show partiality.[864] However, they have in common the fact that the interests they aim to represent go beyond the particular case in which they intervene.[865] This makes them different from actual third-party interveners, as explained in the next section.

3.2. ACTUAL THIRD-PARTY INTERVENTIONS

In addition to amicus curiae interventions, Article 36(2) ECHR allows for 'actual' third-party interventions; in other words, interventions by natural and legal persons implicated in the facts of the case and who were usually a party to the case at the domestic level.[866] It follows from this definition that these interventions are the most relevant type of interventions for this study. More specifically, Article 36(2) ECHR implies that the disappeared party, i.e. the party involved in the conflict at the domestic level and who has not lodged the application with the Court, has a procedural opportunity to intervene in the verticalised case before the Court and present his own account of the rights and interests at stake.

Actual third-party interventions involve clearly 'private interest-based'[867] third-party participation. Unlike amicus curiae interveners, actual third-party interveners have a direct and personal interest in the case, and this interest, moreover, is limited to the outcome of the case in which they intervene.[868] This implies that, unlike amicus curiae interventions, the opportunity for actual third-party interventions is not included in the Convention for the purpose of protecting the public interest. On the contrary, it has been observed that actual third-party interventions are allowed under the Convention primarily for reasons of due process, i.e. to serve the proper

---

861 *MGN Limited v. the United Kingdom* App No 39401/04 (ECtHR 18 January 2011), paras. 184–191. Joint submissions were made by Open Society Justice Initiative, Media Legal Defence Initiative, Index on Censorship, the English PEN, Global Witness and Human Rights Watch.

862 Bürli 2017 (n 795), pp. 20ff. See also: Bartholomeusz 2005 (n 795), p. 241; Sicilianos 2005 (n 795), p. 124; Van den Eynde 2013 (n 841), pp. 273–274.

863 Bürli 2017 (n 795), pp. 21–22.

864 See also Wiik 2018 (n 809), p. 237.

865 Hennebel 2007 (n 808), p. 653.

866 Bürli 2017 (n 795), p. 9.

867 Wiik 2018 (n 809), pp. 140ff.

868 Hennebel 2007 (n 808), p. 655.

administration of justice.[869] More specifically, the main purpose of permitting actual third-party interventions seems to be to give third parties the opportunity to be heard before the Court issues a judgment that could affect their legal interests.[870] This is explained by the fact that although the proceedings before the Court are of a vertical nature (involving a private party and the State), the private party involved in the conflict at the domestic level may still have an interest in the case before the Court because of being implicated in the facts of the case or possible even being affected by a judgment of the Court.[871]

Actual third-party interveners can thus provide the Court with more information on the rights and private interests at stake by, for example, specifying and explaining the exact meaning and importance of these rights and interests, as illustrated by cases in which an actual third party intervened. In, for example, *Perna*[872], a journalist complained about his conviction for defaming the public prosecutor by alleging abuse of position for political ends. The journalist had accused the public prosecutor of being a politically militant officer and committing abuse of authority by taking part in a plan by the Italian communist party to gain control over the public prosecutors' offices.[873] In the proceedings before the Court, the public prosecutor was granted leave to intervene and submitted that the domestic courts had never established his militancy, while also arguing that he had never hidden his beliefs and that these should not be confused with militancy.[874] Besides the case of *Perna,* several examples discussed in Chapter 6 can be recalled, including the case of *Taşkin and Others*[875] concerning the domestic authorities' decision to issue a permit to use a cyanidation operating process in a gold mine. In the Court's proceedings, the receiver of the permit, the Normandy Madencilik A.S. Company, intervened as a third party. In this capacity, the company stressed that it had received the necessary permits for operating the goldmine in question and referred to several reports that concluded the risks involved to be negligible.[876] Another example is the case *Mandet*[877], concerning the right to private and family life and in which the legal parents and the child claimed before the Court that recognition of the biological father's paternity had violated their right to private and family life. The biological father intervened in the Court's proceedings, submitting that the mother had obstructed any contact between him and the child, and that this had led him to initiate proceedings

---

869 Bartholomeusz 2005 (n 795), p. 241; Sicilianos 2005 (n 795), p. 124; Bürli 2017 (n 795), p. 160; Pastor Vilanova 2019 (n 821), p. 383.

870 Bartholomeusz 2005 (n 795), p. 236.

871 Sicilianos 2005 (n 795), p. 133; Hennebel 2007 (n 808), p. 655; Wiik 2018 (n 809), p. 140. This was also discussed extensively in Chapters 7 and 8 of this study.

872 *Perna v. Italy* App No 48898/99 (ECtHR (GC) 6 May 2003).

873 *Perna v. Italy* App No 48898/99 (ECtHR (GC) 6 May 2003), para. 37.

874 *Perna v. Italy* App No 48898/99 (ECtHR (GC) 6 May 2003), para. 38.

875 *Taşkin and Others v. Turkey* App No 46117/99 (ECtHR 10 November 2004), as discussed in Chapter 6 (Section 3.1).

876 *Taşkin and Others v. Turkey* App No 46117/99 (ECtHR 10 November 2004), paras. 82–88.

877 *Mandet v. France* App No 30955/12 (ECtHR 14 January 2016). This case was discussed in Chapter 6 (Section 3.3).

in order to have his paternity legally established.[878] As a final example, the case of *Schüth* concerned the dismissal of a church employee after the employee's divorce and second marriage.[879] In this case, a representative of the employer, the Catholic Diocese of Essen, intervened in the Court's proceedings. As a third-party intervener, the employer's representative submitted that 'the finding of a violation of the Convention would be seen as a serious interference with consequences not only for the Diocese, but also for all the contracts of employment of the Catholic and Protestant Churches'.[880] In the Diocese's opinion, 'the employing Churches would then find themselves unable to require their employees to comply with particular occupational duties corresponding to their specific missions'.[881]

These examples show that the possibility of actual third-party intervention gives natural and legal persons implicated in the facts of the case and who were usually a party to the case at the domestic level the opportunity to provide the Court with information on the rights and private interests at stake. They also show that actual third-party interventions are private interest-based and give third parties the opportunity to be heard before the Court issues a judgment that could affect their legal interests.

Nevertheless, it should be recalled that actual third-party interventions are not common in practice and that such would-be interveners are not frequently granted leave to intervene by the Court. Compared to amicus curiae interventions and interventions by Convention States, actual third-party interventions are the least frequent type of interventions in the Court's proceedings.[882] To illustrate, Bürli identified 391 judgments between 1979 and August 2016 in which leave to intervene was granted to a total of 661 interveners.[883] Of these 661 interventions, only 33 (in 32 cases) were actual third-party interventions.[884] In the sample of cases analysed for the present study, meanwhile, 9 of the 77 cases involved an actual third-party intervention.[885]

---

878 *Mandet v. France* App No 30955/12 (ECtHR 14 January 2016), para. 42.

879 *Schüth v. Germany* App No 1620/03 (ECtHR 23 September 2010). See similarly the cases of *Obst v. Germany* App No 425/03 (ECtHR 23 September 2010) and *Siebenhaar v. Germany* App No 18136/02 (ECtHR 3 February 2011). As in *Schüth*, the church, acting as an employer, was granted leave to intervene in the Court's proceedings (see also Chapter 6 (Section 3.4)).

880 *Schüth v. Germany* App No 1620/03 (ECtHR 23 September 2010), para. 52.

881 *Schüth v. Germany* App No 1620/03 (ECtHR 23 September 2010), para. 52.

882 Bürli 2017 (n 795), pp. 6, 177, 193.

883 Bürli 2017 (n 795), p. 3. The numbers of 391 and 661 are mentioned in the introduction. In different parts of the study slightly different numbers are mentioned (for example, 397 on page 184, and 667 on page 6). This inconsistency does, however, not affect the conclusion that actual third-party intervention is least seen in the Court's proceedings.

884 Bürli 2017 (n 795), p. 193. A similar remark as made in footnote 86 applies here. On page 177, Bürli speaks of 27 actual third-party interventions. The table of cases with interventions count, however, 33 actual third-party interventions (for the table of cases see xiii-xlvii).

885 This are the following nine cases: *Von Hannover v. Germany (No. 1)* App No 59320/00 (ECtHR 24 June 2004) (intervention by media company responsible for the publication of the photos); *Von Hannover v. Germany (No. 2)* App Nos 40660/08 and 60641/08 (ECtHR (GC) 7 February 2012) (intervention by media company responsible for the publication of the photos); *Hokkanen v. Finland* App No 19823/92 (ECtHR 23 September 1994) (intervention by the grandparents of the child); *Mandet v. France* App No 30955/12 (ECtHR 14 January 2016) (intervention by the biological father of the child);

In seeking to explain this relatively low number of actual third-party interventions, Bürli suggested that requests submitted by actual third-party interveners may sometimes be rejected because the Court may be cautious about accepting and dealing with actual third-party interventions as it does not want to act as a court of fourth instance.[886] Similarly, Judge Pastor Vilanova mentioned in a scholarly publication that while the Court is very liberal in accepting interventions of Member States and amicus curiae, it is very cautious with regard to actual third-party interveners.[887] Such explanations, however, must be treated with caution as the Court rarely indicates in its judgments whether and why it has denied a request for a third-party intervention. In other words, although it is clear that actual third-party interventions are the least common form of third-party intervention in the Court's practice, it is difficult to establish how many requests for such interventions are actually made and rejected, and nor is it easy to find out the Court's exact policy is in this regard.

3.3. CONCLUSION

The previous subsections explained that the Convention provides for various types of third-party intervention: interventions by Convention States, by the Council of Europe Commissioner for Human Rights, by amici curiae and by actual third parties. It was also explained that these different types of third-party intervention serve different aims. Amicus curiae interventions, for example, are allowed in order to protect the public interest, whereas actual third-party interventions seems to be allowed under the Convention for the purpose of protecting private interests and ensuring due process in individual cases.

Taken together, the diverse range of actors with a right to intervene or who may be granted leave to intervene in the Court's proceedings, and the different rationales for allowing these persons to intervene, show that the Convention takes quite a liberal approach with regard to the instrument of third-party intervention. As a result, natural and legal persons implicated in the facts of the case and who were usually a party to the case at the domestic level (i.e. the disappeared party) may have the opportunity to provide the Court with information on the rights and private interests at stake. It should be noted, however, that this possibility is not often used in practice and that this type of would-be intervener is not frequently granted leave to intervene by the Court. Indeed, the majority of third-party interventions before the Court are amicus curiae

Hatton and Others v. the United Kingdom App No 36022/97 (ECtHR (GC) 8 July 2003) (intervention by airplane company); *Taşkin and Others v. Turkey* App No 46117/99 (ECtHR 10 November 2004) (intervention by the receiver of the permit); *Schüth v. Germany* App No 1620/03 (ECtHR 23 September 2010) (intervention by a representative of the employer); *Obst v. Germany* App No 425/03 (ECtHR 23 September 2010) (intervention by the employer); *Siebenhaar v. Germany* App No 18136/02 (ECtHR 3 February 2011) (intervention by the employer).

886 Bürli 2017 (n 795), p. 178. For a discussion of the no fourth-instance court doctrine, see Chapter 3 (Section 3.2.1) of this study.

887 Pastor Vilanova 2019 (n 821), p. 381.

interventions, while actual third-party interventions are the least common in the Court's proceedings.

The next section examines whether this liberal approach is also reflected in the Court's approach to third-party submissions in its judgments and, more specifically, considers the Court's receptiveness to third-party submissions and the influence of such submissions on the Court's reasoning and its case law.

4. INFLUENCE OF THIRD-PARTY INTERVENTIONS ON THE COURT'S JUDGMENTS

The previous two sections provided an overview of the rules stated by Article 36 ECHR in relation to the third-party intervention procedure and the Court's policy in this regard, with particular attention being paid to the different types of third-party intervention allowed under the Convention. This discussion showed the Court to take a relatively liberal approach regarding the actors who may be granted leave to intervene in its proceedings. This, in turn, raises the question as to how the Court deals with third-party submissions in its judgments. In other words, how receptive is the Court to facts and arguments presented by third-party interveners? Does it deal differently with submissions by Convention States, amicus curiae interveners and actual third-party interveners? These questions are the focus of the present section, which completes the introduction to the third-party intervention procedure in its current form.

Bürli distinguishes three ways in which the Court deals with third-party submissions in its judgments: it may provide a summary of the intervener's main arguments or refer directly to the third-party submissions in its reasoning, or judges may include references to third-party submissions in their separate opinions.[888] Of these three options, the Court has chosen to provide a summary of the third-party submissions in most of the cases in which a third party was granted leave to intervene. Only occasionally has the Court referred directly to third-party submissions in its reasoning.[889] This makes it difficult to examine the influence of third-party submissions on the Court's reasoning[890], given that a summary of such submissions provided in the Court's judgment does not actually say much about the value the Court accords to them. Similarly, the absence of direct references to third-party submissions in the Court's reasoning, does not necessarily mean that the third-party submissions did not influence the Court's heuristic process.

Several scholars have nevertheless tried to provide some insight into the Court's receptiveness to arguments presented by third-party interveners and to shed some light on whether the Court deals differently with submissions by Convention States, amici

888 Bürli 2017 (n 795), p. 12.
889 Bürli 2017 (n 795), pp. 12–13.
890 See also Sicilianos 2005 (n 795), p. 136; Hennebel 2007 (n 808), p. 667; Glas 2016 (n 827), pp. 555–556; Bürli 2017 (n 795), p. 189; Wiik 2018 (n 809), p. 443.

curiae and actual third parties.[891] These scholars share the finding that, of the three different types of third-party intervention, amicus curiae interventions seem to have the most profound impact on the Court's case law.[892] It is submitted that, particularly in morally or politically sensitive cases, these interventions may significantly influence the development of the Court's case law.[893] Bürli gives the example, in this respect, of judgments relating to the rights of detainees, LGBTs and travellers, in which the Court followed the evolutive interpretation of the Convention suggested by amicus curiae interveners, often in support of arguments presented by the respective applicants.[894] With regard, for example, to LGBT rights, the Court's 2010 judgment in *Schalk and Kopf*[895] was the first time that it found the relationship of cohabiting same-sex couples living in a stable partnership to fall within the notion of 'family life' within the meaning of Article 8 ECHR[896], noting a 'rapid evolution of social attitudes towards same-sex couples'.[897] Before this landmark case, the Court had either left this question to the Convention States[898] or had left it open.[899, 900] As in previous cases concerning LGBT rights, amicus curiae interveners submitted in *Schalk and Kopf* that 'the Court should rule on the question whether a same-sex relationship of cohabiting partners fell under the notion of "family life" within the meaning of Article 8 of the Convention'[901] and that 'by now it was generally accepted that same-sex couples had the same capacity to establish a long-term emotional and sexual relationship as different-sex couples and, thus, had the same needs as different-sex couples to have their relationship recognised by law'.[902] Although the Court did not explicitly refer to the third-party submissions in its reasoning, the amicus curiae submissions are quite likely to have helped the Court, at least to some extent, to take note of and understand the societal changes on this particular issue.[903]

It should also be noted that amicus curiae interventions providing international comparative law studies seem to have influenced the Court's case law[904], as illustrated by the case of *Aydin* discussed in Section 3.1. As explained above, Amnesty International intervened as a third party in this case to provide the Court with information on how

891 E.g. Sicilianos 2005 (n 795); Hennebel 2007 (n 808); Van den Eynde 2013 (n 841); Glas 2016 (n 827); Bürli 2017 (n 795); Wiik 2018 (n 809).

892 Sicilianos 2005 (n 795), p. 143; Hennebel 2007 (n 808), p. 667; Bürli 2017 (n 795), pp. 188ff.

893 Bürli 2017 (n 795), pp. 129 and 189–190. See also Sicilianos 2005 (n 795), p. 139 and Wiik 2018 (n 809), pp. 445–446.

894 Bürli 2017 (n 795), p. 129.

895 *Schalk and Kopf v. Austria* App No 30141/04 (ECtHR 24 June 2010).

896 *Schalk and Kopf v. Austria* App No 30141/04 (ECtHR 24 June 2010), paras. 94–95.

897 *Schalk and Kopf v. Austria* App No 30141/04 (ECtHR 24 June 2010), para. 93.

898 For example, *Mata Estevez v. Spain* App No 56501/00 (ECtHR 10 May 2001 (dec.)).

899 For example, *Karner v. Austria* App No 40016/98 (ECtHR 24 July 2003).

900 For a detailed analysis of the development of the Court's case law on this issue, see N. Koffeman, *Morally sensitive issues and cross-border movement in the EU. The cases of reproductive matter and legal recognition of same-sex relationships,* Intersentia 2015, pp. 347ff.

901 *Schalk and Kopf v. Austria* App No 30141/04 (ECtHR 24 June 2010), para 84.

902 *Schalk and Kopf v. Austria* App No 30141/04 (ECtHR 24 June 2010), para 84.

903 See also Wiik 2018 (n 809), pp. 445–446.

904 Sicilianos 2005 (n 795), p. 139; Bürli 2017 (n 795), p. 190; Wiik 2018 (n 809), p. 445.

other international and regional legal systems interpret the prohibition of torture. In line with the submissions by Amnesty International, but without referring to them, the Court held that the rape of a female detainee by a State agent in order, for example, to extract information or confessions, or the humiliation, punishment or intimidation of the victim, amounted to an act of torture in breach of Article 3 ECHR.[905] By providing this information, Amnesty International may have contributed to the harmonisation of international law and to the development of the Court's case law on this particular issue.[906] Besides *Aydin,* Section 3.1 discussed the case of *Kurt,* concerning domestic violence. This case is an example in which the Court actually referred to third-party comments in its reasoning. As explained, several amicus curiae interveners provided the Court with information on the need for risk assessments to protect victims of domestic violence. In its general considerations on positive obligations under Article 2 in the context of domestic violence, the Court then set out a detailed obligation for States to carry out a risk assessment, referring to the submissions by GREVIO and as illustrated by the Court's reasoning that:

> according to GREVIO, the competent authorities should carry out ... a risk assessment for victims as of receipt of a complaint, ideally using standardised, internationally recognised and research-based tools with pre-established questions that the authorities should systematically ask and answer. The system in place should afford law-enforcement officials clear guidelines and criteria governing action or intervention in sensitive situations (see the third-party submissions by GREVIO, paragraph 140 above). The Court considers this approach to be relevant for the member States' positive obligations under Article 2 in the context of domestic violence.[907]

Compared to amicus curiae interventions, interventions by Convention States and actual third-party interventions seem to have less impact, with the latter having the least impact of all.[908] Or, as Bürli puts it, 'the intervener with the most serious interests at stake seems to be the one with the least impact'.[909] This statement follows from her finding that the Court tends to make only brief references to actual third-party submissions, or no reference to them at all, meaning there is rarely any sign in the Court's reasoning that it has actually considered the interests of the actual third-party intervener.[910] Similarly, Harvey has concluded that:

> once leave to intervene is given, the most effective interventions are those which respect the Court's request not to comment on the merits of the case, those which do not seek to advance

---

905 *Aydin v. Turkey* App No 23178/94 (ECtHR (GC) 25 September 1997), para. 86.

906 See also Sicilianos 2005 (n 795), p. 139.

907 *Kurt v. Austria* App No 62903/15 (ECtHR (GC) 15 June 2021), paras. 167–168. See paras. 171ff for more references to the third-party submissions.

908 Bürli 2017 (n 795), pp. 153, 178, 192–193. On interventions by Convention States see also Glas 2016 (n 827).

909 Bürli 2017 (n 795), p. 192.

910 Bürli 2017 (n 795), p. 193.

their own interests and, above all, those which, in good faith, seek to provide real assistance to the Court in its adjudicative task.[911]

The verticalised cases analysed for this study support these findings. As noted in Section 3.2, 9 of the 77 cases analysed for this study involved an actual third-party intervention. The Court dealt with these third-party submissions by providing a summary of the comments in its judgment.[912] In the cases studied, the Court did not refer directly to third-party submissions in its reasoning. Indeed, it was rare for the Court's reasoning to show any sign of having taken account of the third-party submissions. An example of this is the Court's judgment in the employer-employee case of *Schüth,* where, as explained above, a representative of the employer intervened in the Court's proceedings to provide information on the employer's interests and the consequences for the employer if the Court were to find a violation. The Court's reasoning shows that it considered the employer's interests, as also discussed in Chapter 6 (Section 3.4), by mentioning, for example, that 'it is true that, under the Convention, an employer whose ethos is based on religion or on a philosophical belief may impose specific duties of loyalty on its employees'.[913] Although this shows some awareness of the employer's interests, it remains difficult to establish whether this was directly related to the third-party submissions and whether the Court would have arrived at the same line of reasoning regardless of the employer's intervention.

It follows from the above that the Court does not appear to take much account of submissions by actual third parties, although amicus curiae interventions may occasionally influence its reasoning. The Court's liberal approach regarding the persons who may be granted leave to intervene in its proceedings is less visible, therefore, in the way it actually deals with third-party submissions in its judgments, and it is consequently difficult to estimate the exact influence of third-party interventions on the Court's reasoning.

5. CONCLUSION

This chapter has provided an introduction to the third-party intervention procedure laid down in Article 36 of the Convention, with attention being paid to the procedural rules governing third-party interventions, the different types of third-party interventions allowed under the Convention, and the influence of third-party submissions on the Court's reasoning and its case law. It was explained that the Convention allows different

911 P. Harvey, 'Third party interventions before the ECtHR: a rough guide' (2015) *Strasbourg Observers* 24 February 2015 <www.strasbourgobservers.com/2015/02/24/third-party-interventions-before-the-ecthr-a-rough-guide/> accessed 31 January 2022.

912 Only in the case of *Hokkanen v. Finland* App No 19823/92 (ECtHR 23 September 1994) did the Court fail to provide a summary of the actual third-party submissions in its judgment.

913 *Schüth v. Germany* App No 1620/03 (ECtHR 23 September 2010), para. 69.

types of third-party intervention: intervention by Convention States, by the Council of Europe Commissioner for Human Rights, by amici curiae and by actual third parties. These different types of third-party intervention show that the Convention takes a relatively liberal approach with regard to this instrument. Indeed, the Court has granted leave to intervene to intergovernmental organisations, NGOs, religious groups, academic institutions, trade unions, and also individuals. The fact that private parties involved in the conflict at the domestic level (i.e. the disappeared party) may be granted leave to intervene in the Court's proceedings should be emphasised, given the importance of this aspect for this research.

It was also explained that the third-party intervention procedure as laid down in the Convention serves different aims. Convention States' right to intervene when a case is brought against another Convention State by one of their nationals, for example, reflects the right to diplomatic protection, while the rationale for allowing amicus curiae interventions is the protection of the public interest, and actual third-party interventions primarily concern the protection of private interests, due process and serving the proper administration of justice.

However, the Court's liberal approach with regard to allowing third parties to intervene appears to be less visible in its approach to third-party submissions. More specifically, it was discussed that although amicus curiae interventions seem to have some influence on the Court's reasoning and thus some impact on the Court's case law, interventions by Convention States and actual third parties seem to have little or no impact at all on the Court's reasoning. In this regard, however, it should be mentioned that the exact influence of third-party interventions on the Court's reasoning remains difficult to establish. Indeed, the limited direct references to third-party submissions mean it cannot be readily concluded whether they had any influence, indirect or otherwise, on the Court's heuristics and findings.

CHAPTER 10

PROPOSAL TO REDESIGN THE THIRD-PARTY INTERVENTION PROCEDURE

1. INTRODUCTION

The previous chapter showed that the third-party intervention procedure laid down in Article 36 of the Convention allows for intervention by actual third parties. It was explained that actual third parties are natural and legal persons implicated in the facts of the case and who were usually a party to the case at the domestic level. In other words, a private party involved in the conflict at the domestic level, but who is not the applicant in the case before the Court (i.e. the disappeared party) can request leave to intervene in the Court's proceedings. The chapter also showed that this particular type of third-party intervention is clearly 'private interest-based', meaning that it gives actual third parties the opportunity to provide the Court with more information on the rights and private interests at stake, including the exact meaning and importance of these rights and interests. Hence, actual third-party intervention is allowed under the Convention for due process reasons; it gives third parties the opportunity to be heard before a Court judgment that could affect their legal interests is issued.

The third-party intervention procedure laid down in Article 36 thus seems, at least in theory, to be an instrument that is already available in the Convention system for addressing the problems arising in verticalised cases. In practice, however, little use is made of this instrument, as shown in the analysis presented in Chapter 6 and further explained in the previous chapter. It also seems that even when an actual third party is granted leave to intervene in the Court's proceedings, the Court does not appear to take much account of that party's submissions. In other words, the instrument of third-party intervention, in its current form, does not seem to be realising its potential to resolve problems arising in verticalised cases. Illustrative in this regard is that Judges Ravarani and Elósegui stressed the 'need to reconsider the third-party intervention mechanism under Article 36(2) of the Convention, in order to make it more concrete and effective'.[914]

The current chapter consequently proposes to redesign the third-party intervention procedure to make it fit for addressing the problems arising in verticalised cases.

[914] Joint Concurring Opinion of Judges Ravarani and Elósegui in *A.M. and Others v. Russia*, App No 47220/19 (ECtHR 6 July 2021), para. 9.

More specifically, it is argued that, in contrast to the provisions in the current text of Article 36, actual third-party interveners should be granted a *right* to intervene in the Court's proceedings.[915] The subsequent sections discuss in more detail how such a right can be designed. Attention is first paid to the personal and procedural scope of a right to intervene for actual third parties (Section 2). This is followed by an exploration of additional procedural issues, such as how to become aware of the Court's proceedings and the possibility of intervening, and how the Court should deal with third-party submissions in its reasoning (Section 3). These separate issues are approached in a way that aims to follow the line taken throughout this study; in other words, the perspective of all the different actors – private parties, Convention States and the Court itself – should be considered when analysing the notion of verticalised cases. It is acknowledged, for example, that granting a right to actual third parties to intervene in the Court's proceedings can have a significant impact on the Court's workload.

This discussion of the procedural framework of the redesigned third-party intervention procedure is followed by discussion of the added value of the proposed new approach and how a right to intervene in the Court's proceedings could work out in practice (Section 4), with the aim being to show how redesigning the procedure can address the problems arising in verticalised cases and be of benefit to private actors, Convention States and the Court.

2. SCOPE OF A RIGHT TO THIRD-PARTY INTERVENTION FOR ACTUAL THIRD PARTIES

Section 2 of the previous chapter explained that the Convention grants Convention States – if the applicant is a national of the relevant State – and the Council of Europe Commissioner for Human Rights the right to intervene in the Court's proceedings.

915 See also N. Bürli, *Third-party interventions before the European Court of Human Rights: Amicus Curiae, Member-State and Third-Party interventions*, Intersentia 2017, pp. 161ff; P. Pastor Vilanova, 'Third parties involved in international litigation proceedings. What are the challenges for the ECHR?' in P. Pinto de Albuquerque and K. Wojtyczek (eds.), *Judical power in a globalized world (Liber amicorum Vincent de Gaetano),* Springer 2019, pp. 377–393, pp. 378ff; G. Ravarani, 'Third parties – poor relations in proceedings before the European Court of Human Rights' (2021) (on file with the author). See similarly A. Nussberger, '"Second-hand justice" and the rule of law. Dilemmas in implementing the judgments of the European Court of Human Rights' in R. Spano et al (eds.) *Fair trial: regional and international perspectives (Liber amicorum Linos-Alexandre Sicilianos),* Anthemis 2020, pp. 349–363, p. 358. Nussberger does not specifically refer to a right to intervene, but notes that the current situation in which the admission of actual third parties as third-party interveners depends on the President's discretion 'is a clear deficiency of the Court's procedure which has to be remedied'. Wojtyczek too, does not specifically refer to a right to intervene, but instead proposes that 'all person who may be directly affected by the final judicial decision or interim measures in the proceedings before the ECtHR should have the status of a party to these proceedings' (K. Wojtyczek, 'Procedural Justice and the Proceedings Before the European Court of Human Rights: Who Should Have the Right to be Heard?' in R. Spano et al (eds.), *Fair trial: regional and international perspectives (Liber amicorum Linos-Alexandre Sicilianos),* Anthemis 2020, pp. 741–755, p. 753).

By contrast, other Convention States, amici curiae and actual third parties wanting to intervene on the basis of Article 36(2) do not have a right to intervene and can do so only at the Court's discretion. It is proposed changing this situation by giving actual third parties a right to intervene in the Court's proceedings and, therefore, a different status from that of Convention States and amici curiae wanting to intervene on the basis of Article 36(2).[916] In practice, this could entail the second paragraph of Article 36 ECHR being split into two separate provisions, each covering a different type of third-party intervention. What is more important, however, is the scope of such a right to third-party intervention for actual third parties, which is discussed in more detail below. First, attention is paid to the personal scope of a right to such intervention for actual third parties (Section 2.1). Second, the exact features, that is the procedural scope, of a right to such intervention are discussed (Section 2.2).

2.1. PERSONAL SCOPE

This section aims to define the personal scope of the envisaged right to third-party intervention by setting criteria for determining whether a party is eligible to intervene in the Court's proceedings. The current text of Article 36(2) ECHR states that 'any person concerned' may be granted leave to intervene if this serves the 'proper administration of justice'.[917] This rather imprecise criterion does not give much clarity or guidance[918] in that, for example, it does not provide the Court with clear tools to determine whether a party may be granted leave to intervene, and nor does it give Convention States and private actors much information on who is eligible to intervene. It is therefore proposed to define the personal scope of the envisaged right to third-party intervention on the basis of a different notion, and specifically the notion of 'actual third parties'. Setting out criteria that establish whether someone qualifies as an actual third party will define and, thereby, limit the personal scope of the envisaged right to third-party intervention. This is important as, in contrast to the current situation, it will enable the Court to apply a standard set of criteria to determine whether a party qualifies for the right to third-party intervention. Furthermore, it will ensure that only a limited number of parties can claim the right to such intervention, which is important from a perspective of the Court's workload. Finally, a clear definition of the personal scope of a right to third-party intervention will create legal certainty for private actors and Convention States alike.

Section 3.2 of the previous chapter explained that actual third-party interventions are interventions by natural and legal persons implicated in the facts of the case and who were usually a party to the case at the domestic level. As such, it provides a basis for explaining how the exact scope of a right for actual third parties to intervene can be

916 See also Bürli 2017 (n 915), pp. 161ff; Pastor Vilanova 2019 (n 915), pp. 378ff.

917 See further Chapter 9 (Section 2).

918 See also Joint Concurring Opinion of Judges Ravarani and Elósegui in *A.M. and Others v. Russia*, App No 47220/19 (ECtHR 6 July 2021), para. 9.

defined. In this regard, it is useful to take a closer look at the work of Bürli.[919] When arguing that actual third parties should have a right to intervene in the Court's proceedings, Bürli submitted that this right should apply to actual third parties with a legal interest in the case. She defines these parties as those 'affected in [their] human rights by individual measures taken by the respondent state in order to comply with the Court's judgment'.[920] With regard to 'being affected in one's human rights', Bürli stipulates that only entities protected by the Convention can qualify as actual third parties, that human rights interests are those interests protected by the Convention, and that those interests have to be in conflict with the rights of the applicant.[921] Finally, with regard to the 'individual measures', Bürli emphasises that actual third parties are affected by individual measures such as the reopening of domestic proceedings, and thus not by the awarding of just satisfaction.[922]

Bürli's work provides an important basis for determining the exact scope of the right to third-party intervention. Indeed, building on this work, it is argued that, in order to qualify for a right to third-party intervention, the third party should have a legal interest in the case; in other words, the third party was involved in the conflict at the domestic level, this party's human rights interests are in conflict with the rights and interests of the applicant, and these interests are protected by the Convention. If these conditions are met, the actual third party wanting to intervene should be presumed to be affected by a judgment of the Court. In other words, the questions of whether the human rights interests are protected by the Convention and whether these interests are in conflict with the rights of the applicant should be indicators for determining whether the actual third party might be affected by a judgment of the Court.[923]

In practice, the envisaged personal scope of a right to third-party intervention for actual third parties would mean that the original party to the conflict at the domestic level would most often be eligible to intervene in the Court's proceedings. This is particularly true for verticalised cases involving a conflict between the right to reputation and private life and the right to freedom of expression and for verticalised family life cases. In such cases it is very clear that the human rights interests of the disappeared party are protected by the Convention and are in conflict with the rights of the applicant.[924] If, for example, an individual complains about domestic courts' refusal to grant an injunction against the publication of photos or an article, the journalist responsible for the publication is no longer formally involved in the Court's proceedings. However, the applicant's right to reputation and private life has to be balanced against the journalist's

919 Bürli 2017 (n 915).
920 Bürli 2017 (n 915), p. 161.
921 Bürli 2017 (n 915), pp. 161, 173.
922 Bürli 2017 (n 915), pp. 161ff.
923 See also Bürli who held that 'whether a third party is affected by an individual measure depends not only on domestic laws regulating the execution of judgments, but also on the conflict of rights that arose between the applicant and the third party' (Bürli 2017 (n 915), p. 165).
924 See Part II of this study for more details.

right to freedom of expression. To give another example: if a child complains about the refusal to take a paternity test, the complaint also touches on the right to private life of the alleged father, who was involved in the conflict at the domestic level. In such cases it is clear that the human rights interests of the disappeared party are protected by the Convention and that these rights are in conflict with the rights of the applicant. This is further illustrated by the fact that, in such cases, a party can claim violation of Convention rights regardless of the outcome of the proceedings before the domestic courts.[925] Thus, in verticalised cases involving a conflict between the right to reputation and private life and the right to freedom of expression, and also in verticalised family life cases, the disappeared party would, in principle, qualify for the right to third-party intervention.

In verticalised employer-employee cases, by contrast, the disappeared party may not always be eligible to intervene in the Court's proceedings. In such cases, the interests of the disappeared party, often the employer[926], are less frequently protected by the Convention. This is because these interests may be business interests, such as ensuring the smooth running of a company. In some instances, such business interests may be protected under Article 1 of Protocol No. 1 which provides for a right to property. However, this may not necessarily be the case if the business interests are limited, for example, to an adverse impact on the company's brand or image.[927] In addition to Article 1 of Protocol No. 1, the examples discussed in Chapter 6 showed that, in some verticalised employer-employee cases previously dealt with by the Court, the rights and interests of the employee could conflict with the employer's right to freedom of religion (Article 9 ECHR). Depending, therefore, on the nature of the rights and interests at stake, the disappeared party in verticalised employer-employee cases can fall within the scope of the envisaged right for actual third parties to intervene.

In addition to the three types of verticalised cases discussed above, cases related to one's surroundings are another type of verticalised case examined in depth for this study. For this particular category, whether the party involved in the conflict at the domestic level qualifies for a right to third-party intervention will depend on the nature of the specific case. As in employer-employee cases, the interests of the disappeared party may be protected under the right to property. In the cases, for example, of *Hatton and Others* and *Taşkin and Others* discussed in Chapter 6, the disappeared parties were an airplane operator and the operator of a gold mine respectively. In such cases, the interests of the disappeared party may be protected by Article 1 Protocol No. 1 because, for example, the measures in question strongly affect the company's activities. The Court, however, would have to determine whether the interests are indeed protected

925 See the 'converse situation test' as designed by Smet as one of the conditions for the identification of a genuine human rights conflict (S. Smet, *Resolving conflicts between human rights: the judge's dilemma*, Routledge 2017, pp. 62–63).

926 This followed from the case law analysis of verticalised employer-employee cases discussed in Sections 2.4 and 3.4 of Chapter 6.

927 See, for example, *Eweida and Others v. the United Kingdom* App No 48420/10 (ECtHR 15 January 2013), discussed in Chapter 6.

by the Convention. It is questionable, for example, whether the interests of the bars or discotheques responsible for the noise disturbance complained of are protected by Article 1 Protocol No. 1.[928]

On a final note, it should be noted that cases related to one's surroundings underscore the importance of clearly defining and limiting the personal scope of a right to intervene. In Part III it was explained that, in cases related to one's surroundings, the fact that one of the original parties to the conflict is not involved in the Court's proceedings does not lead to substantial problems during the proceedings and that this is due to the specific nature of these cases and the Court's approach to them.[929] This illustrates that it is not necessary for all parties involved in the conflict at the domestic level to automatically qualify for a right to third-party intervention, but only parties whose interests are protected by the Convention and whose interests are in conflict with the rights and interests of the applicant.

2.2. PROCEDURAL SCOPE

In addition to delineating the personal scope of a right to third-party intervention for actual third parties, the procedural scope of such a right has to be elaborated on. In other words, what rights would actual third parties have if they were allowed to intervene in the Court's proceedings? This question is particularly important from the perspective of private actors since it determines whether a right to third-party intervention creates a 'genuine and effective' opportunity to participate in the Court's proceedings.[930]

Bürli, Judge Pastor Vilanova and Judge Wojtyczek believe that actual third parties should be granted full litigation rights.[931] This would mean that actual third parties would have to be served all the relevant documents, including the written observations of the applicant and the State, and that they should be heard in public hearings. Bürli and the two judges have also argued that actual third parties should have the opportunity to apply for legal aid and be able to apply to the Grand Chamber for the case to be reheard.[932] Although only Wojtyczek has spoken of it explicitly[933], granting

928 See, for example, *Moreno Gómez v. Spain* App No 4143/02 (ECtHR 16 November 2004) and *Olujić v. Croatia* App No 61260/08 (ECtHR 20 May 2010), discussed in Chapter 6.

929 See Chapter 7 (Section 2.1).

930 The phrasing 'genuine and effective' is taken from the work of Pastor Vilanova (see Pastor Vilanova 2019 (n 915), p. 379).

931 Bürli 2017 (n 915), p. 181; Pastor Vilanova 2019 (n 915), pp. 391–392; Wojtyczek 2020 (n 915), pp. 752ff. See, similarly, Ravarani 2021 (n 915). Judge Ravarani seems to support the ideas of Bürli, Pastor Vilanova and Wojtyczek, but presents them more as possible solutions, holding, for instance, that '[t]he … proposals are not intended to constitute operational solutions; they should be seen as an invitation for the Court to reflect on its own practice and to engage in a serious discussion on the need for an enhanced role for interested third parties' (Ravarani 2021 (n 915), concluding remarks).

932 Bürli 2017 (n 915), p. 181; Pastor Vilanova 2019 (n 915), pp. 391–392; Wojtyczek 2020 (n 915), pp. 752ff.

933 Wojtyczek 2020 (n 915), p. 753.

such full litigation rights would entail actual third parties obtaining a status close or similar to that of a party to the Court's proceedings. From the perspective of private actors, and with a view to guaranteeing their procedural rights, such a far-reaching right is a very appealing scenario. However, the procedural scope of a right for actual third parties to intervene has to be balanced against the need to duly consider the Court and the Convention States. In other words, the aim should be to find an appropriate balance between creating a genuine and effective opportunity to participate in the Court's proceedings and creating a situation that remains workable from the perspective of the Court and the Convention States.

It is consequently proposed that the extent of the right to intervene for actual third parties should follow the current rules on the existing right to third-party intervention for Convention States and the Council of Europe Commissioner for Human Rights. Accordingly, it is not submitted that actual third parties should be granted full litigation rights, such as having automatic access to the complete case file, the opportunity to apply for legal aid or obtaining the right to request leave to appeal to the Grand Chamber. However, and in contrast to the current practice of interventions by actual third parties, the Court will no longer be able to set certain conditions as to the matters that can be covered by the intervention.[934] Indeed, according to the Rules of Court, the Court has this authority solely in relation to situations in which parties are *not* granted a right to intervene; that is, interventions under Article 36(2) ECHR.[935] As explained in Section 2 of the previous chapter, such conditions may restrict the matters that can be covered by the intervention: intervening parties may be requested, for example, not to directly address the facts of the case. If it is no longer possible to set conditions for the matters that can be covered by the intervention, disappeared parties will be free to explain and define the rights and interests at stake in a way they think is best suited to the case. In view, however, of the impact that a right for actual third parties to intervene will have on the Court's workload, it is submitted that the Court should be allowed to set a maximum length, such as ten pages, for the written submissions. Like limiting the personal scope of a right to intervene, limiting the length of the written submissions will considerably reduce the impact of the proposed change on the Court's workload.

Regarding access to the complete case file, Article 40(2) ECHR states that 'documents deposited with the Registrar shall be accessible to the public unless the President of the Court decides otherwise'. Accordingly, documents deposited by the Registry, by the parties or by any third party can be consulted upon submission of a written request to the Registrar.[936] Although this does not mean the third-party intervener is automatically served with the relevant documents, they are available upon request, at least in theory, on the basis of Article 40(2). In other words, the

934 See also Ravarani who has held that '[i]t could be envisaged to give interveners more freedom regarding the content of their submissions' (Ravarani 2021 (n 915), section 'extending third parties' possibilities to intervene').

935 See Rule 44(5) Rules of Court.

936 See also Rule 33 Rules of Court.

current system already has a mechanism in place to compensate interveners for lack of automatic access to the complete case file.

Finally, and regarding taking part in hearings, it should first be recalled that oral hearings are held in only a limited number of cases. A decision on admissibility, or a judgment on the merits of the case, is generally made on the basis of written submissions. This differs only for Grand Chamber cases, which generally involve a hearing.[937] If a hearing takes place, the current text of Article 36(2) ECHR provides that any person granted leave to intervene may take part in a hearing, albeit that the Rules of Court restrict this possibility to 'exceptional cases'.[938] Transposing these current procedural rules to the envisaged right to third-party intervention for actual third parties would mean that actual third parties are allowed to take part in a hearing, but it is up to the Court to decide whether this is necessary. Given, however, that hearings are held in only a very limited number of cases, it is proposed that the Rules of Court should no longer restrict the possibility of being involved in a hearing to exceptional cases. The fact that a hearing is held means a case is already a rather exceptional Chamber or Grand Chamber case. Combined with guaranteeing procedural rights, the right to be heard and the principle of equality of arms in particular, actual third-party interveners should, therefore, be allowed to take part in any hearing organised.

3. ADDITIONAL PROCEDURAL ISSUES IN RELATION TO A RIGHT TO THIRD-PARTY INTERVENTION

In addition to the scope of a right to third-party intervention for actual third parties, other issues may be relevant when creating a genuine and effective opportunity to participate in the Court's proceedings and, thereby, addressing the problems arising in verticalised cases. This is illustrated by the two additional procedural issues discussed below in relation to a right to third-party intervention for actual third parties. First, the question is considered as to whether and how an actual third party should be made aware of proceedings pending before the Court and the possibility of intervention (Section 3.1). This question relates very clearly to the effectiveness of a right to intervene for actual third parties. Judge Pastor Vilanova, for example, submitted that '[t]o be effective, such a right should entail notification by the Court to the original parties of the existence of the proceedings in question'.[939]

The second question concerns how the Court should deal with third-party submissions by actual third parties in its reasoning (Section 3.2). This issue is important both for Convention States and private actors. If it is unclear whether and how third-party submissions are taken into account by the Court, it is difficult for domestic courts,

937 As explained in Part I, Chapter 4 (Section 2.2).

938 Rule 44(3a) Rules of Court. This was also discussed in Chapter 9 (Section 2).

939 Pastor Vilanova 2019 (n 915), p. 379; See also Joint Concurring Opinion Judges Ravarani and Elósegui in *A.M. and Others v. Russia* App No 47220/19 (ECtHR 6 July 2021), para. 9.

for example, to determine whether the Court's judgment gives a complete picture of the legal positions and interests involved. With regard to private actors, the issue is explored in the light of the discussion in Part I of this study, where it was explained that the right to a reasoned judgment serves to demonstrate that the parties have been heard. This is particularly important if a submission is fundamental to the outcome of the case. If so, a court must always specifically deal with the submission in its judgment.[940] Although it is not submitted that actual third parties acting as third-party interveners should become an official party to the case, it is nevertheless important for them to know that they have been heard by the Court and that their right to third-party intervention is consequently an effective right. This reflects the analysis presented in Parts II and III, in which it was concluded that actual third parties are involved in the facts of the case and have a direct legal interest in it because their own rights and interests may be affected by a judgment of the Court.

3.1. BECOMING AWARE OF THE COURT'S PROCEEDINGS AND THE POSSIBILITY OF INTERVENING

In the current system, it is the responsibility of persons wanting to intervene to become aware of proceedings pending before the Court. After the respondent State has been notified of the application, interested parties have twelve weeks to inform the Court that they want to intervene.[941] However, the only place where interested parties can find out that the respondent State has been notified is through the Court's website or database (HUDOC), and finding this information is no easy task.[942] It is also important to recall that the case law examples discussed in Part II showed that the parties involved in verticalised cases before the Court can include a wide variety of actors, such as parents, adult/minor children, journalists, publishers and private employers. Whether such private actors can be expected to be aware that proceedings originating from the conflict they were involved in at the domestic level have been initiated at the Court and also to know about the possibility for them to intervene in these proceedings is certainly open to question, particularly in the case of private individuals such as parents or adult/minor children, for whom finding their way to the Court is likely to be less easy than, say, for large companies.

To make actual third parties aware of Court's proceedings and, thereby, to guarantee their procedural rights more effectively, several judges at the Court have proposed changing the current procedure. Pastor Vilanova submitted, for example, that the Court should be obliged to inform all potentially concerned parties about a pending procedure before the Court.[943] Similarly to Pastor Vilanova, Judge Wojtyczek argued

940 This was discussed in Section 3.1 of Chapter 4 on the right to a reasoned judgment.

941 Rule 44(3b) Rules of Court.

942 See also Pastor Vilanova 2019 (n 915), p. 390; Wojtyczek 2020 (n 915), p. 752; Ravarani 2021 (n 915), section on 'the information issue'.

943 Pastor Vilanova 2019 (n 915), pp. 390–391.

in his concurring opinion to the case of *A and B*, concerning allegations of child sexual abuse, that the Court should have invited the father to present his observations, both as the father and legal representative of the applicant, and as a party whose own rights and interests might have been affected by the outcome of the proceedings.[944] Finally, Ravarani and Elósegui submitted in their joint concurring opinion to the case of *A.M. and Others* that the third-party intervention mechanism could be made more effective by 'implementing systematic notification of pending cases to all persons defined as "concerned" in relation to those cases'.[945] This case concerned the restricting of parental rights and the deprivation of contact after the applicant had undergone a medical and legal gender transition. In addition to the above-mentioned joint concurring opinion, Judge Elósegui wrote a concurring opinion in which she considered that, in this case, 'the Court could have informed the ex-spouse and biological mother of the children about the present proceedings before it, even if she was not a party to them'.[946]

The previous chapter explained that, under the current rules, the Court can already invite a State, an individual or an organisation to intervene in the Court's proceedings. Currently, however, this is neither an obligation for the Court, nor standard practice. Indeed, the Court only occasionally makes use of the opportunity to invite a third party to intervene in the proceedings, as, for example, in *Strand Lobben* in which the Court invited the adoptive parents of the second applicant to intervene.[947] According to Pastor Vilanova, one of the judges in this case, the Court was able to do so by asking the respondent State to provide the identity and contact details of potential third parties.[948] In other words, the Court and the respective Convention State worked together in inviting the second applicant's adoptive parents to intervene. In should also be recalled that Germany has legislation in place that requires third parties to be informed by the government agent whenever it becomes apparent that their interests would be affected in proceedings before the Court, and that legal aid can be provided if this party wishes to appear before the Court.[949] This legislation was enacted in response to the criticism by the German Federal Constitutional Court that an ECtHR judgment may not necessarily give a complete picture of the legal positions and interests involved, and that this might be unfair to the parties to the original case.

It is consequently proposed that actual third parties should be made aware of the Court's proceedings and their opportunity to intervene, and that Convention States and the Court have a shared responsibility in this respect. It would be the Court's responsibility to first determine who should be informed about the pending

---

944 Concurring Opinion Judge Wojtyczek in *A and B v. Croatia* App No 7144/15 (ECtHR 20 June 2019), para. 6.

945 Joint Concurring Opinion Judges Ravarani and Elósegui in *A.M. and Others v. Russia* App No 47220/19 (ECtHR 6 July 2021), para. 9.

946 Concurring opinion Judge Elósegui in *A.M. and Others v. Russia* App No 47220/19 (ECtHR 6 July 2021), para. 11.

947 Pastor Vilanova 2019 (n 915), p. 388. Pastor Vilanova was one of the judges in this case. See also Section 2 of Chapter 9.

948 Pastor Vilanova 2019 (n 915), p. 391.

949 See Chapter 8 (Section 4).

proceedings, and the Convention States would then be responsible for informing this party, or at least making a reasonable effort to do so. This shared responsibility is based on the idea that it is the Court's task to determine who qualifies for a right to intervene, while Convention States are in the best position to inform actual third parties. The weakness of this approach is that the effectiveness of actual third parties' right to intervene will partly depend on cooperation with Convention States and that, accordingly, differences may arise between Convention States. In fact, States will have no legal obligation to inform actual third parties about pending proceedings unless this is laid down in the official text of the Convention. And even if this obligation were to be part of the Convention, not all Convention States would necessarily adhere to this rule in every case. However, the alternative of assigning sole responsibility to the Court also has its drawbacks: such an obligation would have a more profound impact on the Court's workload and would not alter the fact that the Court depends on the cooperation of Convention States to trace and contact the actual third party. The application form submitted by the applicant, for example, will not contain much helpful information in this regard. The fact that the Court depends on Convention States was also illustrated above, when it was explained that the Court could invite third parties to intervene in the Court's proceedings by asking the respondent State to provide the identity and contact details of these individuals. A shared responsibility construction, as proposed above, would therefore seem to be the best approach. It is important to recall, in this regard, that the current approach to verticalised cases not only poses problems for private actors, but also for Convention States and the Court. In other words, it also important for Convention States and the Court for actual third parties to be put in a position in which they can effectively claim their right to third-party intervention.

3.2. THIRD-PARTY SUBMISSIONS AND THE COURT'S REASONING

Another procedural issue to be discussed is how the Court should deal with third-party submissions by actual third parties in its reasoning. The analysis presented in Part II and the previous chapter showed that the Court's current practice in relation to third-party submissions is to include a summary of these submissions in its judgment. However, the Court only occasionally refers directly to third-party submissions in its reasoning, while the analysis of the verticalised cases examined for this study showed that the Court never referred directly to third-party submissions in cases when an actual third party was granted leave to intervene in the Court's proceedings.[950]

With regard to guaranteeing a genuine and effective right to intervene, the question arises as to whether the Court should continue the above practice when actual third parties are granted a right to intervene. By not referring directly to third-party submissions, the Court leaves it unclear as to whether and how these submissions

[950] See Chapter 6 (Section 3).

were taken into account. It can certainly be said that, in the current practice, third-party interveners are left in the dark. Even if their submissions have influenced the Court, there is no guarantee that this will be noted in the Court's reasoning. As a result, actual third parties will not know whether they have been heard by the Court, whereas one of the purposes served by the right to a reasoned judgment is the purpose of demonstrating that parties have actually been heard.[951]

The lack of clarity on whether and how third-party submissions are taken into account also has implications for Convention States, and for domestic courts in particular. As the German Federal Constitutional Court clearly explained, domestic courts may face problems when they have to apply and enforce a judgment of the Court in a verticalised case as this judgment may not necessarily give a complete picture of the legal positions and interests involved.[952] This is because the Court proceedings involve an applicant-State relationship, whereas the original and continued, reopened or newly initiated proceedings involve a different – that is, horizontal – relationship. If the original parties to the proceedings at the domestic level are granted a right to intervene, the Court judgment may give a better picture of the legal positions and interests involved. But if the Court does not refer to the arguments as provided in the third-party submissions, it will remain difficult for domestic courts to determine whether this is indeed the case.

For the above reasons, it is proposed that the Court should refer directly to a third-party submission if this influenced the Court's reasoning. In other words, the Court should rely more often on the second way of dealing with third-party submissions, as identified by Bürli. To briefly reiterate, Bürli distinguished three ways in which the Court deals with third-party submissions: it may provide a summary of the intervener's main arguments or it may refer directly to the third-party submissions in its reasoning, or judges may include references to third-party submissions in their separate opinions.[953] It is proposed that the Court should, in principle, combine the first and second ways of dealing with third-party submissions, with an example of what this could look like in practice being discussed in Section 4 of the previous chapter. This example concerned the case *Kurt*, in which the Court referred directly to the third-party submissions by GREVIO by adding references, in brackets, to these submissions. For verticalised cases, this could mean that the Court refers to submissions by the actual third party if it relied on these submissions for obtaining a well-informed view of the exact meaning and importance of the rights and interests of the actual third party. In, for instance, the discussed case of *Schüth*, concerning the dismissal of an employee, the Court could have made reference to the third-party submissions by the employer when describing the latter's interests. This particular example is given here since the Court's reasoning seems to suggest that the Court was aware of the employer's interests and that the third-party submissions by the employer had provided the Court with information

951 See Chapter 4 (Section 3.1).
952 The reasoning of the German Federal Constitutional Court is discussed in detail in Chapter 8 (Section 3).
953 This is discussed in Chapter 9 (Section 4).

on the exact meaning and importance of these interests.[954] Although the proposed approach does not guarantee that the Court will consider a third-party submission and give weight to the arguments and interests presented, it would at least provide more clarity on whether a third-party submission had influenced the Court's reasoning. This is important both for private actors and for Convention States, as was discussed above.

4. REDESIGNED THIRD-PARTY INTERVENTION PROCEDURE IN PRACTICE

In the previous sections it was proposed that the third-party intervention procedure of Article 36 ECHR should be redesigned so that actual third parties are granted a *right* to intervene in the Court's proceedings. With regard to the personal scope of such a right to intervene it was explained that, to qualify for such a right, actual third parties must have a legal interest in the case. More specifically, they must have been involved in the conflict at the domestic level, their human rights interests must be in conflict with the rights and interests of the applicant, and these interests must be protected by the Convention. If these conditions are met, it should be presumed that the actual third party wanting to intervene might be affected by a judgment of the Court. Regarding the procedural scope, and in order to guarantee a genuine and effective right to intervene, it was submitted that a right for actual third parties should follow the current rules on the right to third-party intervention for Convention States and the Council of Europe Commissioner for Human Rights. In practice, this should ensure that actual third parties are free to explain and define the rights and interests at stake in a way they think is best suited to the case. In order also to ensure that actual third parties are aware of the Court's proceedings and the possibility of intervening, it was proposed that the Court and Convention States should have a shared responsibility for informing such parties about a pending procedure before the Court. Finally, it was suggested that the Court should make it explicit in its judgments if third-party submissions have influenced its reasoning, even though this does not entail an obligation for the Court to consider such submissions.

If actual third parties are granted a right to intervene in the Court's proceedings, the possibility of intervening will no longer be at the Court's discretion. This, combined with the various features envisaged for a right to third-party intervention, should create a situation in which the original party to the conflict at the domestic level has a genuine and effective opportunity to intervene in Court proceedings and, thus, the ability to defend or explain his acts, interests or rights in these proceedings. This will be beneficial not only for private actors, but also for Convention States and the Court itself. The benefit for Convention States it that they will be confronted less often with situations in which they have to defend the rights and interests of the disappeared party and will instead

954 See also Chapter 6 (Section 3.4).

be able to refer to third-party submissions. From the Court's perspective, the proposed solution is beneficial as it will allow the Court to base its judgments on a fuller and more balanced account of the rights and interests at stake and the legal positions involved. This, in turn, will minimise the problems faced by domestic courts when applying and enforcing a judgment of the Court in a verticalised case since the Court's judgment will provide a more complete picture of the legal positions and interests involved.

This can be further illustrated by returning to the different types of verticalised cases used throughout this study as illustrative case studies for unravelling the notion of such cases and the Court's approach to them. These different types of verticalised cases are used below to describe how the redesigned third-party intervention procedure could work out in practice. First, verticalised cases involving a conflict between the right to reputation and private life and the right to freedom of expression are discussed, followed by verticalised family life cases. Finally, attention is paid to verticalised employer-employee cases. Verticalised cases related to one's surroundings are not discussed separately, given that it was concluded in Part III that, in most of these cases, no substantial problems arise due to their specific nature and the Court's approach to them, and also because the disappeared party in such cases will not always qualify as an 'actual third party' under the definition provided above.[955]

4.1. RIGHT TO REPUTATION AND PRIVATE LIFE VERSUS FREEDOM OF EXPRESSION CASES

With regard to verticalised cases involving a conflict between the right to reputation and private life and the right to freedom of expression it was explained that the Court sometimes scrutinises the acts of the private actor not involved in the Court's proceedings, based on the standards it has set for the balancing exercise in its case law.[956] In exercising this scrutiny, the Court relies primarily on the case file and the submissions made by the government and the applicant. If, however, actual third parties are granted a right to intervene and free to explain and define the rights and interests at stake, the Court can rely, instead, on the third-party submissions. A journalist, for instance, can provide the Court with more information about how a publication came about and the consequences of an injunction for the journalist's right to freedom of expression, while, in the opposite scenario, individuals can provide the Court with information on their role or function and the impact of the publication on their right to reputation and private life. This information relates directly to the substantive criteria identified and listed by the Court for the balancing exercise. Accordingly, the Court will have a more complete picture of the facts and the rights and interests at stake when it compares the domestic courts' assessment with its own assessment for each standard laid down in the Court's case law.

955 See Section 2.1 of the present chapter.
956 See Chapter 6 (Section 3.2).

With regard to this type of verticalised case, it was explained, furthermore, that the Court may also rely on a procedural review instead of a substantive review. The Court then reviews the national judicial decision-making process by focusing on the balancing exercise conducted by the domestic courts and without performing a substantive balancing exercise of its own, although it may still include some substantive comments in its reasoning. In such cases, too, the Court can benefit from third-party submissions. Submissions such as those described above can help the Court to obtain a fuller account of the rights and interests in conflict with each other and that are central to the balancing exercise. If, for example, the Court examines whether the domestic courts carefully balanced the applicant's right to reputation and private life against the actual third party's right to freedom of expression, it will no longer have a full account of only *one* of the rights and interests at stake, i.e. the right to reputation and private life invoked by the applicant, but of both of them.

4.2. FAMILY LIFE CASES

Verticalised family life cases on custody and access rights, too, provide a good illustration. In general, the Court has been shown to approach such cases by carrying out a procedural review in the classic sense; in other words, a procedural review focusing on the fairness of the decision-making process as a whole.[957] When doing so, it considers whether all persons concerned were involved in the decision-making process and whether the best interests of the child prevailed in this process. As in verticalised cases involving a conflict between the right to reputation and private life and the right to freedom of expression, the Court's examination relies primarily on the case file and the submissions made by the government and the applicant(s). If actual third parties are granted a right to intervene without any restrictions on the subject matter of the intervention, parents who 'won' the case at the domestic level can, for example, provide the Court with their own account of the custody and access proceedings at the domestic level and the exact meaning and importance of what is at stake for them.

This is important since verticalised family life cases are the type of verticalised cases in which the Court's judgment can affect the rights and interests of the disappeared party most strongly.[958] Granting the right to intervene will help the Court to have a full and balanced account of the facts and the rights and interests at stake and thus to be in a better position to evaluate the decision-making process as a whole. More specifically, the Court can then rely on an additional perspective on, for example, the background to the custody and access arrangements and the impact of these arrangements for the right to private and family life, as well as important elements in how the national proceedings were conducted, including the involvement of the parties concerned. Such an additional perspective is particularly important in verticalised cases on custody and access rights

[957] See Chapter 6 (Section 3.3).

[958] See Chapter 8 (Section 2).

for two reasons. First, the particular nature of the conflict means that parents are likely to have a different account of the facts; in other words, the version of the facts presented by the applicant will be rather subjective. Second, and even more importantly, in verticalised family life cases on custody and access rights the question as to whether the child's best interests prevailed in the decision-making process is of fundamental importance to the Court's review.[959] If actual third parties are granted a right to intervene, the parent involved in the proceedings at the domestic level, not being the applicant, can use this opportunity to share his or her views on the best interests of the child. Accordingly, the Court can examine this important question on the basis of the views of both parents, instead of the views of only one of them, i.e. the applicant in the case before the Court.[960]

4.3. EMPLOYER-EMPLOYEE CASES

In relation to employer-employee cases it was observed that the Court either takes a substantive or a mixed substantive and procedural review approach when examining whether a fair balance was struck between the competing rights and interests of the employer and the employee. It was also discerned that, when doing so, the Court sometimes explicitly considered the interests, and sometimes rights, of the disappeared party (often the employer), even though this party was not itself always formally involved in the proceedings before the Court. If the original party to the conflict at the domestic level qualifies for and makes use of the right to intervene, this party will be able to explain the exact meaning and importance of the rights and interests considered by the Court. This is thus quite similar to the examples discussed above. An

---

959 See Chapter 6 (Section 3.3).

960 This issue is closely related to the discussion on the representation and involvement of children in the Court's proceedings when the parents do not agree on the child's best interests. In this regard, it has been put forward that '[i]f the child's rights and best interests are to be taken seriously, the child needs independent representation by a person who is not involved in the underlying conflict and is capable of taking the child's perspective in the matter' (Joint Dissenting Opinion of Judges Koskelo and Nordén on the question of the first applicant's right to represent the second applicant in *Strand Lobben and Others v. Norway* App No 37283/13 (ECtHR (GC) 10 September 2019), para. 7). In other words, it is submitted that the Court should appoint a *curator ad litem* to represent the child if there is a conflict between the parents (see also Concurring Opinion of Judge Wojtyczek in *A and B v Croatia* App No 7144/15 (ECtHR 20 June 2019), para. 5; Partly dissenting opinion of Judge Wojtyczek in *L.R. v North Macedonia* App No 38067/15 (ECtHR 23 January 2020), para. 12; Joint Concurring Opinion of Judges Ravarani and Elósegui in *A.M. and Others v. Russia,* App No 47220/19 (ECtHR 6 July 2021), para. 11; Concurring Opinion of Judge Elósegui in *A.M. and Others v Russia,* App No 47220/19 (ECtHR 6 July 2021), paras. 4ff). On this issue, see also, for example, L. Acconciamessa, 'Bringing the child's procedural rights before the ECtHR through interpretative tools. Access to justice, participation and representation' in P. Czech et al. (eds.), *European Yearbook on Human Rights 2020,* Intersentia 2020, pp. 49–77; E. Merckx, 'The ECtHR on parental authority and contact after separation. Towards a more child-centred perspective?' in P. Czech et al. (eds.), *European Yearbook on Human Rights 2020,* Intersentia 2020, pp. 97–133. For a more general discussion of children's right to participate in family law proceedings see, for example, C.R. Mol, *The child's right to participate in family law disputes. Represented, heard or silenced?,* Intersentia 2022.

illustrative case for explaining more concretely how a right to third-party intervention for actual third parties could work in practice in verticalised employer-employee cases is that of *Bărbulescu*, concerning an employer monitoring the communications of its employees.[961] This was the first case in which the Court listed substantive criteria to be taken into account by the domestic courts when examining the proportionality of surveillance measures and balancing the competing rights and interests at stake.[962] When examining the merits, the Court found in *Bărbulescu* that the domestic court had failed to determine, inter alia, whether the applicant had received prior notice from the employer and the specific reasons justifying the introduction of the monitoring measures. However, six dissenting judges did not agree with these findings of the majority and reasoned, by contrast, that the domestic courts had considered the question of prior notification and, more generally, had carried out a careful balancing exercise between the interests of the employee and the employer. The employer, being the disappeared party, was not involved in the Court's proceedings by way of third-party intervention. The disagreement between the judges shows that the Court could indeed have benefited from third-party submissions, which would have provided it with additional information on, for example, the question of prior notification and the reasons justifying the monitoring, as well as on the extent to which these issues had been part of the domestic proceedings.

This example of verticalised employer-employee cases was the final category discussed. By providing various examples of how the proposed redesigned third-party intervention procedure could work out in practice, this section aimed to illustrate that redesigning this procedure is a possible way to address the problems in verticalised cases and will be of benefit to private actors, Convention States and the Court alike.

961 For a detailed discussion and analysis of this case, see Chapter 6 (Section 3.4).

962 For these criteria, see Chapter 5 (Section 3.7).

CONCLUSION

The first three parts of this study provided an introduction to the Convention system and an analysis of the characteristics of verticalised cases and the Court's approach to them, and identified problems arising in verticalised cases. To address the problems identified in Part III, the fourth and final part of this study outlined a new approach to verticalised cases, while taking account of the characteristics of the Convention system in general and of verticalised cases in particular.

This proposed new approach to verticalised cases consists in redesigning the third-party intervention procedure. On the basis of the current third-party intervention procedure, as laid down in Article 36 ECHR and as discussed in Chapter 9, private actors involved in the conflict at the domestic level (i.e. the disappeared party) *may* be granted leave to intervene in the Court's proceedings. To build on the potential of this existing Convention instrument, while also making it fit to address the problems arising in verticalised cases, it was proposed redesigning the third-party intervention procedure so as to grant actual third parties a *right* to intervene in the Court's proceedings. This means that actual third parties with a legal interest in the case before the Court will no longer depend on the Court's discretion to intervene in its proceedings. Instead, providing they were involved in the conflict at the domestic level, their human rights interests are in conflict with the rights and interests of the applicant, and these interests are protected by the Convention, they will have a guaranteed opportunity to defend or explain their acts, interests or rights in the Court's proceedings. To ensure that this opportunity is genuine and effective, the proposal contains suggestions for the procedural scope of the right to third-party intervention, for becoming aware of the Court's proceedings, and for third-party submissions and the Court's reasoning.

As well as creating a genuine and effective opportunity to participate in the Court's proceedings, the aim was to create a situation that is workable both for the Court and the Convention States. To this end, the personal scope of the envisaged right to third-party intervention was clearly defined and limited, with attention also being paid to the length of third-party submissions and finding an appropriate balance between the need to make actual third parties aware of the Court's proceedings and the burden this will put on Convention States and the Court.

The concluding section of Chapter 10 illustrated how the proposed redesigned third-party intervention procedure addresses the problems arising in verticalised cases from the perspective of private actors, Convention States and the Court alike. More specifically, it was explained that all actors will benefit from the disappeared party's improved opportunity to defend and explain his acts, interests or rights, which may be part of the Court's examination and which may be affected by a judgment of the Court. If the original party to the conflict at the domestic level is involved in the Court's proceedings by way of third-party intervention, the procedural standards formulated for domestic judicial proceedings, as well as more general procedural justice principles, will be better reflected in the Court's proceedings. Furthermore, the Court will be better equipped to base its judgment on a complete and balanced account of the facts and the rights and interests at stake. Accordingly, this judgment will provide a better picture of the legal positions and interests involved. This, in turn, will be of benefit to domestic courts having to apply and enforce a judgment of the Court in reopened, continued, or new proceedings involving the original parties to the conflict.

Although the proposed new approach to verticalised cases is a rather generic approach, applying to all verticalised cases, it allows the Court to tailor its review to the particular nature of the verticalised case before it. As such, it acknowledges that the notion of verticalised cases covers a wide variety of cases and that the Court may need to conduct different types of review when examining them. Hence, it is important that, regardless of the nature of the Court's review (substantive, procedural or a combination of the two), a right to intervene for actual third parties will guarantee that the original party to the conflict at the domestic level has the opportunity to explain and defend his acts, interests and rights, while also putting the Court in a better position to examine the case, without disregarding its position in the Convention system.

CONCLUSION

CHAPTER 11
CONCLUSION

1. INTRODUCTION

In a speech marking the Convention's 70th anniversary in autumn 2020, former President of the Court Sicilianos described the Convention system as a 'unique international instrument' that 'has developed an unparalleled dynamic in its 70 years of existence'.[963] Cases coming before the Court that originate from a conflict between private actors at the domestic level, termed 'verticalised' cases in this study[964], are a notable aspect of this unique system, making up a large share of the Court's case law. This has been illustrated throughout this study, starting with the case of *Von Hannover (No. 2)* in Chapter 1. The applicants in this case, Princess Caroline von Hannover and her husband, had first brought domestic proceedings against several publishing companies to prevent the (further) publication of photos of their private life, and then complained before the Court about the lack of adequate State protection of their right to respect for private life (Article 8 ECHR). In other words, a case between two private actors (i.e. a 'horizontal' case) at the domestic level transformed into a case between an individual and the State (i.e. a 'vertical' case) at the Court. The case of *Von Hannover (No. 2)*, involving a conflict between the right to reputation and private life and the right to freedom of expression of two private individuals, is just one example of a verticalised case. Cases about family life, cases about the relationship between an employee and an employer, and cases related to one's surroundings – such as a case about serious health damage caused by a privately owned factory's emissions – are other examples of cases coming before the Court that can originate from a conflict between private actors at the domestic level. For example, a conflict at the domestic level between separated or divorced parents about custody or access rights can transform into a case between an individual and the State if one of the parents complains at the Court about the State's failure to enforce the custody agreement.

This tendency towards 'verticalisation' can be explained by Article 34 of the Convention, which contains the right for individuals to petition to the Court. Under

963 Speech by Linos-Alexandre Sicilianos (former President of the Court) during a conference marking the 70th anniversary of the Convention ('The European Convention on Human Rights at 70: milestones and major achievements'), Strasbourg 18 September 2020 [translation by the author].

964 On the definition of 'verticalised' cases, in particular the delineation of the notion of verticalised cases as used in the current study, see Chapter 1 (Section 3).

this provision, complaints have to be directed against one of the Convention States to be admissible. Accordingly, complaints directed against private actors are incompatible *ratione personae* with the provisions of the Convention.[965] Chapters 1 and 2 explained that Article 34 ECHR has to be seen in the light of the drafting history of the Convention system. The rule that complaints have to be directed against one of the Convention States is a reflection of the Convention's primary aim to protect individuals against violations of fundamental rights by the State. This does not mean, however, that the Convention system has ignored infringements of the values, rights and liberties enshrined in the Convention by private actors in its 70 years of existence. The overview of horizontal positive obligations in Chapter 5 clearly showed that, over the years, the Court has increasingly offered substantive protection of Convention rights by requiring States to take action to secure the rights and liberties guaranteed in the Convention in relations between private actors. These horizontal positive obligations have been formulated in relation to a broad variety of relations between private actors and Convention rights and have in common that they are often imposed in cases originating from a conflict between private actors at the domestic level.

But although verticalised cases are thus an explainable aspect of the Convention system, and make up a large share of the Court's case law, they have remained underexplored. This makes the phenomenon as such relatively unknown, in particular when it comes to its characteristics, the Court's approach to it, and the exact extent and implications of procedural issues arising in verticalised cases, given that the Convention system was not originally designed to deal with such cases. To fill this gap, this research has provided an in-depth analysis of verticalised cases, with the more specific aims of offering insight into the characteristics of such cases and the Court's approach to them; evaluating the problems of the Court's current approach to verticalised cases for private actors, Convention States and the Court itself; and offering a solution for these problems by designing an alternative approach to verticalised cases.[966] These issues have been explored in the various parts of this book by means of a detailed analysis of four types of verticalised cases: cases related to one's surroundings, cases involving a conflict between the right to reputation and private life and the right to freedom of expression, family life cases, and employer-employee cases. To conclude this study, this final chapter provides a synthesis of the most important findings and, thereby, an answer to the main research question underlying this study: *what are the characteristics of ECtHR cases originating from a conflict between two private actors and how can the Court deal with such verticalised cases while taking due care of the procedural rights of private actors, as well as the position of Convention States and the Court itself?*

In line with the structure of this study, Section 2 first discusses the main findings in relation to the characteristics of verticalised cases and the Court's approach to them. This is followed by a discussion of the problems in verticalised cases (Section 3) and the proposed new approach to such cases (Section 4), with the main findings being linked

965 The admissibility criteria were discussed in detail in Chapter 4 (Section 2.1).
966 For a discussion of the research aim and questions, see also Chapter 1 (Section 2).

to each other throughout these sections. Section 5 rounds off this conclusion with some final remarks.

2. CHARACTERISTICS OF VERTICALISED CASES AND THE COURT'S APPROACH TO THEM

To understand the nature of verticalised cases and the problems arising in them it is necessary to examine their characteristics; that is, the underlying conflicts and the parties involved in them. The previous section briefly explained that the notion of verticalised cases covers different types of cases coming before the Court and that these can originate from a wide range of conflicts between private actors, including conflicts between the right to reputation and private life of one individual and the right to freedom of expression of another individual, conflicts about custody and access rights, work-related conflicts, conflicts related to one's surroundings, conflicts concerning a private insurance contract, or property-related conflicts. In view of the many differences between these cases, there is not just one type of verticalised case, and the underlying conflicts and the parties involved in them can vary substantially. This is further illustrated by the four types of verticalised cases examined for this study in order to provide an in-depth analysis of such cases before the Court.

Verticalised cases involving a conflict between the right to reputation and private life and the right to freedom of expression can originate from a conflict between a private individual and a journalist or publishing company and concern, for example, rectification of an article concerning one's private life or an injunction on the publication of certain photos. Depending on the outcome of the case at the domestic level, one of the two private actors can lodge a complaint at the Court. Because of the vertical nature of the Court's proceedings, this complaint has to be directed against the State. If, for example, the domestic courts decide not to grant an injunction, private individuals seeking redress at the Court can complain about a lack of State protection of their right to reputation and private life. In the opposite scenario, journalists or publishing companies can complain about a violation of their right to freedom of expression on the basis of the domestic courts' decision to grant the injunction. As a result of this verticalisation, one of the private actors involved in the conflict at the domestic level is not formally involved as a party in the subsequent ECtHR proceedings. If, say, a publications' alleged victim lodges a complaint with the Court, the publishing company directly responsible for the publication is not involved in the Court's proceedings, whereas if, on the other hand, the journalist or publishing company brings a case before the Court, the individual who experienced harm from the publication is not a formal party to the Court's proceedings.

Although very different in nature, a similar scenario unfolds in verticalised family life cases. This research distinguished two types of verticalised family life cases: cases involving custody and access to a child, and cases on access to information about one's origins. Cases before the Court concerning custody and access rights often arise from a conflict between separated or divorced parents at the domestic level. After parents have separated or divorced, one of them may start domestic judicial proceedings to obtain custody and or access rights or to seek enforcement of these rights. Depending on the outcome of the domestic case, one of the parents can lodge a complaint at the Court, claiming that the decision or approach of the domestic courts violated his or her right to private and family life. In such cases, the other parent involved in the proceedings at the domestic level does not play a formal role in the proceedings before the Court. In contrast, however, to verticalised cases involving a conflict between the right to reputation and private life and the right to freedom of expression, these verticalised family life cases involve a conflict between the same Convention provision (Article 8 ECHR) rather than a conflict between two different Convention provisions (Articles 8 and 10 ECHR).

The same holds true for verticalised family life cases on access to information about one's origins. Rather than arising from a conflict between two parents at the domestic level, such cases originate from a conflict between a minor or adult child and a parent (or alleged parent). A child may start civil proceedings at the domestic level to establish, for example, whether a man who denies paternity is his or her biological father. Depending on the outcome of the domestic proceedings, one of these two individuals can subsequently seek redress by lodging an application with the ECtHR. If, for example, the domestic courts decide to order a paternity test, the alleged father can complain to the Court that his right to private life has been violated. The child who initiated the proceedings at the domestic level is not then part of the ECtHR proceedings.

Another type of verticalised cases, employer-employee cases, generally arise from a conflict concerning an employee's dismissal by an employer, such as when an employee is dismissed after being monitored by his employer, or an employment contract is terminated because of an employee wearing religious symbols at work or making certain political statements. If the domestic courts uphold the dismissal, the employee can subsequently complain to the Court about this decision by the domestic courts. Such a complaint can be based on various Convention provisions, depending on the reason for the dismissal: the right to private life, the right to freedom of religion, or the right to freedom of expression, for example. These Convention rights may be in conflict with the right to property of the employer who was involved in the conflict at the domestic level, but who is not a formal party to the ECtHR proceedings. However, it may also be interests, rather than rights, that are in conflict with each other, such as the employer's interest in the smooth running of the company.

The final type of verticalised cases discussed here are cases related to one's surroundings. These are slightly different from the cases discussed above and may concern, for example, noise disturbance caused by private bars or discotheques, or nuisance caused by industrial plants. Such cases do not always clearly originate from a conflict between private actors. Although a private actor may be directly responsible for the nuisance complained of, the responsibility can often be regarded as combined or shared because the contested harmful activity is, in fact, caused by two connected sets of activities. Taken in combination, for example, the actual activities of the private actor involved and the granting of a permit by the domestic authorities may result in an interference with the fundamental rights of an individual. In other words, the alleged harmful activity often depends on, or is legitimised by, domestic regulations or concrete decisions by national authorities. As a result of this combined or shared responsibility, the actual involvement of the State authorities may be so strong that, already at the domestic level, the conflict involves not only two private actors, but also State authorities. At the same time, and because of this shared responsibility, two private actors are involved, at least at some point, in the domestic conflict, whereas one of them will be no longer involved in the proceedings when the case comes before the ECtHR.

The characteristics of the four types of verticalised cases examined for this study illustrate that verticalised cases are rooted in different types of horizontal conflicts at the domestic level, involve different types of private actors, and concern different Convention rights. These differences notwithstanding, they all have in common the fact that one of the private actors involved in the conflict at the domestic level is not part of the proceedings at the Court.

Turning to the Court's approach to verticalised cases, this study investigated whether the differences between verticalised cases are reflected in the Court's approach and how the Court deals with the rights and interests of the party not involved in the proceedings before it. To answer these questions, the Court's approach was analysed for the four types of verticalised cases selected for this study, with a specific focus on the Court's type of review (procedural, substantive, or a combination of the two), the rights and interests that are taken into account by the Court when it examines a verticalised case, and the question of whether the private party involved in the conflict at the domestic level, not being the applicant, is involved in the Court's proceedings by way of third-party intervention. The conclusion that can be derived from this analysis is that the wide variety of verticalised cases is reflected in the approach taken by the Court in assessing them.

The Court often approaches verticalised cases by examining whether a fair balance was struck between the rights and interests of two private actors; that is, the applicant and the private actor involved in the conflict at the domestic level. This is different, however, for verticalised cases related to one's surroundings. In these cases, the Court examines whether a fair balance was struck between the interests of the individual and the community as a whole. This different approach may be explained by the shared or combined responsibility discussed above. In other words, the fact that the harmful activity of a private actor depends on, or is legitimised by, domestic regulations or concrete decisions by national authorities may explain why, in the Court's reasoning and judgment, the activities and interests of the private actor involved in the conflict at the domestic level do not as such play a role, even though this private actor may be the direct source of the nuisance complained of.

Although the Court approaches the other three types of verticalised cases by examining whether a fair balance was struck between the rights and interests of two private actors, the type of review performed by the Court for this purpose varies between review of a more or less procedural or substantive nature, review of a semi-procedural nature, and mixed/combined review. In this respect, differences exist not only between the different types of verticalised cases, but even within specific types of verticalised cases. Illustrative for the former are the differences between the Court's type of review in verticalised employer-employee cases and verticalised family life cases. In verticalised employer-employee cases, the Court often conducts a mixed or combined substantive and procedural review of the national judicial decision-making process, which means the Court includes substantive comments of its own when assessing the domestic courts' balancing exercise.[967] In, for instance, cases concerning surveillance measures by employers, the Court has formulated a set of criteria domestic courts have to take into account when they examine the proportionality of such surveillance measures and balance the different rights and interests at stake. These criteria are often quite substantive in nature, such as the extent of the monitoring by the employer and the degree of intrusion into the employee's privacy. This may explain why the Court may include substantive findings in its reasoning when examining whether the domestic courts took the criteria into account when deciding on the case. By contrast, the Court approaches verticalised family life cases by conducting a strongly procedural type of review, which is also characterised by a focus on procedural safeguards in relation to the decision-making process as a whole. Indeed, the Court consistently approaches such cases by examining the fairness of the decision-making process at the domestic level and, in doing so, pays particular attention to whether all parties concerned were involved in the decision-making process, whether the domestic courts adduced relevant reasons to justify their decision, and whether the best interests of the child prevailed in the decision-making process.

Verticalised cases involving a conflict between the right to reputation and private life and the right to freedom of expression illustrate that differences even exist within a specific type of verticalised case. In these cases, the Court usually starts its reasoning with the standard formula that '[w]here the balancing exercise has been undertaken by the national authorities in conformity with the criteria laid down in the Court's case-law, the Court would require strong reasons to substitute its view for that of the domestic courts'.[968] This suggests that the Court's review is predominantly procedural in nature and that it will therefore examine the judicial decision-making process at the domestic level, without conducting a substantive balancing exercise of its own. However, the case law analysis revealed that the features of the Court's actual review differ and that the Court is not necessarily consistent in its approach. It may still, for example, carry out a substantive approach by re-doing the balancing exercise conducted by the domestic courts and by taking an independent stance of its own as to where the balance should be struck, even if it is not evident from the Court's reasoning that it has

[967] The discussion of the Court's approach to verticalised employer-employee cases in Chapter 6 (Section 3.4) also included an example of a case in which the Court conducted a substantive review.

[968] The Court developed this standard line of reasoning in *Von Hannover v. Germany (No. 2)* App Nos 40660/08 and 60641/08 (ECtHR (GC) 7 February 2012), para. 107. For a detailed discussion, see Chapter 6 (Section 3.2).

much cause to do so. The Court may also conduct a mixed or combined procedural and substantive review by including substantive comments of its own when assessing whether the domestic courts took all the criteria into account when engaging in the balancing exercise. Some of these differences may be explained by the fact that, as in verticalised employer-employee cases, the criteria listed by the Court are of a rather substantive nature, such as contribution to a debate of general interest; the content, form and consequences of the publication; or the circumstances in which the photos were taken, or the information obtained. As a result, it may be difficult for the Court to clearly distinguish between procedural and substantive review.

In addition to the Court's type of review, attention was also paid to how the Court deals with the rights and interests of the private actor who was involved in the conflict at the domestic level, but does not play a formal role in the Court's proceedings. It followed from this analysis that, in verticalised cases involving a conflict between the right to reputation and private life and the right to freedom of expression, the Court may scrutinise the acts and interests of the private actor not involved in the Court's proceedings on the basis of the criteria it has laid down for the balancing exercise. To illustrate, in cases in which Article 8 is invoked, the Court may consider whether the journalist acted in good faith or properly verified the facts. Conversely, in cases in which Article 10 is invoked, the Court can examine the role and function of the victim of the alleged harmful publication, the victim's prior conduct, or the impact of the publication on that person's private life. In other words, since some of the criteria listed by the Court as relevant for the balancing exercise relate directly to the acts and interests of the private actor involved in the conflict at the domestic level, not being the applicant, the Court may scrutinise the acts of this private actor on the basis of the criteria. It also followed from the case law analysis that, to exercise this scrutiny, the Court relies primarily on the case file and the submissions made by the government and the applicant(s). Indeed, in only two of the cases examined for this study was the private actor involved in the conflict, not being the applicant, involved in the Court's proceedings by way of third-party intervention.

The fact that some of the criteria listed by the Court as relevant for the balancing exercise relate directly to the acts and interests of the private actor not involved in the Court's proceedings also applies to verticalised employer-employee cases concerning surveillance measures by employers. This is illustrated by criteria such as whether the employee received prior notification of the surveillance measures and whether the employer has provided legitimate reasons to justify the monitoring. In verticalised employer-employee cases, however, the Court generally tends to take account, at least to some extent, of the rights and interests of the private party not involved in the proceedings, often the employer. Indeed, the Court sometimes explicitly considers the interests, and sometimes rights, of the employer, regardless of whether the employer submitted a third-party intervention in the Court's proceedings.[969] This is thus different from verticalised

[969] The employer – that is, the original party to the conflict at the domestic level, not being the applicant – was granted leave to intervene in three of the verticalised employer-employee cases examined for this study (see further Chapter 6 (Section 3.4) and Chapter 9 (Section 3.2)).

cases involving a conflict between the right to reputation and private life and the right to freedom of expression, in which the Court sometimes merely scrutinises the acts of the private party involved in the conflict at the domestic level, not being the applicant.

Finally, it can be mentioned that, in verticalised family life cases, the Court, as part of its specific focus on the fairness of the decision-making process as a whole, tends not to focus on the conflict between the competing rights and interests as such, but on the best interests of the child. Furthermore, the private actor involved in the conflict at the domestic level was found to be involved in the Court's proceedings by way of third-party intervention in only two of the verticalised family life cases examined for this study. This suggests that the Court bases its examination of the decision-making process on the information provided in the case file and the submissions made by the government and the applicant(s).

The Court's approach to the four types of verticalised cases examined for this study shows, therefore, that the Court carries out different types of review and that these may be more or less procedural or substantive in nature, or semi-procedural or mixed/combined. Differences also exist with regard to how the Court deals with the rights and interests of the private actor involved in the conflict at the domestic level, but who does not play a formal role in the Court's proceedings. These differences do not seem to be influenced by whether the private party involved in the conflict at the domestic level submits a third-party intervention in the Court's proceedings. It was only in relatively few cases examined for this study that the private actor, not being the applicant, intervened as a third party in the case before the ECtHR. In the rare case of a third-party intervention, it is difficult to examine whether and how the intervention influenced the Court's reasoning since the Court does not expressly refer to the submissions in its reasoning.

3. PROBLEMS IN VERTICALISED CASES

As discussed above, the first steps in providing an in-depth analysis of verticalised cases were descriptive and analytical in nature, resulting in the identification and description of the particular characteristics of verticalised cases and the Court's approach to them. To take the analysis a step further, a more evaluative approach was adopted in Part III by examining the procedural implications of verticalisation. This was done in the light of the procedural issues identified by several scholars and ECtHR judges, as well as the procedural standards discussed in Chapter 4.[970] To determine the exact extent and implications of these issues, the problems of the Court's current approach to verticalised cases were examined for private actors, Convention States and the Court itself, with attention being paid both to problems arising *during* the Court's proceedings and problems manifesting themselves *after* a judgment of the Court in a verticalised case.

[970] For a discussion of these issues raised by scholars and ECtHR judges, see Chapter 1 (Section 1), the general introduction to Part IV and Chapter 10.

The analysis of the characteristics of verticalised cases made clear that an important feature of such cases is that one of the original parties to the conflict at the domestic level is not involved in the ECtHR proceedings. Thus, one of the original parties 'disappears' from the case when it comes before the Court. A close analysis of the problems arising during the Court's proceedings and after the Court issues a judgment in a verticalised case shows that this particular situation has implications for private actors, Convention States and the Court itself.

For private actors it means that the disappeared party is not represented in the Court's proceedings unless he intervenes as a third party.[971] When the disappeared party is not involved in the Court's proceeding, this party will be unable to defend or explain his acts, interests or rights. At the same time, and with the exception of cases related to one's surroundings, these acts, interests or rights may be part of the Court's examination. To reiterate, in verticalised cases involving a conflict between the right to reputation and private life and the right to freedom of expression, the Court may, for example, scrutinise the acts and interests of the private actor not involved in the Court's proceedings on the basis of the standards it has laid down for the balancing exercise in its own precedents. Accordingly, it can examine whether a journalist, who on the domestic level was found to have violated someone's reputation, acted in good faith or properly verified the facts, without having information provided by the disappeared party itself. Similarly, in verticalised employer-employee cases, the Court may explicitly consider the interests, and sometimes rights, of the employer (often the disappeared party), even though the employer is not always formally involved in the proceedings before the Court. The disappeared party is then not able to defend his rights or interests himself by, for example, providing the Court with information on the exact meaning and importance of these rights and interests. Finally, in verticalised family life cases, in which the Court's review is predominantly procedural in nature, one of the parents involved in the conflict at the domestic level, or the mother or father (or presumed mother or father) or a child seeking information about his or her origins, will not be able to provide the Court with their own account of the domestic proceedings and the exact meaning and importance of what is at stake for them. This is particularly important since these family life cases are the type of verticalised cases in which the judgment of the Court can affect the rights and interests of the disappeared party most strongly.

Thus, the main problem arising for private actors during the Court's proceedings is that the original party to the conflict at the domestic level, not being the applicant, is not heard in the Court's proceedings, while his acts, interests and rights may be part of the Court's examination and this party may eventually be affected by a judgment of the Court. The latter was confirmed by the analysis of the execution process in the verticalised cases examined for this study.[972] More specifically, it followed from this

[971] This opportunity is offered by Article 36(2) ECHR which provides that a third party may be granted leave to intervene in the Court's proceedings. A detailed analysis of the form and features of the current third-party intervention procedure can be found in Chapter 9.

[972] See Chapter 8 (Section 2.2).

analysis that a Court judgment in a verticalised case can impact on the legal situation at the domestic level, for example when the Court judgment is followed by domestic proceedings. This applies in particular to verticalised family life cases, when the reopening, continuing or initiating of new domestic proceedings after a judgment of the Court has led, for example, to the granting of custody or access rights or the establishing of paternity.

The fact that the disappeared party is not heard in the Court's proceedings is problematic in the light of the procedural standards discussed in Part I of this study, where it was explained that it is necessary and important for the Court to adhere to the procedural standards it has set for domestic judicial proceedings and to comply with general procedural justice principles.[973] These include the right to be heard, the principle of equality of arms, the right to a reasoned judgment, and the general procedural justice principle of participation. The extent to which a third party is affected by a judgment is generally considered an important factor in determining whether this party has a right to be heard. The right to be heard requires, moreover, that observations are not only listened to by a court, but also duly considered when a decision is being reached. It is also important to recall that the general procedural justice principle of participation requires the Court not only to represent the different viewpoints of the parties in its judgments and to carefully assess the merits of each argument, but also to pay attention to stakeholders who may not be a formal party in the case.[974] The above discussion and the discussion in Section 2 of Chapter 7 showed, however, that the Court's current approach to verticalised cases is not in complete conformity with these procedural standards. Although the existing Convention instrument of third-party intervention offers the disappeared party the possibility of being granted leave to intervene in the Court's proceedings, the analysis of the characteristics of verticalised cases and the Court's approach to them showed this to be the exception rather than the rule. Only in a few cases examined for this study was the disappeared party involved in the Court's proceedings by way of third-party intervention.[975] It was also explained that, in the rare event of the disappeared party intervening, the Court does not expressly refer to this party's submissions in its reasoning. This then makes it difficult for this party to verify whether his submissions were actually considered by the Court.

In addition to the problems arising for private actors, the Court's current approach to verticalised cases has implications for Convention States. Again, these problems originate from the fact that, in verticalised cases, one of the original parties to the

---

973 See in particular Chapter 4.

974 This concerns an application of the general procedural justice principle of participation, as proposed by Brems and Lavyrsen (E. Brems and L. Lavrysen, 'Procedural justice in human rights adjudication: the European Court of Human Rights' (2013) 35 *Human Rights Quarterly* 176). For a detailed discussion, see Chapter 4 (Section 3.2).

975 This is supported by Bürli, who found 'actual third-party interventions' to be the type of interventions seen least in the Court's proceedings (N. Bürli, *Third-party interventions before the European Court of Human Rights: Amicus Curiae, Member-State and Third-Party interventions*, Intersentia 2017, pp. 6, 7, 193). For a detailed discussion of Bürli's study, see Chapter 9,

conflict at the domestic level is not involved in the Court's proceedings. Since the disappeared party is not able to present and defend his acts, interests and rights himself, Convention States may be asked to take on this role.[976] The latter, however, may be unwilling to do so or incapable of such as part of their role of defending the national position in the Court's proceedings. The respondent State may not, for example, have all the information needed to provide the Court with a full and correct account of the rights and interests of the disappeared party, while the interests of the disappeared party may even be in conflict with those of the respondent State.

The non-involvement of the disappeared party also means that, in most verticalised cases, the Court receives only the version of the facts and arguments presented by the applicant(s) and the Convention States, supplemented with the information provided in the case file. Although the latter can contain detailed information on the domestic proceedings, a manifest problem for the Court is that it may have to examine a verticalised case without having access to a full and balanced account of the facts of the case, the different rights and interests at stake, and the exact meaning and importance of these rights and interests. Indeed, judges at the Court have expressed concerns in this regard by pointing out that the Court may lack essential information for forming a full and balanced view in a verticalised case.[977] For this reason, they have referred to a 'flawed'[978] balancing exercise and a 'blind spot'[979] in such cases.

This situation, in turn, may give rise to problems for domestic courts having to apply and enforce a judgment of the Court in a verticalised case. In the frequently cited judgment in *Görgülü*[980], for example, the German Federal Constitutional Court reasoned that a Court judgment in a verticalised case may not necessarily give a complete picture of the legal positions and interests involved. The reason for this is that the ECtHR proceedings involve an applicant-State relationship, whereas the original and continued or reopened proceedings involve different parties and may be a multi-dimensional, multi-subject case. Hence, the German Federal Constitutional Court held that domestic courts have to evaluate the ECtHR judgment when taking it into account in a reopened or continued case between the original parties to the case.[981] For similar reasons, Switzerland and the Republic of Moldova introduced legislation that allows the federal tribunal to invite every party to the original proceedings that led to the application to the

976 In Chapter 7 (Section 3.1) it was illustrated on the basis of submissions by States that governments are sometimes under the impression that they are actually being asked to defend the acts of a private actor.

977 Joint Concurring Opinion of Judges Ravarani and Elósegui in *A.M. and Others v. Russia*, App No 47220/19 (ECtHR 6 July 2021), para. 1. For a detailed discussion, see Chapter 7 (Section 3.2).

978 Concurring Opinion of Judge Wojtyczek in *A and B v. Croatia* App No 7144/15 (ECtHR 20 June 2019), para. 3.

979 Joint Concurring Opinion of Judges Ravarani and Elósegui in *A.M. and Others v. Russia*, App No 47220/19 (ECtHR 6 July 2021), para. 6.

980 BVerfGE, Order of the Second Senate of 14 October 2004, 2 BvR 1481/04 (*Görgülü*) (official English translation). For a detailed discussion of this judgment, see Chapter 8 (Section 3).

981 BVerfGE, Order of the Second Senate of 14 October 2004, 2 BvR 1481/04 (*Görgülü*) (official English translation), paras. 50 and 59.

Court to give their written observations or oral pleadings when domestic proceedings are reopened.[982] This shows that, in applying and enforcing a judgment of the Court in a verticalised case, domestic courts may be charged with an additional responsibility to compensate for the fact that the judgment of the Court may not necessarily have given a complete picture of the legal positions and interests involved.

Finally, the difficulties domestic courts encounter when applying and enforcing a judgment of the Court in a verticalised case also have implications for the Court itself, in particular for its role in the broader Convention system. As discussed in Section 3 of Chapter 8, such a situation may put pressure on the authority of the Court's judgments. This, in turn, may adversely affect the relationship between the Court and domestic courts, while, as explained in Chapter 3, this relationship is crucial for the effective functioning of the Convention system as a whole.

4. TOWARDS A NEW APPROACH TO VERTICALISED CASES

The Court's current approach to verticalised cases clearly gives rise to problems for private actors, Convention States (including domestic courts) and the Court itself. To offer a solution to these problems, the final part of this study (Part IV) focused on designing an alternative approach to such cases. In designing this alternative approach, it was chosen to concentrate on the procedural framework rather, for example, than on the Court's argumentation in verticalised cases. The wide variety of verticalised cases and the differences between them make it difficult to design a one-size-fits-all approach directed at the Court's reasoning, let alone apply in practice. Such an approach could also leave the Court too little room to tailor its review to the particular nature of the case before it. A procedural change, by contrast, gives the Court flexibility to adapt its review and reasoning to the particular case before it.

In focusing on a procedural solution, it was also decided to stay close to the characteristics of the Convention system by exploring the potential of an already existing Convention instrument: the third-party intervention procedure of Article 36 ECHR. The proposal presented in this study is to redesign the third-party intervention procedure such that third parties with a legal interest in the case ('actual third parties') are granted a *right* – rather than just a possibility – to intervene in the Court's proceedings. In further developing this proposal, attention was paid to the perspectives of private actors, Convention States and the Court. It was consequently proposed to redesign the third-party intervention procedure in such a way that it can properly address the problems arising in verticalised cases for private actors, Convention States and the Court alike, while also giving careful consideration to the practical implications of a redesigned third-party intervention procedure, including its implications for the Court's workload.

---

982 See Chapter 8 (Section 4).

Based on the above, the features of the proposed redesigned third-party intervention procedure can be summarised as follows. First, in order to qualify for the proposed right to intervene, disappeared parties must have a legal interest in the case. This means that they must have been involved in the conflict at the domestic level, their fundamental rights interests must conflict with the rights and interests of the applicant, and these interests must be protected by the Convention. If these conditions are met, it can be presumed that the actual third party wanting to intervene may be affected by a Court judgment in the case brought by the applicant. Setting out these criteria helps to clearly define and limit the scope of the envisaged right to intervene by enabling the Court to determine, based on a standard set of criteria, whether a party qualifies for the right to third-party intervention. At the same time, it will ensure that only a limited number of parties can claim the proposed right to third-party intervention, which is important in the light of the Court's workload. Finally, the criteria provide Convention States and private actors with clarity and certainty as to who is eligible to intervene in the Court's proceedings.

In addition to the personal scope, the procedural scope of the proposed right to intervene has to be delineated. In doing so, it is important to find an appropriate balance between, on the one hand, creating a genuine and effective possibility for third parties to usefully participate in the Court's proceedings and, on the other hand, generating a situation that remains workable from the perspective of the Court and the Convention States. Against this background, it is proposed that a right to intervene for actual third parties should be based on the current rules for the existing right to third-party intervention for Convention States and the Council of Europe Commissioner for Human Rights. This means that 'actual' third parties will not be granted full litigation rights, such as having automatic access to the complete case file or having the opportunity to apply for legal aid or the right to request leave to appeal to the Grand Chamber.[983] Nevertheless, it will still guarantee a genuine and effective right to intervene by ensuring that actual third parties are free to explain and define the rights and interests at stake in a way they think is best suited to the case. To take account of the Court's workload it was also submitted that that the Court should be allowed to set a maximum length – ten pages, for example – for the written submissions.

To guarantee a genuine and effective right to intervene that is used more often than the current opportunity to intervene, it is also proposed that the Court and the Convention States should have a shared responsibility for informing actual third parties about a pending procedure before the Court. To ensure that such parties are aware of the Court's proceedings and able to make use of their right to intervene, it is the Court's responsibility to first determine who should be informed about the pending proceedings. The Convention States then have the task of actually informing this party, thus making use of their more direct access to information about the party.

---

983 As discussed in Chapter 10 (Section 2.2), such full litigation rights have been proposed by some scholars and ECtHR judges.

Finally, it is proposed that the Court should make it explicit in its judgments when third-party submissions have influenced its reasoning. This means, for example, that the Court should refer to the submissions by the actual third party if it relied on these submissions to get a well-informed view of the exact meaning and importance of the actual third party's rights and interests. Even though this does not entail an obligation for the Court to substantively consider third-party submissions and explain how they influenced its judgment, it has the benefit of providing more clarity as to whether the third-party submissions had an impact on the Court's reasoning. This is important in the light of the right to a reasoned judgment, which serves the purpose, among other things, of demonstrating that parties have been heard. In addition, it makes it easier for domestic courts to determine whether the judgment of the Court gives a complete picture of all the legal positions and interests involved.

It follows from the above that the proposed redesigned third-party intervention procedure can help to address the problems arising in verticalised cases by creating a situation in which the original party to the conflict at the domestic level has a genuine and effective opportunity to intervene in the Court's proceedings and thus the ability to defend or explain his acts, interests or rights in the Court's proceedings. In verticalised cases involving, for example, a conflict between the right to reputation and private life and the right to freedom of expression, the redesigned procedure will enable journalists to provide the Court with more information about how a publication came about and the consequences of an injunction for their right to freedom of expression. In the opposite scenario, it will allow a private individual who suffered as a result of a publication to provide the Court with information on his or her role or function or the impact of the publication on his or her right to reputation and private life. Meanwhile, even in verticalised cases involving a conflict between the right to reputation and private life and the right to freedom of expression in which the Court relies primarily on a procedural review, third-party submissions by the disappeared party can help the Court to gain a fuller account of the conflicting rights and interests that were central to the national judicial balancing exercise it has to examine. The redesigned procedure also has benefits for verticalised employer-employee cases, such as cases concerning surveillance measures by an employer. If the disappeared party, often the employer, qualifies for the proposed right to intervene in such cases, this party will have the opportunity to provide additional information on, for example, questions of prior notification and reasons justifying the monitoring, and the exact meaning and importance of its own rights and interests. Lastly, in verticalised family life cases, the redesigned procedure will make it possible, for example, for a parent who 'won' the case at the domestic level to provide the Court with an additional perspective on matters such as the background to the custody and access arrangements and the impact of these arrangements on the right to private and family life, as well as on important elements relating to how the national proceedings were conducted, including the involvement of the parties concerned.

Finally, it should be noted that the existence of a genuine and effective opportunity to defend or explain their acts, interests or rights in the Court's proceedings will be beneficial not only for the private actors involved in the conflict at the domestic level. The above examples also illustrate that a right to third-party intervention for actual third parties will allow the Court to base its judgment on a fuller and more balanced account of the facts of the case, the rights and interests at stake, and the legal positions involved. This, in turn, will make it easier for domestic courts to apply and enforce judgments of the Court in verticalised cases since these judgments will give a more complete picture of the legal positions and interests involved. The proposed redesigned third-party intervention procedure can thus address the problems arising in verticalised cases for all actors involved; in other words, not only for private actors, but also for Convention States and the Court.

5. FINAL REMARKS

This final chapter started with a quotation from a speech by former President of the Court Sicilianos marking the 70th anniversary of the Convention. In this speech, Sicilianos said that 'continuous adaptation of the working methods of the Court' is one of the five institutional features explaining the unique character and dynamics of the Convention system.[984] In other words, an important feature of the Convention system is that the Court is able to adapt its working methods to deal with new challenges. This study shows that verticalised cases represent precisely such a challenge, given that they give rise to particular issues for private actors, Convention States and the Court alike, while also forming a notable aspect of the Convention system, and comprising a large share of the Court's case law. As such cases are likely to play an even more prominent role in the Convention system in the future, it is particularly important for the Court to adopt an approach to verticalised cases that allows it to deal with them satisfactorily, while also paying due attention to the procedural rights of private actors and to the position of Convention States and the Court itself. The final part of this study showed that adapting the working methods of the Court by redesigning the third-party intervention procedure of Article 36 ECHR comprises precisely such an approach in that it addresses many of the problems arising in verticalised cases, while making use of an existing Convention instrument. As such, it represents an approach to verticalised cases that builds on existing features of the Convention system and thus does not detract from the Convention's original function and characteristics.

984 Speech by Linos-Alexandre Sicilianos (former President of the Court) during a conference marking the 70th anniversary of the Convention ('The European Convention on Human Rights at 70: milestones and major achievements'), Strasbourg 18 September 2020 [translation by the author]. The other four institutional features mentioned by Sicilianos are the unconditional right of individual application, the permanent character of the Court, the unique execution mechanism, and the dialogue with national authorities. See also L.A. Sicilianos, 'The European Convention on Human Rights at 70: the dynamic of a unique international instrument' in P. Czech et al. (eds.), *European Yearbook on Human Rights 2020,* Intersentia 2020, pp. 3–15, p. 15.

SUMMARY IN DUTCH

1. INLEIDING

De zaak *Von Hannover (Nr. 2)*[985] is misschien wel een van de meest bekende en belangwekkende uitspraken van het Europees Hof voor de Rechten van de Mens (hierna: EHRM of Hof). De klaagster in deze zaak, prinses Caroline von Hannover, had op nationaal niveau verschillende rechtszaken aangespannen tegen Duitse uitgevers om de publicatie van foto's van haar privéleven een halt toe te roepen. Voor de prinses hadden deze zaken niet de gewenste uitkomst, omdat de Duitse rechter alleen de publicatie van een paar foto's verbood en de uitgevers dus geen totaalverbod oplegde. Dit gaf de prinses en haar man aanleiding om een klacht in te dienen bij het EHRM. In Straatsburg klaagden zij dat de Duitse overheid onvoldoende had gedaan om hun recht op privéleven (artikel 8 Europees Verdrag voor de Rechten van de Mens (hierna: EVRM)) te beschermen. Anders dan de prinses en haar man betoogden, overwoog het Hof dat de Duitse rechters hadden voldaan aan hun positieve verplichtingen onder artikel 8 EVRM nu zij het recht op privéleven van klagers zorgvuldig hadden afgewogen tegen het recht op vrijheid van meningsuiting van de uitgevers. Om deze conclusie te ondersteunen formuleerde het Hof verschillende criteria die nationale rechters in acht moeten nemen wanneer zij een belangenafweging moeten maken tussen het recht op privéleven en het recht op vrijheid van meningsuiting.

Alhoewel de zaak *Von Hannover (Nr. 2)* bekend is geworden vanwege de criteria die het Hof formuleerde, speelde er nog iets anders in deze zaak. Wat gebeurde in *Von Hannover (Nr. 2)* is dat een private partij, na een procedure op nationaal niveau tegen een andere private partij, bij het EHRM een klacht indient tegen de staat over deze zaak. Oftewel, een 'horizontale' zaak (een zaak tussen private partijen) op nationaal niveau verandert in een 'verticale' zaak (een zaak tussen een private partij en de staat) bij het EHRM. Deze 'verticalisering' is inherent aan de werking van het EVRM-systeem. Op basis van artikel 34 EVRM kan ieder natuurlijk persoon, niet-gouvernementele organisatie of iedere groep personen namelijk alleen een klacht indienen over een schending van het EVRM door een van de verdragsstaten. Het is dus niet mogelijk om bij het EHRM een klacht in te dienen tegen een private partij, bijvoorbeeld een individu of een bedrijf.

Dat bij het EHRM alleen kan worden geklaagd over het handelen of nalaten van staten moet in het licht worden gezien van de totstandkomingsgeschiedenis van het

985 *Von Hannover t. Duitsland (Nr. 2)* (EHRM (GK) 7 februari 2012, nrs. 40660/08 en 60641/08).

EVRM. Het EVRM is opgesteld in de jaren na de Tweede Wereldoorlog – een oorlog die op verschrikkelijke wijze heeft laten zien hoe staten hun macht kunnen misbruiken om inbreuk te maken op de autonomie, menselijke waardigheid en vrijheid van personen. In de jaren na de Tweede Wereldoorlog werd de angst voor het communisme en een derde wereldoorlog tussen het oosten en het westen bovendien steeds groter. Tegen deze achtergrond is het niet moeilijk te begrijpen dat het EVRM is opgesteld met de risico's van totalitarisme in het achterhoofd, en dat het tot doel heeft om individuen te beschermen tegen grondrechtenschendingen door staten.

Toch illustreert de zaak *Von Hannover (Nr. 2)* dat het EVRM-systeem ook aandacht heeft voor grondrechtenschendingen door private partijen. Door de jaren heen heeft het EHRM steeds vaker voorzien in materiële bescherming van EVRM-rechten in relaties tussen private partijen. Dat heeft het vooral gedaan door aan staten horizontale positieve verplichtingen op te leggen. Dit betekent dat het Hof staten verplicht om maatregelen te nemen om de rechten en vrijheden zoals neergelegd in het EVRM te beschermen in private verhoudingen. Dat kan een staat bijvoorbeeld doen door middel van wetgeving, door het garanderen van effectieve rechtshandhaving, door het nemen van preventieve maatregelen of door te voorzien in effectieve rechtsbescherming. Deze horizontale positieve verplichtingen vloeien voort uit de verantwoordelijkheid van staten voor hun eigen handelen en nalaten in relatie tot het handelen van private partijen en uit de verplichting tot het garanderen van effectieve bescherming van EVRM-rechten.

Horizontale positieve verplichtingen worden door het Hof vaak geformuleerd in wat in dit onderzoek 'geverticaliseerde zaken' worden genoemd. Het gaat dan om zaken die hun oorsprong vinden in een conflict tussen private partijen op nationaal niveau. De zaak *Von Hannover (Nr. 2)*, die ging over een conflict tussen het recht op reputatie en privéleven en het recht op vrijheid van meningsuiting, is een voorbeeld van zo'n geverticaliseerde zaak, maar er zijn veel meer voorbeelden denkbaar. Geverticaliseerde zaken kunnen bijvoorbeeld ook betrekking hebben op familieverhoudingen, bijvoorbeeld zaken over ouderlijke macht en omgangsrechten die voortkomen uit een conflict tussen gescheiden ouders of zaken waar een kind een rechtszaak begint om vast te stellen of een man die zijn vaderschap ontkent toch de biologische vader is. Verder kan gedacht worden aan arbeidsgerelateerde zaken, bijvoorbeeld wanneer een werknemer wordt ontslagen voor het dragen van religieuze symbolen op de werkvloer, of zaken met betrekking tot de leefomgeving, bijvoorbeeld schadelijke uitstoot door fabrieken of geluidsoverlast door vliegtuigen of cafés. Dergelijke zaken kunnen allemaal worden omschreven als geverticaliseerde zaken, omdat ze hun oorsprong vinden in een conflict tussen twee private partijen op nationaal niveau (een horizontaal conflict) en daarom moeten worden getransformeerd tot een zaak tussen een private partij en de staat (een verticale zaak) om ontvankelijk te zijn bij het EHRM.

Hoewel het bestaan van geverticaliseerde zaken al langere tijd wordt erkend en deze zaken een aanzienlijk deel van de rechtspraak van het Hof beslaan, is het een aspect van het EVRM-systeem waar nauwelijks onderzoek naar is gedaan. Hierdoor zijn geverticaliseerde zaken een relatief onbekend fenomeen en is weinig bekend over de precieze aard van de onderliggende conflicten en de partijen die in de conflicten een rol spelen alsmede de manier waarop deze zaken door het EHRM worden beoordeeld. Daardoor is er ook weinig inzicht in de procedurele vraagstukken die zich in geverticaliseerde zaken kunnen voordoen als gevolg van het feit dat het EVRM-systeem eigenlijk niet is ontworpen om dergelijke zaken te behandelen. Alhoewel enkele auteurs en rechters bij het EHRM al eerder op deze problemen hebben gewezen, vergen hun precieze omvang en implicaties nader onderzoek. Om in deze hiaten te voorzien, biedt deze studie een gedetailleerde analyse van geverticaliseerde zaken en verschaft deze inzicht in de aard en kenmerken van geverticaliseerde zaken en de manier waarop ze door het Hof worden beoordeeld. Daarnaast zijn de procedurele problemen die zich voordoen in geverticaliseerde zaken onderzocht en in kaart gebracht voor verschillende betrokken actoren (private partijen, verdragsstaten en het Hof zelf). Tot slot wordt een oplossing voor deze problemen aangereikt in de vorm van een voorstel voor een nieuwe aanpak van geverticaliseerde zaken. Hieronder worden de belangrijkste bevindingen samengevat, waarbij de structuur van het boek wordt gevolgd.

2. DE AARD VAN GEVERTICALISEERDE ZAKEN EN DE AANPAK VAN HET EHRM

Om geverticaliseerde zaken te begrijpen, alsmede de problemen die zich in deze zaken voordoen, moet eerst inzicht worden verkregen in de conflicten die aan geverticaliseerde zaken ten grondslag liggen. In het voorgaande werd al aangestipt dat een breed scala aan zaken dat bij het EHRM terechtkomt als geverticaliseerde zaak kan worden aangemerkt. Deze zaken vinden hun oorsprong in uiteenlopende conflicten tussen private partijen, bijvoorbeeld conflicten over botsingen tussen het recht op reputatie en privéleven en het recht op vrijheid van meningsuiting, conflicten over ouderlijke macht of omgangsrechten, arbeidsgerelateerde conflicten, conflicten over de woon- en leefomgeving, conflicten over verzekeringscontracten of conflicten over eigendomskwesties. Dit laat zien dat er niet één type geverticaliseerde zaak is en dat er substantiële verschillen kunnen bestaan tussen de geschillen die aan een geverticaliseerde zaak ten grondslag liggen. Dit wordt verder geïllustreerd door vier groepen van geverticaliseerde zaken die voor dit onderzoek zijn bestudeerd.

Allereerst is nader onderzoek gedaan naar geverticaliseerde zaken die gaan over een conflict tussen het recht op reputatie en privéleven en het recht op vrijheid van meningsuiting. Dergelijke zaken kunnen hun oorsprong vinden in een conflict tussen een individu en een journalist of uitgever over bijvoorbeeld de rectificatie van een artikel dat informatie bevat over iemands privéleven of een verbod om bepaalde foto's te publiceren. Afhankelijk van de uitkomst van de zaak op nationaal niveau kan een van de twee private partijen een klacht indienen bij het EHRM. Vanwege de verticale aard van de procedure in Straatsburg moet deze klacht gaan over het handelen of nalaten van de staat. Wanneer de nationale rechter bijvoorbeeld besluit om de publicatie van bepaalde foto's niet te verbieden, kan een individu bij het Hof klagen dat de staat onvoldoende heeft gedaan om zijn of haar recht op reputatie en privéleven te beschermen. Tegelijkertijd kan een journalist bij het Hof klagen over een schending van zijn recht op vrijheid van meningsuiting door de staat wanneer de nationale rechter juist wel een verbod oplegt of de rectificatie van een artikel beveelt. Als gevolg van deze verticalisering is een van de twee private partijen die op nationaal niveau betrokken was in het conflict niet langer formeel betrokken in de procedure bij het EHRM. Wanneer een persoon die beweert slachtoffer te zijn van een bepaalde publicatie een klacht indient bij het EHRM is de journalist of de uitgever die verantwoordelijk is voor de publicatie niet meer betrokken in de procedure bij het EHRM. Wanneer daarentegen de journalist of de uitgever klaagt over een schending van zijn recht op vrijheid van meningsuiting is juist de persoon die onder de publicatie heeft geleden niet meer betrokken in de procedure in Straatsburg.

Hoewel de aard van het conflict geheel anders is, doet een vergelijkbare situatie zich voor in familiezaken. In dit onderzoek is een onderscheid gemaakt tussen twee soorten familiezaken: zaken die gaan over ouderlijke macht en omgangsrechten en zaken over toegang tot informatie over iemands afkomst. Zaken bij het EHRM over ouderlijke macht en omgangsrechten ontstaan vaak uit een conflict op nationaal niveau tussen gescheiden ouders. Wanneer ouders uit elkaar gaan, kunnen zij op nationaal niveau verwikkeld raken in rechtszaken over de toekenning of handhaving van de ouderlijke macht en omgangsrechten. Na een dergelijke procedure op nationaal niveau kan een van de ouders een klacht indienen bij het EHRM, met als inhoud dat de beslissing of aanpak van de nationale rechter een schending oplevert van het recht op privé- en familieleven. De andere ouder die betrokken was in de zaak op nationaal niveau is dan niet langer formeel betrokken in de procedure bij het EHRM. In tegenstelling tot geverticaliseerde zaken over een conflict tussen het recht op reputatie en privéleven en het recht op vrijheid van meningsuiting gaan deze geverticaliseerde familiezaken over een conflict tussen eenzelfde EVRM-bepaling (artikel 8 EVRM) en niet over een conflict tussen twee verschillende EVRM-bepalingen (bijvoorbeeld artikel 8 en 10 EVRM in het zaaktype van de reputatie- versus uitingsrechten).

Ook in geverticaliseerde familiezaken over toegang tot informatie over iemands afkomst is maar één EVRM-bepaling betrokken. In plaats van uit een conflict tussen gescheiden ouders, ontstaan dergelijke zaken uit een conflict tussen een kind en een (vermeende) ouder. Een kind kan bijvoorbeeld op nationaal niveau een rechtszaak starten om vastgesteld te krijgen dat een man die het vaderschap ontkent zijn of haar biologische ouder is. Afhankelijk van de beslissing van de nationale rechter kan een van deze partijen vervolgens een klacht indienen bij het EHRM. Wanneer bijvoorbeeld de nationale rechter oordeelt dat de vermeende vader een vaderschapstest dient te ondergaan, kan deze persoon bij het EHRM klagen over een schending van zijn recht op privéleven. Het kind dat op nationaal niveau de procedure was gestart is dan geen partij in de procedure bij het EHRM.

Conflicten tussen werkgevers en werknemers kunnen resulteren in een derde type geverticaliseerde zaken. Dergelijke conflicten kunnen zich bijvoorbeeld voordoen wanneer een werknemer is ontslagen nadat de werkgever de communicatie van de werknemer heeft gemonitord of wanneer een arbeidsovereenkomst wordt beëindigd omdat de werknemer religieuze symbolen draagt op de werkvloer of bepaalde politieke uitlatingen heeft gedaan. Wanneer het ontslag door de nationale rechter in stand wordt gehouden, kan de werknemer een klacht over deze beslissing indienen bij het EHRM. Afhankelijk van de reden van het ontslag kan een dergelijke klacht over verschillende EVRM-bepalingen gaan, zoals het recht op privéleven, het recht op vrijheid van godsdienst of het recht op vrijheid van meningsuiting. Deze EVRM-rechten kunnen conflicteren met het eigendomsrecht van de werkgever of het belang van de werkgever dat gediend is met een soepele bedrijfsvoering. Deze werkgever was op nationaal niveau betrokken in het geschil, maar is bij het EHRM geen formele partij in de procedure.

Omgevingsgerelateerde zaken vormen een ander, en laatste, soort geverticaliseerde zaak dat onderdeel heeft uitgemaakt van de analyse. Omgevingsgerelateerde zaken gaan over de woon- en leefomgeving en betreffen bijvoorbeeld schadelijke uitstoot door fabrieken, overlast door overvliegende vliegtuigen of geluidsoverlast door cafés of discotheken. Deze zaken wijken af van andere geverticaliseerde zaken in de zin dat bij nadere bestudering blijkt dat ze vaak niet ontstaan uit een conflict dat puur horizontaal van aard is. Alhoewel een private partij over het algemeen direct verantwoordelijk is voor de hinder waarover wordt geklaagd, gaat het vaak om een gecombineerde of gedeelde verantwoordelijkheid van een private partij en de staat. Naast het directe handelen van de private partij speelt het handelen van de overheid namelijk vaak een belangrijke rol, bijvoorbeeld omdat de overheid een vergunning heeft afgegeven of onvoldoende toezicht heeft gehouden. Oftewel, het handelen van de private partij is vaak afhankelijk van, of gelegitimeerd door nationale wetgeving of concrete overheidsbesluiten. Vanwege deze gecombineerde of gedeelde verantwoordelijkheid kan al op nationaal niveau de staat betrokken zijn in het conflict, waardoor het conflict niet puur horizontaal van aard is. Dit doet echter niet af aan het feit dat twee private partijen in het conflict op nationaal niveau betrokken zijn en dat een van deze twee partijen niet meer betrokken is in de procedure wanneer de zaak bij het EHRM komt.

De karakteristieken van de vier verschillende soorten geverticaliseerde zaken die voor dit onderzoek zijn onderzocht laten zien dat geverticaliseerde zaken hun oorsprong vinden in verschillende horizontale conflicten op nationaal niveau, dat verschillende soorten private partijen in deze conflicten betrokken zijn en dat verschillende EVRM-rechten in het geding kunnen zijn. Tegelijkertijd hebben de zaken gemeen dat een van de private partijen betrokken in het conflict op nationaal niveau geen formele partij is in de procedure bij het EHRM.

Naast de aard van geverticaliseerde zaken is onderzocht in hoeverre de verschillen tussen geverticaliseerde zaken terug te zien zijn in de beoordeling van het EHRM en hoe het EHRM omgaat met de rechten en belangen van de private partij die niet formeel bij de procedure is betrokken, maar die wel onderdeel uitmaakte van het conflict op nationaal niveau waaruit de zaak is ontstaan. Om deze vragen te beantwoorden is de beoordeling van het Hof geanalyseerd voor de vier soorten geverticaliseerde zaken die voor dit onderzoek zijn geselecteerd. Hierbij is in het bijzonder aandacht besteed aan het soort toetsing (procedureel, materieel of een combinatie van de twee), aan de rechten en belangen die het Hof in zijn beoordeling meeneemt en aan de vraag of de private partij die betrokken was in het conflict op nationaal niveau, niet zijnde de klager, ook betrokken is in de procedure bij het EHRM door middel van derde-partij-interventie. Uit deze analyse is gebleken dat het feit dat er niet één type geverticaliseerde zaak is ook terug te zien is in de wijze van beoordeling van de zaak.

Over het algemeen beoordeelt het Hof in geverticaliseerde zaken of een eerlijke afweging (*fair balance*) is gemaakt tussen de rechten en belangen van twee private partijen, dus de klager en de andere private partij betrokken in het conflict op nationaal niveau. Dit is alleen anders in omgevingsgerelateerde zaken. In deze zaken beoordeelt het Hof of een eerlijke afweging is gemaakt tussen de rechten en belangen van de klager en die van de samenleving als geheel. Een mogelijke verklaring hiervoor kan worden gevonden in de gedeelde of gecombineerde verantwoordelijkheid die dit type zaken kenmerkt. Specifieker, het feit dat het schadelijk handelen van een private partij afhankelijk is van of wordt gelegitimeerd door nationale wetgeving of concrete overheidsbesluiten kan verklaren waarom in de beoordeling en uitspraak van het Hof de activiteiten en belangen van de private partij die betrokken was in het conflict op nationaal niveau als zodanig geen rol spelen, terwijl deze private partij direct verantwoordelijk kan zijn voor de hinder waarover wordt geklaagd.

Zoals gezegd beoordeelt het Hof in de andere drie soorten geverticaliseerde zaken of een eerlijke afweging is gemaakt tussen de rechten en belangen van twee private partijen. De manier waarop het Hof dit toetst varieert. Uit de analyse is gebleken dat het Hof verschillende soorten toetsing hanteert in de zin dat de toetsing procedureel of materieel van aard kan zijn of een combinatie van de twee. Deze verschillen zijn niet alleen terug te zien tussen de verschillende soorten geverticaliseerde zaken, maar ook binnen één type geverticaliseerde zaak. Illustratief voor verschillen *tussen* de typen geverticaliseerde zaken is het verschil tussen werkgever/werknemerszaken en familiezaken. In werkgever/werknemerszaken past het Hof vaak een combinatie toe van materiële en procedurele toetsing om de belangenafweging door de nationale rechter te beoordelen. Zo heeft het Hof voor zaken over de inzet van surveillancetechnologie door werkgevers een set criteria geformuleerd die nationale rechters in acht moeten nemen wanneer zij de proportionaliteit van surveillancemaatregelen beoordelen en de verschillende rechten en belangen tegen elkaar afwegen. Een aantal van deze criteria is behoorlijk materieel van aard, bijvoorbeeld als het gaat om de omvang van de surveillance en de mate waarin hiermee inbreuk is gemaakt op het privéleven van de werknemer. Dit kan een verklaring zijn voor het feit dat de redenering van het Hof vaak materiële overwegingen bevat wanneer het beoordeelt of de nationale rechters alle criteria mee hebben genomen bij het beoordelen van de zaak.

In tegenstelling tot werkgever/werknemerszaken, is de toetsing van het Hof in geverticaliseerde familiezaken sterk procedureel van aard. Deze procedurele toets kenmerkt zich bovendien door een bijzondere aandacht voor procedurele waarborgen in relatie tot het gehele besluitvormingsproces op nationaal niveau. Concreter: de aanpak van het Hof in geverticaliseerde familiezaken kenmerkt zich door een consistente beoordeling van de eerlijkheid van het besluitvormingsproces op nationaal niveau. Hierbij besteedt het Hof aandacht aan de vraag of alle relevante partijen betrokken zijn geweest in de procedure, of de nationale rechters hun beslissing voldoende hebben gemotiveerd en of voorrang is gegeven aan de rechten en belangen van het kind.

Geverticaliseerde zaken die gaan over een conflict tussen het recht op reputatie en privéleven en het recht op vrijheid van meningsuiting zijn illustratief voor het feit dat de beoordeling van het Hof niet alleen varieert per type geverticaliseerde zaak, maar dat ook verschillen bestaan *binnen* een bepaald soort zaak. Over het algemeen gaat het Hof er in deze zaken van uit dat wanneer de nationale autoriteiten een belangenafweging hebben gemaakt in overeenstemming met de in de EHRM-rechtspraak neergelegde criteria, het Hof van de uitkomst daarvan alleen mag afwijken als daarvoor zwaarwegende redenen bestaan.[986] Dit suggereert dat het Hof in principe de nationale rechterlijke procedure toetst zonder de zaak zelf inhoudelijk te beoordelen en dat de beoordeling dus hoofdzakelijk procedureel van aard is. De rechtspraakanalyse heeft echter laten zien dat de precieze beoordeling van het Hof per zaak kan verschillen en dat het Hof niet altijd consistent is in zijn aanpak. Het Hof kan bijvoorbeeld een inhoudelijke toets uitvoeren door de belangenafweging die op nationaal niveau heeft plaatsgevonden over te doen en tot een eigen oordeel te komen over hoe deze afweging moet uitvallen, zonder dat uit de redenering van het Hof blijkt dat er aanleiding bestaat om dit te doen. Ook kan de beoordeling door Hof bestaan uit een gecombineerde procedurele en materiële toets. Dit betekent dat de redenering van het Hof ook materiële overwegingen bevat wanneer het beoordeelt of de nationale rechters alle criteria in acht hebben genomen bij het maken van de belangenafweging. Net als bij geverticaliseerde werkgever/werknemerszaken kan een verklaring voor deze verschillen schuilen in het feit dat de criteria die door het Hof zijn geformuleerd behoorlijk materieel van aard zijn, zoals de bijdrage aan een debat van algemeen belang, de vorm en gevolgen van een publicatie of de omstandigheden waarin de foto's zijn genomen of de informatie is verkregen. Als gevolg van dergelijke criteria kan het voor het Hof lastig zijn om een duidelijk onderscheid te maken tussen procedurele en materiële toetsing.

Naast het soort toetsing is ook onderzocht hoe het Hof omgaat met de rechten en belangen van de private partij die betrokken was in het conflict op nationaal niveau, maar die geen formele partij is in de procedure bij het EHRM. Hieruit blijkt dat in geverticaliseerde zaken over een conflict tussen het recht op reputatie en privéleven en het recht op vrijheid van meningsuiting het Hof aan de hand van de criteria die het heeft geformuleerd voor de belangenafweging op nationaal niveau soms kritisch kijkt naar het handelen en de belangen van de private partij die niet is betrokken in de procedure in Straatsburg. In zaken waarin artikel 8 EVRM wordt ingeroepen kan het

[986] Het EHRM gebruikte deze standaardredenering voor het eerst in *Von Hannover t. Duitsland (Nr. 2)* (EHRM (GK) 7 februari 2012, nrs. 40660/08 en 60641/08, par. 107).

Hof bijvoorbeeld nagaan of de journalist die verantwoordelijk is voor de publicatie te goeder trouw heeft gehandeld of zorgvuldig de feiten heeft geverifieerd. Wanneer een beroep wordt gedaan op artikel 10 EVRM, het tegenovergestelde scenario, besteedt het Hof soms aandacht aan de rol en de functie van de persoon die heeft geleden onder de publicatie in kwestie, het gedrag van deze persoon in het verleden of de impact van de publicatie op zijn of haar privéleven. Dat betekent dat een aantal van de geformuleerde criteria rechtstreeks verband houdt met het handelen en de belangen van de private partij betrokken in het conflict op nationaal niveau, niet zijnde de klager, die voor het EHRM niet vertegenwoordigd is. Uit de analyse is gebleken dat het Hof hiervoor hoofdzakelijk leunt op informatie uit het dossier en de argumenten van de klager(s) en de staat. In slechts twee van de voor deze studie geanalyseerde zaken was de private partij betrokken in het conflict op nationaal niveau, niet zijnde de klager, betrokken in de procedure bij het Hof door middel van derde-partij-interventie.

Dat een aantal van de door het Hof geformuleerde criteria voor de belangenafweging op nationaal niveau direct verband houdt met het handelen en de belangen van de private partij niet formeel betrokken in de procedure bij het EHRM geldt ook voor geverticaliseerde werkgever/werknemerszaken over surveillancemaatregelen. Dit wordt geïllustreerd door criteria die zien op de vraag of de werknemer voorafgaand aan de inzet van surveillancemaatregelen is geïnformeerd en of de werkgever legitieme redenen heeft aangedragen om het toezicht te rechtvaardigen. In werkgever/werknemerszaken kan het Hof echter ook aandacht hebben voor de rechten en belangen van de werkgever; meestal de private partij die niet langer betrokken is in de procedure wanneer de zaak bij het EHRM komt. Dit betekent dat het Hof soms expliciet, en onafhankelijk van de vraag of de werkgever betrokken is in de procedure door middel van derde-partij-interventie, de belangen, en soms rechten, van een niet in de procedure betrokken partij in zijn beoordeling betrekt. Dit is dus anders dan bij geverticaliseerde zaken over een conflict tussen het recht op reputatie en privéleven en het recht op vrijheid van meningsuiting, waarin het Hof soms enkel het handelen van de private partij, niet zijnde de klager, kritisch onder de loep neemt.

Tot slot gaat in geverticaliseerde familiezaken de aandacht van het Hof gewoonlijk niet zozeer uit naar de conflicterende rechten en belangen, maar naar het belang van het kind. Dit als onderdeel van de specifieke focus van het Hof in deze zaken op de vraag of het gehele besluitvormingsproces op nationaal niveau eerlijk is verlopen. Uit de analyse van geverticaliseerde familiezaken blijkt dat slechts in twee van de geanalyseerde zaken de private partij betrokken in het conflict op nationaal niveau door middel van derde-partij-interventie betrokken was in de procedure bij het EHRM. Dus ook in deze zaken lijkt het Hof zijn beoordeling van de nationale procedure hoofdzakelijk te baseren op de informatie die het krijgt aangereikt in het dossier en via de argumenten van klager(s) en de staat.

De beoordeling door het Hof van de vier soorten geverticaliseerde zaken die voor dit onderzoek zijn bestudeerd laat zien dat het Hof verschillende soorten toetsing hanteert. Deze toetsing kan meer of minder procedureel of materieel van aard zijn of kan de vorm hebben van een combinatie van procedurele en materiële toetsing. Naast deze verschillen in toetsing bestaan er ook verschillen in de manier waarop het Hof omgaat met de rechten en belangen van de private partij die betrokken was in het conflict op nationaal niveau maar die geen formele partij is in de procedure bij het EHRM. Een verklaring voor deze verschillen is niet gelegen in de vraag of de private partij betrokken in het conflict op nationaal niveau als derde partij intervenieert in de procedure bij het EHRM. Dit was namelijk slechts het geval in enkele zaken die voor dit onderzoek zijn bestudeerd. In het zeldzame geval van derde-partij-interventie is het bovendien lastig om na te gaan of en in hoeverre de interventie invloed heeft gehad op de beoordeling, omdat het Hof in zijn overwegingen niet verwijst naar de derde-partij-interventie.

3. PROBLEMEN IN GEVERTICALISEERDE ZAKEN

In aanvulling op de hiervoor samengevatte rechtspraakanalyse is in Deel III van deze studie voor een meer evaluerende aanpak gekozen om de procedurele gevolgen van verticalisering in kaart te brengen. In het licht van een nadere analyse van de achtergronden en doelstellingen van het EVRM-systeem en van de procedurele rechten die voor de verschillende betrokken actoren moeten worden erkend, is in dit kader gekeken naar problemen die zich voordoen voor private partijen, verdragsstaten en het Hof. Daarbij is een onderscheid gemaakt tussen problemen *tijdens* de procedure bij het Hof en problemen die zich manifesteren *na* een uitspraak van het Hof in een geverticaliseerde zaak.

De analyse van de karakteristieken van geverticaliseerde zaken maakte duidelijk dat een belangrijk kenmerk van deze zaken is dat een van de private partijen die betrokken was in het conflict op nationaal niveau geen formele partij is in de procedure bij het EHRM. Oftewel, een van de twee partijen 'verdwijnt' uit het conflict wanneer de zaak bij het EHRM komt. Uit het onderzoek naar problemen die zich voordoen tijdens de procedure bij het Hof en nadat het Hof uitspraak heeft gedaan in een geverticaliseerde zaak blijkt dat deze situatie gevolgen heeft voor private partijen, verdragsstaten en het Hof zelf.

Voor private partijen betekent het dat de verdwenen partij niet vertegenwoordigd is in de procedure bij het EHRM, tenzij hij als derde partij intervenieert in de procedure. Wanneer de verdwenen partij niet betrokken is in de procedure, is het voor deze partij niet mogelijk om zijn handelen, belangen of rechten te verdedigen of nader toe te lichten. Tegelijkertijd is gebleken dat, met uitzondering van omgevingsgerelateerde zaken, de handelingen, belangen en rechten van de verdwenen partij wel degelijk onderdeel kunnen zijn van de beoordeling door het Hof. Zo kan in herinnering worden geroepen dat het Hof in geverticaliseerde zaken over een conflict tussen het recht op reputatie en privéleven en het recht op vrijheid van meningsuiting het handelen van de niet betrokken private partij soms kritisch bekijkt aan de hand van de criteria die het heeft geformuleerd voor de belangenafweging op nationaal niveau. Het Hof kan bijvoorbeeld nagaan of een journalist die op nationaal niveau verantwoordelijk is gehouden voor de schending van iemands reputatie te goeder trouw heeft gehandeld en de feiten zorgvuldig heeft geverifieerd, zonder dat het Hof over informatie hierover beschikt die door deze partij zelf is aangeleverd. In geverticaliseerde werkgever/werknemerszaken kan het Hof daarnaast expliciet aandacht besteden aan de belangen, en soms rechten, van de werkgever (over het algemeen de verdwenen partij), terwijl de werkgever vaak niet formeel is betrokken in de procedure bij het Hof. Daardoor heeft de werkgever niet de mogelijkheid om op te komen voor zijn rechten en belangen, bijvoorbeeld door het Hof meer inzicht te verschaffen in wat er precies voor hem op het spel staat. Tot slot geldt in geverticaliseerde familiezaken, waarin het Hof sterk procedureel toetst, dat een van de ouders die betrokken was in het conflict op nationaal niveau (of de (vermeende) moeder of vader of een kind dat meer te weten wil komen over zijn of haar afkomst) het Hof geen uitleg kan geven over zijn of haar kijk op de procedure op nationaal niveau en de precieze betekenis en het belang van wat voor deze partij op het spel staat. Nu juist in geverticaliseerde familiezaken de uitspraak van het Hof veel impact kan hebben op de rechten en belangen van de verdwenen partij is dat bijzonder problematisch.

Het probleem dat zich dus tijdens de procedure bij het EHRM voor private partijen voordoet is dat een van de twee private personen die partij was in het conflict op nationaal niveau niet wordt gehoord in de procedure bij het EHRM, terwijl zijn handelen, rechten en belangen wel voorwerp kunnen vormen van de beoordeling en deze partij uiteindelijk kan worden geraakt door de uitspraak van het Hof. Dit laatste is bevestigd door een analyse van de tenuitvoerlegging van de geverticaliseerde zaken die voor deze studie zijn onderzocht. Uit deze analyse is gebleken dat een uitspraak van het Hof in een geverticaliseerde zaak gevolgen kan hebben voor de rechten en belangen van de private partij die betrokken was in het conflict op nationaal niveau. Dit geldt in het bijzonder voor geverticaliseerde familiezaken. In deze zaken kan de heropening, continuering of initiëring van een nieuwe rechtszaak op nationaal niveau na een uitspraak van het Hof bijvoorbeeld leiden tot het toekennen van omgangsrechten of de vaststelling van vaderschap.

Het feit dat de verdwenen partij niet wordt gehoord in de procedure bij het Hof is problematisch in het licht van de procedurele standaarden die in dit boek zijn uitgewerkt. Uiteen gezet is dat het voor het Hof belangrijk en noodzakelijk is om zich te houden aan de procedurele standaarden die het zelf heeft geformuleerd voor nationale procedures en te handelen conform algemene beginselen van procedurele rechtvaardigheid. Hieronder vallen onder meer het recht om gehoord te worden, het beginsel van *equality of arms*, het recht op een gemotiveerde beslissing en participatie als algemeen beginsel van procedurele rechtvaardigheid. De mate waarin een derde partij wordt geraakt door een uitspraak wordt bijvoorbeeld meestal gezien als een factor die een belangrijke rol speelt bij het bepalen of deze partij het recht heeft om gehoord te worden. Het recht om gehoord te worden vereist bovendien dat een partij niet alleen gehoord wordt, maar dat de argumenten die deze partij naar voren brengt ook daadwerkelijk worden meegenomen. In dit kader is het ook belangrijk om te noemen dat het participatiebeginsel zoals uitgelegd door Brems en Lavrysen vereist dat het EHRM in een uitspraak niet alleen aandacht besteedt aan de standpunten van de klager en de staat in kwestie, maar ook kijkt naar belangrijke stakeholders die geen formele partij zijn in de procedure bij het Hof.

Uit de geschetste probleemanalyse blijkt dat de huidige aanpak van geverticaliseerde zaken niet geheel in overeenstemming is met deze procedurele standaarden. Hoewel de verdwenen partij op basis van het bestaande instrument van derde-partij-interventie toestemming kan worden verleend om in de procedure te interveniëren en dus zijn belangen en stellingen naar voren kan brengen, is uit de analyse van de karakteristieken van geverticaliseerde zaken en de aanpak van het Hof gebleken dat dit maar heel weinig voorkomt. Slechts in een beperkt aantal zaken die voor deze studie zijn onderzocht was de verdwenen partij in de procedure bij het Hof betrokken door middel van derde-partij-interventie. Daarnaast is uitgelegd dat in het uitzonderlijke geval dat de verdwenen partij intervenieert in de procedure, het Hof niet expliciet aandacht besteedt aan de informatie of de standpunten die deze partij naar voren heeft gebracht. Als gevolg daarvan is het voor deze partij lastig om na te gaan of zijn inbreng een rol heeft gespeeld in de beoordeling van de zaak door het Hof.

Naast de problemen voor private partijen, heeft de huidige aanpak van geverticaliseerde zaken ook gevolgen voor de verdragsstaten. Ook hier geldt dat deze problemen worden veroorzaakt door het feit dat in geverticaliseerde zaken een van twee private partijen die betrokken was in het conflict op nationaal niveau geen onderdeel uitmaakt van de procedure bij het EHRM. Doordat de verdwenen partij niet zelf zijn handelen, rechten en belangen kan verdedigen en toelichten kan het aan verdragsstaten zijn om deze taak op zich te nemen. Verdragsstaten kunnen hiertoe echter niet altijd bereid of in staat zijn, omdat zij de nationale positie verdedigen in de procedure bij het Hof. De betreffende staat kan bijvoorbeeld niet alle informatie hebben om het Hof te voorzien van een volledige en juiste weergave van de rechten en belangen van de verdwenen partij. Deze rechten en belangen kunnen bovendien conflicteren met die van de staat.

Dat de verdwenen partij niet is betrokken in de procedure bij het EHRM betekent ook dat in veel van de geverticaliseerde zaken het Hof alleen beschikking heeft over de versie van de feiten zoals gepresenteerd door klager(s) en de staat, de argumenten van deze twee partijen en aanvullende informatie uit het dossier. Hoewel het dossier gedetailleerde informatie kan bevatten over de nationale procedure, is een probleem voor het Hof dat het een geverticaliseerde zaak moet beoordelen zonder toegang te hebben tot een volledig en evenwichtig overzicht van de feiten van de zaak, de verschillende rechten en belangen die in het geding zijn en de precieze betekenis van deze rechten en belangen. EHRM-rechters hebben hierover ook hun zorgen geuit door erop te wijzen dat het Hof essentiële informatie kan missen die nodig is om tot een volledig en afgewogen oordeel te komen in een geverticaliseerde zaak. In dit licht spreken zij van een 'gebrekkige belangenafweging' of een 'blinde vlek' in geverticaliseerde zaken.

Deze situatie heeft op haar beurt gevolgen voor nationale rechters wanneer zij uitvoering moeten geven aan een uitspraak van het Hof in een geverticaliseerde zaak. In de *Görgülü*-uitspraak[987] overwoog het Duitse *Bundesverfassungsgericht* bijvoorbeeld dat een uitspraak van het EHRM in een geverticaliseerde zaak niet noodzakelijkerwijs een volledig beeld geeft van de verschillende rechten en belangen die in het geding zijn. De oorzaak hiervan schuilt erin dat de procedure bij het EHRM een klager-staat-constructie kent, terwijl de zaak op nationaal niveau een multidimensionaal karakter heeft doordat hierbij verschillende private partijen betrokken zijn. Daarom heeft het *Bundesverfassungsgericht* overwogen dat nationale rechters een EHRM-uitspraak zorgvuldig moeten evalueren wanneer deze uitspraak een rol speelt in een heropende of gecontinueerde zaak tussen de twee private partijen die oorspronkelijk bij het conflict betrokken waren. Om vergelijkbare redenen hebben Zwitserland en Moldavië wetgeving geïntroduceerd die het voor rechters mogelijk maakt om alle partijen die betrokken waren in het conflict dat leidde tot de klacht bij het EHRM uit te nodigen wanneer de uitspraak van het EHRM wordt gevolgd door een nieuwe procedure. Dit laat zien dat wanneer nationale rechters uitvoering moeten geven aan een EHRM-uitspraak in een geverticaliseerde zaak op hen de verantwoordelijkheid kan rusten om op enige wijze te compenseren voor het feit dat de uitspraak van het EHRM niet noodzakelijkerwijs een volledig beeld geeft van de betrokken rechten en belangen.

Tot slot heeft de situatie waarmee nationale rechters geconfronteerd kunnen worden ook gevolgen voor het Hof, in het bijzonder voor de rol van het Hof in het EVRM-systeem. Het gezag van de uitspraken van het Hof kan hierdoor namelijk onder druk komen te staan. Dit kan op zijn beurt een negatief effect hebben op de relatie tussen het Hof en nationale rechters, terwijl deze relatie cruciaal is voor het effectief functioneren van het EVRM-systeem.

4. NAAR EEN NIEUWE AANPAK VAN GEVERTICALISEERDE ZAKEN

De huidige aanpak van het Hof van geverticaliseerde zaken leidt dus tot problemen voor private partijen, verdragsstaten (inclusief nationale rechters) en het Hof zelf. Om een oplossing voor deze problemen aan te reiken, heeft deze studie zich tot slot gericht op het ontwerpen van een alternatieve aanpak van geverticaliseerde zaken. Daarbij is gekozen voor een focus op de procedure in plaats van op bijvoorbeeld de argumentatie van het Hof in geverticaliseerde zaken. Het brede scala aan geverticaliseerde zaken en de verschillen tussen deze zaken maakt het immers lastig om een *one-size-fits-all*-aanpak te kiezen die gericht is op de argumentatie van het Hof. Een dergelijke aanpak zou het Hof te weinig ruimte laten om de beoordeling toe te spitsen op de specifieke kenmerken van de zaak die het moet beoordelen. Bij een procedurele verandering

[987] BVerfGe (order of the second senate) 14 oktober 2004, 2 BvR 1481/04 (*Görgülü*) (officiële Engelstalige versie).

behoudt het Hof daarentegen de nodige vrijheid en flexibiliteit om zijn beoordeling en argumentatie aan te passen aan de voorliggende zaak.

Verder is ervoor gekozen om bij het ontwerpen van een procedurele oplossing dicht bij de aard van het EVRM-systeem te blijven. Dit is gedaan door de potentie van een al bestaand Conventie-instrument te benutten, namelijk de mogelijkheid van derde-partij-interventie zoals neergelegd in artikel 36 EVRM. In het kort komt het voorstel voor een nieuwe aanpak van geverticaliseerde zaken erop neer dat de huidige derde-partij-interventieprocedure zo moet worden vormgegeven dat derde partijen met een juridisch belang in de zaak (*actual third parties*) het recht krijgen om als derde partij te interveniëren in de procedure. Bij de uitwerking van dit voorstel is aandacht besteed aan het perspectief van private partijen, verdragsstaten en het Hof. Zo wordt voorgesteld om de derde-partij-interventieprocedure zo aan te passen dat die een oplossing biedt voor de problemen die ontstaan in geverticaliseerde zaken voor private partijen, verdragsstaten en het Hof en tegelijkertijd de praktische implicaties van een vernieuwde derde-partij-interventieprocedure beperkt worden gehouden, waaronder de gevolgen voor de werklast van het Hof.

De kenmerken van de voorgestelde aangepaste derde-partij-interventieprocedure kunnen als volgt worden samengevat. Om in aanmerking te komen voor het voorgestelde recht op derde-partij-interventie moet de verdwenen partij een juridisch belang hebben bij de zaak. Dit betekent dat de partij betrokken moet zijn geweest in het conflict op nationaal niveau, dat haar belangen moeten conflicteren met de rechten en belangen van de klager en dat deze belangen worden beschermd door het EVRM. Wanneer aan deze voorwaarden is voldaan, kan worden verondersteld dat de partij die wil interveniëren kan worden geraakt door een uitspraak van het Hof in de geverticaliseerde zaak die door klager aanhangig is gemaakt. Verder zorgen deze criteria ervoor dat het toepassingsbereik van het voorgestelde recht op derde-partij-interventie duidelijk wordt gedefinieerd en afgebakend. Hierdoor zal slechts een beperkte groep aanspraak kunnen maken op het voorgestelde recht op derde-partij-interventie, wat belangrijk is in het licht van de werklast van het Hof. Daarnaast bieden de criteria verdragsstaten en private partijen duidelijkheid en zekerheid met betrekking tot de vraag wie in aanmerking komt voor het recht op derde-partij-interventie.

Naast het toepassingsbereik zijn ook de procedurele rechten afgebakend die kunnen worden ontleend aan het voorgestelde recht op derde-partij-interventie. Hierbij is het van belang om een balans te vinden tussen het creëren van een reële en effectieve mogelijkheid voor derde partijen om te participeren in de procedure bij het Hof en een situatie die werkbaar is voor het Hof en verdragsstaten. Met dit in gedachten wordt voorgesteld dat het recht op derde-partij-interventie voor verdwenen partijen op dezelfde manier moet worden vormgegeven als het al bestaande recht op interventie voor verdragsstaten en de mensenrechtencommissaris van de Raad van Europa. Dit betekent dat daadwerkelijke derde partijen, zoals de verdwenen partijen vaak ook wel worden genoemd, geen volledige procedurele rechten krijgen. Zij kunnen bijvoorbeeld geen aanspraak maken op automatische toegang tot het complete dossier, de mogelijkheid om een beroep te doen op financiële rechtsbijstand of het recht om te verzoeken dat de zaak wordt doorverwezen naar de Grote Kamer van het EHRM. Tegelijkertijd wordt een reëel en effectief recht op derde-partij-interventie op deze manier nog steeds gecreëerd, nu verdwenen partijen het recht krijgen om zonder inhoudelijke beperkingen hun kant van het verhaal te laten horen. Met het oog op de werklast voor het Hof is wel voorgesteld om een maximum te stellen aan het aantal pagina's dat een schriftelijke interventie mag hebben.

Om ervoor te zorgen dat het voorgestelde recht op derde-partij-interventie vaker wordt gebruikt dan de al bestaande mogelijkheid om toestemming te vragen om te interveniëren in de procedure bij het Hof wordt voorgesteld dat het Hof en de verdragsstaten een gedeelde verantwoordelijkheid hebben om verdwenen partijen te informeren over een aanhangig gemaakte procedure bij het EHRM. Daarbij is het de verantwoordelijkheid van het Hof om eerst vast te stellen wie moet worden geïnformeerd over de lopende procedure. Vervolgens is het aan de verdragsstaten om deze partij daadwerkelijk te informeren aangezien zij eenvoudiger dan het Hof kunnen beschikken over de contactgegevens van deze partij.

Tot slot wordt voorgesteld dat het Hof in zijn uitspraken expliciet moet maken wanneer een derde-partij-interventie van invloed is geweest op de redenering en de uitkomst in de zaak. Dit betekent bijvoorbeeld dat het Hof moet verwijzen naar de derde-partij-interventie wanneer het de interventie heeft gebruikt om tot een geïnformeerde beoordeling te komen van de precieze omvang van de rechten en belangen van de verdwenen partij. Alhoewel dit het Hof niet verplicht om een derde-partij-interventie altijd mee te nemen in zijn overwegingen, heeft het als voordeel dat het leidt tot een situatie waarin meer duidelijkheid wordt gecreëerd over de vraag of een derde-partij-interventie van invloed is geweest op de beoordeling van de zaak. Dit is van belang in het licht van het recht op een gemotiveerde beslissing dat onder meer tot doel heeft om te laten zien dat partijen zijn gehoord. Daarnaast zal het hierdoor voor nationale rechters eenvoudiger zijn om na te gaan of de uitspraak van het Hof in een geverticaliseerde zaak een compleet beeld geeft van alle rechten en belangen die op het spel staan.

Uit het voorgaande blijkt dat het voorstel voor een vernieuwde derde-partij-interventieprocedure een oplossing biedt voor de problemen in geverticaliseerde zaken, omdat het een situatie creëert waarin de verdwenen partij een reële en effectieve mogelijkheid heeft om in de procedure bij het Hof te interveniëren en daardoor de kans heeft om zijn handelen, rechten en belangen toe te lichten en te verdedigen. In geverticaliseerde zaken over een conflict tussen het recht op reputatie en privéleven en het recht op vrijheid van meningsuiting geeft de voorgestelde procedure journalisten bijvoorbeeld de mogelijkheid om het Hof inzicht te verschaffen over de totstandkoming van de publicatie in kwestie en de gevolgen van een gebod voor zijn recht op vrijheid van meningsuiting. In het tegenovergestelde scenario zal het de private partij die heeft geleden onder de publicatie de kans geven om informatie te geven over zijn of haar rol of functie en de impact van de publicatie op zijn of haar recht op reputatie en privéleven.

De voorgestelde procedure is ook van toegevoegde waarde voor geverticaliseerde werkgever/werknemerszaken, zoals zaken over surveillancemaatregelen door een werkgever. Wanneer de verdwenen partij, vaak de werkgever, in aanmerking komt voor het recht op derde-partij-interventie zal deze partij het Hof meer kunnen vertellen over zaken als kennisgeving vooraf en de redenen voor de monitoring alsmede de precieze omvang van de rechten en belangen die voor hem in het geding zijn. Voor geverticaliseerde familiezaken zal de voorgestelde procedure het voor bijvoorbeeld de ouder die op nationaal niveau aan het langste eind heeft getrokken mogelijk maken om het Hof te laten beschikken over een aanvullend gezichtspunt, bijvoorbeeld met betrekking tot de achtergrond van de ouderschaps- en omgangsregeling en de gevolgen hiervan voor zijn of haar recht op privé- en familieleven. Ook kan de derde partij in dergelijke zaken belangrijke informatie geven over hoe de nationale procedure is verlopen, waaronder de participatie van alle betrokken partijen.

Het is belangrijk om te benadrukken dat het creëren van een reële en effectieve mogelijkheid voor de verdwenen partij om te participeren in de procedure bij het Hof niet alleen voor private partijen voordelen heeft. De genoemde voorbeelden laten zien dat een recht op derde-partij-interventie ook het Hof zelf in de gelegenheid stelt om zijn uitspraak te baseren op een completer en evenwichtiger beeld van de feiten van de zaak en de verschillende rechten en belangen die in de zaak een rol spelen. Dit zal het bovendien voor nationale rechters eenvoudiger maken om een EHRM-uitspraak in een geverticaliseerde zaak toe te passen, omdat deze uitspraak een vollediger beeld geeft van de betrokken rechten en belangen. De voorgestelde vernieuwde derde-partij-interventieprocedure biedt dus vanuit het perspectief van alle betrokken actoren – private partijen, verdragsstaten en het Hof zelf – een oplossing voor de problemen in geverticaliseerde zaken

5. AFSLUITING

In een speech ter gelegenheid van de 70e verjaardag van het EVRM zei de voormalig voorzitter van het EHRM, Sicilianos, dat de voortdurende ontwikkeling van de werkmethoden van het Hof één van de vijf institutionele kenmerken is die het unieke karakter en de ongeëvenaarde dynamiek van het EVRM-systeem verklaren.[988] Oftewel, een belangrijke eigenschap van het EVRM-systeem is dat het Hof in staat is gebleken om zijn procedures aan te passen aan nieuwe uitdagingen. Dit onderzoek heeft laten zien dat geverticaliseerde zaken precies zo'n nieuwe uitdaging zijn. Ze leiden tot problemen voor private partijen, verdragsstaten en het Hof zelf, terwijl ze tegelijkertijd een belangrijk

[988] Speech Linos-Alexandre Sicilianos (voormalig voorzitter van het EHRM) tijdens een conferentie ter gelegenheid van de 70e verjaardag van het EVRM ('The European Convention on Human Rights at 70: milestones and major achievements'), Straatsburg 18 september 2020. De andere vier kenmerken die Sicilianos noemt zijn het individueel klachtrecht, het permanente karakter van het EHRM, het unieke tenuitvoerleggingsmechanisme en de dialoog met nationale autoriteiten.

onderdeel van het EVRM-systeem vormen door een aanzienlijk deel van de rechtspraak van het Hof te beslaan. Nu het bovendien voor de hand ligt dat geverticaliseerde zaken in de toekomst een nog belangrijkere plaats zullen innemen, is het bijzonder belangrijk dat een aanpak van geverticaliseerde zaken wordt ontwikkeld die het Hof in staat stelt deze zaken goed te behandelen en aandacht te hebben voor de procedurele rechten van private partijen en de positie van verdragsstaten. Deze studie heeft laten zien dat een vernieuwde derde-partij-interventieprocedure zo'n aanpak kan zijn. Doordat het een oplossing biedt voor de problemen in geverticaliseerde zaken door gebruik te maken van een al bestaand instrument bouwt de voorgestelde aanpak bovendien voort op het huidige EVRM-systeem en doet het geen afbreuk aan de oorspronkelijke functie en kenmerken van het systeem.

BIBLIOGRAPHY

E. Abdelgawad, 'The execution of the judgments of the European Court of Human Rights: towards a non-coercive and participatory model of accountability' (2009) 69 *ZaöRV* 2009 471.

L. Acconciamessa, 'Bringing the child's procedural rights before the ECtHR through interpretative tools. Access to justice, participation and representation' in P. Czech, L. Heschl, K. Lukas, M. Nowak, G. Oberleitner (eds.), *European Yearbook on Human Rights 2020*, Intersentia 2020, pp. 49–77.

M. Addo, 'The reality of the United Nations Guiding Principles on Business and Human Rights' (2014) 14 *Human Rights Law Review* 133.

Y. Arai-Takahashi, *The margin of appreciation doctrine and the principle of proportionality in the jurisprudence of the ECHR*, Intersentia 2002.

Y. Arai-Takahashi, 'The margin of appreciation doctrine: a theoretical analysis of Strasbourg's variable geometry' in A. Føllesdal, B. Peters, G. Ulfstein (eds.) *Constituting Europe: The European Court of Human Rights in a National, European and Global Context*, Cambridge University Press 2013, pp. 62–105.

O.M. Arnardóttir, 'Organised retreat? The move from "substantive" to "procedural" review in the ECtHR's case law on the margin of appreciation' (2015) *European Society of International Law Annual Conference*.

O.M. Arnardóttir, 'Rethinking the two margins of appreciation' (2016) 12 *European Constitutional Law Review* 27.

O.M. Arnardóttir, 'The "procedural turn" under the European Convention on Human Rights and presumptions of Convention compliance' (2017) 15 *International Journal of Constitutional Law* 9.

O.M. Arnardóttir, 'The Brighton aftermath and the changing role of the European Court of Human Rights' (2018) 9 *Journal of International Dispute Settlement* 223.

I. Bar-Siman-Tov, 'Semi-procedural Judicial Review' (2012) 6 *Legisprudence* 271.

T. Barkhuysen and M. van Emmerik, 'A comparative view on the execution of judgments of the European Court of Human Rights' in T. Christou and J.P. Raymond (eds.), *European Court of Human Rights. Remedies and execution of judgments*, British Institute of International and Comparative Law 2005, pp. 1–23.

T. Barkhuysen and M. van Emmerik, 'Legitimacy of European Court of Human Rights Judgments: Procedural Aspects' in N. Huls, M. Adams, J. Bomhoff (eds.), *The Legitimacy of Highest Courts' Rulings: Judicial Deliberations and Beyond*, TMC Asser Press 2009, pp. 437–449.

T. Barkhuysen, M. van Emmerik, O. Jansen, M. Fedorova, 'Right to a fair trial' in P. van Dijk, F. van Hoof, A. van Rijn, L. Zwaak (eds.), *Theory and practice of the European Convention on Human Rights*, Intersentia 2018 (5th edition), pp. 497–654.

L. Bartholomeusz, 'The *Amicus Curiae* before International Courts and Tribunals' (2005) 5 *Non-State Actors and International Law* 209.

E. Bates, *The evolution of the European Convention on Human Rights: from its inception to the creation of a permanent Court of Human Rights*, Oxford University Press 2010.

E. Bates, 'The birth of the European Convention on Human Rights' in J. Christoffersen and M.R. Madsen (eds.), *The European Court of Human Rights: between law and politics*, Oxford University Press 2011, pp. 17–42.

E. Bates, 'History' in D. Moeckli, S. Shah, S. Sivakumaran (eds.), *International human rights law*, Oxford University Press 2014 (2nd edition), pp. 3–21.

M. Beijer, *The limits of fundamental rights protection by the EU: the scope for the development of positive obligations*, Intersentia 2017.

S. Beljin, 'Bundesverfassungsgericht on the Status of the European Convention of Human Rights and ECHR Decisions in the German Legal Order. Decision of 14 October 2004' (2005) 1 *European Constitutional Law Review* 553.

S. Besson, 'Enforcing the child's right to know her origins: contrasting approaches under the Convention on the Rights of the Child and the European Convention on Human Rights' (2007) 21 *International Journal of Law, Policy and the Family* 137.

E. Brems, 'Introduction' in E. Brems (ed.), *Conflicts between fundamental rights*, Intersentia 2008, pp. 1–16.

E. Brems and L. Lavrysen, 'Procedural justice in human rights adjudication: the European Court of Human Rights' (2013) 35 *Human Rights Quarterly* 176.

E. Brems, 'The "Logics" of Procedural-Type Review by the European Court of Human Rights' in J.H. Gerards and E. Brems (eds.) *Procedural Review in European Fundamental Rights Cases*, Cambridge University Press 2017, pp. 17–39.

M. Breuer, 'Establishing common standards and securing the rule of law' in S. Schmahl and M. Breuer (eds.), *The Council of Europe: its law and policies*, Oxford University Press 2017, pp. 639–670.

A.W. Brian Simpson, *Human rights and the end of empire*, Oxford University Press 2001.

A. Bryman, *Social Research Methods*, Oxford University Press 2008 (3rd edition).

A. Büchler and H. Keller (eds.) *Family forms and parenthood: theory and practice of Article 8 ECHR in Europe*, Intersentia 2016.

N. Bürli, *Third-party interventions before the European Court of Human Rights: Amicus Curiae, Member-State and Third-Party interventions*, Intersentia 2017.

A. Butler, 'Legal aid before human rights treaty monitoring bodies' (2000) 49 *International and Comparative Law Quarterly* 360.

A. Buyse, *Post-conflict housing restitution: the European human rights perspective, with a case study on Bosnia and Herzegovina*, Intersentia 2008.

A. Buyse, 'The pilot judgment procedure at the European Court of Human Rights: possibilities and challenges' (2009) 57 *Nomiko Vina* 1913.

L. Caflisch, 'New practice regarding the implementation of the judgments of the Strasbourg Court' (2005) 15 *Italian Yearbook of International Law* 3.

B. Çali, 'From flexible to variable standards of judicial review: the responsible courts doctrine at the European Court of Human Rights' in O.M. Arnardóttir and A. Buyse (eds.), *Shifting Centres of Gravity in Human Rights Protection: Rethinking relations between the ECHR, EU, and national legal orders'*, Routledge 2016, pp. 144–160.

B. Çali, 'Coping with crisis: wither the variable geometry in the jurisprudence of the European Court of Human Rights' (2018) 35 *Wisconsin International Law Journal* 237.

I. Cameron, 'Protocol 11 to the European Convention on Human Rights: the European Court of Human Rights as a Constitutional Court?' (1995) 15 *Yearbook of European Law* 219.

I. Cameron, *An introduction to the European Convention on Human Rights*, iUSTUS 2018 (8th edition).

J.L. Černič and N.C. Santarelli (eds.), *The future of business and human rights: theoretical and practical considerations for a UN treaty*, Intersentia 2018.

O. Cherednychenko, 'Towards the Control of Private Acts by the European Court of Human Rights?' (2006) 13 *Maastricht Journal of European and Comparative Law* 195.

O. Cherednychenko, *Fundamental rights, contract law and the protection of the weaker party: a comparative analysis of the constitutionalisation of contract law, with emphasis on risky financial transactions*, Sellier, European Law Publishers 2007.

J. Christoffersen, *Fair balance: proportionality, subsidiarity and primarity in the European Convention on Human Rights*, Brill Nijhoff 2009.

J. Christoffersen, 'Individual and constitutional justice: can the power balance of adjudication be reversed?' in J. Christoffersen and M.R. Madsen (eds.), *The European Court of Human Rights: between law and politics*, Oxford University Press 2011, pp. 181–203.

A. Clapham, *Human Rights in the Private Sphere*, Clarendon Press 1993.

V. Colandrea, 'On the power of the European Court of Human Rights to order specific non-monetary measures: some remarks in light of the Assanidze, Broniowski and Sejdovic cases' (2007) 7 *Human Rights Law Review* 396.

P.M. Collins, *Putting human rights to work. Labour law, the ECHR, and the employment relation*, Oxford University Press 2021.

I. Cram, 'Protocol 15 and Articles 10 and 11 ECHR – The partial triumph of political incumbency post-Brighton?' (2018) 67 *International and Comparative Law Quarterly* 477.

H.J. Cremer, 'Zur Bindungswirkung von EGMR-Urteilen – Anmerkung zum Görgülü-Beschluss des BVerfG vom 14.10.2004' (2004) 31 *Europäische Grundrechte-Zeitschrift* 683.

M. Dahlberg, '"…It is not its task to act as a Court of fourth instance": the case of the European Court of Human Rights' (2014) 7 *European Journal of Legal Studies* 84.

M.B. Dembour, '"Finishing off" cases: the radical solution to the problem of the expanding ECtHR caseload' (2002) 5 *European Human Rights Law Review* 604.

S. Deva and D. Bilchitz (eds.), *Building a treaty on business and human rights*, Cambridge University Press 2017.

P. van Dijk, F. van Hoof, A. van Rijn, L. Zwaak (eds.), *Theory and Practice of the European Convention on Human Rights*, Intersentia 2018 (5th edition).

I. Dobinson and J. Francis, 'Legal research as qualitative research' in M. McConville and W. Hong Chui (eds.), *Research methods for law*, Edinburgh University Press 2017 (2nd edition), pp. 18–47.

A. Donald and A.K. Speck, 'The European Court of Human Rights' remedial practice and its impact on the execution of judgments' (2019) 19 *Human Rights Law Review* 83.

O. Dörr, 'European Convention on Human Rights' in S. Schmahl and M. Breuer (eds.), *The Council of Europe: its law and policies* Oxford University Press 2017, pp. 465–506.

F. Dorssemont, K. Lörcher, I. Schömann (eds.), *The European Convention on Human Rights and the Employment Relation*, Hart Publishing 2013.

S. Dothan, 'Judicial tactics in the European Court of Human Rights' (2011) 358 *University of Chicago Public Law & Legal Theory Working Paper* 115.

S. van Drooghenbroeck, 'L'horizontalisation des droits de l'homme' in H. Dumont, F. Ost, S. van Drooghenbroeck (eds.), *La responsabilité, face cachée des droits de l'homme*, Bruylant 2005, pp. 355–390.

A. Drzemczewski, 'The role and authority of the European Court of Human rights', *2018 International Conference: Constitutional Courts and Human Rights Protection*, 1–2 October 2018, organised by Judicial Yuan (Constitutional Court, Taipei, Taiwan).

P. Ducoulombier, 'Conflicts between fundamental rights and the ECHR: an overview' in E. Brems (ed.) *Conflicts between fundamental rights*, Intersentia 2008, pp. 217–247.

J. Dugard, 'Diplomatic Protection', *Max Planck Encyclopedias of International Law*, Oxford University Press 2009.

K. Dzehtsiarou and A. Greene, 'Restructuring the European Court of Human Rights: preserving the right of individual petition and promoting constitutionalism' (2013) *Public Law* 710.

M.A. Eissen, 'The European Convention on Human Rights and the Duties of the Individual' (1962) *Nordisk Tidsskrift for International Ret* 230.

L. van den Eynde, 'An empirical look at the amicus curiae practice of human rights NGOs before the European Court of Human Rights' (2013) 31 *Netherlands Quarterly of Human Rights* 271.

J.H. Gerards, 'Pluralism, Deference and the Margin of Appreciation Doctrine' (2011) 17 *European Law Journal* 80.

J.H. Gerards, 'The European Court of Human Rights and the national courts – giving shape to the notion of "shared responsibility"' in J.H. Gerards and J.W.A. Fleuren (eds.), *Implementation of the European Convention on Human Rights and of the judgments of the ECtHR in national case law. A comparative analysis*, Intersentia 2014, pp. 13–94.

J.H. Gerards, 'Inadmissibility Decisions of the European Court of Human Rights: A Critique of the Lack of Reasoning' (2014) 14 *Human Rights Law Review* 148.

J.H. Gerards and L.R. Glas, 'Access to justice in the European Convention on Human Rights System' (2017) 35 *Netherlands Quarterly of Human Rights* 11.

J.H. Gerards and E. Brems (eds.), *Procedural review in European fundamental rights cases*, Cambridge University Press 2017.

J.H. Gerards, 'Procedural Review by the ECtHR: a Typology' in J.H. Gerards and E. Brems (eds.) *Procedural Review in European Fundamental Rights Cases*, Cambridge University Press 2017, pp. 127–160.

J.H. Gerards, 'The European Court of Human Rights' in A. Jakab, A. Dyevre, G. Itzcovich (eds.), *Comparative Constitutional reasoning*, Cambridge University Press 2017, pp. 237–276.

J.H. Gerards, 'Margin of Appreciation and Incrementalism in the Case Law of the European Court of Human Rights' (2018) 18 *Human Rights Law Review* 495.

J.H. Gerards, *General principles of the European Convention on Human Rights*, Oxford University Press 2019.

J.H. Gerards, 'Advisory Opinion: European Court of Human Rights (ECtHR)', *Max Planck Encyclopedia of International Procedural Law (MPEiPro)*, Oxford University Press 2019.

C. Giannopoulos, 'Considerations on Protocol No. 16: Can the New Advisory Competence of the European Court of Human Rights Breathe New Life into the European Convention on Human Rights?' (2015) 16 *German Law Journal* 337.

L.R. Glas, *The Theory, Potential and Practice of Procedural Dialogue in the European Convention on Human Rights System*, Intersentia 2016.

L.R. Glas, 'State Third-Party Interventions before the European Court of Human Rights: the what and how of intervening' (2016) 5 *European Journal of Human Rights* 539.

L.R. Glas, 'The functioning of the pilot-judgment procedure of the European Court of Human Rights in practice' (2016) 34 *Netherlands Quarterly of Human Rights* 41.

L.R. Glas, 'Translating the Convention's Fairness Standards to the European Court of Human Rights: an exploration with a Case Study on Legal Aid and the Right to a Reasoned Judgment' (2018) 10 *European Journal of Legal Studies* 47.

L.R. Glas, 'The European Court of Human Rights supervising the execution of its judgments' (2019) 37 *Netherlands Quarterly of Human Rights* 228.

L.R. Glas, 'From Interlaken to Copenhagen: What has become of the proposals aiming to reform the functioning of the European Court of Human Rights?' (2020) 20 *Netherlands Quarterly of Human Rights* 121.

C. van de Graaf, 'Procedural fairness: between human rights law and social psychology' (2021) 39 *Netherlands Quarterly of Human Rights* 11.

S. Greer, *The margin of appreciation: interpretation and discretion under the European Convention on Human Rights,* Council of Europe Publishing 2000.

S. Greer, *The European Convention on Human Rights: Achievements, Problems and Prospects,* Cambridge University Press 2006.

S. Greer and L. Wildhaber, 'Revisiting the debate about "constitutionalising" the European Court of Human Rights' (2012) 12 *Human Rights Law Review* 655.

S. Greer, J.H. Gerards, R. Slowe, *Human rights in the Council of Europe and the European Union,* Cambridge University Press 2018.

E. Gruodytė and S. Kirchner, 'Legal aid for intervenors in proceedings before the European Court of Human Rights' (2016) 2 *International Comparative Jurisprudence* 36.

D. Harris, M. O'Boyle, E. Bates, C. Buckley, *Harris, O'Boyle and Warbrick: Law of the European Convention on Human Rights,* Oxford University Press 2018 (4th edition).

M. Hartwig, 'Much ado about human rights: the Federal Constitutional Court confronts the European Court of Human Rights' (2005) 6 *German Law Journal* 869.

P. Harvey, 'Third party interventions before the ECtHR: a rough guide' (2015) *Strasbourg Observers* 24 February 2015 <www.strasbourgobservers.com/2015/02/24/third-party-interventions-before-the-ecthr-a-rough-guide/> accessed 31 January 2022.

L. Hennebel, 'Le rôle des amici curiae devant la Cour Européenne des Droits de l'Homme', (2007) 71 *Revue Trimestrielle des droits de l'homme* 641.

P. Hirvelä and S. Heikkilä, *Right to a fair trial. A practical guide to the Article 6 case-law of the European Court of Human Rights,* Intersentia 2021.

L. Huijbers, 'Procedural-type review: a more neutral approach to human rights protection by the European Court of Human Rights?' (2017) *European Society of International Law Conference Paper Series.*

L. Huijbers, *Process-based fundamental rights review. Practice, concept and theory,* Intersentia 2019.

T. Hutchinson, 'The doctrinal method: incorporating interdisciplinary methods in reforming the law' (2015) 3 *Erasmus Law Review* 130.

A. Ieven, 'Privacy rights in conflict: in search of the theoretical framework behind the European Court of Human Rights' balancing of private life against other rights' in E. Brems (ed.) *Conflicts between fundamental rights,* Intersentia 2008, pp. 39–67.

N. Ismaïli, *Who cares for the child?: regulating custody and access in family and migration law in the Netherlands, the European Union and the Council of Europe*, VU Amsterdam (diss.) 2018.

N. Jägers, 'UN Guiding Principles on Business and Human Rights: making headway towards real corporate accountability' (2011) 29 *Netherlands Quarterly of Human Rights* 159.

J. Jahn, 'Ruling (in)directly through individual measures? Effect and legitimacy of the ECtHR's new remedial power' (2014) 74 *ZaöRV* 1.

T. de Jong, *Procedurele waarborgen in materiële EVRM-rechten* [Procedural guarantees in substantive ECHR provisions], Wolters Kluwer 2017.

R. Kay, 'The European Convention on Human Rights and the control of private law' (2005) 5 *European Human Rights Law Review* 466.

K. Keith, 'Procedural fairness in the international legal tradition: the fundamentals of judicial procedure' in A. Sarvarian, F. Fontanelli, R. Baker, T. Vassilis (eds.), *Procedural fairness in international courts and tribunals,* British Institute of International and Comparative Law 2015, pp. 39–57.

H. Keller and C. Marti, 'Reconceptualizing implementation: the judicialization of the execution of the European Court of Human Rights' judgments' (2016) 25 *European Journal of International Law* 829.

A. Kjeldgaard-Pedersen, *The international legal personality of the individual,* Oxford University Press 2018.

T. Kleinlein, 'The procedural approach of the European Court of Human Rights: between subsidiarity and dynamic evolution' (2019) 68 *International and Comparative Law Quarterly* 91.

N. Koffeman, *Morally sensitive issues and cross-border movement in the EU. The cases of reproductive matter and legal recognition of same-sex relationships,* Intersentia 2015.

J. Kratochvil, 'The inflation of the margin of appreciation doctrine by the European Court of Human Rights' (2011) 29 *Netherlands Quarterly of Human Rights* 324.

D. Kurban, 'Forsaking individual justice: the implications of the European Court of Human Rights' Pilot judgment procedure for victims of gross and systematic violations' (2016) 16 *Human Rights Law Review* 731.

P. Lauren, *The evolution of international human rights: visions seen,* University of Pennsylvania Press 2011 (3rd edition).

L. Lavrysen, *Human rights in a positive state: rethinking the relationship between positive and negative obligations under the European Convention on Human Rights,* Intersentia 2016.

L. Lavrysen, 'System of restrictions' in P. van Dijk, F. van Hoof, A. van Rijn, L. Zwaak (eds.), *Theory and practice of the European Convention on Human Rights,* Intersentia 2018 (5th edition), pp. 307–330.

L. Lavrysen and N. Mavronicola (eds.), *Coercive Human Rights: Positive Duties to Mobilise the Criminal Law under the ECHR,* Hart Publishing 2020.

L. Lazarus, 'Positive obligations and Criminal Justice: Duties to Protect or Coerce' in J. Roberts and L. Zedner (eds.), *Principled and values in Criminal Law and Criminal Justice: Essays in Honour of Professor Andrew Ashworth,* Oxford University Press 2012, pp. 135–155.

L. Lazarus, 'Preventive obligations, risk and coercive overreach' in L. Lavrysen and N. Mavronicola (eds.), *Coercive Human Rights: Positive Duties to Mobilise the Criminal Law under the ECHR,* Hart Publishing 2020, pp. 249–266.

P. Leach, H. Hardman, S. Stephenson, 'Can the European Court's pilot judgment help resolve systematic human rights violations? *Burdov* and the failure to implement domestic court decisions in Russia' (2010) 10 *Human Rights Law Review* 346.

P. Leach, 'No longer offering fine mantras to a parched child? The European Court's developing approach to remedies' in A. Føllesdal, B. Peters, G. Ulfstein (eds.), *Constituting Europe: the*

European Court of Human Rights in a national, European and global context, Cambridge University Press 2013, pp. 142–180.

P. Leach, *Taking a case to the European Court of Human Rights,* Oxford University Press 2017 (4th edition).

I. Leigh, 'Horizontal rights, the Human Rights Act and Privacy: lessons from the Commonwealth' (1999) 48 *International and Comparative Law Quarterly* 57.

N. van Leuven, *Contracten en mensenrechten: een mensenrechtelijke lezing van het contractenrecht* [Contract law and human rights], Intersentia 2009.

L. Lixinski, 'Procedural fairness in human rights systems' in A. Sarvarian, F. Fontanelli, R. Baker, V. Tsevelekos (eds.), *Procedural fairness in international courts and tribunals,* British Institute of International and Comparative Law 2015, pp. 325–342.

F. de Londras, 'Dual functionality and the persistent frailty of the European Court of Human Rights' (2013) 1 *European Human Rights Law Review* 38.

C.M.S. Loven, 'Milieudefensie summons Shell: similar obligations for States and companies when it comes to CO2 reduction?' (2019), *Blog of the Montaigne Centre for Rule of Law and Administration of Justice* 26 June 2019 <www.blog.montaignecentre.com/en/milieudefensie-summons-shell-similar-obligations-for-states-and-companies-when-it-comes-to-co2-reduction-2/> accessed 31 January 2022.

C.M.S. Loven, 'A and B v. Croatia and the concurring opinion of Judge Wojtyczek: the procedural status of the "disappearing party"' (2019), *Strasbourg Observers* 16 July 2019 <www.strasbourgobservers.com/2019/07/16/a-and-b-v-croatia-and-the-concurring-opinion-of-judge-wojtyczek-the-procedural-status-of-the-disappearing-party/> accessed 31 January 2022.

C.M.S. Loven, '"Verticalised" cases before the European Court of Human Rights unravelled: an analysis of their characteristics and the Court's approach to them' (2020) 38 *Netherlands Quarterly of Human Rights* 246.

C.M.S. Loven, 'Horizontale positieve verplichtingen in de rechtspraak van het Europees Hof voor de Rechten van Mens' [Horizontal positive obligations and the case law of the European Court of Human Rights] (2020) 45 *Nederlands Tijdschrift voor de Mensenrechten* 479.

M.R. Madsen, 'From cold war instrument to Supreme European Court: the European Court of Human Rights at the crossroads of international and national law and politics' (2007) 32 *Law & Social Inquiry* 137.

P. Mahoney, 'New challenges for the European Court of Human Rights resulting from the expanding case load and membership' (2002) 21 *Penn State International Law Review* 101.

P. Mahoney, 'Commentaire' in H. Ruiz Fabri and J.M. Sorel (eds.), *La tiers à l'instance devant les juridictions internationales,* Pedone 2005, pp. 151–161.

R. Mares (ed.), *The UN Guiding Principles on Business and Human Rights – foundations and implementation,* Martinus Nijhoff Publishers 2012.

M. McConville and W. Hong Chui, 'Introduction and overview' in M. McConville and W. Hong Chui (eds.), *Research methods for law,* Edinburgh: Edinburgh University Press 2017 (2nd edition), pp. 1–17.

R. McCorquodale, 'The individual and the international legal system' in M. Evans (ed.), *International law,* Oxford University Press 2014 (4th edition), pp. 280–305.

F. Mégret, 'Nature of obligations' in D. Moeckli, S. Shah, S. Sivakumaran (eds.), *International human rights law,* Oxford University Press 2014 (2nd edition), pp. 86–109.

E. Merckx, 'The ECtHR on parental authority and contact after separation. Towards a more child-centred perspective?' in P. Czech, L. Heschl, K. Lukas, M. Nowak, G. Oberleitner (eds.), *European Yearbook on Human Rights 2020*, Intersentia 2020, pp. 97–133.

J.G. Merrills and A.H. Robertson, *Human rights in Europe: a study of the ECHR*, Manchester University Press 2001 (4th edition).

D. Moeckli, S. Shah, S. Sivakumaran (eds.), *International human rights law*, Oxford University Press 2014 (2nd edition).

C.R. Mol, *The child's right to participate in family law disputes. Represented, heard or silenced?*, Intersentia 2022

N. Mole and C. Harby, *The right to a fair trial*, Council of Europe Human Rights Handbook No. 3, 2006 (2nd edition).

A. Moravcsik, 'The origins of Human Rights Regimes: Democratic Delegation in Postwar Europe' (2000) 54 *International organisation* 217.

J. Morsink, *The Universal Declaration of Human Rights: origins, drafting and intent*, University of Pennsylvania Press 1999.

A. Mowbray, 'The creativity of the European Court of Human Rights' (2005) 5 *Human Rights Law Review* 57.

A. Mowbray, 'The Interlaken Declaration: The beginning of a new era for the European Court of Human Rights?' (2010) 10 *Human Rights Law Review* 519.

A. Mowbray, 'Subsidiarity and the European Convention on Human Rights' (2015) 15 *Human Rights Law Review* 313.

D. Nicol, 'Original intent and the European Convention on Human Rights' (2005) *Public Law* 152.

A. Nussberger, 'Subsidiarity in the Control of Decisions Based on Proportionality: An Analysis of the Basis of the Implementation of ECtHR judgments into German Law' in A. Seibert-Fohr and M. Villiger, *Judgments of the European Court of Human Rights: Effects and Implementation*, Nomos Verlagsgesellschaft 2014, pp. 165–185.

A. Nussberger, 'Procedural Review by the ECHR: View from the Court' in J.H. Gerards and E. Brems (eds.), *Procedural Review in European Fundamental Rights Cases*, Cambridge University Press 2017, pp. 161–176.

A. Nussberger, '"Second-hand justice" and the rule of law. Dilemmas in implementing the judgments of the European Court of Human Rights' in R. Spano et al (eds.) *Fair trial: regional and international perspectives (Liber amicorum Linos-Alexandre Sicilianos)*, Anthemis 2020, pp. 349–363.

S. Ouald Chaib, 'Suku Phull v. France rewritten from a procedural justice perspective: taking religious minorities seriously' in E. Brems (ed.) *Diversity and European human rights. Rewriting judgments of the ECHR*, Cambridge University Press 2013, pp. 218–240.

A. Paprocka and M. Ziółkowski, 'Advisory opinions under Protocol No. 16 to the European Convention on Human Rights' (2015) 11 *European Constitutional Law Review* 274.

P. Pastor Vilanova, 'Third parties involved in international litigation proceedings. What are the challenges for the ECHR?' in P. Pinto de Albuquerque and K. Wojtyczek (eds.), *Judical power in a globalized world (Liber amicorum Vincent de Gaetano)*, Springer 2019, pp. 377–393.

P. Pastor Vilanova, 'Le juge européen est-il tenu par les règles du procès équitable?' in R. Spano et al. (eds.), *Fair trial: regional and international perspectives (Liber amicorum Linos-Alexandre Sicilianos)*, Anthemis 2020, pp. 391–405.

P. Popelier and C. van de Heyning, 'Procedural rationality: giving teeth to the proportionality analysis' (2013) 9 *European Constitutional Law Review* 230.

P. Popelier and C. van de Heyning, 'Subsidiarity post-Brighton: procedural rationality an answer?' (2017) 30 *Leiden Journal of International Law* 5.

B. Rainey (ed.), *Jacobs, White and Ovey: the European Convention on Human Rights,* Oxford University Press 2017 (7th edition).

G. Ravarani, 'The Fairness of Proceedings before the European Court of Human Rights' in R. Spano et al. (eds.), *Fair trial: regional and international perspectives (Liber amicorum Linos-Alexandre Sicilianos),* Anthemis 2020, pp. 453–470.

G. Ravarani, 'Third parties – poor relations in proceedings before the European Court of Human Rights' (2021) (on file with the author).

G. Ress, 'The effect of decisions and judgments of the European Court of Human Rights in the domestic legal order' (2005) 40 *Texas International Law Journal* 359.

D. Rietiker, 'The principle of "effectiveness" in the recent jurisprudence of the European Court of Human Rights: its different dimensions and its consistency with the public international law – No need for the concept of treaty sui generis' (2010) 79 *Nordic Journal of International Law* 245.

N. Rodley, 'International human rights law' in M. Evans (ed.) *International law,* Oxford University Press 2014 (4th edition), pp. 783–820.

W. Sadurski, 'Partnering with Strasbourg: constitutionalisation of the European Court of Human Rights, the accession of Central and East European States to the Council of Europe, and the idea of pilot judgments' (2009) 9 *Human Rights Law Review* 397.

D. Sanderink, *Het EVRM en het materiële omgevingsrecht* [The relationship between the ECHR and substantive environmental and planning law], Kluwer 2015.

O. de Schutter, 'Towards a new treaty on business and human rights' (2016) 1 *Business and human rights journal* 41.

G. Serghides, 'The Principle of Effectiveness in the European Convention on Human Rights. In Particular its Relationship to the other Convention Principles' in J. Vidmar (ed.) *Hague Yearbook of International Law* (Vol. 30), Brill Nijhoff 2017, pp. 1–16.

S. Shah, 'Detention and trial' in D. Moeckli, S. Shah, S. Sivakumaran (eds.), *International human rights law,* Oxford University Press 2014 (2nd edition), pp. 252–277.

D. Shelton (ed.), *The Oxford Handbook of International Human Rights,* Oxford University Press 2013.

D. Shelton, 'Significantly disadvantaged? Shrinking access to the European Court of Human Rights' (2016) 16 *Human Rights Law Review* 303.

L.A. Sicilianos, 'La tierce intervention devant la Cour Européenne des Droits de l'Homme', in H. Ruiz Fabri and J.M. Sorel (eds.), *La tiers à l'instance devant les juridictions internationales,* Pedone 2005, pp. 123–150.

L.A. Sicilianos, 'The involvement of the European Court of Human Rights in the implementation of its judgments: recent developments under Article 46 ECHR' (2014) 32 *Netherlands Quarterly of Human Rights* 235.

L.A. Sicilianos and M.A. Kostopoulou, *The individual application under the European Convention on Human Rights,* Council of Europe 2019.

L.A. Sicilianos, 'The European Convention on Human Rights at 70: the dynamic of a unique international instrument' in P. Czech, L. Heschl, K. Lukas, M. Nowak, G. Oberleitner, Gerd (eds.), *European Yearbook on Human Rights 2020,* Intersentia 2020, pp. 3–15.

O. Sidhu, *The Concept of Equality of Arms in Criminal Proceedings under Article 6 of the European Convention on Human Rights*, Intersentia 2017.

S. Smet, 'Freedom of expression and the right to reputation: human rights in conflict' (2010) 26 *American University International Law Review* 183.

S. Smet, *Resolving conflicts between human rights: a legal theoretical analysis in the context of the ECHR*, Ghent University (diss.) 2014.

S. Smet, *Resolving conflicts between human rights: the judge's dilemma*, Routledge 2017.

J.M. Smits, 'What is legal doctrine? On the aims and methods of legal-dogmatic research' in R. van Gestel, H.W. Micklitz and E.L. Rubin (eds.), *Rethinking legal scholarship. A transatlantic dialogue*, Cambridge University Press 2017, pp. 207–228.

R. Spano, 'Universality or diversity of human rights? Strasbourg in the age of subsidiarity', (2014) 14 *Human Rights Law Review* 487.

R. Spano, 'Future of the European Court of Human Rights – Subsidiarity, process-based review and the rule of law' (2018) 18 *Human Rights Law Review* 473.

D. Spielmann, *L'effet potentiel de la Convention européenne des droits de l'homme entre personnes privées*, Bruylant 1995.

D. Spielmann, 'The European Convention on Human Rights. The European Court of Human Rights' in J. Fedtke and D. Oliver (eds.) *Human rights and the private sphere: a comparative study*, Routledge-Cavendish 2007, pp. 427–464.

D. Spielmann, 'Allowing the right margin: the European Court of Human Rights and the national margin of appreciation doctrine: waiver or subsidiarity of European review?' (2012) *Cambridge Yearbook of European Legal Studies 2011–2012*, pp. 381–418.

D. Spielmann, 'Whither the margin of appreciation?' (2014) 67 *Current Legal Problems* 49.

J. Sweeney, *The European Court of Human Rights in the post-Cold War era: universality in transition*, Taylor and Francis 2013.

V. Stoyanova, 'The disjunctive juncture of positive rights under the European Convention on Human Rights' (2018) 87 *Nordic Journal of International Law* 344.

V. Stoyanova, 'Common law tort of negligence as a tool for deconstructing positive obligations under the European Convention on Human Rights' (2020) 24 *The International Journal of Human Rights* 632.

J. Thibaut and L. Walker, *Procedural justice: a psychological analysis*, L. Erlbaum Associates 1975.

C. Tomuschat, *Human rights: between idealism and realism*, Oxford University Press 2014 (3rd edition).

G. Ulfstein, 'The European Court of Human Rights and national courts: a constitutional relationship?' in O.M. Arnardóttir and A. Buyse (eds.), *Shifting Centres of Gravity in Human Rights Protection: Rethinking relations between the ECHR, EU, and national legal orders'*, Routledge 2016, pp. 46–58.

T. Voland and B. Schiebel, 'Advisory opinions of the European Court of Human Rights: unbalancing the system of human rights protection in Europe?' (2017) 17 *Human Rights Law Review* 73.

J. Vranken, 'Exciting times for legal scholarship' (2012) 2 *Law and Method* 2012 42.

H. de Vylder, 'Stensholt v. Norway: Why single judge decisions undermine the Court's legitimacy' (2014) *Strasbourg Observers* 28 May 2014, <https://strasbourgobservers.com/2014/05/28/stensholt-v-norway-why-single-judge-decisions-undermine-the-courts-legitimacy-2/> accessed 31 January 2022.

J. Wadham and T. Said, 'What price the right of individual petition: report of the evaluation group to the Committee of Ministers on the European Court of Human Rights' (2002) 2 *European Human Rights Law Review* 169.

D. Walton, 'Subsidiarity and the Brighton Declaration' in A. Seibert-Fohr and M. Villiger, *Judgments of the European Court of Human Rights: Effects and Implementation,* Nomos Verlagsgesellschaft 2014, pp. 193–206.

N. Weiss, 'Origin and further development' in S. Schmahl and M. Breuer (eds.), *The Council of Europe: its law and policies,* Oxford University Press 2017, pp. 3–22.

A. Wiik, *Amicus curiae before international courts and tribunals,* Nomos Verlagsgesellschaft 2018.

L. Wildhaber, 'A constitutional future for the European Court on Human Rights?' (2002) 25 *Human Rights Law Journal* 161.

L. Wildhaber, *The European Court of Human Rights 1998–2006: history, achievements, reform,* N.P. Engel Publisher 2006.

K. Wojtyczek, 'Procedural Justice and the Proceedings Before the European Court of Human Rights: Who Should Have the Right to be Heard?' in R. Spano et al (eds.), *Fair trial: regional and international perspectives (Liber amicorum Linos-Alexandre Sicilianos),* Anthemis 2020, pp. 741–755.

J. Wouters, C. Ryngaert, T. Ruys, G. de Baere (eds.), *International law: a European perspective,* Hart Publishing 2019.

D. Xenos, *The positive obligations of the state under the European Convention of Human Rights,* Routledge 2012.

L. Zwaak, Y. Haeck, C. Burbano Herrera, 'Procedure before the Court' in P. van Dijk, F. van Hoof, A. van Rijn, L. Zwaak (eds.), *Theory and practice of the European Convention on Human Rights*, Intersentia 2018 (5th edition), pp. 79–271.

APPENDIX I: OVERVIEW CASE LAW SAMPLE

CASES RELATED TO ONE'S SURROUNDINGS

Powell and Rayner v the United Kingdom App No 9310/81 (ECtHR 21 February 1990).
López Ostra v Spain App No 16798/90 (ECtHR 9 December 1994).
Guerra and Others v Italy App No 14967/89 (ECtHR (GC) 19 February 1998).
Hatton and Others v the United Kingdom App No 36022/97 (ECtHR (GC) 8 July 2003).
Surugiu v Romania App No 48995/99 (ECtHR 20 April 2004).
Taşkın and Others v Turkey App No 46117/99 (ECtHR 10 November 2004).
Moreno Gómez v Spain App No 4143/02 (ECtHR 16 November 2004).
Fadeyeva v Russia App No 55723/00 (ECtHR 9 June 2005).
Giacomelli v Italy App No 59909/00 (ECtHR 2 November 2006).
Tătar v Romania App No 67021/01 (ECtHR 27 January 2009).
Bacila v Romania App No 19234/04 (ECtHR 30 March 2010).
Oluic v Croatia App No 61260/08 (ECtHR 20 May 2010).
Deés v Hungary App No 2345/06 (ECtHR 9 November 2010).
Mileva and Others v Bulgaria App No 43449/02 (ECtHR 25 November 2010).
Zammit Maempel v Malta App No 24202/10 (ECtHR 22 November 2011).
Cevrioğlu v Turkey App No 69546/12 (ECtHR 4 October 2016).
Cordella and Others v Italy App No 54414/13 (ECtHR 24 January 2019).

CASES INVOLVING A CONFLICT BETWEEN THE RIGHT TO REPUTATION AND PRIVATE LIFE AND THE RIGHT TO FREEDOM OF EXPRESSION

Lingens v Austria App No 9815/82 (ECtHR 8 July 1986).
Von Hannover v Germany (No. 1) App No 59320/00 (ECtHR 24 June 2004).
Chauvy and Others v France App No 64915/01 (ECtHR 29 June 2004).
Ukrainian Media Group v Ukraine App No 72713/01 (ECtHR 29 March 2005).
White v Sweden App No 42435/02 (ECtHR 19 September 2006).
Kanellopoulou v Greece App No 28504/05 (ECtHR 11 October 2007).
A. v Norway App No 28070/06 (ECtHR 9 April 2009).
Karakó v Hungary App No 39311/05 (ECtHR 28 April 2009).
Polanco Torres and Movilla Polanco v Spain App No 34147/06 (ECtHR 21 September 2010).
M.G.N. Limited v the United Kingdom App No 39401/04 (ECtHR 18 January 2011).
Von Hannover v Germany (No. 2) App No 40660/08 (ECtHR (GC) 7 February 2012).

Axel Springer AG v Germany App No 39954/08 (ECtHR (GC) 7 February 2012).
Aksu v Turkey App No 4149/04 (ECtHR (GC) 15 March 2012).
Tanasoaica v Romania App No 3490/03 (ECtHR 19 June 2012).
Ageyevy v Russia App No 7075/10 (ECtHR 18 April 2013).
Ärztekammer für Wien and Dorner v Austria App No 8895/10 (ECtHR 16 February 2016).
Rubio Dosamantes v Spain App No 20996/10 (ECtHR 21 February 2017).
Medžlis Islamske Zajednici Brčko and Others v Bosnia and Herzegovina App No 17224/11 (ECtHR (GC) 27 June 2017).
Rodina v Latvia App No 48534/10 (ECtHR 14 May 2020).
Petro Carbo Chem S.E. v Romania App No 21768/12 (ECtHR 30 June 2020).
Dupate v Latvia App No 18068/11 (ECtHR 19 November 2020).
Gheorghe-Florin Popescu v Romania App No 79671/13 (ECtHR 12 January 2021).
Société Editrice de Mediapart and Others v France App No 281/15 (ECtHR 14 January 2021).
Budinova and Charprazov v Bulgaria App No 12567/13 (ECtHR 16 February 2021).

FAMILY LIFE CASES

Hokkanen v Finland App No 19823/92 (ECtHR 23 September 1994).
Salgueiro da Silva Mouta v Portugal App No 33290/96 (ECtHR 21 December 1999).
Ignaccolo-Zenide v Romania App No 31679/96 (ECtHR 25 January 2000).
Mikulić v Croatia App No 53176/99 (ECtHR 7 February 2002).
Sahin v Germany App No 30943/96 (ECtHR (GC) 8 July 2003).
Görgülü v Germany App No 74969/01 (ECtHR 26 February 2004).
Jäggi v Switzerland App No 58757/00 (ECtHR 13 July 2006).
V.A.M. v Serbia App No 39177/05 (ECtHR 13 March 2007).
Bevacqua and S. v Bulgaria App No 71127/01 (ECtHR 12 June 2008).
Mijuskovic v Montenegro App No 49337/07 (ECtHR 21 September 2010).
Gluhaković v Croatia App No 21188/09 (ECtHR 12 April 2011).
A.M.M. v Romania App No 2151/10 (ECtHR 14 February 2012).
Godelli v Italy App No 33783/09 (ECtHR 25 September 2012).
Mandet v France App No 30955/12 (ECtHR 14 January 2016).
Fröhlich v Germany App No 16112/15 (ECtHR 26 July 2018).
Petrov and X. v Russia App No 23608/16 (ECtHR 23 October 2018).
Mifsud v Malta App No 62257/15 (ECtHR 29 January 2019).
Milovanovic v Serbia App No 56065/10 (ECtHR 8 October 2019).
Koychev v Bulgaria App No 32495/15 (ECtHR 13 October 2020).
Honner v France App No 19511/16 (ECtHR 12 November 2020).
A.M. and Others v Russia App No 47220/19 (ECtHR 6 July 2021).

EMPLOYER-EMPLOYEE CASES

Wilson, National Union of Journalists and Others v the United Kingdom App No 30668/96 (ECtHR 2 July 2002).
Sørensen and Rasmussen v Denmark App No 52562/99 (ECtHR (GC) 11 January 2006).
Schüth v Germany App No 1620/03 (ECtHR 23 September 2010).
Obst v Germany App No 425/03 (ECtHR 23 September 2010).
Köpke v Germany App No 420/07 (ECtHR 5 October 2010 (dec.)).
Siebenhaar v Germany App No 18136/02 (ECtHR 3 February 2011).
Heinisch v Germany App No 28274/08 (ECtHR 21 July 2011).[989]
Palomo Sánchez and Others v Spain App No 28955/06 (ECtHR (GC) 12 September 2011).
Redfearn v the United Kingdom App No 47335/06 (ECtHR 6 November 2012).
Eweida and Others v the United Kingdom App No 48420/10 (ECtHR 15 January 2013).
I.B. v Greece App No 552/10 (ECtHR 3 October 2013).
Bărbulescu v Romania App No 61496/08 (ECtHR (GC) 5 September 2017).
López Ribalda and Others v Spain App No 1874/13 (ECtHR (GC) 17 October 2019).
Herbai v Hungary App No 11608/15 (ECtHR 5 November 2019).
Halet v Luxembourg App No 21884/18 (ECtHR 11 May 2021).[990]

989 The applicant in this case, the dismissed employee, had been working for a limited liability company specialised in health care, geriatrics, and assistance to the elderly. Although this company is majority-owned by the State, the case has been included in the sample because the employer is not considered a public authority (cf. *Libert v. France* App No 588/13 (ECtHR 22 February 2018) in which the Court held that the French national railway company SNCF was a public authority, because it was supervised by the State, with State-appointed directors, provided a public service, held a monopoly and enjoyed implicit State guarantee (para. 38)).

990 This case has been referred to the Grand Chamber on 6 September 2021.

CURRICULUM VITAE

Claire Loven (1993) obtained a bachelor's degree in law and in human geography and urban planning at the University of Amsterdam and a master's degree in constitutional and administrative law at Utrecht University. During her studies, Claire worked as a research intern at the National Ombudsman. As part of this research internship, she contributed to the report entitled ‹Woonwagenbewoner zoekt standplaats› (Traveller in search of caravan sites). After her internship, Claire continued to work on this topic. She published several articles on human rights of travellers (co-authored with dr. L.M. Huijbers) and has been coordinator of the traveller's policy case file at the Public Interest Litigation Project (PILP) of the Dutch Section of the International Commission of Jurists (NJCM). In September 2018, Claire started her PhD at Utrecht University's Montaigne Centre for Rule of Law and Administration of Justice. During her PhD, she has written several case notes on judgments of the European Court of Human Rights, published two peer-reviewed articles on the topic of her research and contributed to periodicals on the Court's case law and developments within the Council of Europe more generally. As part of her PhD research, Claire has also been a visiting researcher at the European Court of Human Rights for a period of three months. From September 2022, Claire is an assistant professor at the department of constitutional and administrative law and legal theory (Utrecht University) and continues her work as a researcher at the university's Montaigne Centre for Rule of Law and Administration of Justice.

Human Rights Research Series

The Human Rights Research Series' central research theme is the nature and meaning of international standards in the field of human rights, their application and promotion in the national legal order, their interplay with national standards, and the international supervision of such application. Anyone directly involved in the definition, study, implementation, monitoring, or enforcement of human rights will find this series an indispensable reference tool.
The Series is published together with the world famous Netherlands Network for Human Rights Research (formerly School of Human Rights Research), a joint effort by human rights researchers in the Netherlands.

 For previous volumes in the series, please visit http://shr.intersentia.com.

Published titles within the Series:

89. Vincent Willem Vleugel, *Culture in the State Reporting Procedure of the UN Human Rights Treaty Bodies. How the HRC, the CESCR and the CEDAWCee use human rights as a sword to protect and promote culture, and as a shield to protect against harmful culture*
ISBN 978-1-83970-006-4
90. Laura Íñigo Álvarez, *Towards a Regime of Responsibility of Armed Groups in International Law*
ISBN 978-1-83970-004-0
91. Getahun A. Mosissa, *A Re-examination of Economic, Social and Cultural Rights in a Political Society in the Light of the Principle of Human Dignity*
ISBN 978-1-78068-987-6
92. Veronika Flegar, *The Transformative Potential of a Vulnerability Focus in Basic Assistance Policies*
ISBN 978-1-83970-039-2
93. Marieke J. Hopman, *Looking at Law through Children's Eyes*
ISBN 978-1-83970-101-6
94. Daniela Heerdt, *Blurred Lines of Responsibility and Accountability. Human Rights Abuses at Mega-Sporting Events*
ISBN 978-1-83970-117-7
95. Annick Pijnenburg, *At the Frontiers of State Responsibility. Socio-economic Rights and Cooperation on Migration*
ISBN 978-1-83970-148-1
96. Amy Weatherburn, *Labour Exploitation in Human Trafficking Law*
ISBN 978-1-83970-154-2
97. Caia Vlieks, *Nationality and Statelessness in Europe. European Law on Preventing and Solving Statelessness*
ISBN 978-1-83970-261-7

www.ingramcontent.com/pod-product-compliance
Ingram Content Group UK Ltd.
Pitfield, Milton Keynes, MK11 3LW, UK
UKHW051921100926
8556IPUK00021B/1311

9 781839 702839